Controlling Immigration
A Global Perspective

PUBLISHED IN ASSOCIATION WITH THE
CENTER FOR U.S.-MEXICAN STUDIES
UNIVERSITY OF CALIFORNIA, SAN DIEGO

Controlling Immigration

A GLOBAL PERSPECTIVE

Edited by

Wayne A. Cornelius
Philip L. Martin
and
James F. Hollifield

STANFORD UNIVERSITY PRESS, STANFORD, CALIFORNIA

Cover photograph: "Too Hungry to Knock," ©1992 Don Bartletti. Having caught U.S. Border Patrol agents off guard before dawn, a group of young men make *el brinco* (the jump) down the north side of the U.S.–Mexico border fence.

Stanford University Press, Stanford, California
©1994 by the Board of Trustees of the
Leland Stanford Junior University
Printed in the United States of America

Stanford University Press publications are distributed exclusively by Stanford University Press within the United States, Canada, Mexico, and Central America; they are distributed exclusively by Cambridge University Press throughout the rest of the world.

Original printing 1994
Last figure below indicates year of this printing:
04   03   02   01   00   99   98   97   96   95

Library of Congress Cataloging-in-Publication Data

Controlling immigration : a global perspective / edited by Wayne A. Cornelius, Philip L. Martin, and James F. Hollifield
    p. cm.
Includes bibliographical references and index.
ISBN 0-8047-2497-0 (alk. paper) : —ISBN 0-8047-2498-9 (alk. paper : pbk.) :
1. Emigration and immigration—Government policy. 2. Immigrants—Government policy. 3. Human rights. I. Cornelius, Wayne A., 1945–   . II. Martin, Philip L., 1949–   . III. Hollifield, James Frank, 1954–   .
JV6271.C66 1995. 325'.1—dc20. 94-40568 CIP

This book is printed on acid-free paper.

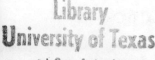

Contents

Preface

This book reports the work of an interdisciplinary research team of immigration specialists, based in the Center for U.S.-Mexican Studies at the University of California, San Diego from 1990 through 1993. The members of this highly interactive research group met weekly during the period of January–March 1993 and on many subsequent occasions. The principal researchers included Wayne A. Cornelius (political scientist, University of California, San Diego; principal investigator for the project), Kitty Calavita (sociologist, University of California, Irvine), Manuel García y Griego (demographer and political scientist, University of California, Irvine), James F. Hollifield (political scientist, Auburn University), Philip L. Martin (economist, University of California, Davis), and Marcelo Suárez-Orozco (anthropologist, University of California, San Diego).

Kitty Calavita merits special recognition for encouraging us to pursue such a wide-ranging and ambitious, fieldwork-based project. Several graduate students at the University of California, San Diego and the University of California, Berkeley made valuable contributions to the project, especially Cynthia R. Hibbs, Takeyuki Tsuda, Jeffrey Weldon, and Scott Morgenstern.

Our work has benefited greatly from the comments of numerous discussants who participated in an international research workshop held at the Center for U.S.-Mexican Studies in March 1993, during which first drafts of the principal papers included in this book were presented and critiqued. Fifteen of the commentaries presented at the 1993 workshop have been included in this volume, thus giving the reader a sense of the diversity of scholarly interpretations on the subject of immigration control and providing grist for ongoing academic and policy debates in the field.

The research for this book included hundreds of personal interviews with government officials, academic experts, representatives of nongovernmental social service organizations, business and labor leaders, and other key informants in the nine countries represented in the study. We are most grateful to these individuals for sharing so generously with us their data, insights, and experiences. Information has also been drawn from public opinion surveys; government documents and reports; public statements and reports by private business associations, labor unions, political parties, and other nongovernmental organizations; newspapers; unpublished papers by academic researchers; and the published scientific literature.

Most of the field research for the in-depth country case studies included in this book was undertaken in 1992 and 1993. The data collection, analysis, and write-up, as well as the project workshop held in March 1993, were supported by generous grants from the Law and Social Science Program of the National Science Foundation (grant #SES 9113739), the Ford Foundation, the Andrew W. Mellon Foundation, the Japan Foundation Center for Global Partnership (through the Social Science Research Council), the University of California's Pacific Rim Research Program, and the Center for German and European Studies at the University of California, Berkeley. Supplemental support for book preparation and dissemination of the research findings was provided by the Center for Iberian and Latin American Studies (CILAS) at the University of California, San Diego. The editors and other contributing authors are solely responsible for all facts and interpretations presented in this book.

Finally, Wayne Cornelius wishes to express deepest gratitude to Grant Barnes, Director Emeritus of the Stanford University Press, for his patience and encouragement over many years. This book has taken a form quite different from the work that we jointly envisioned during the early phase of research on the current wave of Mexican migration to the United States. The final product reflects both changing economic, social, and political realities (i.e., the spread of the perceived "crisis" of immigration control to most of the world's industrialized democracies) and a belated recognition of the analytic payoffs of the comparative method in understanding what is unique and what is generalizable about the contemporary U.S. experience with Third World immigration.

Wayne A. Cornelius
Philip L. Martin
James F. Hollifield

La Jolla, California
August 1994

Contributors

WALTER ACTIS is a sociologist and member of the Madrid-based research team Colectivo Ioé, which studies migration, social movements, and related issues. Actis collaborated in Ioé's seminal study of Spain's immigrant population and has prepared reports for the European Commission, the government of Spain, universities in Spain and abroad, nongovernmental organizations, and trade unions. The Ioé research team has published several books, including *Los inmigrantes en España* (1987) and *La inmigración extranjera en Catalunya: balance y perspectivas* (1992).

ROGERS BRUBAKER is Associate Professor of Sociology at the University of California, Los Angeles. He is author, most recently, of *Citizenship and Nationhood in France and Germany* (1992). His current work centers on the triangular interplay, in post-Soviet Eurasia, between national minorities (especially Russians and Hungarians), the newly nationalizing states in which they live, and the external national "homelands" (i.e., Russia and Hungary) to which they belong by ethnic affinity but not legal citizenship.

KITTY CALAVITA is Associate Professor of Criminology/Law and Society at the University of California, Irvine. She is the author of many articles and books on immigration history and policy, including *Inside the State: The Bracero Program, Immigration and the INS* (1992). She has lived and traveled extensively in Italy, where she held a Fulbright award in 1984 to study Italian labor law and occupational safety and health policy. She has been studying Italian immigration policy and its relationship to domestic labor law since the late 1980s.

WAYNE A. CORNELIUS is the Gildred Professor of U.S.-Mexican Relations and the founding Director of the Center for U.S.-Mexican Studies at the University of California, San Diego, where he is also Professor of

Political Science. In 1992–1993 he was an Abe Fellow of the Japan Foundation Center for Global Partnership, conducting research on immigration policy in Japan. His numerous publications on Mexican labor migration to the United States include, most recently, "The Uncertain Connection: Free Trade and Rural Mexican Migration to the United States," *International Migration Review* (with Philip L. Martin, Fall 1993). Other recent articles include "Controlling Latin American Migration to Industrialized Countries: The U.S. and Japanese Experiences," *Annals of Latin American Studies* (Japan, 1994) and "The 'New' Immigration and the Politics of Cultural Diversity in the United States and Japan," *Asian and Pacific Migration Journal* (Philippines, 1993). His current research deals with the educational needs of immigrant children in California and the impact of business cycles on the demand for foreign-born labor in Japan and the United States.

MIGUEL A. DE PRADA is a sociologist and member of the Colectivo Ioé research team in Madrid. The group's research on migration, social movements, and related issues includes the first empirical study of Spain's foreign-born population, *Los inmigrantes en España* (1987). Ioé members have prepared numerous reports for the European Commission, the government of Spain, universities in Spain and abroad, nongovernmental organizations, and trade unions.

MIRIAM FELDBLUM is Assistant Professor of Politics at the University of San Francisco. She received her Ph.D. from Yale University and has been a Visiting Scholar at the Center for European Studies at Stanford University. She has published articles on Franco-North Africans, ethnic politics in France, French citizenship, and immigration politics in Europe and the United States. Currently she is working on a comparative study of citizenship and immigration in Europe.

GARY P. FREEMAN is Professor of Government at the University of Texas at Austin. He is the author of *Immigrant Labor and Racial Conflict in Industrial Societies: The French and British Experience, 1945–75* (1979) and coeditor of *Nations of Immigrants: Australia, the United States, and International Migration* (1992). His recent articles on migration include "From 'Populate or Perish' to 'Diversity or Decline': Immigration and Australian National Security," in *International Migration and Security* (edited by Myron Weiner, 1993), and "Can Liberal States Control Unwanted Migration?" *The Annals* (July 1994).

MANUEL GARCIA Y GRIEGO is Assistant Professor of Social Sciences at the University of California, Irvine, and Associate Professor of International Studies at El Colegio de México, in Mexico City. He has written widely on international migration and on U.S.-Mexico relations. His recent articles include "Policymaking at the Apex: International Migration, State Autonomy, and Societal Constraints," in *U.S.-Mexican Relations: Labor Market Interdependence* (edited by J.A. Bustamante, C.W. Reynolds, and R.A. Hinojosa Ojeda, 1992).

JAMES C. HATHAWAY is Professor of Law at York University in Toronto, Canada, where he teaches in the fields of international human rights law and refugee law. He is also Associate Director of York University's Centre for Refugee Studies. He has served as Consultant on Special Legal Assistance for the Disadvantaged for the Canadian Department of Justice. He is the author of numerous articles on international refugee law and a treatise on the scope of the refugee definition, *The Law of Refugee Status* (1991).

JAMES F. HOLLIFIELD is the Alumni Associate Professor of Political Science at Auburn University, where he teaches comparative and international political economy. He has served as Associate Director of Research at the CNRS and the Centre d'Etudes et de Recherches Internationales of the FNSP in Paris, and was an associate at Harvard's Center for International Affairs. A specialist on France as well as comparative immigration studies, his books include *Immigrants, Markets, and States* (1992) and *Searching for the New France* (coedited with G. Ross, 1991). His most recent work is on migration as an issue area in international relations.

ELMAR HÖNEKOPP is an economist and Senior Researcher at the Institute for Employment Research in Nuremberg, Germany. His work deals with various aspects of international labor markets. He is coauthor and editor of *Economic Aspects of the Employment of Foreign Workers in Germany* (1987) and coeditor of *European Integration and the Labour Market: Basic Questions and Perspectives* (1994). His current work focuses on economic and labor market development in Eastern Europe and its consequences for Germany and Western Europe.

ZIG LAYTON-HENRY is Director of the ESRC Centre for Research in Ethnic Relations at the University of Warwick. He is the author of *The Politics of Race in Britain* (1984) and *The Politics of Immigration: Immigration, Race and Race Relations in Britain* (1992), and editor of *The Political Rights of Migrant Workers in Western Europe* (1990). He is researching issues of citizenship, discrimination, and racism in Britain and Germany.

DAVID A. MARTIN is the Henry L. & Grace Doherty Professor of Law at the University of Virginia, teaching immigration, constitutional law, and international human rights. From 1978 to 1980 he served in the Human Rights Bureau of the U.S. Department of State, where he worked on both human rights and refugee matters and was involved in the drafting of the U.S. Refugee Act of 1980. He has published numerous works on immigration, refugees, international human rights, and constitutional law, including a leading casebook on U.S. immigration law.

PHILIP L. MARTIN is Professor of Agricultural Economics at the University of California, Davis. He was a Fulbright Fellow at the University of Göttingen in Germany in 1974 and has served as staff associate at the Brookings Institution and as an economist for the Select Commission on Immigration and Refugee Policy. His research on immigration and labor market issues covers the United States, Germany, Turkey, Egypt, and Mexico. He was a member of the Commission on Agricultural Workers established by the Immigration Reform and Control Act of 1986. He recently completed a book on Turkish labor migration to Western Europe and is writing another on the resurgence of farm labor contractors in the United States.

MARK J. MILLER is Professor of Political Science and International Relations at the University of Delaware. He is coauthor of *The Age of Migration: International Population Movements in the Modern World* (1993). Miller has served as the assistant editor of the *International Migration Review* since 1984 and was formerly the U.S. correspondent to the OECD's SOPEMI group of migration specialists. He has published and testified extensively on employer sanctions enforcement and guest-worker programs in Western Europe.

CHRISTOPHER MITCHELL is Professor of Politics and Director of the Center for Latin American and Caribbean Studies at New York University. He is the author of "International Migration, International Relations and Foreign Policy," *International Migration Review* (Fall 1989), and editor of *Western Hemisphere Immigration and United States Foreign Policy* (1992).

JEFFREY S. PASSEL is the Director of the Urban Institute's Program for Research on Immigration Policy, based in Washington, D.C. Prior to joining the Urban Institute, Dr. Passel spent most of his career as an analyst with the U.S. Bureau of the Census. His research has focused on the demography of immigration and the integration of immigrants into American society. His most recent books include *Immigration and Immigrants: Setting the Record Straight* (with Michael Fix, 1994) and *Immigration and Ethnicity: The Integration of America's Newest Immigrants* (coedited with Barry Edmonston, 1994).

CARLOS PEREDA OLARTE, a sociologist, is a cofounder of the Madrid-based research team Colectivo Ioé. The group specializes in issues relating to migration and social movements. It conducted the first comprehensive study of Spain's immigrant population and has prepared reports for the European Commission, the government of Spain, universities in Spain and abroad, and trade unions. Among the books Pereda has coauthored with his Ioé colleagues are *Informe sobre trabajadoras del servicio doméstico en Madrid* (1991) and *La inmigración extranjera en Catalunya: balance y perspectivas* (1992).

EUGEEN E. ROOSENS is Professor and Head of the Department of Anthropology at the Catholic University at Leuven, Belgium. He has been a visiting professor at the University of California, Berkeley. He has done extensive fieldwork in Zaire among the Yaka, in Quebec among the Huron Indians, and in Geel, Belgium. Since 1974 he has directed the Cultural Identity of Ethnic Minorities project, a long-term field study being conducted by a team of scholars operating in several countries.

MARCELO M. SUÁREZ-OROZCO is Associate Professor of Anthropology at the University of California, San Diego. He has been a visiting professor at the Catholic University of Leuven, Belgium, and at Harvard University. His books include *Central American Refugees and U.S. High Schools* (1989) and *Status Inequality: The Self in Culture* (with George A. De Vos, 1990). With Carola Suárez-Orozco as coauthor, he is completing a book entitled *Latino Cultural Psychology*. His primary research interests are the psychocultural aspects of immigration, particularly in the adaptation of the children of immigrants in comparative perspective.

GEORGES P. TAPINOS is Professor of Economics and Demography at the Institut d'Etudes Politiques de Paris and Researcher in Economic Demography at the Institut National d'Etudes Démographiques. He served as Secretary General/Treasurer of the International Union for the Scientific Study of Population from 1981 to 1989. His books include *L'Economie des migrations internationales* (1974), *L'Immigration étrangère en France* (1975), and *Inmigración e integración en Europa* (1993).

ALESSANDRA VENTURINI is a member of the economics faculty at Bergamo University, Italy. Her research focuses on European labor markets and the impact that foreign workers have on them. Among her publications are "Italy in the Context of European Migration," *Regional Development Dialogue* (Autumn 1991), and "Trade, Aid and Migration: Some Basic Policy Issues," *European Economic Review* (April 1993).

PATRICK WEIL, a political scientist, is Professor at the Institut d'Etudes Politiques de Paris, Université de Paris IX, and Director of the European Community Today and Tomorrow program. Among his recent books are *France and Its Foreigners: The Adventure of an Immigration Policy, 1938–1991*

(1991) and *State Strategies and Immigrations* (coedited with Jacqueline Costa-Lascoux, 1992).

KEIKO YAMANAKA is a Research Associate at the Institute for the Study of Social Change, University of California, Berkeley. She has taught at Ithaca College and Grinnell College, and was an Advanced Research Fellow in the Program on U.S.-Japan Relations at Harvard University. As an Abe Fellow in 1993, she conducted research on immigrant workers in Japan. Her recent publications include "New Immigration Policy and Unskilled Foreign Workers in Japan," *Pacific Affairs* (Spring 1993).

PART I

OVERVIEW

1

Introduction: The Ambivalent Quest for Immigration Control

Wayne A. Cornelius, Philip L. Martin, and James F. Hollifield

This book is a systematic, comparative study of immigration policy and policy outcomes in nine industrialized democracies: the United States, Canada, Britain, France, Germany, Belgium, Italy, Spain, and Japan. It has two central, interrelated theses. The first, which we call the *"convergence hypothesis,"* is that there is growing similarity among industrialized, labor-importing countries in terms of (1) the policy instruments chosen for controlling immigration, especially unauthorized immigration and refugee flows from less developed countries; (2) the results or efficacy of immigration control measures; (3) social integration policies (the measures adopted by labor-importing countries that affect the extent and rate of social, economic, and political integration among immigrants who become long-term residents); and (4) general-public reactions to current immigrant flows and evaluations of government efforts to control immigration.

Second, we argue that the gap between the *goals* of national immigration policy (laws, regulations, executive actions, etc.) and the actual results of policies in this area (policy *outcomes*) is wide and growing wider in all major industrialized democracies, thus provoking greater public hostility toward immigrants in general (regardless of legal status) and putting intense pressure on political parties and government officials to adopt more restrictive policies. We refer to this as the *"gap hypothesis."*

Beyond testing these general hypotheses against the comparative evidence gathered in the nine countries represented in the book, we seek

The helpful comments of Lawrence H. Fuchs, Brandeis University, on an earlier draft of this chapter and other parts of this book are gratefully acknowledged.

to *explain* the declining efficacy of immigration control measures in today's labor-importing countries, in an era of unprecedented international labor mobility. In each of the in-depth country profiles presented in the book, the author explains why certain immigration control measures were chosen (or *not* chosen) by that country, and why these measures usually failed to achieve their stated objectives.

Our findings generally support the hypothesis of increased "convergence" among industrialized, labor-importing countries, along the lines described above, as well as the "gap" hypothesis emphasizing the divergence between immigration policies and policy outcomes. Despite significant increases in immigration control efforts in several of the countries under study (especially France, Germany, and the United States) and the tightening of entry restrictions and monitoring of unauthorized immigrants already working in other countries (e.g., Japan, Spain), we found less confidence today among officials that they could effectively regulate immigration flows and employment of unauthorized foreign workers than there was fifteen years ago. There appears to be a "hardening" of employer demand for foreign labor in key sectors of these countries' economies—i.e., the hiring or continued employment of foreign workers, regardless of legal status, is increasingly insensitive to cyclical economic fluctuations, as measured by unemployment rates in the labor-importing countries.[1] However, the supply of immigrant labor in these countries is now determined mainly by conditions in the principal sending countries, combined with the expansion of already established transborder social and labor brokerage networks promoting migration for family reunification or economic gain.

The country studies highlight the administrative, political, and economic difficulties that hinder enforcement of laws and regulations against unauthorized labor migration in relatively open and pluralistic societies. In countries like those represented in this book, where bureaucratic power is routinely open to contestation by a variety of social and economic groups, reducing the "demand-pull" factors that attract migrants is extremely difficult. Competing interests in pluralistic societies lead to policy-making gridlock which, in the face of ever stronger economic incentives, permits immigration to continue in one form or another. Such policy paralysis also sends mixed signals to prospective migrants in the labor-exporting countries, encouraging them to overcome whatever new obstacles may be placed in their path. This helps to explain, for example, the cross-national failure of laws penalizing em-

---

[1]For example, in the United States, until some point in the 1970s there was a clear relationship between the availability of labor for agricultural work and the urban unemployment rate. Similarly, in the 1960s a large portion of the variance in Turkish emigration to Germany could be explained by fluctuations in the German unemployment rate. Today neither correlation would be statistically significant.

ployers who hire unauthorized foreign workers to reduce illegal immigration over the long term.

On the other hand, industrialized countries cannot, at least in the short term, realistically hope to reduce the "supply-push" pressures in the principal labor-exporting countries to which they are now linked through trade liberalization, direct foreign investment, or various forms of development assistance. And as the case studies in this book show, severing the family- and employer-based network "bridges" that link high-emigration and labor-importing nations seems to be getting harder rather than easier.

At the same time, "fixing" immigration control systems that are buckling under the pressure of new waves of refugees and economic migrants has become a political imperative in most of the countries we have studied. The principal exceptions are Canada, Spain, Italy, and Japan, where the numbers of new immigrants are still relatively small, general public hostility to them remains relatively low, and foreign workers can still be absorbed easily into labor-short sectors of the formal economy or the burgeoning informal ("black" or "underground") economy.

However, even in these de facto countries of immigration, general publics and the politicians and political parties that respond to them are increasingly uneasy about the long-term implications of current immigration flows from Third World countries for maintenance of national culture, language, and identity. Even if foreign workers and their dependents living in industrialized democracies are not *illegal* aliens (e.g., there are millions of settled, legally admitted foreign "guest-workers" in European countries), they are still *unwanted* as a permanent component of the population, often for noneconomic reasons (e.g., low tolerance for cultural, racial, and ethnic diversity; fear of crime; overcrowding in major urban areas).

This situation generates strong incentives for public officials in labor-importing industrial democracies to redouble their efforts at immigration control, by fine-tuning existing control measures like employer sanctions, investing more heavily in border enforcement, and pursuing new experiments to restore at least the appearance of control. The more advanced agenda of anti-immigration forces in these countries today is to (1) curtail the access of illegal immigrants to tax-supported public services, including education and nonemergency health care; (2) block any policies and programs that would accelerate the socioeconomic and cultural integration of settled immigrants and their offspring; and (3) take symbolically important steps to discourage permanent settlement, such as tightening citizenship requirements for legal immigrants, or denying citizenship to the native-born children of illegal immigrants. It remains to be seen how much of this agenda can be translated into law and public policy in each of the labor-importing countries, and if so, whether such measures can serve as an effective deterrent to future unwanted migration.[2]

Immigration Control in Industrialized Democracies: The Nature of the Dilemma

In the last decades of the twentieth century, immigration has become a central issue of politics and public policy in the advanced industrial democracies. In Europe, immigration is already a driving factor in electoral politics, and it is becoming an increasingly potent electoral issue in the United States (at least in the five states most impacted by illegal immigration).[3] After decades of importing foreign labor as "guests," many European nations are now confronted with the unexpected and unwanted challenge of assimilating large numbers of culturally different, permanent resident aliens and their offspring. In Japan, the recent influx of foreign workers eagerly sought by labor-hungry, small and medium-sized employers into a racially and culturally homogeneous society looms as a volatile issue of national policy in the 1990s. In the United States, the latest waves of largely Hispanic and Asian immigrants have yet to provoke the same degree of nativist political reaction and violence observable in Europe since the late 1980s; but there is no question that a broadly based, anti-immigration backlash—supported even by mainstream-liberal intellectuals who warn of the "Balkanization" of America—is building.[4]

The increasing international mobility of workers and their dependents has had a dramatic impact on relations among states. The major industrial democracies have scrambled to find ways to consult with each

---

[2]A related issue is the way in which *subnational* units of government may respond to the immigrant populations within their jurisdictions. Even where efforts to exclude immigrants from public programs and services funded primarily by national governments may fail, subnational governments may seek to deny or restrict immigrants' access to services that they provide, such as public education and various social welfare programs. The most extreme example of this phenomenon in the U.S. context is the "S.O.S." ("Save Our State") voter initiative in the state of California, which if approved in the November 1994 election would deny all public services to illegal immigrants and their children except emergency health care, and require police, educators, social workers, and other service providers to report suspected illegal aliens to state or federal authorities. More than 600,000 Californians signed petitions to put the "S.O.S." initiative on the ballot. For case studies of the efforts of two other U.S. states (Massachusetts and Texas) to develop their own policies in this area, see Zimmerman and Fix 1994: 287–316. For examples of subnational units that have opted for more *inclusionary* social policies toward immigrants than the national government has been willing to sanction, see Cornelius on Japan, this volume.

[3]The states of California, Texas, New York, Illinois, and Florida accounted for 81 percent of the 3.2 million illegal immigrants that the U.S. Immigration and Naturalization Service estimated were present in the United States in 1992.

[4]For examples of the "Balkanization" argument, see Schlesinger 1992; Johnson 1994, especially 261–93; *Wall Street Journal* 1994. On recent general trends in U.S. public opinion toward immigration, see Espenshade and Calhoun 1993; R. Simon 1993; Simon and Alexander 1993.

other and coordinate policies for controlling migration, especially refugee flows. This new dynamic in international relations, to which we will return later in this chapter, is particularly evident in Europe, where the relaxation of internal borders (associated with the Single Market initiative and the drive for economic and political union) is pushing states to seek common visa and asylum policies.

The end of the Cold War has contributed to this sea change in international relations by increasing the movement of populations from east to west, but *without* slowing or stopping south-to-north migration flows. As a policy issue, international migration has moved from the realm of "low politics" (i.e., problems of domestic governance, especially labor market and demographic policies) to the realm of "high politics" (i.e., problems affecting relations between states, including questions of war and peace). The former Yugoslavia and Haiti provide perhaps the best current examples of this phenomenon. Attempts have been made by governments to recast international migration as a problem of national security, and international organizations, such as the United Nations High Commission for Refugees, have come under intense pressure to help states manage the increasing flows.

Should we therefore conclude that increased movements of people across national borders are primarily a function of changes in the international system? Clearly there is a connection between certain changes in the international political economy and the increasing mobility of people (see Hollifield 1992a). But we shall argue that *endogenous* factors are the key determinants. As much as Europe, North America, and Japan may wish to ignore or avoid dealing with these factors, they must eventually recognize that the "crisis of immigration control" which they are experiencing derives largely from political, economic, and social changes occurring *within* the major labor-importing countries.

On the economic side, neoclassical "push-pull" arguments provide us with a simple and straightforward explanation for increases in immigration. Demand-pull in the U.S. and European economies during the 1950s and 1960s was so great as to stimulate large-scale migrations from the poorer economies of the "periphery" (Mexico, Turkey, North Africa, etc.).[5] These labor migrations were initiated and legitimized by the receiving states, in Western Europe through the so-called guest-worker programs, and in the United States through the Bracero Program of contract labor importation (1942–1964). But what started as an optimal movement of labor from south to north became, in the 1970s and 1980s, a sociopolitical liability as economic growth in Western Europe and North America slowed in the aftermath of the first big postwar recession (1973–1974).

---

[5] For general accounts of the role of labor migration in the economies of post-World War II Europe, see Tapinos 1974; Böhning 1984; Hollifield 1992b; Castles and Miller 1993.

But stopping immigration, even during a period of sharp economic contraction, proved exceedingly difficult, in part because of powerful, underlying push-pull factors. Demand-pull migration had initiated processes that continued to have unanticipated consequences, from the micro level (e.g., employers wanting to retain their "guestworkers" indefinitely) to the macro (e.g., the increasingly large role of immigration in host-country population and labor force growth; the multi-billion-dollar dependence of sending-country economies on migrant remittances[6]). Moreover, supply-push migration reached new heights as the populations of peripheral countries like Turkey, Mexico, and Algeria grew at a very rapid pace, even as their economies also slowed as a result of the global recession. Finally, migration networks had developed during the years of expansionary immigration policies, helping to spread information about job opportunities and modes of entry and residence in the receiving countries to the smallest villages. These transnational social networks, perhaps more than any other factor, helped to sustain migration—especially family reunification immigration to Europe and illegal labor migration from Mexico to the United States—during periods of high uncertainty regarding employment prospects in the labor-importing countries.[7] Thus, despite the economic recessions of 1973–1974, 1981, and 1991 to the present, immigration has continued at historically high levels, and governments have scrambled to redesign immigration control and refugee admission policies to cope with the rising tides.

Push-pull forces and the imbalances between economies of the North and South (as well as West and East within Europe) provide *necessary* but not *sufficient* conditions for immigration, especially on the scale experienced during the last fifteen years. To explain the "crisis of immigration control" in the last decades of the twentieth century, we must look beyond macro- and microeconomics, and even social networks, to trends in the *political* development of the major receiving countries.

The difficulties of immigration control in industrialized democracies today are closely linked to the rise of rights-based politics in postwar Western Europe and the United States (see Hollifield 1992b, especially chaps. 1 and 8). This new brand of politics is especially evident in debates over immigration, naturalization, and asylum policies in the larger

---

[6]See, for example, Asch 1994. With specific reference to Mexico, see Lozano Ascencio 1993; Massey and Parrado 1994.

[7]For a general perspective on the evolution of the immigrant network phenomenon in U.S. history, see Tilly 1980. A valuable case study of the insertion and consolidation of immigrant networks in a particular segment of the New York City labor market is provided in Waldinger 1994. In the case of Japan, the relative *weakness* of family-based migration networks—most of which date only from the late 1980s—may help to account for the apparent leveling off of the unauthorized immigrant population during Japan's recession of the 1990s, despite persistently strong push factors in the principal sending countries.

republican democracies: France, Germany, and the United States. The newer, de facto countries of immigration—Spain, Italy, and Japan—are just beginning to put into place policies for coping with the arrival of foreign workers; but they, too, must face the issues of how many migrants to accept, from which countries, and what rights and social services to provide to them. Individual rights-based policies help immigrants not only to get in (e.g., as asylum claimants) but to *stay* in labor-importing countries. In sum, it is to both political and economic changes in these states that we must look for an adequate explanation of the increasing difficulty of immigration control in industrialized democracies.

Rights-based Liberalism

The gradual extension of rights to ethnic minorities and foreigners over a period of several decades, from the 1960s through the 1980s, is one of the most salient aspects of political development in the advanced industrial democracies. The creation of new legal spaces for marginal groups (including foreigners) in societies as different as Germany and the United States is linked to a much broader change in democratic politics, which originates in the American civil rights struggle. A new type of liberal *republicanism* has taken shape at many levels of the democratic polity: in legislative acts, partisan and interest group (especially ethnic) politics, and most important of all, in judicial rulings.[8] Judicial activism of this sort has gained many supporters and detractors, and has helped to spawn a plethora of advocacy groups, ranging from social movements and political parties of the extreme right (such as the Front National in France and the "skinheads" in Germany) to civil rights groups (e.g., S.O.S. Racisme and France Plus, in France; S.O.S. Racismo in Spain).

Even though the history of rights-based politics in the United States is quite different than in Europe, the impact on politics and immigration policy has been much the same: expanded rights for marginal and ethnic groups, including foreigners. These historical developments have provoked a rethinking of classical liberal theory in the works of scholars who place human (and especially civil and social) rights squarely at the center of a new social contract (see, for example, Rawls 1971; Walzer 1983; Hirsch 1992). Redefining the relationship between individuals, groups, and the state, through a process of political struggle, has had a great impact on the capacity of democratic states to control immigration. While judicial rulings of

---

[8]By far the most important of these rulings in the U.S. context came in the 1982 U.S. Supreme Court case *Plyer vs. Doe*, which assured the right to free public education to illegal alien children residing anywhere in the United States. The rationale behind the lower-court ruling that was affirmed in *Plyer vs. Doe* is explained in Cornelius and Anzaldúa Montoya 1983: 172–77.

recent years have whittled away at some of the rights and protections previously accorded to immigrants in the United States and Europe, the legal and political legacy of the 1960s, 1970s, and 1980s continues to constrain the executive authorities of democratic states in their attempts to achieve territorial closure and to exclude certain individuals and groups from membership in society.[9]

It is the confluence of *markets* (the push-pull factors described above) and *rights* that explains much of the contemporary difficulty of immigration control in Europe and the United States. This new political-economic dynamic seems to have broken or seriously weakened the historically close linkage between business cycles and "admissionist" or "restrictionist" immigration policies.[10] Recent efforts by democratic states to regain control of their borders all point to a gradual recognition that effective control of immigration requires a rollback of civil and human rights for noncitizens. Examples include the U.S. policy of interdicting Haitian and Chinese refugees on the high seas (to prevent them from reaching U.S. territory and gaining access to the refugee admissions process), the German decision to radically tighten the provisions of its asylum law (formerly the most liberal in Europe), and new powers granted to the police in France and Spain to carry out random identity checks on any suspicious (or foreign-looking!) individual.

Obviously, the development of rights-based politics in a number of West European countries has not prevented or dampened a nationalist backlash against immigration in the 1980s and 1990s. The French Front National is perhaps the most widely known of the new anti-immigrant political movements, but many others have emerged in almost every industrialized country that has experienced large-scale immigration in recent decades, and even in one (the United Kingdom) that has not.[11] The backlash is nationalist, particularist, and exclusionary in character. Its principal target is immigrants, but criticisms are also leveled at liberal parties and politicians who support the expansion or preservation of civil and political rights for ethnic minorities.

The assault from the extreme right places politicians of the left and center-right under tremendous electoral pressures. For example, how can a "liberal" society tolerate the presence of individuals who are *members* but not *citizens* of that society? Should not all individuals who are members (i.e., permanent residents) of a liberal society be ac-

---

[9] One of the best illustrations of the impact of these earlier changes in political and legal culture on immigration policy in the United States can be found in Schuck 1984.

[10] For evidence to substantiate this argument, see, for example, Hollifield 1992b: chap. 5.

[11] For a detailed profile of the most important anti-immigrant movement in Germany, see Veen et al. 1993. See also Suárez-Orozco's discussion of the Vlaams Blok party (this volume) and Layton-Henry's discussion of the British National Party (this volume).

corded the full panoply of rights (social and political as well as civil) enjoyed by those who are citizens?[12] This is the dilemma that "liberals" must face, and it is particularly acute in a country like Germany, which has a large, multigenerational resident alien population (mostly Turks) that remains just outside of the confines of the social contract.[13] In sum, immigration in most of the countries represented in this book can no longer be debated strictly in economic or demographic terms; the terms of citizenship, membership in national and local communities, and basic human rights must also be addressed.

Countries of Immigration: The North American Experience

The United States: Conflict and Contradictions

Of all the countries included in this study, the United States has by far the largest gap between the stated goal of controlling immigration and the actual results of policy: ever increasing numbers of both legal and illegal immigrants. In her treatment of the U.S. case, Kitty Calavita views immigration and immigration policy in the post-World War II period as a history of "paired oppositions": (1) between *employers*, seeking a cheap and tractable source of labor, and U.S.-born *workers*, whose bargaining power is threatened by an influx of nonunionized, immigrant labor; (2) between an *economy* that generates a high demand for unskilled labor (whose importation is periodically sanctioned and promoted by the state) and a *political class* unwilling to confront the social conflicts associated with that demand; and (3) between the *human rights* associated with liberal democracy and the exigencies of *border controls*. These "oppositions" or tensions have come to the fore during recessionary periods, leading to outbreaks of xenophobia and restrictionism and making it increasingly difficult for the state to articulate a coherent immigration policy.

The 1986 Immigration Reform and Control Act (IRCA) exemplifies the contradictions that run throughout recent attempts at immigration reform in the United States. The main purpose of IRCA was ostensibly to attack the problem of illegal immigration and regain control of the borders. To accomplish this, an employer sanctions law was enacted for the first time in American history, to placate restrictionists. But this key element of IRCA was weakened from the outset by legal protections afforded employers, who are not required to verify the authenticity of documents (social security cards, permanent resident-alien cards, etc.) presented to them by prospective

---

[12]Our reference here is to the "trilogy" of rights—civil, political, and social—defined by T.H. Marshall (1950: chap. 4).

[13]On the problems faced by the Turkish minority in Germany, see Faist 1993, 1994.

employees.[14] In addition, IRCA offered a generous amnesty (or legalization) to illegal aliens and created a Special Agricultural Workers (SAW) program, both of which contributed to a further influx of immigrant workers into the U.S. labor market. Thus IRCA attempted to reconcile the rising political clamor for border control with the continuing demand for cheap immigrant labor. The result was to increase the gap between the goals and outcomes of U.S. immigration policy.

Calavita points out that IRCA is simply the latest chapter in a long history of state sponsorship of large-scale immigration of unskilled labor, which can be traced initially to the Bracero Program begun in 1942, but which has its origins in the earliest decades of the Republic. Throughout the nineteenth century, especially during the height of the industrial revolution following the Civil War, U.S. immigration policy was geared to creating a low-cost, tractable, and unlimited supply of labor. What distinguishes the earlier eras from today's situation is the restructuring of the U.S. economy, which has moved away from heavy manufacturing with more or less stable, semiskilled production line jobs to a service economy with a much higher percentage of temporary, unskilled jobs. Immigrants have rushed into the American labor market to fill these jobs, continuing to perform the same economic function as in earlier periods. The long-standing contradictions inherent in American immigration policy thus remain unresolved.

Philip Martin also points to the failures of U.S. policy, which he views largely as a consequence of "benign neglect." Unlike Calavita, however, he argues that it may be possible for the United States to articulate a coherent immigration policy and regain control of its borders *if* there is a clear consensus on what "the problem" is, what has caused it, and what must be done to close the gap between goals and outcomes of policy. Martin defines "the problem" as illegal immigration, specifically the recent waves of largely unskilled immigrants, whose presence magnifies the inequalities in American society and who may find themselves confined to a permanent underclass. If steps are not taken to

---

[14]It took eight years, from the enactment of IRCA, for the first southern California employer to be indicted on criminal charges of repeatedly accepting false documents from illegal alien job applicants (López 1994). A belated attempt to close the gaping loophole that has made it so difficult to enforce employer sanctions in the United States may result from the work of the U.S. Commission on Immigration Reform, which in August 1994 recommended the creation of a national, computerized registry containing the names and social security numbers of all persons authorized to work in the United States, coupled with a telephone verification system. While stopping short of calling for a new, national identification card, the Commission also recommended the issuance of counterfeit-resistant versions of commonly used identifiers, such as social security cards and driver's licenses. Implementing these immigration control measures may require new legislation at both federal and state levels. In addition, there are a number of serious practical obstacles to be overcome, such as the common practice of using valid social security numbers borrowed from relatives or friends to gain employment, and the use of fraudulent base documents (e.g., birth certificates) to obtain even the new "tamper-proof" social security cards.

stem the tide of illegal immigration, he argues, the United States may end up with an "hourglass-shaped" society, characterized by a wealthy (but isolated) upper class, and a large, uneducated lower class. Martin attributes the failure of policy makers to address this problem to two principal factors: (1) a lack of consensus on policy options, which translates too often into a lack of concern (benign neglect); and (2) a lack of understanding of the root causes of illegal immigration.

The lack of consensus can be explained in part by the fact that the United States still perceives itself as a nation of immigrants—a tradition that makes it difficult to restrict or control any type of immigration. Moreover, immigration generates immediate benefits for many groups (business owners, middle-class consumers, etc.), while the costs of immigration (especially in terms of the long-term impacts of unskilled and illegal immigration on society) are deferred. But pressures on the U.S. system of immigration control are now building as never before because of the large economic and demographic imbalances between developed and developing nations. For this reason, according to Martin, it is essential for high-immigration countries like the United States to understand clearly the causes and consequences of unauthorized immigration, and to design policies to head off excessive social costs in the future.

Martin views immigration as a result of (1) demand-pull factors, (2) supply-push pressures, and (3) migration networks. He argues that governments of developed countries have some control over each of these factors, but they should focus on those over which they have greatest control—i.e., the demand for unskilled, immigrant labor (especially in the service sector, which he believes should be more tightly regulated) and migration networks (especially professional smuggling rings, which should be broken up). If such steps are not taken, in Martin's view, the gap between the goals and consequences of immigration policy in the United States will continue to widen; social inequality will increase; and the probability of a generalized xenophobic backlash will rise. Martin proposes a "grand bargain": preventing as much as possible of new illegal immigration, in order to integrate the resident-alien (settled) population and to avoid the creation of a new underclass.

Canada: Low-conflict Incrementalism

Among the countries represented in this book, Canada seems to be most comfortable with its immigration policy. Canada's is a consensual and relatively open approach to immigration, reminiscent of earlier periods of U.S. history, when immigration was generally viewed as a great asset. Manuel García y Griego's analysis of the recent Canadian experience reveals a much smaller gap between immigration policy goals and outcomes than in the other countries that we have examined, with the

partial exception of refugee and asylum policies. This is partly attributable to the fact that immigration remains a vital part of Canada's national
development strategy, but also to the fact that Canada (unlike the United
States) has not experienced a large, uncontrolled influx of unskilled,
illegal immigrants. Temporary agricultural workers are imported on a
small scale (e.g., a total of 12,237 such workers were admitted in 1989–
1990) under bilateral agreements with Mexico and several West Indian
countries.

García y Griego attributes the success of Canadian immigration
policy to a variety of factors: the flexibility of policy makers (who have
been able to administer and manage immigration flows with reassuring
competence); the self-confidence of the Canadian public, much of which
has a multicultural outlook as a result of having two "founding nationalities"; and the increasing rationalization of immigration policy, as the
country moved gradually away from the "white Canada" policy of the
pre-World War II era toward a neatly prioritized system of control,
epitomized by the point system.

While there have been some minor problems in the area of asylum
claims and occasional outbreaks of concern over illegal immigration, the
Canadians would seem to be fortunate in that their large neighbor to the
south helps deflect pressures that arise in these two areas. García y
Griego points out that many potential refugees and "illegals" either
remain in the United States or flee there if denied entry or residence in
Canada.

If there is a gap between policy goals and outcomes in Canada, it is
to be found primarily in the large backlog of asylum cases created by a
complicated appeal process, which is not uncommon in other liberal
democracies. Thus, in spite of the similarities between the U.S. and
Canadian immigration experiences—both are, by tradition and self-
image, "nations of immigrants"—the nature and severity of problems
associated with contemporary immigration are quite different.

There are, nevertheless, a few signs of convergence. In the fall 1993
electoral campaign, the Reform Party attacked federal spending on
activities intended to promote tolerance for multiculturalism and called
for a reduction in total annual immigration from 250,000 to 150,000, in
light of Canada's persistently high unemployment rate (11 percent in
1994). Nevertheless, in 1994 the Canadian government maintained its
original targets for immigration and refugee admissions, even while
stationing immigration officers at some overseas airports to prevent
aliens deemed likely to request asylum in Canada from boarding planes
that would fly them there. Linguistically based tensions have also begun
to develop between immigrant minorities and the majority French-
speaking population in the province of Quebec. Newly arrived immigrants in Montreal have tended to adopt English rather than French as
their language, for economic reasons (Raskin 1993: 70–73).

Reluctant Countries of Immigration: The West European Experience

France: The Republican Model of Immigration Policy

James Hollifield argues in this volume that in France the strength of the political ideology of republicanism—initially a form of left-wing, rights-based politics—buttressed by the labor requirements of French capitalism and the policy preferences of government economic planners enabled successive post-World War II governments to justify liberal immigration and naturalization policies. Such policies also derived from the early establishment, in the nineteenth century, of a pattern whereby immigrant labor was privately recruited by French industry, often with government sanction but with very little state control. The organization of foreign labor importation by the private sector largely bypassed official institutions created to manage immigration flows. The historical pattern has been for such flows to accelerate to the point where the state is compelled, for political reasons, to intervene and try to regain control.

French immigration policy was complicated by the country's highly conflictive experience with decolonization in the 1950s and 1960s, which created a special class of protected immigrants who were quasi-citizens of France. Decolonization created ethnic and racial fault lines in French society that set the stage for the immigration control controversies of the 1970s and 1980s, leading to policies designed to discourage permanent settlement of some nationalities, especially Algerians and other North Africans.

Prior to the oil shocks of 1973, various government attempts at tighter immigration control were defeated by a combination of the high demand for labor, the ambiguous status of citizens of France's former colonies, and deeply rooted respect for the civil and human rights of foreigners. But France was not impervious to the anti-immigrant tide that swept Western Europe in 1973–1974. Henceforth, government policy was to treat foreigners as "guests" rather than potential permanent settlers, and public opinion turned sharply against immigration, which was widely blamed for exacerbating the deteriorating economic situation.

Post-1974 government attempts to halt foreign worker immigration and induce the repatriation of foreigners already in France only had the effect of stimulating more "backdoor" immigration: family reunification immigration, seasonal worker admissions, and clandestine immigration under the guise of tourism. The weight of republican tradition and the continuing power of rights-based politics championed by nongovernmental organizations (NGOs) reinforced the economic market forces that continued to draw Third World immigrants into the French economy during the remainder of the 1970s and 1980s, despite persistently high (averaging 10 percent) rates of domestic unemployment. Gaps in the labor market for construction and service industries that had been created by the suspension of legal guestworker immigration were filled by new "backdoor" flows.

As in Germany in the 1990s, second-generation immigrants in France became increasingly willing to assert their political rights and cultural identities during the 1980s. Foreign workers and their offspring were increasingly able to exit from declining manufacturing industries and move into jobs in the more dynamic service sector. These developments, together with a generous amnesty program in the early 1980s, which regularized about 140,000 illegal immigrants, further anchored the foreign worker population in France and fueled a public backlash against immigration in general that was effectively channeled by Jean-Marie Le Pen's Front National.

Subsequent political and legislative assaults on the "French republican model" for dealing with immigrants have had little impact on the objective situation of the foreign-born and second-generation populations in France. For example, by contrast with Germany, the French naturalization process has remained relatively open, and no significant obstacles to continued assimilation of the foreign population have been erected.

Immigration nevertheless remains a politically potent issue, with about one-third of the French electorate disposed to support highly restrictive policies. As isolated episodes of "cultural militancy" by members of the North African Muslim community inflamed public opinion, debates over immigration control have been eclipsed at least temporarily by concerns over sociocultural assimilation (the specter of American-style multiculturalism). As in the United States, however, it is likely that the immigration control and immigrant integration debates will become increasingly linked, with advocates of immigration reduction utilizing "cultural threat" arguments to justify their position.[15]

The ongoing process of European integration has introduced additional, politically sensitive issues into France's immigration debate. For example, the Maastricht Treaty contains a provision that would establish a common tourist visa policy that could be used to exclude certain ethnic and nationality groups—a kind of national-origins quota system. Another provision would enfranchise European Community nationals to participate in local and Europe-wide elections, wherever they may be living.

The post-Cold War surge in refugees and asylum seekers from Eastern Europe has been felt in France, but Germany has clearly borne

---

[15]France's new rightist government has already signaled that it will no longer tolerate multiculturalism, at least in the form of the spread of Muslim customs in the public school system. Moroccan girls wearing traditional head scarves to school have been suspended, and Islamic leaders who defended them were deported or put under house arrest. See Riding 1993.

the brunt of these population movements, and until recently it has been conspicuously less successful than France in controlling the influx of refugees. Nevertheless, France, like all other countries represented in this book, has failed to prevent would-be asylees whose claims are rejected from staying and joining the clandestine workforce of illegal immigrants.

Hollifield points out that, despite all of the recent political turmoil over immigration, France's level of legal immigration has remained essentially unchanged, at slightly over 100,000 per year. Officially, immigration has fallen off somewhat, by 10,000–20,000 per year. But Hollifield surmises that the reduction may be more artificial than real: a higher percentage of the newest arrivals seem to have "gone underground." Even the election in 1993 of a new, rightist government espousing a militantly restrictionist line (France is "a country of immigration that no longer wishes to be"[16]) and a full constitutional debate on immigration policy have yielded only the types of controls that are likely to be more symbolic than effective in stopping new immigration, such as random identity checks by police. While maintaining (or restoring) high rates of economic growth is no longer a politically adequate rationale for an expansionary immigration policy in France, the legitimacy still attached to immigration by the "republican model" has proven strong enough to sustain a relatively generous policy of legal immigration.

Germany: Ineffectual Immigration Control and a Violent Response

The Federal Republic of Germany, formerly the "guestworker" country par excellence, now recoils from the wave of foreigners that has descended upon it since the collapse of East European Communism in 1989, and which has been adding almost 1 percent annually to the German population. The arrival in Germany of 1 million foreigners— including ethnic Germans relocating from the former Soviet Union and its satellites, relatives of immigrants already settled in Germany, applicants for political asylum, and legal and illegal foreign workers—in the year 1990 alone made it by far the leading recipient of immigrants among OECD nations, even while German leaders declared that their country "is not, nor shall it become, a country of immigration." Germans tend to see themselves as the paymasters of Europe ("We have one-quarter of the population and economy, and three-quarters of the immigrants!") and increasingly resent it.

Philip Martin observes in this volume that Germany did, in fact, become a country of immigration, in part because it pursued inherently flawed policies that worked *as intended* the first time they were applied. For example, a recession in 1967 led to the departure of most of the "guestworkers" who had lost their jobs, thereby reinforcing the notion

---

[16]Statement by the newly installed French Interior Minister Charles Pasqua.

that foreign migrant workers could be rotated easily into and out of the German labor market as they were needed. Similarly, when Germany first experienced a rush of asylum seekers in 1980, the crisis seemed to be resolved simply by requiring entry visas of Turks, who comprised half of the 110,000 applicants for asylum in that year. In the long run, neither rotating "guestworkers" nor using visa requirements to deter economic migrants from seeking asylum status proved to be effective policies for Germany, but the search for durable immigration controls was delayed because these flawed policies seemed at first to work.

The millions of foreign "guestworkers" who were recruited under government-to-government agreements between Germany and Spain, Greece, Portugal, and Turkey during the 1960s and early 1970s—reaching a peak of 2.6 million guestworkers in 1972, equivalent to 12 percent of the total workforce—made possible a remarkable economic recovery and expansion that could not possibly have been achieved using Germany's shrinking domestic labor supply alone. However, the "strict rotation" principle on which the guestworker program was originally based began to break down almost immediately, because a rotation policy was not in the interests of either the migrants or their employers. As in France, the abrupt "immigration stop" declared by the German government in 1973 failed to prevent the number of foreigners in Germany from rising; in fact, it actually enlarged the foreign-born population. Migrants' fears of a permanently "closing door" prompted them to remain and, eventually, to bring their dependents to Germany, which the German government allowed them to do if certain requirements were met. The German public was suddenly confronted with the unexpected and unwelcome reality of a large, settled population of Turks, Yugoslavs, and other non-European Community migrants.

Several other government attempts to regulate the behavior of the foreign population during the 1970s and 1980s through restrictions on their geographic mobility, financial incentives, and other measures similarly backfired, creating the image of a government that was hopelessly incapable of controlling immigration flows and equally ineffective in dealing with the challenges of integrating, socially and culturally, the settled population of 6.5 million foreign-born residents and their offspring. The uncontrolled flood of returning ethnic Germans and asylum seekers who began to enter Germany in the late 1980s only compounded this widely held impression of governmental ineffectiveness and loss of control.

The emergence of a powerful anti-immigrant backlash in the early 1990s—including over 2,300 physical attacks on foreigners in 1992 alone—set the stage for a significant tightening of Germany's highly liberal, post-World War II asylum law and regulations, and the imposition of an annual limit on the number of ethnic Germans allowed to return to Germany.[17] German authorities report a sharp drop in asylum applications since the revision of the Basic Law in early 1993. However, there has been no systematic roundup and deportation of the hundreds of thousands of asylum seekers whose claims were rejected in previous years.[18]

The ongoing immigration debate in Germany is being shaped by three key factors: projections of a declining labor force; the need to politically and socially integrate long-settled guestworkers and their offspring from countries like Turkey; and fears of massive, uncontrolled population movements from Eastern Europe. Martin and other observers expect Germany to accept during the 1990s its de facto status as a country of immigration and establish a ceiling of perhaps 200,000–400,000 newcomers (of all types) per year. Setting such an overall annual quota may prove to be less contentious than allocating entries through the returning "ethnic German" citizen, family unification, economic need, and humanitarian entry doors.

Martin suggests that the average German might be willing to accept a situation in which the government makes it easier for foreign residents to become naturalized citizens, in exchange for reduced levels of future immigration. However, any such trade-off will only be proposed, and accepted, with considerable reluctance. As Martin notes, the majority of German politicians as well as average citizens "still cling to the belief that Germany is not a country of immigration, and while they may deplore the [recent] violence against foreigners, they are likely to argue that violence against foreigners is another reason *not* to become an immigration country."

Belgium: The Making of an Immigration Non-Policy

Belgium today is a country more deeply divided than ever along cultural, linguistic, social class, ethnic, and religious lines. Contemporary immigration, mostly from Muslim countries in Africa, has played a major role in deepening and politicizing these cleavages. Like France and Germany, Belgium practiced active recruitment of foreign workers during most of the post-World War II period up to 1974. During the post-1974 period, the principal sources for Belgium's immigration have shifted from Spain, Italy, and other European Community countries to mostly non-EC nations, and the composition of the flow changed from legal "guestworkers" to clandestine immigrants and asylum seekers.

---

[17]For example, a limit of 225,000 has been set on the number of ethnic Germans who can immigrate from the former Soviet Union.

[18]The stock of such denied (but unremoved) asylum applicants in Germany grew rapidly in the late 1980s and early 1990s. In 1991, for example, the number of rejected asylum claimants actually removed from Germany (10,622) represented only 6.5 percent of the number of asylum claims refused in that year (163,637 out of 438,200 claims filed) (Coleman 1994: tables 11, 12).

The new immigrants are perceived not only as a threat to the survival of the dominant Flemish culture but as a major source of crime.

Stepped-up government efforts to discourage family reunification immigration employing bogus marriages and divorces have been largely unsuccessful. As in most of the countries represented in this book, fines and criminal penalties prescribed for employers who hire unauthorized immigrants are rarely enforced and provide no credible deterrent to such hiring. Belgium carefully maintains a "non-policy" on asylum seeking, to avoid setting precedents that large numbers of economic migrants might abuse. Nevertheless, a long (commonly three-year) adjudication process enables most fraudulent applicants to disappear into the labor market. Repatriation of denied asylum seekers whose cases are actually decided is rare; thus, the asylum mechanism continues to function as a key "backdoor" for new immigrants and their dependents, along with bogus tourism. Illegal immigrants stopped by the local police are not detained and expelled; they are simply "invited to leave" the country. Most just move to another town. The repeat offenders who are deported typically are dumped over the Netherlands border, much as the vast majority of undocumented Mexicans apprehended by the U.S. Border Patrol are "voluntarily repatriated" to Tijuana and other Mexican border cities, thereby assuring their swift return.

Despite the extreme weakness of its regulatory regime, which virtually guarantees continued growth of the foreign-born, non-EC population, Belgium is far from having accepted this outcome. Indeed, the evidence reported by Marcelo Suárez-Orozco in this volume suggests that most Belgians flatly reject the notion that a multicultural society could be something positive, enriching, or politically viable. They have no confidence that the new Islamic immigrants can be assimilated. Feeling both culturally and economically insecure in the midst of a steep economic downturn, growing numbers of Belgians have been giving their votes to an extreme-right political party, the Vlaams Blok, that advocates draconian immigration restriction.

Nevertheless, the demand for inexpensive, flexible, low-skilled foreign workers persists in certain sectors of the Belgian economy. Hiring illegal immigrants "off the books" enables employers to bypass Belgium's costly social security system. The phenomenon of "black" (underground) employment is widely accepted, as it is in other West European countries, especially Spain and Italy. There is no evidence of job competition between natives and immigrants, since the latter are typically employed in jobs shunned by natives (e.g., seasonal agriculture, working with toxic chemicals, etc.) even under conditions of high unemployment among the native-born (12 percent in 1993). The hidden consensus seems to be that expelling the foreigners and their offspring who are already integrated into Belgium's economy would be too costly and disruptive. Meanwhile, the consolidation of immigrant communities, especially in big cities like Brussels and Antwerp, acts as a magnet for new entrants.

Despite rising public concern about the continuing influx of foreigners and clear indications of assimilation problems among second- and third-generation immigrants from non-EC countries (elevated school dropout rates, drug use, and other forms of delinquency), most establishment politicians in Belgium see nothing to be gained from a more open, vigorous public debate over immigration policy, which would only generate more fodder for right-wing extremists. The result, as described by Suárez-Orozco, is "non-policy as policy." He predicts that loud official condemnations of illegal immigration will continue to be accompanied by "symbolic—and equivocal—enforcement of controls," at least so long as the political pressures generated by nativist groups can be contained.

British Exceptionalism

Great Britain is *not* a nation of immigrants, and it is emphatically not a "country of immigration"; nevertheless, it continues to experience immigration on a small scale.[19] The British experience is also different from most other cases represented in this volume to the extent that British authorities have been able to set targets for controlling immigration and to stick to them. Zig Layton-Henry offers several explanations for this British exceptionalism. First, successive governments have tenaciously protected British sovereignty in the area of immigration control, even when this has meant marching out of step with Britain's European Community partners. Second, Britain possesses a built-in supply of "immigrant" labor, in the Republic of Ireland, which has long performed the role of industrial reserve army for Britain.[20] Third, British governments have been willing to discriminate in their immigration and naturalization policies, even against former British subjects in the Commonwealth countries. Finally, Britain was for much of its history a country of emigration, conquering and settling many parts of the world; it was only in the 1930s that Britain began to experience significant (non-Irish) immigration.

Britain did experience significant problems of immigrant control after World War II, primarily as a result of decolonization. This was a problem that the British shared with the French and other colonial powers, but the resolution of the problem was very different in Britain.

---

[19]For example, in 1993 some 55,000 legal immigrants were granted residence in the United Kingdom (over half of them from former British colonies), and 22,400 new applications were received from asylum seekers.

[20]For a brief period British Commonwealth states in the Caribbean also supplied contract labor, but fewer than 10,000 workers were recruited from this region (directly by British companies, with no government encouragement), and controls on such labor recruitment were imposed in 1962. See Peach 1991.

Unlike the French, the British did not hesitate to deny the rights of settlement and citizenship to former colonial subjects. As Layton-Henry demonstrates, the postwar history of British immigration and naturalization policy is replete with restrictionist—even racist—legislation, designed explicitly to cut off the flow of nonwhite, non-European immigration.

Perhaps the biggest turning point came in 1981 with the adoption of a new British Nationality Act, which created a kind of gradational citizenship, severely limiting the rights of Commonwealth "citizens" to settle in the United Kingdom. In many ways, this Nationality Act, pushed through by the Conservative Thatcher government, was simply the culmination of a series of policies pursued over a twenty-year period to shut down "coloured" or "black" immigration. But the 1981 Nationality Act clearly marked the end of the imperial policy of *Civic Britanicus Sum*. On the refugee admissions front, British governments have been equally severe in curtailing the right to asylum, accepting only a few thousand persons per year, even during the period of intense refugee movements in the late 1980s and early 1990s.[21]

To what can we attribute the greater British capacity for immigration control? Layton-Henry suggests that this capacity is, at least in part, a function of the stringency of parliamentary government, which makes British governments more responsive to xenophobic public opinion. He also attributes British policy to a greater willingness to discriminate, which is a reflection of a special elite political culture. Nonetheless, he points out that immigration has persisted in Britain, albeit at modest levels, and other close observers suspect that the stock of illegal immigrants (especially of those aptly described by Layton-Henry as "insiders" or "welcome outsiders") is much larger than the country's meager apprehension statistics (fewer than 4,000 cases in 1993) would suggest (Thomas Cordi, personal communication). Moreover, pressures on the British immigration system are mounting as a result of European integration and the desire to create a border-free Europe. Thus far, British governments have resisted these pressures and insisted upon the need for tight border controls to maintain good race relations. However, the necessity for stricter internal controls (e.g., mandatory identification cards, increased random and systematic identity checks by law enforcement personnel) is being discussed quietly within the bureaucracy.

Latecomers to Immigration: Italy, Spain, and Japan

Italy, Spain, and Japan are immigration latecomers in the industrialized world. Modern Italy and Spain were powerfully shaped by emigration, and even Japan exported over 1 million of its workers during the period

---

[21] For a summary of recent developments in British refugee policy, see Randall 1994.

from 1868–1989.[22] However, until recently, all three of these countries have been marked by the absence of significant immigration. Today, fewer than 1 percent of these three nations' 200 million inhabitants are foreigners; if they were to have foreign populations accounting for 8 percent of the total, as in Northern Europe and North America, the number of foreign-born people in them would increase tenfold, to more than 16 million. All three "latecomers" are expected to experience increased immigration in the 1990s, but the increase will be from a very small base.

Italy: Immigrants in a Dual Economy

Among the latecomer immigration countries, Italy has the largest number of recently arrived, noncitizen residents: about 1 million, or 2 percent of the population. These immigrants trickled in after 1975, in response to the Italian "economic miracle" of the 1960s and the suspension of guestworker recruitment in Northern Europe. Almost 80 percent of Italy's foreigners today are from non-European Community countries, with the vast majority originating in northern and sub-Saharan Africa and Asia.

Italy has a dual economy. The northern part of the country has most of the manufacturing jobs, found in large firms (including multinationals) whose workforces are usually unionized, as well as in thousands of small, often family-owned businesses. These family firms are the backbone of Italy's large informal economy, which is estimated to account for one-sixth to one-third of the country's GNP. Regional differences in immigrant employment reflect the underlying economic structure. Immigrants find manufacturing jobs in the industrial north, and farm jobs in the agricultural south. In northern Italy, illegal immigrants are concentrated in the service sector of the informal economy. In her chapter on the Italian case, Kitty Calavita argues that immigrant workers—legal and illegal—provide the flexibility that informal-sector enterprises need to survive in a modern economy.

As a country with a long tradition of emigration, Italy is sensitive about conditions for immigrants. Through three different amnesty programs, conducted from 1982 to 1990, Italy offered legal status to employed aliens whose employers also agreed to pay back taxes and regularize the employment relationship; either the alien or the employer could initiate the legalization process. As a result, Italy today has Europe's largest population of "amnestied" foreign workers.

Nevertheless, there still appear to be significant numbers of illegal immigrants in the labor force, and some have advocated yet another

---

[22]The largest single receiving country was Brazil, which absorbed more than 260,000 Japanese workers, thereby establishing the community of Japanese-Brazilians (*Nikkeijin*) from which Japan has drawn the largest number of its legal immigrants since the late 1980s. See Watanabe 1994: table 2.

legalization program. Such suggestions are meeting resistance, however. A rising proportion of the Italian population—over 60 percent in a 1991 survey—believe that immigration is mostly (or *only*) bad for the country. Economic recession and rising unemployment in the 1990s have made Italians less hospitable to foreigners. Incidents of anti-immigrant violence occurred for the first time in 1993, in both Rome and small agricultural communities in the southern region.

Italian labor unions, well entrenched in the formal economy and thus largely insulated from immigrant-worker competition, have been strong supporters of rights for foreign workers. Calavita argues that union and church support for immigrants, as well as the fear in established political parties that open discussion of immigration policy would benefit only the new, anti-immigrant parties, explains why there is so little public debate on immigration in Italy today. She warns, however, that this silence may be short lived. Italian unions remain supportive of immigrant workers, and established Italian political parties prefer not to discuss their presence; but a continuing influx of unauthorized immigrants and asylum seekers, in the face of an increasingly hostile public opinion, may eventually force a more serious effort to restrict the flows. Government officials already are calling for tougher legislation and other control measures, including a crackdown on tourist visas routinely issued by the Vatican to nationals of East European countries with large Roman Catholic communities.

Spain: The Front Door Is Still Open

Like Italy, Spain's experience with immigration—especially from developing countries—is very limited. Only since the mid-1980s have Third World migrant workers replaced "sunbird" northern Europeans as the most numerous foreigners in Spain. Wayne Cornelius's chapter on Spain reveals a country grappling with the issue of how to preserve legal access for the foreign workers on which major parts of its economy depend, while not allowing illegal immigration to get out of control and thus create opportunities for political extremists of the sort now plaguing other European countries.

As of 1993, there were more than 600,000 immigrants in Spain, including an estimated 200,000–300,000 illegals. Unauthorized migrants slip into Spain primarily along with the 50 million legitimate tourists who come annually, then overstay their tourist visas. Others arrive as asylum seekers or enter clandestinely by crossing the virtually unguarded Portuguese-Spanish border; a few brave the Strait of Gibraltar in small boats originating in North Africa. As in Italy, most illegal immigrants in Spain work in service industries, agriculture, and construction. Within these sectors, they are concentrated in the lowest-wage and often seasonal segment of the labor market. Spaniards generally shun these jobs or take them only long enough to qualify for unemployment benefits.

Spain first adopted a comprehensive immigration law in 1985, in anticipation of entry into the European Community on January 1, 1986. This law ostensibly sought to discourage foreign worker employment by forcing aliens to run a bureaucratic gauntlet: first obtaining work contracts from Spanish employers, then soliciting linked work and residence permits from two different government ministries. The result of this complex and inefficient system, whether intended or unintended, has been to confine an ever-growing, unauthorized foreign labor force to Spain's large underground economy or to firms that employ such aliens "off-the-books." Ministry of Labor inspectors are responsible for enforcing Spain's employer sanctions law, but inspection efforts focus on other types of violations (e.g., nonpayment of payroll taxes). If labor law enforcement were to be strengthened, it is anticipated that many labor-intensive manufacturing businesses would move offshore—a phenomenon already well under way.

Since 1985 Spain has carried out three legalization programs, and their effects are more visible than the government's efforts to deter illegal immigration. The programs legalized a total of nearly 150,000 aliens, the largest contingent of whom are Moroccans. Legalization is acknowledged to be incomplete (as indicated by recent estimates of 200,000–300,000 still irregular foreign workers in the country), but Spanish authorities rule out another amnesty program, arguing that it would attract more illegal immigrants.

Opinion surveys reveal most Spaniards to be sympathetic to legal immigrants but increasingly intolerant of illegal immigrants, especially those coming from North Africa. Opposition politicians have been unable to exploit this nascent anti-immigration sentiment because nativist appeals would be perceived as a throwback to the discredited Franco era. Cornelius points out that pressure from the European Community was a crucial stimulus to enactment of those immigration control measures that Spain now possesses; he suggests that any future efforts to strengthen these controls will probably be made under EC pressure as well. Until the global recession of the 1990s hit Spain hard, its government was considering a generous quota system permitting the entry of up to 100,000 temporary and permanent foreign workers per year. The economics and politics of the recession caused the quota to be scaled back drastically, to slightly more than 20,000 in the first year (1993). Nevertheless, Spain's demographic profile (rock-bottom fertility rates, rapid population aging) will make foreign labor importation on a significant scale virtually inevitable to head off labor shortages in certain economic sectors and regions.

Japan: The Loss of Immigration Exceptionalism

Japan is the most celebrated "exception" among the industrialized nations. Its export-oriented manufacturers consistently have rung up huge trade surpluses and given Japan the industrialized world's highest per capita GNP, supposedly with little or no reliance on foreign labor. While Japan today has the lowest percentage of foreigners in its labor force among industrialized nations (less than 0.5 percent), demographic and economic forces are transforming it into a major destination for migrant workers from throughout the Pacific Basin.

In his chapter on the Japanese case, Cornelius identifies five key factors responsible for this transformation: demography (below-replacement fertility rates and rapid population aging), the exhaustion of domestic labor reserves, changing lifestyles and attitudes toward manual work, the longest economic boom in Japan's post-World War II history (up to the 1990s recession), and the strength of the yen in relation to other Asia-Pacific region currencies.

Cornelius notes that most Japanese academics, business leaders, and many public policy makers believe that this combination of factors will sustain a strong demand for foreign workers, especially in the small and medium-sized businesses that have suffered from chronic labor shortages even during the current recession. These firms, many of them subcontractors, are hardly marginal to the Japanese economy. Major companies tend to rely upon several layers of subcontractors; and the lower the "layer" of subcontract work, the lower the pay, the fewer the fringe benefits, and the higher the proportion of female and foreign workers. The extensive use of subcontractors is a critical ingredient of Japan's highly successful system of "just-in-time" mass production, consisting of a tightly integrated series of small-lot production processes (see Sayer and Walker 1992: 162–90).

How will heretofore "immigrant-free" Japan respond to a structural demand for foreign labor? The initial adjustments are already evident. Since 1989, Japan has been making it easy for nonimmigrant "temporary" foreign workers—even unskilled ones—to legally gain employment through a variety of "backdoor" or "side door" mechanisms: "company trainee" programs, a liberal supply of "student" visas, and a policy of essentially unlimited admission of ethnic Japanese workers from Latin America, approximately 160,000 of whom are already in Japan's labor force.

Japan faces a growing gap between immigration policy goals and outcomes because the numbers of both legal and illegal foreign workers are rising even as Japan's official, highly restrictive stance on low-skill and permanent immigration remains unchanged. Cornelius outlines the three central tenets of Japanese immigration policy as follows: (1) foreign workers can be admitted only as a last resort; (2) no unskilled foreign workers are to be admitted; and (3) all foreign workers are short-term "guests" in Japan—not potential permanent settlers. He shows how all three of these supposedly inviolable principles have been eroded by current de facto immigration policies. Moreover, employer sanctions introduced in 1990 to curb hiring of unauthorized foreign workers (virtually all of whom are visa overstayers) are rarely enforced.

Japan's economic success has been credited in part to the fact that it was a latecomer, able to install the newest technologies in its postwar factories. Will Japan also benefit in immigration policy making by being a latecomer? Cornelius argues that the United States and West European countries have mostly "mismanaged" immigration, leaving a legacy of policies to be avoided rather than emulated. He highlights the proposals of some leading Japanese immigration specialists who advocate acceptance of the inevitability of immigration (at all skill levels), gradual expansion of the number of legal immigrants, and admission of them through a newly opened front door rather than through "backdoor" or "side door" devices that merely disguise social and economic reality and delay the formulation of explicit national policies and programs to facilitate the social integration of settled immigrants.

Immigration Control and the International System

If many of the major industrial democracies have experienced growing problems of immigration control since 1945, as our country studies indicate, to what extent do these problems reflect changes in international relations? Is contemporary international migration simply another indicator of growing interdependence, in which a variety of transnational flows of capital, labor, goods, and services have led to a weakening of the sovereignty of the nation-state, or what James Rosenau (1990) and others have referred to as the "individualization of the world"? Do these transnational flows, especially labor migration, put such enormous pressure on states as to render Westphalian notions of sovereignty moot? In short, as we move into an era of unprecedented international labor mobility,[23] will it no longer be possible for states to exercise control over their populations and to achieve territorial closure?

Clearly, the difficulty that many industrialized democracies have encountered in their efforts to control immigration would indicate that, at the very least, we must reconsider classical, realist notions of the state

---

[23] According to United Nations estimates, about 100 million people were living outside their countries of birth in 1993. While refugees fleeing war, civil violence, direct political persecution, and environmental catastrophes doubled in numbers during the 1980s, they still comprised only 37 percent of the total of migrants by 1993; the remainder were economic migrants seeking employment or higher incomes (United Nations 1993). The number of long-term migrants from developing to developed countries increased fourfold, from about 230,000 per annum in the early 1960s to about 940,000 per year by the late 1980s (Population Action International 1994).

as a sovereign and autonomous actor in the international system. But the findings reported in this book would seem to argue strongly against the elimination of the nation-state from our analysis, even though we have seen major increases in a variety of transnational flows over the past several decades. States have struggled to master these flows, and their struggles are reflected in a range of public policies, of which immigration and refugee policies, along with trade, are perhaps the best examples.

Theories of international relations offer three competing perspectives which can help to illuminate the evolution of international migration and problems of immigration control since 1945. The first of these perspectives is *realism*, which, in its classical formulation, is designed to explain issues of "high politics" — primarily war and peace.[24] It does not deal with transnational and economic issues like migration, which are relegated to the realm of "low politics." However, the realist view of international relations, conceiving the state as a unitary and sovereign actor, has been used to explain a wide range of transnational phenomena, from international trade and finance to European integration. The basic assumptions of realist theory would lead us to expect sovereign states to act according to their national interests to control immigration. National interests could include a desire to limit population growth, regulate the supply of and demand for labor, improve the human capital stock, maintain the cultural or ethnic "balance" of society, and so on.

In fact, we can find evidence of all these factors at work in the immigration policies of the countries examined in this book. In a world of sovereign states, governments are under constant pressure to adopt and enforce rules and laws affecting the entry and residence of foreign nationals. Moreover, since foreigners presumably have no rights other than those accorded to them by sovereign states, levels of immigration should conform to the dictates of policy. Following the logic of realist theory, if states do not succeed in controlling their borders, it must be from a lack of political will on the part of governments, or because immigration policies have been flawed in design or inadequately implemented. The evidence presented in this volume clearly indicates that states indeed have had increasing difficulty in controlling immigration, but in most cases realist arguments offer very little in the way of explanation for the large and growing gap between the goals of policy and actual outcomes.

Dependency theory, which is rooted in classical Marxist-Leninist theory, offers a second perspective on the political economy of international migration. Its adherents seek to explain migration and problems of immigration control in terms of the massive socioeconomic inequalities that exist between north and south, or between rich and poor

---

[24]For a review of realist theory, see Waltz 1979.

countries. From this perspective, international migration is largely a function of the contradictions of capitalism, which requires an industrial reserve army to overcome periodic crises in the process of production and accumulation.[25] International migration is initially a consequence of the imperialist expansion of capitalist economies, which seek to export their surplus populations of displaced and unemployed workers and peasants; thus the great transatlantic migrations of the nineteenth and early twentieth centuries were a direct result of capitalist expansion and industrialization in Europe. Later in the twentieth century, emigration is replaced by immigration, as advanced capitalist societies seek to recover an industrial reserve army—in the European case, coming largely from former colonies—during periods of high economic growth, especially after 1945.[26]

Dependency theory (and its cousin, *world systems theory*) is very seductive because it would seem to explain why the movement of people from one state or economy to another does not conform neatly to some realist-statist logic; rather, such movements are viewed as the consequence of deeply embedded structural factors operating in domestic and international economic systems. If we take this approach, it would be easier to understand why immigration policies in contemporary industrialized democracies fail: essentially because states are helpless in the face of a powerful structural dynamic. Policies are driven purely by the economic interests of business (read: the capitalist class), and the built-in flaws that eventually render them ineffectual are a direct result of this dynamic.

It is precisely because the dependency argument relies so heavily on economic/structural factors, however, that it fails ultimately to explain contemporary immigration and the problems of immigration control, at least in the countries that we have studied. Immigration levels in today's industrialized democracies clearly are *not* purely a function of business cycles (indeed, as we have pointed out, such flows appear increasingly *less* sensitive to cyclical economic fluctuations). Moreover, immigration policy is *not* made solely in the interests of the business community, as the following chapters demonstrate. Powerful economic forces, in both sending and receiving countries, unquestionably underlie a large part of today's global pattern of migratory movements. But we should not view these forces deterministically, as entirely motivating or thwarting the makers of immigration policy in industrialized democracies, nor as precluding all meaningful policy innovation. The recent spate of fairly drastic immigration policy experiments in labor-importing countries (e.g., the implementation of a "blockade" enforcement strategy along

---

[25] A good example of the application of dependency theory to international migration can be found in Sassen 1988. See also Portes and Walton 1981.

[26] The best illustration of the use of this argument in explaining the development of post-World War II Europe is Castles and Kosack 1973.

portions of the U.S.-Mexico border, the proposed national registry system to reduce employment opportunities for illegal immigrants in the United States, the sweeping 1993 amendments to the German Constitution to deter bogus asylum seekers) all suggest that the political process on immigration matters is not paralyzed by economic/structural forces.

What we are left with are basically liberal theories of international exchange, especially *trade theory* and the *theory of complex interdependence*. Trade theory is perhaps the most purely "liberal" perspective, in the sense that it is derived from microeconomic theory and is, for the most part, apolitical. It runs directly counter to the realist-statist arguments outlined above, which would tend to view international migration as a function of national interests and security. According to classical trade theory, transborder migration must be viewed in the rationalist context of utility/profit maximization, cost/benefit analysis, and push-pull factors. To understand migration (and by extension, the problems of immigration control in liberal democracies), we must study the disequilibria (inequalities) that exist in the international economy, especially differing factor endowments, differential returns to labor and capital, and so forth. A full appreciation of these disequilibria will then allow us to specify the conditions under which migration is likely to occur, and to identify push-pull factors. In short, we must be able to identify the parameters of an evolving transnational labor market, in which states should not interfere.[27]

The theory of complex interdependence rests in part on liberal trade theory, yet it recognizes the important role of state power in guaranteeing an open (or liberal) international order (see, for example, Keohane and Nye 1977). But these arguments about the importance of trade and other transnational flows, as they have evolved since Bretton Woods, offer us only a partial explanation for the rise in international migration since 1980 and the difficulties of immigration control in industrialized democracies. Growing interdependence (through trade) together with long periods of prosperity and economic growth (fostered by American hegemony) have led to greater international cooperation and openness, and may eventually lead to factor-price equalization. But immigration still depends heavily on certain domestic political developments in the receiving states.

From the studies of France, Germany, and the United States presented in this volume, we can readily see the importance of national immigration policies in promoting the recruitment of foreign labor

---

[27]The *Wall Street Journal*, for example, has editorialized frequently for a policy of open borders with Mexico as a way to bring about more rapid factor-price equalization. A more moderate version of the same argument has often been made by economist Clark W. Reynolds (see especially Reynolds 1992). For a rigorously neoclassical view of the political economy of international migration, see J. Simon 1989.

during the first decades of the post-World War II period. Similarly, in Canada immigration has come to be seen as an important human capital asset, to be managed by the state (through a point system).[28] In Japan, a small temporary worker program (the "company trainee" program) has been launched, similar in some respects to the old guestworker program of the Federal Republic of Germany. These concerted efforts by states to encourage international labor migration led to the creation of transnational labor markets in Europe and North America, and it appears that Japan and the principal labor exporters of the Asia-Pacific region are heading in the same direction.

These regional labor markets, which are driven in part by family- and employer-based networks as well as market forces of supply and demand, have developed important political and humanitarian dimensions, even though these have not been fully institutionalized. The fact that waves of economic migration in the 1960s and 1970s have been followed by political or refugee migrations in the 1980s and 1990s is further evidence of the growing political dimension of international migration, which has an important "rights" dimension to it. Thus legal protections afforded economic migrants and political refugees, either through national constitutions or international organizations and treaties (the European Community, the Geneva Convention, the International Convention on the Rights of All Migrant Workers and Members of Their Families,[29] etc.), have given greater political legitimacy to international migration. Trade theory cannot account for these developments.

So we must look, finally, to *second-image theories* for clues to the links between international migration and the international system in the post-World War II era (see Gourevitch 1978). From this perspective, higher levels of immigration and the increasing difficulty of immigration control are a reflection of liberal developments in the international system, which are not purely economic but derive, in part, from political coalitions that seek to promote civil and human rights. Following the arguments of John Ruggie (1982), we can conclude that the postwar order has, embedded within it, certain liberal notions of rights, norms, and principles, which have been partially institutionalized. What we have not seen, however, is the emergence of a full-blown "international migration regime," equivalent to existing regimes for trade and finance that act to constrain the sovereignty and autonomy of nation-states in those areas of international relations.

---

[28] A similar stance is taken by Australia, which also has had a long history of relatively open immigration. For a detailed analysis of the Australian experience and its points of convergence and divergence with the United States, see Freeman and Jupp 1992.

[29] See the special issue of *International Migration Review* (25:4 [Winter 1991]) devoted to the new United Nations convention on migrant workers, adopted by the General Assembly on December 18, 1990; see also Cator and Niessen 1994.

The reasons for incomplete institutionalization in the migration area are fairly obvious. The incentives for states to cooperate in managing or controlling migration are very different than in the areas of trade and finance. With regard to trade, such international regimes as GATT (and its proposed successor, the World Trade Organization), the European Community (which is actually an international organization), and the North American Free Trade Agreement (NAFTA) help to maintain a more open world economy in the face of strong domestic political pressures for protectionism. Free trade only affects issues of national sovereignty and national identity at the margins, and the case for economic benefits is strong and clear. With respect to international finance, the gains from exchange rate stability and the coordination of macroeconomic policy (through the G-7) are also quite clear; thus a small sacrifice in sovereignty (in setting interest rates, for example) can result in tremendous economic benefits. Finally, if states want the benefits of international trade and finance regimes, they have to play by their rules; in the immigration area, however, industrialized nations want to retain the capacity to make up their own rules.

On the other hand, international labor migration is a much more difficult issue to address through multilateralism because the costs (in terms of loss of sovereignty and threats to national identity) are much higher, and the benefits (greater control over immigration levels, sudden refugee flows, etc.) are more difficult to realize. Notwithstanding these difficulties, the European Community has taken several steps in the direction of an international regime for controlling immigration and refugee flows. The principal vehicles have been the Schengen Agreement, which calls for an eventually border-free Europe and common visa policies, and the Dublin and Trevi groups, which have been pushing for harmonization of refugee and asylum policies and greater information sharing and cooperation among police authorities to control illegal immigration (see Hollifield 1992a; Callovi 1992).

The construction of a partial international migration regime in Europe has also established the principle of freedom of movement for citizens of EC member states, and the Maastricht Treaty (ratified in 1993) pushes the logic of a border-free Europe one step farther by endorsing limited political rights (i.e., voting in local elections) for nationals of one member state who reside in another member state. This would seem to be the first step in the creation of a kind of EC citizenship, albeit a very limited one. The problem remains, however, of how to deal with the nationals of *non*-EC states who have acquired legal permanent resident status in an EC country; in 1990, there were some 9.3 million of these "third-country nationals." Should a Turk residing in Germany be able to move and work freely within the twelve-nation European Union? The answer from member states, thus far, is "no."

European governments and European Union officials are still grappling with the challenge of fully implementing a border-free Europe while providing adequate protections against illegal immigration, false asylum claims, drug smuggling, and terrorism. While EU bureaucrats are convinced that harmonized immigration and asylum policies are needed now more than ever, national governments (not just the British) are dragging their feet. Even the signatories to the Schengen Agreement appear to be having second thoughts; in 1994 they missed their fourth deadline for the elimination of internal border controls.

No such even partial international migration regimes have emerged as yet in the North American or East Asian regions. Indeed, transborder labor mobility was explicitly kept "off the table" in negotiating the 1993 North American Free Trade Agreement, at the insistence of the United States. Within these regions, immigration policy remains the exclusive prerogative of the sovereign states. However, bilateral cooperation on some immigration-related issues (e.g., combatting the professional smuggling rings that bring groups of illegal immigrants into the United States and Japan) may become both politically feasible and necessary in the foreseeable future.

In the absence of a fully institutionalized international regime or organization to manage and structure the movements of people (be they refugees, economic migrants, or skilled professionals), the rules of entry of nation-states themselves continue to prevail, and the constitutional/administrative procedures defining the rights of aliens in these countries predominate. What can be seen from the country studies that follow, however, is a marked convergence of national policies, norms, and procedures, despite major differences in the domestic political economies of the principal receiving states.

It remains to be seen what features of the liberal, post-Cold War world order (e.g., sweeping guarantees of political asylum for those fleeing persecution) can be maintained in the face of strong (and rising) domestic opposition to the current influx of foreigners and the collapse of some rights-based political coalitions. As can be seen most clearly in the French, German, and U.S. cases, civil rights coalitions are under increasing pressure, and immigration and refugee policies are becoming more restrictionist, even though actual levels of entries in these major labor-importing countries have remained at historically high levels. It seems highly unlikely, however, that the ongoing "rights rollback" and other policy reversals will succeed in fully restoring the sovereignty and autonomy of industrialized democracies with respect to immigration and border control.

Alternative Futures for Reluctant Labor Importers

As the twentieth century draws to a close, virtually all of the industrialized countries examined in this volume, with the partial exception of

Canada, would prefer to classify themselves as "reluctant" or "unwilling" importers of foreign labor. In each of these cases, we can observe the interaction of the four key trends: (1) high migration from less developed countries (especially those deemed by native-born citizens as "problem nationalities"), where economic and demographic push factors are strong and likely to remain so in the foreseeable future; (2) in the receiving countries, economic contraction, volatility, or sluggish growth accompanied by stubbornly high unemployment rates; (3) the persistence in industrialized economies of employer demand for low-cost, flexible labor—a *structural* demand that has become decoupled from the business cycle; and (4) the rising frequency of symbolic efforts by governments to deter immigration and discourage permanent settlement, e.g., by rolling back the social service entitlements formerly enjoyed by immigrants and would-be refugees, under pressure from an increasingly hostile public opinion.

These cases also vividly illustrate the limited effectiveness of most attempts by governments of industrial democracies to intervene in the migration process linking them to Third World labor-exporting countries, at this point in time. As Philip Martin comments in his analysis of the German case, "Industrial democracies do not want to reduce the demand-pull factors that attract migrants, and they cannot in the short term reduce supply-push emigration pressures." Martin also observes that breaking the intervening variables in the international migratory process—such as the increasingly pervasive family- and employer-based networks that assist new arrivals with job seeking, housing, and financing for migration—seems to be getting harder rather than easier, because of revolutions in communications, transportation, and civil and human rights that have facilitated migration and constrained government regulatory capacity. The de facto situation in the major labor-importing countries today could be described as "If you get in, you can stay."

As noted above, the seemingly intractable nature of the regulatory problem in this area has not discouraged the governments of several of the industrialized countries examined in this book from taking some drastic and unprecedented steps to control immigrant and refugee flows. However, the long-run effects of these "drastic" policy changes often cannot be envisioned at the time of implementation, and the historical record provides ample reason for skepticism that they will counteract the fundamental demand-pull, supply-push, and network factors that we have emphasized.

As the case studies included in this book reveal, that record is littered with the wreckage of government interventions that appeared to work reasonably well at first but had little staying power, or which had long-term consequences that were exactly the opposite of the initial, intended effects. For example, the 1986 U.S. Immigration Reform and Control Act (specifically, the employer sanctions component) appeared to be effectively deterring illegal immigration during the first two to three years following its implementation; then the long-term, upward trend reasserted itself. Apprehensions of illegal entrants crossing the southern U.S. border fell from 1.8 million in 1986 to 954,000 in 1989; by 1993, however, the number of apprehensions had risen to 1.2 million. The legalization components of the 1986 law—most notably the Special Agricultural Workers (SAW) program—attracted many first-time migrants from Mexico into the U.S. labor force, a large portion of whom did not actually qualify for amnesty (see, for example, the evidence in Bean et al. 1990: 183–210, 227–49), and subsequent family reunification immigration by ineligible wives and children further increased the stock of illegal immigrants. Moreover, both employer sanctions and the SAW program created enormous economies of scale in fraudulent document production by creating both a demand and supply of such papers. The easy availability of false documents in turn rendered the 1986 law's employer sanctions virtually unenforceable.

More recently, U.S. immigration authorities have trumpeted the success of "Operation Hold-the-Line," a highly concentrated enforcement strategy used by the Border Patrol in the El Paso, Texas sector since September 1993, which reduced apprehensions from 700 to about 200 per day. Whatever the long-term efficacy of the strategy (if maintained) along this segment of the U.S.-Mexico border, a careful study has already found that the El Paso "blockade" has failed almost completely to deter long-distance, illegal labor migration (Bean et al. 1994). It *has* reduced local border-crossing activity by some types of unauthorized commuter migrants (street vendors, older female domestic workers) and juvenile delinquents from nearby Ciudad Juárez, while apparently diverting long-distance migrants to other border-crossing points in the state of Arizona, where apprehensions rose by more than 60 percent in the same period. Thus the drastic change in border enforcement tactics has "solved" a highly localized problem, leaving unaffected the larger phenomenon of illegal entry by migrants from the interior of Mexico, who can simply go around the "line."

Similarly, in Germany today one finds a remarkable degree of optimism that unauthorized immigration is now under control because of the 1993 revision of the asylum law. The principal basis for this conviction that the policy change has "worked" is the sharp decline in new asylum applications, from 438,000 in 1992 (before the tightening of requirements) to perhaps 108,000 in 1994. However, a large part of the decline could be attributable to other factors, including weakness in the German economy (GDP was growing at an annualized rate of only 2.2 percent by mid-1994), unauthorized migrants entering by other means (including illegal border crossings), and the fact that would-be asylum claimants are still at the beginning of the learning curve, figuring out how to cope with the changed legal structure. But already they are learning. Most asylum seekers no longer arrive in Germany with passports or other documents identifying their country of origin, because if they do, and their home country appears on the very long list of "safe" countries from which asylum applicants are no longer accepted, they will be deported immediately. Asylum seekers getting into Germany without papers are thus more difficult and time-consuming to process.

These few examples must suffice to make our point. It is easy to be deceived by the apparent short-term efficacy of some of the sweeping changes in the rules of the immigration game now being implemented or considered. There is still no basis for claiming that these drastic remedies have actually "worked" where they have been tried, at least in the terms specified by their advocates. Nor are there, necessarily, grounds for believing that with the passage of more time, with more "fine-tuning," more public education, etc., such measures will sharply and durably modify patterns of migration and employer behavior in the anticipated way. There are many routes to failure and frustration.

At what point in the future will the new politics of restrictionism collide with the national interests of the receiving nations, defined in terms of economic growth and global competitiveness—not to mention the interest of individual citizens in maintaining life styles often made possible by immigrant service providers and producers of low-cost goods? When that point is reached, the goals of national immigration policy may have to be redefined, to reduce the large and constantly widening gap between policy goals and outcomes, and thus restore at least the *appearance* of control by receiving-country governments.[30]

This could happen with relatively little political pain to incumbent governments if the economies of the labor-importing countries rebound to the point that immigrants are no longer needed as scapegoats and most citizens no longer live in fear of losing their jobs due to corporate downsizing, the globalization of production, and other forces beyond their control. Such restructuring has led in the industrial democracies to a sense that no job is secure and that if a job is lost, the 80 percent of the workforce with less than a college education faces reemployment at drastically lower wages. Conceivably, regional economic integration in both Europe and North America during the last half of the 1990s and beyond could prove to be such a stimulus to economic growth in industrialized countries with rapidly aging and low-fertility populations that immigration at some relatively high level could once again be viewed as essential, as it was in the 1950s and 1960s.

Nevertheless, even with robust and sustained economic recovery, it is possible that the ethnic and cultural balance within industrialized

---

[30]For a provocative argument on the importance of restoring the *image* of state control in the area of immigration, see Portes 1983. See also Calavita 1989.

countries has been so shifted by the 1980s–1990s wave of Third World immigration that native-born populations will continue to press for restrictive measures out of fear that the "core culture" of their nation is being assaulted, diluted, or transformed to an unacceptable degree by culturally distinct immigrants. In that scenario, some countries—especially France, Germany, and Japan—face a potentially wrenching debate over redefining national identity and citizenship. Should these concepts become more inclusive (i.e., less ethnically, racially, and culturally based), or must traditional, exclusivist concepts of nationality and citizenship be reaffirmed?

A major question, repeatedly posed but necessarily unresolved in this book, concerns the extent to which future governments in the labor-importing countries will succeed in rolling back the "civil rights and social entitlements revolution" of recent decades that has made it easier for unauthorized immigrants who have entered one of these countries to remain, if they are determined to stay. Curtailing the legal, political, and basic human rights of "within-country" immigrants is a much easier remedy for governments of industrialized countries to pursue than attempting to change the basic market and demographic forces (in both sending and receiving countries) that now drive most Third World migration to these countries. This approach also avoids or mitigates most of the diplomatic costs associated with more stringent border enforcement or imposing tough visa restrictions on the nationals of certain high-emigration countries. However, our research indicates that it is unlikely to stem the flow of new migrants appreciably, since there is little empirical evidence for the proposition that availability of social services or entitlements is a powerful magnet for would-be illegal entrants, as compared with other demand-pull factors.

Redefining the goals of their immigration policies will also force industrialized countries to squarely confront rather than ignore or downplay the trade-offs between more effective immigration control and other societal goals and principles. What basic values, what civil liberties, how much in tax revenues, and how much future economic growth are to be sacrificed in order to gain greater control of the immigrant influx and reduce the size of the extant foreign-born population?

The outcomes of these debates will determine whether persistently high levels of immigration from less developed countries—in whatever form—will be tolerated in the foreseeable future. It is entirely possible that the political and cultural objections to liberal immigration policies will be sufficiently intense to override economic considerations, regardless of how strong the demand-pull factors become in industrialized nations. In that scenario, we could expect today's labor-importing countries to make further efforts to deal quietly with "spot" labor shortages in specific sectors of their economies through a variety of Japanese-style "backdoor" or "side door" labor importation programs, rather than pursue more generalized, openly expansionary immigration policies that would inflame anti-immigrant public opinion.

The immigration debates to come in industrialized countries will also determine whether governments will, at long last, abandon the myths of "temporariness" and enforceable rotation of workers, and take the steps necessary to promote the sociocultural integration and economic mobility of settled immigrants and their children—especially those not currently viewed as easily assimilable (Mexicans in the United States, Turks in Germany, North Africans in France and Spain, etc.). Will governments opt to *invest* in the human capital that they are now receiving from Third World countries (rather than simply bemoan these foreign workers' initially low educational and occupational skill levels[31]) and facilitate their incorporation into labor-hungry sectors of the economy, while protecting their labor and human rights? These are among the most critical policy choices that will confront the governments of reluctantly labor-importing industrialized countries in the remainder of the 1990s and beyond.

References

Asch, Beth J., ed. 1994. *Emigration and Its Effects on the Sending Country.* Santa Monica, Calif.: Center for Research on Immigration Policy, Rand Corporation.

Bean, Frank D., Barry Edmonston, and Jeffrey S. Passel, eds. 1990. *Undocumented Migration to the United States: IRCA and the Experience of the 1980s.* Washington, D.C.: Urban Institute Press.

Bean, Frank D., et al. 1994. "Illegal Mexican Migration and the United States/ Mexico Border: The Effects of Operation Hold-the-Line on El Paso/Juárez." Report prepared for the U.S. Commission on Immigration Reform, July 15.

Böhning, W.R. 1984. *Studies in International Labor Migration.* London: Macmillan.

Borjas, George J., and Richard B. Freeman, eds. 1992. *Immigration and the Work Force: Economic Consequences for the United States and Source Areas.* Chicago: University of Chicago Press.

Calavita, Kitty. 1989. "The Immigration Policy Debate: Critical Analysis and Policy Options." In *Mexican Migration to the United States,* edited by Wayne A. Cornelius and Jorge A. Bustamante. La Jolla: Center for U.S.-Mexican Studies, University of California, San Diego, for the Bilateral Commission on the Future of United States-Mexican Relations.

Callovi, G. 1992. "Regulation of Immigration in 1993: Pieces of the European Community Jig-saw Puzzle," *International Migration Review* 26:2:353–72.

Castles, Stephen, and Godula Kosack. 1973. *Immigrant Workers and Class Structure in Western Europe.* London: Oxford University Press.

Castles, Stephen, and Mark J. Miller. 1993. *The Age of Migration: International Population Movements in the Modern World.* New York: Guilford Press.

---

[31] For one side of the debate over the "declining quality" of immigrant cohorts in the U.S. context, see Borjas and Freeman 1992. For an alternative view, see Fix and Passel 1994.

Cator, Julie, and Jan Niessen, eds. 1994. *The Use of International Conventions to Protect the Rights of Migrants and Ethnic Minorities*. Strasbourg: Churches' Commission for Migrants in Europe and Commission of the European Communities.

Coleman, David A. 1994. "Europe under Migration Pressure: Some Facts on Immigration." Paper presented at the workshop on "Immigration into Western Societies: Implications and Policy Choices," European Community Studies Association and South Carolina Institute of International Studies, Charleston, S.C., May 13–14.

Cornelius, Wayne A., and Ricardo Anzaldúa Montoya, eds. 1983. *America's New Immigration Law: Origins, Rationales, and Potential Consequences*. Monograph Series, no. 11. La Jolla: Center for U.S.-Mexican Studies, University of California, San Diego.

Espenshade, Thomas J., and Charles A. Calhoun. 1993. "An Analysis of Public Opinion toward Undocumented Immigration," *Population Research and Policy Review* 12:189–224.

Faist, Thomas. 1993. "From School to Work: Public Policy and Underclass Formation among Young Turks in Germany during the 1980s," *International Migration Review* 27:2 (Summer): 306–31.

———. 1994. "States, Markets, and Immigrant Minorities: Second-Generation Turks in Germany and Mexican-Americans in the United States in the 1980s," *Comparative Politics* 26:4 (July): 439–60.

Fix, Michael, and Jeffrey S. Passel. 1994. *Immigration and Immigrants: Setting the Record Straight*. Washington, D.C.: Urban Institute Press.

Freeman, Gary P., and James Jupp, eds. 1992. *Nations of Immigrants: Australia, the United States, and International Migration*. Melbourne: Oxford University Press.

Gourevitch, Peter A. 1978. "The Second Image Reversed: International Sources of Domestic Conflict," *International Organization* 32:3:881–911.

Hirsch, Harry N. 1992. *A Theory of Liberty: The Constitution and Minorities*. New York: Routledge.

Hollifield, James F. 1992a. "Migration and International Relations: Conflict and Control in the European Community," *International Migration Review* 26:2:568–95.

———. 1992b. *Immigrants, Markets and States*. Cambridge, Mass.: Harvard University Press.

Johnson, Haynes. 1994. *Divided We Fall: Gambling with History in the Nineties*. New York: Norton.

Keohane, Robert O., and Joseph Nye. 1977. *Power and Interdependence*. Boston: Little, Brown.

López, Robert J. 1994. "'86 Immigrant Hiring Ban Used in L.A. Case," *Los Angeles Times*, August 9.

Lozano Ascencio, Fernando. 1993. *Bringing It Back Home: Remittances to Mexico from Migrant Workers in the United States*. Monograph Series, no. 37. La Jolla: Center for U.S.-Mexican Studies, University of California, San Diego.

Marshall, T.H. 1950. *Class, Citizenship, and Social Development*. Cambridge: Cambridge University Press.

Massey, Douglas S., and Emilio Parrado. 1994. "Migradollars: The Remittances and Savings of Mexican Migrants to the USA," *Population Research and Policy Review* 13:3–30.

Peach, G.C.K. 1991. *The Caribbean in Europe: Contrasting Patterns of Migration and Settlement in Britain, France, and the Netherlands*. Warwick, England: Centre for Research in Ethnic Relations, University of Warwick.

Population Action International. 1994. *Global Migration: People on the Move*. Washington, D.C.: Population Action International.

Portes, Alejandro. 1983. "Of Borders and States: A Skeptical Note on the Legislative Control of Immigration." In *America's New Immigration Law: Origins, Rationales, and Potential Consequences*, edited by Wayne A. Cornelius and Ricardo Anzaldúa Montoya. Monograph Series, no. 11. La Jolla: Center for U.S.-Mexican Studies, University of California, San Diego.

Portes, Alejandro, and John Walton. 1981. *Labor, Class, and the International System*. New York: Academic Press.

Randall, Chris. 1994. "An Asylum Policy for the U.K." In *Strangers and Citizens: A Positive Approach to Migrants and Refugees*, edited by Sarah Spencer. London: Institute for Public Policy Research/Rivers Oram Press.

Raskin, Carl. 1993. "De Facto Discrimination, Immigrant Workers and Ethnic Minorities: A Canadian Overview." Working Paper MIG WP.72. Geneva: World Employment Programme, International Labour Organisation, February.

Rawls, John. 1971. *A Theory of Justice*. Cambridge, Mass.: Harvard University Press.

Reynolds, Clark. 1992. "Will a Free Trade Agreement Lead to Wage Convergence? Implications for Mexico and the United States." In *U.S.-Mexico Relations: Labor Market Interdependence*, edited by Jorge A. Bustamante, Clark W. Reynolds, and Raúl A. Hinojosa Ojeda. Stanford, Calif.: Stanford University Press.

Riding, Alan. 1993. "France, Reversing Course, Fights Immigrants' Refusal to Be French," *New York Times*, December 5.

Rosenau, James. 1990. *Turbulence in World Politics*. Princeton, N.J.: Princeton University Press.

Ruggie, John G. 1982. "International Regimes, Transactions, and Change: Embedded Liberalism in the Postwar Economic Order," *International Organization* 36:2:379–415.

Sassen, Saskia. 1988. *The Mobility of Labor and Capital: A Study in International Investment and Labor Flow*. Cambridge: Cambridge University Press.

Sayer, Andrew, and Richard Walker. 1992. *The New Social Economy: Reworking the Division of Labor*. Cambridge, Mass.: Blackwell.

Schlesinger, Arthur M., Jr. 1992. *The Disuniting of America: Reflections on a Multicultural Society*. Boston: Houghton Mifflin.

Schuck, Peter H. 1984. "The Transformation of Immigration Law," *Columbia Law Review* 84 (January): 1–90.

Simon, Julian. 1989. *The Economic Consequences of Immigration*. Oxford: Basil Blackwell/Cato Institute.

Simon, Rita J. 1993. "Old Minorities, New Immigrants: Aspirations, Hopes, and Fears," *Annals of the American Academy of Political and Social Science* 530 (November): 61–73.

Simon, Rita J., and Susan H. Alexander. 1993. *The Ambivalent Welcome: Print Media, Public Opinion, and Immigration*. Westport, Conn.: Praeger.

Tapinos, Georges. 1974. *L'économie des migrations internationales*. Paris: A. Colin and Presses de la FNSP.

Tilly, Charles. 1990. "Transplanted Networks." In *Immigration Reconsidered: History, Sociology, and Politics*, edited by Virginia Yans-McLaughlin. New York: Oxford University Press.

United Nations Population Fund. 1993. *The State of World Population, 1993*. New York: United Nations.

Veen, Hans-Joachim, Norbert Lepszy, and Peter Mnich. 1993. *The Republikaner Party in Germany: Right-Wing Menace or Protest Catchall?* Westport, Conn.: Praeger.

Waldinger, Roger. 1994. "The Making of an Immigrant Niche," *International Migration Review* 28:1 (Spring): 3–30.

Wall Street Journal. 1994. "Migration Trends Hint at 'Balkanizing' Pattern," January 18.

Waltz, Kenneth. 1979. *Theory of International Relations*. Reading, Mass.: Addison-Wesley.

Walzer, Michael. 1983. *Spheres of Justice: A Defense of Pluralism and Equality*. New York: Basic Books.

Watanabe, Susumu. 1994. "The Lewisian Turning Point and International Migration: The Case of Japan," *Asian and Pacific Migration Journal* 3:1.

Zimmermann, Wendy, and Michael Fix. 1994. "Immigrant Policy in the States: A Wavering Welcome." In *Immigration and Ethnicity: The Integration of America's Newest Arrivals*, edited by Barry Edmonston and Jeffrey S. Passel. Washington, D.C.: Urban Institute Press.

Commentary

Factoring Administration, Law, and Foreign Policy into the Study of Immigration Policy Making

Christopher Mitchell

The emphasis that the essays in this volume place on legislative, legal, and administrative aspects of immigration policy is welcome indeed. These concerns have sometimes remained in the background in the political science literature dealing with international migration during the past ten years, and they deserve attention. One finds in the studies collected here, as well, ample empirical data to assist well-ordered comparison of policy steps across national settings.

The country studies in this book provide a variety of insights relating to law and administration. First, many chapters clarify the administrative difficulties that hinder the enforcement of legislation and regulations against unauthorized labor migration in relatively pluralistic and open societies. For example, in nations such as those examined here, where bureaucratic power is routinely open to contestation and where plural social interests enjoy access to political influence, employer sanctions very seldom restrain labor migration over the long term. The key flaw in the United States' plan for employer sanctions, as analyzed by Kitty Calavita, was in relieving employers of any responsibility to verify the authenticity of identity documents, leaving the door open to widespread forgery. The Spanish effort has been ineffective, argues Wayne Cornelius, due to causes including low fines, few inspectors, division among enforcement agencies, and the informalization of a large segment of the nation's economy.

On the other hand, administrative measures have quite often proved effective in reducing the flow of migrants claiming refugee status. Would-be refugees or asylum claimants are less likely than labor migrants to have already entered the national territory. They may be deterred from embarking, or deported immediately upon entry. In Canada after 1987, stricter regulations somewhat narrowed the flow of asylum claimants from abroad, and Britain has used visa requirements, fines against airlines, and other measures to discourage the arrival of migrants likely to request asylum. Calavita discusses the United States' lamentable success in blockading most Haitian asylum claimants from entering the jurisdiction of U.S. courts through use of the Coast Guard and Navy. Germany also hopes, through legal and constitutional changes, to limit refugee inflows by narrowing access to the German Basic Law's guarantee of a welcome to all foreigners who are politically persecuted. One should observe, however, that none of the refugee-admitting countries examined in this volume has the administrative ability to track and deport rejected asylum applicants who are within its borders. Such persons, in each of these countries, probably number in the tens of thousands.

Third, the case studies presented in this volume emphasize that constitutionalism and the availability of judicial review in some nations may constrain state authority in dealing with migration issues. In France during the late 1970s, the semi-judicial Council of State deflected the executive power's efforts to narrow migrants' rights to family reunification. Citing legal and constitutional issues, the Council of State also persuaded the French government to give up efforts to repatriate migrant workers forcibly, largely to Algeria. In Australia—an interesting comparative case that does not happen to be covered in the current work—judicial review has tended in recent years to liberalize national immigration policy. Australian court decisions have often set aside administrative efforts to tighten immigration controls, instead favoring efforts by migrants to obtain permanent residence on grounds of marriage or the danger of human-rights abuses in their nations of origin.

We should also note that the bureaucracies charged with enforcing immigration restrictions may adapt to legal challenges, frustrating migrants' efforts to gain court protection. For example, Washington's interception policy against sea-borne Haitian migrants came in response to the painful progress that Haitian asylum applicants had achieved through litigation in the early 1980s. The "interdiction" policy was resoundingly endorsed in June 1993 by an 8-to-1 majority of the United States Supreme Court in *Sale v. Haitian Centers Council*.

An administrative and legal focus also reminds us with special vividness that the impact of policy measures is often quite hard to predict and to duplicate. New policies may have inverse effects from those that were intended or, if efficacious in the short term, may lull decision makers into a false sense that underlying social trends have been thwarted. Thus, as Philip Martin notes, the United States did not intend that the 1965 amendments to the Immigration and Nationality Act would greatly increase migration flows from the Third World. The West German state derived an illusory sense of accomplishment from its fleeting successes in reducing guestworker employment in the late 1960s and in reducing asylum claims by requiring Turks to obtain visas beginning in 1980. These findings suggest that states should examine carefully what policy measures have been effective *over the long term* in other societies. The essays in this book and other comparative studies should assist with that endeavor.

A key pitfall of emphasizing legal and administrative matters—legalism—is avoided in this volume by comparing policy with performance and by linking legal/administrative changes to alterations in the political coalitions affecting immigration policy. At the same time, these country studies make clear that the general public or other relevant constituencies for immigration policy may themselves be excessively legalistic, at least in the short run. Considerable faith may be placed in the efficacy of new laws on migration, confidence that may be undercut by the practical difficulties frequently encountered once enforcement is attempted. The United States' experience with the Immigration Reform and Control Act of 1986 is almost a textbook illustration of this syndrome.

One notes in this volume a proper concern with the impact of national myths and self-images on immigration policies. The ability to depict a preferred outcome in immigration policy as consonant with a nation's self-identity or aspirations often becomes a political resource that is sought by contending forces in domestic debates. National immigration myths are not always clear, to be sure. In at least half of the cases examined here—France, Germany, Spain, and the United States—there is significant ambiguity in national "ideologies of immigration."

In controversies over policy, advocates of continued immigration may evoke links between national identity and relatively liberal immigration policies. Such bonds have been easiest to cite in the United States with its "Statue of Liberty" and "melting pot" myths. Hollifield also underscores the importance to French immigration policy of the "republican synthesis" in political ideals that emerged between 1890 and 1914. The universalist and humanitarian implications of republican values, in turn, fostered a pro-immigration policy after World War II that also suited the labor needs of French capital and the *populationnisme* of the new Gaullist political right.

A call to atone for past national errors may also prove a potent ideological instrument in immigration debates. The determination of Germany's post-World War II constitutional framers to shed the Nazi image helped create a deep-seated admissionist policy toward asylum claimants, and Cornelius reports that in Spain xenophobic appeals are rare in part because they would imply an association with the discredited Franco regime. The memory of the U.S. government's failure to admit enough European refugees in the 1930s to blunt the effects of the Holocaust remains a potent appeal in U.S. politics that favors refugee admissions.

As most of these essays also explicitly note, all the belief systems on immigration in the nations studied are currently subject to challenge and change. No national myth or immigration ideology is now so strong as entirely to negate pressure from global economic trends. Japan's de facto utilization of unskilled foreign labor, despite the absence of a national immigration tradition, well illustrates this point. Recent German immigration policy also underscores the continued demand by some sectors in modern industrial societies for relatively cheap and vulnerable labor. Since 1989 Germany has once again begun admitting "temporary" workers, this time from Eastern Europe. The adoption of these seasonal, apprenticeship, and frontier work programs is especially striking, given the resentment felt by some ethnic Germans toward Turkish "guestworkers" who remained in Germany after the 1960s.

At the same time, it is striking how relatively little emphasis these essays give to the role of international relations in the setting of migration policy. While these studies do not ignore the issue, their brief discussions of it indicate the gains to be made by exploring the issue further. Scholars might elucidate, for example, the effects of a state's current priorities in international relations on its migration choices. In these studies we find that France's interest in restraining immigration from North Africa in the early 1970s was offset by its concern to maintain good relations with Algeria, Morocco, and Tunisia. Spain's 1985 *ley de extranjería* was drafted in large part to conform to European Community policies restricting non-EC immigration, on the eve of Spain's joining the Community. The U.S. government acted harshly (and, it subsequently admitted, illegally) against Salvadoran asylum applicants until 1990, partly to avoid endorsing criticism of human rights violations under its client regime in El Salvador.

Additional insights into policy behavior can also be gained by considering the effects of past imperial roles, obligations, and political self-images on migration policies. Most ex-colonial powers find themselves with special immigration obligations that constrain state policy or require embarrassing modifications of past promises. Zig Layton-Henry effectively analyzes Britain's narrowing of immigration access to the United Kingdom through its redefinition of British nationality, culminating in 1981. Neocolonial world powers do not escape the "migration burden" of empire, as the United States discovered when it (quite creditably) accepted the moral obligation to admit numerous Southeast Asian refugees after 1975. Of the ex-colonial nations studied here, only Belgium minimized its migration duties by the simple and severe expedient of denying any special rights to citizens of Zaire.

Some of the relative effectiveness of Japanese and Canadian immigration control may be attributed to those nations' exceptionalism as major industrial powers that have not been major colonial powers. Australia may well fall into the same category. Immigration policies in that nation over the past twenty years have been shaped by considerations of economic growth, family reunification, and the need felt by many in the political elite to repudiate the "White Australia" policy that had been followed until the 1960s. Australians have been free to pursue these debates, and to vary (over quite a wide range) the numbers of those admitted yearly, without considering obligations to past colonial subjects.

Finally, a nation's concerns about migration may come to affect that country's foreign policy toward (actual or potential) migrant-sending nations. The degree of this influence may vary greatly, of course. It may be limited primarily to the realm of declaratory policy or to the economic field. In the first area, Spain is currently quite ready to describe many sending nations in Africa as democratic, helping to justify Spain's rejection of most asylum claims filed by citizens of those states. In international economics, Germany now extends development assistance to some East European nations so that potential migrants' incentives to move to the Federal Republic may be reduced.

In certain cases, receiving nations are now stimulated to adopt far more active roles, encouraging democracy in specific sending states. The United States' policy toward Haiti is focused at present on reinstating an elected democratic government in Port-au-Prince, largely in order to justify Washington's policy of intercepting Haitian boat people. In the Far East, British governor Chris Patten in Hong Kong has sought since 1992 to expand democratic freedoms for the Crown Colony's population. Britain has agreed to relinquish Hong Kong to the rule of the People's Republic of China in 1997, but only 50,000 selected persons from Hong Kong will be permitted to emigrate to Britain with their families. One motivation for London's extension of new powers to Hong Kong's Legislative Council (for the first time since 1843!) may be the desire to improve the apparent political lot of Hong Kong residents once the territory becomes a "Special Administrative Region" within China.

Commentary

Three Critical Questions about the Study of Immigration Control

James C. Hathaway

The general parameters of the research presented in this volume raise three fundamental issues of concern. First, the project assumes the legitimacy of the legal and policy framework within which immigration is presently controlled. We are asked to assess the effectiveness of a system that has not been shown to have moral or political validity, since the study does not subject the concept of immigration control to critical scrutiny in the light of the right to freedom of international movement. One need not advocate an untrammeled right to migrate in order to share this concern. Those of us who recognize the central importance of boundedness to the viability of genuine community in the extant political context may nonetheless insist that constraints on freedom of international movement be justified. That is, there can be no resort to the facile assumption that unbridled immigration control is an inherent aspect of a state's sovereignty.

Governments, and in particular those that ascribe to liberal values, ought reasonably to be held to account for the restrictions placed on migratory freedom. Bruce Ackerman has attempted to define such an approach in his discussion of the liberal dialogue:

> Since authoritarian revolutions cannot be predicted with accuracy, the most we can demand is that statesmen set an overall [immigration policy] conscious of an immigrant's prima facie *right* to demand entry into a liberal state. Westerners are not entitled to deny this right simply because they have been born on the right side of a boundary line; nor can they escape the de-

mands of dialogue simply because they would find
sharing "their" wealth inconvenient. . . . The *only*
reason for restricting immigration is to protect the
ongoing process of liberal conversation itself. Can our
present immigration practices be rationalized on these
grounds (Ackerman 1980: 95)?

Michael Walzer's test for constraining membership in a state, while
clearly less exacting than that posited by Ackerman, would nonetheless
also require states to consider more than simply the perceived best
interests of their own citizenry in setting immigration policy:

Self-determination in the sphere of membership is not
absolute. . . . It is subject both to internal decisions by
the members themselves (*all* the members, including
those who hold membership simply by right of place)
and to the external principle of mutual aid. Immigration, then, is both a matter of political choice and moral
constraint (Walzer 1983: 62).

The critical concern, then, is that this project has not come to grips
with the basic question of the circumstances in which states may
appropriately resort to particular variants of immigration policy. Absent
this optic, the evaluation of immigration control is little more than a
process of legitimizing the assumed congruity of states as currently
bounded with meaningful forms of community.

A second concern is the pervasiveness in the chapters of references
to the sufficiency of *immigration* control procedures to regulate the entry
of *refugees*. There are, however, good reasons grounded in international
law to insist that refugee admissions be assessed within an alternative
paradigm. Indeed, refugee law is by its very nature a regime consciously
constructed by states in recognition of the nonviability of the panoply of
ordinary immigration rules in the face of involuntary transborder movements.

This is not to say that refugees enjoy an absolute or unqualified right
to asylum: international legislative history is clearly to the contrary. On
the other hand, it is equally obvious that states did *not* intend refugees to
be subject to the general scheme for regulation of entry. The international human right to "seek and to enjoy in other countries asylum from
persecution" outlined in the Universal Declaration of Human Rights, as
well as the existence of a duty to avoid the return of refugees to their
countries of origin, and perhaps most apparently, the explicit prohibition on the imposition of penalties on refugees "on account of their
illegal entry or presence" (from the Convention Relating to the Status of
Refugees) allow no room for the assertion that refugees may be dealt

with in a purely discretionary manner. While state self-interest influences the form and substance of protection, refugees unquestionably benefit from at least a partial abrogation of whatever general prerogative states may be said to enjoy in regard to immigration control. The human rights-driven process within which decisions about the entry of refugees should be made argues, in my view, for a conceptual segregation of this issue from the general concerns of the project.

Third, a purely comparative approach to the study of immigration control may seriously understate the nature of the challenge that many contemporary migrants face. It is increasingly the case that states act not autonomously, but rather collectively, in the setting of immigration control policies. In Europe, the TREVI ("Terrorism, Radicalism, Extremism, and Violence International") and Schengen intergovernmental processes have been particularly successful in facilitating the coordination of migration-hampering strategies by bureaucrats shielded from public scrutiny. European officials have been joined since 1985 by their counterparts from Australia, Canada, and the United States under the rubric of the so-called Informal Consultations, a forum for the sharing of plans and elaboration of common views on migration control.

The critical importance of this emerging intergovernmental approach to the development of migration control policy cannot be overstated. Because central policies are increasingly formulated outside the domestic political process, and indeed outside the bounds of even international or supranational legal accountability, a careful probing of the form and substance of transnational bureaucratic policy making is essential to a meaningful appraisal of the future of immigration control in the developed world.

References

Ackerman, Bruce. 1980. *Social Justice in the Liberal State.* New Haven, Conn.: Yale University Press.

Walzer, Michael. 1983. *Spheres of Justice: A Defence of Pluralism and Equality.* Oxford: M. Robertson.

PART II

COUNTRIES OF IMMIGRATION: THE UNITED STATES AND CANADA

2

U.S. Immigration and Policy Responses: The Limits of Legislation

Kitty Calavita

Introduction

The United States is often described as a land of immigrants. Indeed, the vast majority of the U.S. population is descended from people who arrived on its shores in the last century and a half. From 1820 to 1920, over 35 million immigrants came to the United States, mostly from Europe but also from China, Mexico, and other countries (see table 2.1). While quota restrictions passed in the 1920s temporarily slowed the flow, immigration—disproportionately this time from the Western Hemisphere—continued to provide the United States with a steady influx of new arrivals, some legal and many undocumented.

This chapter briefly traces the history of U.S. immigration and the policies that have both responded to the influx and stimulated and shaped it. It is clearly impossible to do justice to the details of this history in such a brief essay. However, the more general purpose of this chapter is to lay the groundwork for exploring the possibility that a number of patterns can be discerned, and that the nature of these patterns may suggest an ongoing set of dynamics that constrain the immigration policy process. Following a necessarily sketchy outline of the major immigration reforms of the nineteenth and twentieth centuries, including a more in-depth discussion of the Immigration Reform and Control Act of 1986, the chapter concludes by proposing that three "paired oppositions," or contradictions, pervade the U.S. experience with immigration and the efforts to regulate it.

TABLE 2.1

FLOW OF LEGAL IMMIGRANTS TO THE UNITED STATES, 1821–1990

Period	Immigrants Admitted (000,000s)	Rate[1]	Percentage of Population Foreign Born[2]
1821–1830	.14	na	na
1831–1840	.60	na	na
1841–1850	1.7	na	na
1851–1860	2.6	na	na
1861–1870	2.3	na	na
1871–1880	2.8	na	na
1881–1890	5.25	na	na
1891–1900	3.7	na	na
1900–1910	8.8	10.4	na
1911–1920	5.7	5.7	13.2
1921–1930	4.1	3.5	11.6
1931–1940	0.5	0.4	8.8
1941–1950	1.0	0.7	6.9
1951–1960	2.5	1.5	5.4
1961–1970	3.3	1.7	4.7
1971–1980	4.5	2.1	6.7
1981–1990	7.3	3.0	8.6

[1] Annual rate per 1,000 U.S. population
[2] Includes both undocumented and documented foreign-born residents.

Sources: 1821–1900, U.S. Immigration and Naturalization Service; 1901–1900, U.S. Bureau of the Census, *Statistical Abstract of the United States,* 11th ed. (Washington, D.C., 1991): tables 5 and 46.

The Door Opens: European Immigration to the United States

In early 1791, Alexander Hamilton warned Congress that if the United States were to develop into an industrial power, immigration would haveto be encouraged so as to offset the "scarcity of hands" and the "dearness of labor" (Hamilton 1791: 123). The nineteenth century witnessed recruitment efforts by the U.S. government and the states, as well as private employers, who saturated Europe with promotional campaigns to stir up emigration to the United States. As Andrew Carnegie (1886: 34–35) explained it, "The value to the country of the annual foreign influx is very great indeed. . . . These adults are surely worth $1500 each—for in former days an efficient slave sold for that sum." Later in the passage, Carnegie referred to immigration as "a golden stream which flows into the country each year." The *New York Journal of Commerce* expressed it this way: "Men, like cows, are expensive to raise and a gift of either should be gladly received. And a man can be put to more valuable use than a cow" (December 13, 1892, p. 2).

Policy makers throughout the nineteenth century extolled the economic benefits of abundant immigration and fashioned U.S. immigration policies to maximize the flow (Calavita 1984). Until 1875 there were no federal restrictions of any kind, and the individual state laws that did exist were largely confined to regulating the reception process, aiding the destitute, and, in some cases, securing bonds from shipowners. The first comprehensive federal immigration law, passed in 1864, was An Act to Encourage Immigration (U.S. Statutes at Large). This law established the first U.S. Immigration Bureau, whose primary function was to increase immigration so that American industries would have an adequate supply of workers to meet production needs during the Civil War. In addition, in an effort to reduce the number of immigrants who left industry for homesteading or army enlistment, the law made pre-emigration contracts binding. Although the law was repealed in 1868, it spawned the host of private labor recruitment agencies that for many years continued to be a significant force behind European emigration (U.S. Congress, Senate 1864: 1–4).

The late nineteenth and early twentieth centuries saw the enactment of a number of selective measures, among them the exclusion of the Chinese, anyone "likely to become a public charge," those with prearranged work contracts, the criminal, the diseased, and the politically undesirable. In practice, however, these measures excluded only about 1 percent of the total flow (Jenks 1913), in large part because they were designed "along conservative lines [so as to] avoid measures so drastic as to cripple American industry" (*Congressional Record* 1902: 5763–64). The implementation of these restrictions was carefully gauged so that the "golden stream" went uninterrupted. As one immigration inspector of the period explained it, "Better to run the risk of the occasional admission of an alien inadmissible under the law than to slow up the process" (quoted in Van Vleck 1932: 28). Within the context of these formal and informal policies of encouragement, immigration to the United States averaged close to a million entrants annually during the early years of the twentieth century.

By 1909, new immigrants constituted the majority of the industrial working class; that year 60 percent of men and 47 percent of women wageworkers in the twenty largest mining and manufacturing industries in the United States were recent immigrants (U.S. Congress, Senate 1911: 322). Because immigrants almost invariably occupied the least desirable and most unstable positions in each industry, wage reductions and layoffs inevitably hit them first and hardest. It should not be surprising then that these newcomers, driven to desperation, began to fight back.

With the support of the Industrial Workers of the World (IWW) and a variety of small, independent unions, many spontaneous uprisings led by immigrant workers early in the twentieth century stunned both their

employers and, increasingly, their American co-workers. Foreign
workers on streetcars, in the clothing trades, textiles, packinghouses,
and steel mills launched some of the most crippling strikes of the period.
The Lawrence Textile Strike of 1912 is a good example of the new role that
Southern and Eastern European immigrants played in the labor movement. Watching tens of thousands of immigrant mill workers fill the
streets of Lawrence, Massachusetts, in 1912 to protest wage reductions
and line speedups, an observer noted that "the capacity of this great host
of recent immigrants . . . for continuous effective solidarity is one of the
revelations of the present strike" (quoted in Hourwich 1912: 392).
Immigrants continued to strengthen the labor movement by joining
labor unions (those from which they were not excluded). For example,
the International Ladies Garment Workers and the Amalgamated
Clothing Workers of America—each claiming 175,000 members, overwhelmingly Jews, Italians, and Poles—were "two of the strongest labor
unions in America by 1920" (*Congressional Record* 1921: 187).

The Mexican "Backdoor"

Mexican immigration gained momentum in the pre-World War I period,
as the U.S. government and some employers began to reconsider the
costs and benefits of European immigration. By this time, the European
immigrant had developed a reputation as a troublemaker, increasingly
forming the backbone of strikes and, more often than not, remaining to
become a permanent member of society. In 1911, the Dillingham Commission on Immigration, in response to these concerns, noted the
special advantages of Mexican immigrants:

> Because of their strong attachment to their native land-
> . . . and the possibility of their residence here being
> discontinued, few become citizens of the United States.
> The Mexican immigrants are providing a fairly ade-
> quate supply of labor. . . . While they are not easily
> assimilated, this is of no very great importance as long
> as most of them return to their native land. In the case of
> the Mexican, he is less desirable as a citizen than as a
> laborer (U.S. Congress, Senate 1911: 690–91).

Initially the bulk of Mexican migration was legal. In response to
warnings from southwest growers that the success of their harvests
depended on a plentiful supply of Mexican labor, the secretary of labor
temporarily exempted Mexican migrant labor from the literacy test
requirement of 1917, the head tax, and the contract labor clause (Reisler
1976: 27; López 1981: 656). When the Quota Restrictions of 1921 and 1924

reduced European immigration, Mexicans and other Western Hemisphere immigrants were exempt; this "backdoor" was seen as a valuable substitute for European labor—a preferred one, in fact, given Mexico's geographic proximity and the United States' ability to regulate the supply at a moment's notice. One scholar, summarizing the congressional debate over possible restrictions on Mexican immigration in the 1920s, paraphrased Congress's anti-restrictionist sentiment:

> The Mexican, they pointed out, was a vulnerable alien living just a short distance from his homeland. . . . He, unlike Puerto Ricans or Filipinos . . . could easily be deported. No safer or more economical unskilled labor force was imaginable (Reisler 1976: 181, paraphrasing Hearings of the House Committee on Immigration 1929).

Mexicans had been recruited as far north as Canada in the late 1880s after Chinese immigrant labor was barred. Now, with European immigration temporarily halted by World War I, industries from southern California to Chicago began to draw labor from Mexico. Between 1915 and 1920, Mexican migration went from 11,000 per year to 51,000; approximately 500,000 Mexicans crossed into the United States during the 1920s (López 1981: 660).

The shift from European to Mexican immigration as a source of labor did increase flexibility, as evidenced by the deportation of thousands of Mexican workers and their families during the depression of the 1930s and the increasingly rigorous interpretations of the public charge clause, which reduced dramatically the number of legal entrants without resorting to statutory changes. As war production refueled the U.S. economy in the 1940s, Mexican contract laborers were imported through the Bracero Program, a series of bilateral agreements that provided Mexican workers to southwest agriculture.

The Bracero Program is interesting not only because it attempted to institutionalize the flexible and temporary nature of the Mexican labor supply (always recognized as its primary virtue), but also because formal and informal policies during this period contributed to the increase in *illegal* migration that characterizes the contemporary movement (see Calavita 1992). The Bracero agreement of 1949 provided that "illegal workers, when they are located in the United States, shall be given preference under outstanding U.S. Employment Service Certification" (quoted in Galarza 1964: 63). Illegal Mexican immigrants, or "wetbacks," were often "dried out" by the INS Border Patrol, who escorted them to the Mexican border, had them step to the Mexican side, and brought them back as legal braceros. In some cases, the Border Patrol "paroled" illegal immigrants directly to employers (Calavita 1992). The

President's Commission on Migratory Labor estimated in 1951 that from 1947 to 1949 more than 142,000 undocumented Mexican workers were legalized in this way, at a time when only 74,600 new braceros were recruited from Mexico (cited in Samora 1971: 47–48).

In addition to these more or less official policies of encouragement of illegal migration, Immigration and Naturalization Service (INS) district directors exercised benign neglect with regard to undocumented labor. The chief inspector at Tucson, for example, reported that he "received orders from the District Director at El Paso each harvest to stop deporting illegal Mexican labor" (Kirstein 1973: 90). During World War II, the INS district director in Los Angeles explained to the Department of Labor that it was INS policy not to check farms and ranches for illegal aliens while harvest work was being done (Calavita 1992: 33). In 1949, the Idaho State Employment Service reported, "The United States Immigration and Naturalization Service recognizes the need for farm workers in Idaho and . . . withholds its search and deportation until such times as there is not a shortage of farm workers" (quoted in President's Commission on Migratory Labor 1951: 76). The implicit message from Congress was consistent with this laissez-faire approach. As one observer put it, Congress was "splendidly indifferent" to the rising number of illegals, reducing the Border Patrol budget just as undocumented migration increased (Hadley 1956: 334).

A key congressional decision made employers immune to any risk involved in employing the undocumented. In 1952, under pressure from Mexico, the U.S. Congress passed an act that made it illegal to "harbor, transport, or conceal illegal entrants" (PL 283). However, an amendment to the provision (referred to as the Texas Proviso, after the Texas growers to whom it was a concession) excluded employment per se from the category of "harboring." The amendment was ostensibly introduced as a way to protect employers who were unaware of their workers' illegal immigrant status from prosecution under the harboring clause. Despite assurances by Texas Proviso advocates in Congress that it did not provide a loophole for the *knowing* employment of illegal aliens, Congress rejected by a vote of 69 to 12 an amendment actually penalizing such knowing employment (see Calavita 1992: 66–70). The Texas Proviso was subsequently interpreted by the INS as a virtual carte blanche for the employment of undocumented workers (see Greene 1972: 453–55).

Illegal immigration increased rapidly within this political and legal context. From 1942 to 1952, when a total of 818,545 braceros were imported from Mexico, the INS apprehended over 2 million undocumented workers, the vast majority of whom were Mexican (U.S. INS 1959: 54). By 1953 the alarm was sounded that illegal immigration was depressing wages, displacing U.S. workers, and—in this period of Cold War paranoia—jeopardizing the national security by providing an entrée to "potential saboteurs and fifth columnists" (quoted in *Congres-*

sional Record 1954: 2564). In response, "Operation Wetback" was launched, in which hundreds of thousands of Mexicans were rounded up and deported (see Calavita 1992: 46–61). For the rest of the decade, the INS provided U.S. growers with an ample supply of braceros as a substitute for the illegal workers of the past. In fact, INS Commissioner Joseph Swing entered into an informal agreement with growers that if they would cooperate, he would "exchange" their illegal workers for legal braceros. As a result of this agreement, Swing and his agency worked hard to preserve growers' satisfaction with the quantity and quality of their bracero workforce. By the time the Bracero Program ended in 1964, a relationship of symbiosis between Mexican immigrants and U.S. employers had become entrenched, facilitated and nurtured by over fifty years of policy making. Almost 5 million Mexican workers had been brought to the United States as braceros; approximately 5 million illegal aliens were apprehended during the same period (López 1981: 671).

The stage was set for high levels of documented and undocumented immigration. U.S. policies in the post-Bracero Program period have perpetuated this pattern largely by default. Budgetary decisions played a key role because they effectively eliminated the counter-pressure to illegal migration. As the congressional subcommittee that holds the INS purse strings stated in 1981, the agency "has been chronically under-funded, undermanned and neglected" (quoted in Harwood 1983: 108). During the 1950s, congressional members from border states pared down the budget of the Border Patrol to ensure a plentiful supply of labor (Galarza 1964: 61). The INS budget did not fare much better in the 1960s and 1970s. While the number of apprehensions of illegal aliens rose from about 71,000 in 1960 to 345,000 by the end of the decade, the number of permanent INS staff positions remained constant at approximately 6,900 (Congressional Research Service 1980: 65, 76, 90). Apprehensions rose to more than 1 million in 1978, while total INS personnel reached barely 10,000 (Congressional Research Service 1980: 76, 90). In 1980, the Border Patrol allotment for policing almost 6,000 miles of border was only $77 million. As Teitelbaum (1980: 55) pointed out, this is less than the budget of the Baltimore police department and less than half that of the Philadelphia police, which stood at $95 and $221 million, respectively.

The Immigration and Nationality Act

At the same time that U.S. policy makers were carefully crafting the Texas Proviso—thereby providing a loophole for the employment of undocumented workers and ensuring a plentiful supply of Mexican braceros to southwest growers—they were making sweeping changes to the legal immigration system. Congress passed the Immigration and Nationality Act (INA) in 1952 over the strenuous objections and veto of President Truman, who considered the act discriminatory and unnecessarily restrictionist. Known also as the McCarran-Walter Act (after its sponsors in the Senate and House), the INA allotted each country an annual quota of immigrants, based on the proportion of people from that country present in the United States in 1920. It thus perpetuated the so-called national origins system that President Truman and others found offensive. In addition, it put a ceiling of 150,000 individuals on immigration from the Eastern Hemisphere but set no such limit for Western Hemisphere countries. Finally, it established the preference system for immigrant workers and close relatives of U.S. citizens and residents, the basic structure of which remains intact today. In brief, the preference system placed priority on family unification, giving first preference to the immediate family of citizens and legal residents, but still keeping the door open to skilled and unskilled workers in certain occupational categories.

In 1965, with Lyndon Johnson in the presidency and a liberal Congress focused on expanding civil rights, the INA was substantially amended in key respects. The differential treatment of the Western and Eastern Hemispheres was reduced, and the national origins system was eliminated. The amendments placed an annual limit of 170,000 immigrants on Eastern Hemisphere countries, with no more than 20,000 coming from any one country, and a limit of 120,000 on the Western Hemisphere, with no per-country quotas. Within these limits, priority was to be given to persons with close relatives in the United States or individuals with certain needed skills.

Relatively minor adjustments to this basic schema continued throughout the 1970s and 1980s—a period when attention was riveted on the issue of controlling the increasing influx of illegal immigration. Two modifications during this period are especially important. First, in 1978 the separate hemispheric limits were eliminated and a single ceiling of 290,000 was established, with a uniform limit of 20,000 per country. Second, the Refugee Act of 1980 took refugees out of the preference system; the president, after consulting with Congress, would now have the authority to establish annual limits on the number of refugees to be admitted.

Anti-Immigrant Backlashes

Beginning with the Irish immigration of the mid-1800s, an appreciation for the immigrants' economic contribution has almost always come accompanied by anti-immigrant nativism and public pleas for restriction. Based on varying combinations of racism, fears of tax increases, cultural and political protectionism, and organized labor's concerns over bargaining power, these anti-immigrant backlashes have tended to intensify in periods of uncertainty, such as economic crisis and/or perceived threats to the national security (Higham 1955; Cornelius 1982).

Although the reaction against Mexican immigrants is similar in many respects, by the mid-twentieth century it also differed in specific ways from anti-immigrant responses of earlier periods. Most important, because of Mexico's proximity and the undocumented status of many Mexican immigrants, these immigrants have been subject to abrupt policy changes that respond to popular concerns. Mass expulsions and roundups of Mexicans during "Operation Wetback" in 1954, for example, were reminiscent of the depression policies of the 1930s. These periodic tightenings of the U.S.-Mexico border—usually accomplished without recourse to statutory changes—are eminently compatible with the long-standing perception of Mexican migration as a flexible and temporary supply of labor.

In the last two decades, immigrants have been the targets of renewed public alarm. As in the past, a vocal minority in the United States have blamed newly arrived immigrants for virtually every social ill affecting American society, including crime, environmental deterioration, and urban uprisings. And, as in the past, it is in large part *because* immigrants supply a cheap labor force (something that employers and policy makers well realize) that they provide an easy target for apprehensive taxpayers and domestic workers. The predominantly illegal nature of the contemporary flow enhances the reaction. As fear spread in the early 1980s that the United States had "lost control of its borders," immigration restrictionism intensified. Local politicians and taxpayers' associations fueled the backlash, sponsoring a number of studies that purported to demonstrate that undocumented immigrants are a drain on taxpayers (see, for example, Stewart, Gascoigne, and Bannister 1992). Despite extensive research demonstrating precisely the opposite, these new studies have been used to stir up restrictionist fervor and elicit support for politicians who use the immigration issue as a political drawing card. By early 1993, a handful of California politicians, in alliance with a variety of citizen groups, placed over twenty anti-immigrant proposals on the state agenda. These bills propose to bar the children of undocumented immigrants from public schools, engage the police in immigration control, and implement other similar strategies of harassment and/or restriction. Most, if not all, of these bills will ultimately be defeated, but their number and the intensity of the debate signifies a renewed nativism among at least a vocal minority. According to Assemblyman Gil Ferguson (R-Newport Beach), sponsor of two such bills, "This is the hottest button going. As people hear about job losses and the state deficit, the backlash against illegal aliens grows" (quoted in Bailey and Morain 1993: A3).

This new nativism—as well as a more broadly based restriction-ism—are unique in at least one respect. In the past, nativism was correlated with high unemployment rates (Cornelius 1982). Indeed, each serious recession since the mid-nineteenth century has heightened anti-immigrant protest, as new arrivals become the scapegoats for economic downturns (Calavita 1984). The apparent irony of today's restrictionism is that, while its roots can be traced to the "stagflation" of the 1970s, its heightened pitch in the mid-1980s occurred at a time of relatively low unemployment.

This is not to say that restrictionism is unrelated to economic factors. Indeed, the current wave of restrictionism is occurring at a time of major dislocations and a profound transformation of the U.S. economy. As the heavy manufacturing sector contracts and the service sector expands, an increased proportion of new jobs are located in the less desirable secondary labor market. A study prepared for the Congressional Joint Economic Committee estimated that close to 60 percent of the workers added to the labor force between 1979 and 1984 earned less than $7,000 per year (*Los Angeles Times* 1987a). Individual wage and salary income fell 10 percent from 1973 to 1985, and the proportion of households with annual incomes below $20,000 increased by 8 percent in the same period (*Los Angeles Times* 1987b).

In addition, traditionally well-paying and stable jobs are being transformed, as more part-time employment—together with overtime for full-time employees—cuts into wages and benefits and erodes economic security. "Contingent" workers doing part-time work on short-term, terminal contracts now comprise approximately 30 percent of the U.S. workforce, which means that they usually accrue no benefits and no seniority (Ingwerson 1993: 9). According to one economist, "Employment by temporary work agencies has surged to a record level, as has . . . overtime" (Bauder 1993: C-1). In 1982, approximately one-quarter of new jobs were for part-time or temporary work; a decade later, half of all jobs filled were for such "contingent" work (Kilborn 1993: A1). The Bureau of Labor Statistics reported that 90 percent of all new jobs in February 1993 were part-time (cited in Kilborn 1993: A6).

In the past, the rising levels of unemployment that triggered back-lashes against immigrants also temporarily reduced the need for immigrant workers, slowing the influx (as occurred during the 1930s, for example). In contrast, the economic processes under way in the United States since the early 1970s have simultaneously increased the demand for immigrants to fill minimum-wage, unskilled, and part-time jobs, and enhanced anti-immigrant reactions. In other words, the structural transformations in the economy that reproduce a continued demand for immigrants *at the same time* contribute to restrictionist sentiment. As

Americans encounter increasing economic uncertainty, they direct some of their anxiety and hostility toward immigrant newcomers, whose numbers are increasing just as meaningful economic opportunities are dwindling.

This brief historical overview suggests that: (1) immigration to the United States can be characterized from the beginning as the movement of a workforce—a movement firmly rooted in economic realities; (2) U.S. policies have both reflected those realities and catalyzed the movement; (3) anti-immigrant reactions are often juxtaposed with employers' appreciation of the immigrant as a labor source; and (4) a conflict has now emerged between restrictionism, on one hand, and the economic forces that accelerate illegal immigration on the other. It was within this context of contradictory economic and political pressures that the U.S. Congress enacted the Immigration Reform and Control Act of 1986 (IRCA). It will be argued here that IRCA can best be understood as an attempt to respond both to the long-standing economic realities of immigration and to the new restrictionism.

IRCA and Its Impacts

IRCA comprises three fundamental components. First, its legalization provision allowed undocumented immigrants who had been in the United States in an illegal status since before January 1, 1982, to apply for legal residence. Second, employer sanctions made it illegal for an employer to knowingly hire undocumented workers. Finally, the Special Agricultural Workers program allowed certain undocumented workers in the agricultural sector to apply for legalization, and it provided for additional farmworkers to be admitted should a shortage of farm labor develop.

IRCA's roots can be traced to 1971, when Representative Peter Rodino's Subcommittee on Immigration held a lengthy series of hearings on the topic of illegal aliens, a substantial portion of which dealt with the possibility of enacting a federal employer sanctions law. Over the next few years, a number of employer sanctions bills were introduced in both houses of Congress. Consistently, only the House of Representatives took any action on these bills (they passed the House by wide margins in the 92nd and 93rd Congresses). In spite of strong support from both the Nixon and Ford administrations, these employer sanctions bills regularly died in the Senate without a vote, in large part due to the staunch opposition of Senator Eastland (D-Mississippi), then chair of the Senate Judiciary Committee. Eastland, a cotton planter with strong ties to southern agricultural interests, refused to hold hearings on the issue. It is reported that the Senate Subcommittee on Immigration, over which

Eastland resided, did not even meet as a committee during these years (Schuck 1975).

In 1975, the first amnesty provision was attached to the House of Representatives' employer sanctions bill. Public opinion polls have consistently shown that the majority of Americans oppose amnesty for the undocumented. Nevertheless, this provision was instrumental in garnering votes for the reform effort, both from liberal advocates of immigrants' rights and from members of Congress concerned with offsetting the effects of employer sanctions and stabilizing the labor supply. That same year, President Ford established a cabinet-level Domestic Council of Illegal Migration, chaired by the attorney general. The recommendations of this council included both a federal employer sanctions law and a legalization plan.

The Carter administration continued the push for reform and in 1977 introduced a bill that included employer sanctions, legalization, and increased border enforcement. The Carter bill did not get far in either house of Congress. Instead, a prestigious sixteen-member U.S. Select Commission on Immigration and Refugee Policy was appointed. This commission published its report in 1981 and (to no one's surprise) recommended employer sanctions, a legalization program, and increased resources for the Border Patrol. Consistent with earlier congressional proposals, the commission's recommendations included no provision for special agricultural worker programs.

Just one year after the commission published its recommendations, the first Simpson-Mazzoli bill was reported out of the House and Senate judiciary committees. Both versions followed closely the commission's proposals, with only relatively minor differences between them. Once again no mention was made of a special farm labor program, although the Senate bill would have expanded the old H-2 program.[1] The Senate—where Senator Alan Simpson (R-Wyoming) had taken over as chair of the Subcommittee on Immigration—passed its bill by 80 to 19 after only three days of floor debate. The bill foundered in the House, however, where civil rights advocates were concerned over the potential for abuse and discrimination against persons who "sound or look foreign," growers' groups lobbied for additional provisions for foreign labor, and the Chamber of Commerce persistently opposed sanctions against employers. So controversial was the bill in the House that over 300 amendments were introduced in a successful effort to forestall a vote.

---

[1] The H-2 program allows for the seasonal importation of workers to areas where the Department of Labor has certified that a labor shortage exists. Approximately 25,000 temporary workers (the largest single group are agricultural workers) are imported annually under this program. This number has declined steadily since the 1970s. Growers in the Southwest have never made extensive use of the H-2 program, probably because of the ease with which undocumented Mexican labor can be obtained as compared to the difficulties imposed by the bureaucratic regulations and requirements of the H-2 program.

A second Simpson-Mazzoli bill finally passed both houses of Congress in 1984, squeaking by in the House by a vote of 216 to 211, only to come apart in the conference committee, ostensibly over cost issues. Nineteen eighty-four marked an important turning point for the immigration reform effort. First, opposition to employer sanctions (most notably from the Chamber of Commerce) began to subside, placated at least in part by the "affirmative defense" clause that released employers from any obligation to check the authenticity of prospective workers' documents. Second, agricultural employers shifted from opposing employer sanctions to campaigning to secure alternative sources of foreign labor. As opposition to employer sanctions waned and growers' lobbying efforts for extensive temporary worker programs intensified, agricultural worker programs began to outrank the employer sanctions component as the most controversial element of the reform. What had begun as a restrictive effort grounded in employer sanctions had now come full circle, to be mired in a debate over how best to *expand* the supply of foreign labor.

The following year Senator Simpson reintroduced the bill that congressional opponents now called "the Monster from the Blue Lagoon" because of its eerie ability to rise from the dead. By September the Senate version had passed, after an impressive show of strength by the Western Growers' Association. Arguing that employer sanctions would cut off an invaluable source of agricultural labor, Senator Pete Wilson (R-California) introduced an amendment in the closing days of debate to create a temporary farm labor program outside of, and in addition to, the old H-2 program. The amendment was defeated 50 to 48, only to be passed four days later after intensive grower lobbying. The Wilson amendment provided for a short-term guestworker program in which each year up to 350,000 foreign workers would be given visas for a short period to harvest perishable crops.

A number of key House Democrats vowed to kill any bill with such a "de facto slave labor program" attached to it, and it seemed that the controversy might destroy the limited consensus achieved in the House the previous year. However, by the end of the amendment process, House Republicans and Democrats had agreed to a complicated formula that provided temporary residence status and eventual eligibility for citizenship to persons who had worked in agriculture for at least ninety days. It also included a generous future replenishment clause, on the assumption that newly legalized workers might abandon farm labor. The compromise struck a delicate balance between civil rights advocates, who argued against traditional guestworker programs on the grounds that they provided employers with a captive workforce and hence invited abuse, and growers' representatives, who were assured a plentiful and continual supply of foreign labor through the replenishment clause. On October 9, 1986—more than a year after its Senate passage—this unwieldy bill passed the House, and on October 14 House and Senate conferees endorsed a compromise. When President Reagan signed IRCA less than a month later, he noted that the law was "the product of one of the longest and most difficult legislative undertakings of recent memory" (quoted in Montwieler 1987: 18).

IRCA's most significant consequence was the legalization of millions of undocumented immigrants who for years had lived and worked in the shadows. Almost 3 million immigrants applied to one of IRCA's two legalization programs, far more than policy makers had anticipated. Approximately 1.7 million applicants filed for the general legalization program (LAW), with an approval rate at close to 98 percent (Bean, Vernez, and Keely 1989: 68). Another 1.3 million applied for legalization through the Special Agricultural Workers program (SAW). Despite claims that fraud was widespread (U.S. Commission on Agricultural Workers 1992), of individuals who had been processed through SAW by 1989, approximately 94 percent were approved (Bean, Vernez, and Keely 1989: 68). The SAW program vastly exceeded original projections (policy makers had predicted no more than 210,000 applicants [Baker 1990: 165]). The majority of legalized immigrants came from Mexico (69.8 percent of LAW applicants; 81.9 percent of SAW applicants), with significant numbers coming from other Central American countries (13.4 percent of LAW applicants; 4.2 percent of SAW applicants) and from Asia (4.3 percent of LAW applicants; 5.4 percent of SAW applicants) (Bean, Vernez, and Keely 1989: 69). Five states—California, Texas, Illinois, New York, and Florida—accounted for over 80 percent of the applications for legalization (Baker 1990: 165).

Ironically, employer sanctions—IRCA's political centerpiece—have had little concrete impact. Section 101 of IRCA makes it illegal to knowingly employ aliens not authorized to work in the United States. The provision applies to all employers, including those who subcontract all or part of their work, and all workers, including day laborers and temporary workers. Further, the law requires that employers ask all new employees for documentation proving their identity and eligibility to work in the United States, that employers complete and sign an I-9 form for each new hire, listing the specific documents seen and their expiration dates, and that they keep these forms on file. Penalties for violating the "knowing hire" provision range from $250 for the first offense to $10,000 for repeated offenses. A "pattern or practice" of violations may bring criminal penalties, including six months in prison. Fines for paperwork violations related to the I-9 form range from $100 to $1,000 per violation.

The INS's final Rules and Regulations on IRCA (U.S. INS 1987) give employers three business days after the date of hire to complete I-9 forms; employers who hire workers for fewer than three days must complete the paperwork within twenty-four hours. Finally, employers are to be given three days' notice before INS inspections.

During the debates preceding the enactment of employer sanctions, advocates in Congress and in the INS maintained that most employers would voluntarily comply with this law. Admitting that the INS would be able to monitor only a tiny fraction of the nation's approximately 7 million employers each year, employer sanctions proponents argued that this was of little consequence. The deterrent effect of the law, the argument went, would be based on voluntary compliance and the example set by a few well-publicized fines.

After passage of employer sanctions, INS Commissioner Alan Nelson stated that most employers were abiding by the law simply because it was the law. Martin Soblick, INS district counsel in San Diego, spoke enthusiastically of "the success we've had across the board in securing voluntary compliance from employers nationwide" (quoted in *San Diego Union-Tribune*, February 1, 1989). Harold Ezell, then western regional commissioner of the INS, maintained that the fines imposed under employer sanctions operated as a deterrent for those few employers who might not otherwise comply voluntarily (*San Diego Union*, August 31, 1988, p. B-2).

Border apprehension statistics at first seemed to validate the early optimism concerning employer compliance and IRCA's deterrent effect. From fiscal year 1986 to fiscal year 1989, Border Patrol apprehensions along the U.S.-Mexico border, where the overwhelming majority of illegal aliens are detained, dropped from 1,615,854 to 854,939. However, this decline reversed dramatically in the second quarter of 1989. After an initial sharp drop in the first quarter of that year, apprehensions increased more than 32 percent in the last two quarters compared to the same period in 1988 (U.S. Immigration and Naturalization Service, cited in Dillin 1989a), leading one usually circumspect reporter to suggest that the border was "spinning out of control" (Dillin 1989b: 8). The figures for fiscal year 1990 showed an even steeper rise in apprehensions. In the San Diego sector, where most apprehensions are made, December 1989 apprehensions were 89 percent above the number in December 1988; January 1990 saw an increase of 51 percent over the previous January; and apprehensions in February were up 78 percent over the previous period (U.S. Border Patrol, cited in Brossy 1990). Confronted with these statistics, INS spokesperson Duke Austin admitted, "The trend is not in the right direction" (quoted in Brossy 1990: B2).

The most comprehensive study to date of the effect of employer sanctions on illegal border crossings concludes that the initial reduction in apprehensions was less a product of employer sanctions than a predictable consequence of IRCA's legalization provisions (Crane et al. 1990). IRCA legalized close to 3 million immigrants, many of whom had been periodically crossing the border illegally prior to their change of

status. The study further demonstrates that, when controlling for variations in Border Patrol enforcement strategies and resources devoted to
border apprehensions, the three-year apprehension figures do not indicate any substantial deterrent effect from the law. A U.S. Department of
Labor study of the impact of employer sanctions on the labor market
similarly concludes that "the drop in apprehensions in the immediate
post-IRCA years may have been more of a pause than a change in
behavior" (U.S. Department of Labor 1991: 62). The Commission on
Agricultural Workers, established by Congress to trace IRCA's effects on
agricultural conditions, reached similar conclusions (U.S. Commission
on Agricultural Workers 1992), as have most academic studies (see, for
example, Bean, Vernez, and Keely 1989; Fix 1991).

In part, it may be that employer sanctions have had little deterrent
effect because they are not systematically enforced. In its first report to
Congress on the impact of employer sanctions, the General Accounting
Office noted that the INS expected to audit approximately 20,000
employers in fiscal year 1988—in other words, one-third of 1 percent of
the approximately 7 million employers in the United States (U.S. GAO
1987: 27). Records show that the INS fell short of even this goal, having
completed 12,319 inspections, or less than one-fifth of 1 percent of the
nation's employers (U.S. INS 1988). In the first five months of fiscal year
1989, the INS conducted 5,000 inspections, almost exactly replicating the
1988 figures (Bean, Vernez, and Keely 1989: 43). The selection procedure
for inspections reduces even further the chances of an offending employer being detected. In order to "demonstrate that the Service is not
engaging in selective enforcement of the law," a substantial portion of
inspections are initiated on the basis of a random selection process
(referred to as the General Administrative Plan, or GAP) generated by a
listing of 5 million employers across the country (U.S. INS 1987). By early
1989, 25 percent of employer sanctions had been based on this random
procedure, while 75 percent were based on leads (Bean, Vernez, and
Keely 1989: 43). By 1990, the proportion of GAP inspections had risen to
35 percent (U.S. GAO 1990: 94). Even though the GAP procedure nets far
fewer offenders than lead-based inspections, the INS has plans to
increase to 40 percent the number of inspections based on random
selection (Bean, Vernez, and Keely 1989: 43).

However, the most potent ingredient influencing employers' continued hiring of undocumented workers despite employer sanctions may
be the employers' perception that they are protected by the I-9 form. As
noted previously, IRCA requires employers to request documentation
from all new hires and to complete I-9 forms attesting to having seen
these documents. One in-depth study of 100 employers in southern
California (summarized in Calavita 1990) found almost universal compliance with this requirement. All but 5 of the employers reported that
they systematically request documentation and complete the required

paperwork. Rather than seeing the paperwork requirement as burdensome, many employers view the I-9 form as an effective barrier between violation and prosecution. The director of human resources at a large plant—who later told the interviewer, "Evidently we have people who are illegal"—pointed out that "It [the I-9] would help protect us."

Such comments spotlight the paradox in the employer sanctions law. Even if they admit that they employ undocumented workers, employers will probably not be subject to fines under employer sanctions. Instead, as long as they complete the paperwork (as the vast majority do), they are labeled "compliers." A garment shop personnel director, who confided to the interviewer that he had instructed his undocumented workers to "fix" their patently false documents, explained the paradox this way: "The I-9 takes a lot of responsibility off me and puts it back on the employee." To understand fully the prevalence of this illegal hiring activity and employers' relative impunity, we must untangle the dynamics of this shift of responsibility via the I-9 form, a shift that has its source in the law itself.

In 1982, a "good faith" clause was inserted into the Simpson-Mazzoli bill. This clause stipulated that if employers check workers' documents, regardless of the validity of those documents, they will be assumed to have complied with the law. During debate of the final Simpson-Rodino bill, Senator Alan Simpson (R-Wyoming) reiterated this theme: "I can assure my colleagues," he said, "that an innocent employer will be protected by following the verification procedures" (quoted in Montwieler 1987: 255). By the time IRCA was passed in 1986, this protection was carefully spelled out. It included a provision that the required document check, conducted in "good faith," would constitute an "affirmative defense that the person or entity has not violated [the 'knowing hire' clause]." Equally important, it released employers from responsibility for detecting fraudulent documents, stating that "a person or entity has complied with the [document check] requirement . . . if the document reasonably appears on its face to be genuine."

While much of the debate surrounding these protections focused on a concern that employer sanctions might otherwise produce discrimination against individuals who sound or look foreign, the protections' effect was to minimize employer opposition to the law. As early as 1981, when the Senate Subcommittee on Immigration and Refugee Policy held hearings on "The Knowing Employment of Illegal Aliens," acting INS Commissioner Doris Meissner stressed that "implementation of the law is not designed to be and will not be anti employer. . . . Unlike a number of State statutes concerning employer sanctions, the Federal law relative to the knowing hiring of illegal aliens will not require employers to make judgments concerning the authenticity of documentation" (U.S. Congress, Senate 1981: 5). At the same hearing, Senator Simpson repeated, "[Employer sanctions] must be the type of program which does not place an onerous burden upon the employer with respect to what he has to do to avoid a penalty" (p. 86). In 1985, the Chamber of Commerce, convinced that employer sanctions would not pose an "onerous burden," officially *endorsed* the measure.

The affirmative defense clause and the "good faith" document check for all practical purposes redefined compliance. Gerald Riso, then deputy commissioner of the INS, unwittingly summarized this de facto transformation in the meaning of compliance before the House Subcommittee on Immigration, Refugees, and International Law in 1983: "We have made some assumptions that most employers will voluntarily comply *if we make compliance pragmatically easy for them*" (U.S. Congress, House 1983: 265; emphasis added). The Senate Judiciary Committee was more specific, stating confidently, "The Committee believes that the affirmative defense which results from compliance (sic) . . . will encourage the majority of employers to elect to comply" (U.S. Congress, Senate 1985: 32).

A semantic transformation had taken place during the legislative process in which compliance with the paperwork requirement became the proxy for compliance with the heart of the employer sanctions law — the "knowing hire" provision. Transforming the definition of compliance was crucial for eliminating employer opposition to the law. By simultaneously appeasing a public that demanded employer sanctions as well as employers who derived economic benefits from immigrant workers, the Simpson-Rodino bill proved to be a carefully crafted response to an underlying contradiction between political and economic forces.

Not only did the assumption of employer compliance facilitate the redefinition of compliance, but it also allowed congressional sponsors to counter an increasing volume of data indicating that employer sanctions have never worked. Two General Accounting Office studies (U.S. GAO 1982, 1985) documented the difficulties of enforcing employer sanctions in nineteen countries around the world and concluded that only in Hong Kong had sanctions actually reduced undocumented migration. Twelve U.S. states (including California) had experimented with sanctions during the 1970s, and in no case was there any measurable effect. Only a handful of employers had ever been convicted and fined (for the California case, see Calavita 1982). Immigration policy makers, committed to this law that effectively reconciled conflicting demands, countered the mounting evidence by asserting that U.S. employers would voluntarily comply with employer sanctions simply because it was the law.

The move to make employer compliance "pragmatically easy" was based on political necessity and justified on the grounds that "most employers, as generally law-abiding citizens, will uphold the law" (U.S. Congress, Senate 1981: 4). Assuming that employers are law-abiding not only made it important to protect the employer through the affirmative defense provision; it apparently also made it unnecessary to suspect that this protection might become a loophole through which employers could circumvent the law—a possibility left unexplored through five years of congressional debate. The employer sanctions law that resulted, grounded as it was in assumptions about voluntary compliance, virtually guaranteed widespread employer violations. Facing a contradiction between political and economic forces, legislators produced a law whose effect was to be solely symbolic. The point is not simply that Congress passed a toothless law by making compliance easy through the incorporation of loopholes. Rather, the law made *violations* "pragmatically easy." Through the affirmative defense and good faith provisions, Congress guaranteed that conformity with the paperwork requirements would be taken as indicating compliance, thereby ensuring that violations of the "knowing hire" provision—the meat of the law—would be virtually risk free.

Not surprisingly, the number of fines levied for violations of employer sanctions has been relatively low. An Urban Institute study of ten major cities covering all four INS regions found that in El Paso, where the most employer sanctions fines were served, only one fine was levied "for every two months of agent service" (Fix and Hill 1990: 89). The rate in Chicago was one fine per *two years* of agent service. The study concludes with an understatement: "INS enforcement activity could not be characterized as hyperactive" (Fix and Hill 1990: 89). When fines are issued, they are relatively light, varying from $9,459 in the Northern Region to $2,060 in the Southern Region. According to a General Accounting Office study, these fines are usually further reduced by about 59 percent through negotiations (Fix and Hill 1990: 86).

The Immigration Reform and Control Act of 1986 has been hailed both as landmark legislation that will "regain control of our borders" and as an ingenious creation painstakingly fashioned through the political art of compromise and concession. This simplified depiction of IRCA is wrong on both counts. First, while the mandate to regain control of the borders did provide the political motor of the reform effort, the sole restrictive provision of the law—employer sanctions—will remain a symbolic measure with little impact on immigration flows. At the same time, other IRCA provisions, such as the Special Agricultural Workers program, will predictably add to the stock of immigrant workers. Thus, not only does IRCA pull both ways at once, but the long-term impact of this reform, which originated in and was fueled by restrictionist fervor, is likely to be a continued increase in immigration, both documented and undocumented.

This is not to suggest that policy makers deliberately and cynically constructed an immigration reform that would delude restrictionists while catering to immigrant employers. Nor is it to suggest that the complex negotiation process surrounding IRCA can be reduced in its

entirety to economics. As both Fuchs (1990) and Schuck (1992) point out
in their excellent summaries of the history and evolution of IRCA, civil
rights issues and humanitarian concerns informed the debate and
complicated the task. The more general point here, however, is that the
primary restrictive measure in this law and its political engine—employer sanctions—was symbolic and doomed to failure; at the same time,
it was *precisely* the "flaws" of employer sanctions and its essentially
symbolic nature that eased employers' concerns, paving the way for
passage.

The Immigration Act of 1990

Once IRCA had addressed—if not solved—the problem of illegal immigration, policy makers turned their attention to reforming policies
related to legal immigration. Driven primarily by a concern that U.S.
immigration policies did not reflect the shifting economic and labor force
needs of the postindustrial period, Congress passed the Immigration
Act of 1990. As described by Papademetriou (1992: 9–12), three fundamental factors were integral to the debate surrounding this latest reform.
First is the transformation of the U.S. economy, whereby the proportion
of the workforce engaged in manufacturing has fallen as the proportion
working in services has increased. Related to this shift is the concern that
the U.S. workforce can supply neither the highly skilled technicians and
professionals required in the new service sector, nor the large number of
entry-level workers on whom this sector depends. Second, in the past
the bulk of legal immigrants to the United States have settled in the
urban areas of the northeast corridor; yet it is precisely these locations
that have been hardest hit by the shift to a service-oriented economy and
the global competition that has hastened the move of manufacturing out
of these areas in search of cheaper, more flexible labor elsewhere. Third,
there has been a steady decline in U.S. fertility rates, such that immigration now accounts for a substantial portion (approximately 30 percent) of
population growth in the United States, as well as providing over 33
percent of new workforce entrants. Within this context, the congressional debate focused on how to provide workers to the U.S. economy and
thereby enhance its global competitiveness without, however, jeopardizing the interests of U.S. workers by displacing them, depressing
wages, or eroding labor's bargaining position.

Although the debate centered around these economic issues, this
latest immigration reform once again made family unification a central
priority. It leaves unchanged the unlimited visa provision for immediate
relatives of U.S. citizens. In addition, it introduces a ceiling, or "cap," on
overall immigration whereby the immigration of more distant relatives
under the family preference system is limited to 465,000 minus the

number of *immediate* relatives (admitted under the unrestricted visa provision) who were given visas the previous year. In 1995, the number of such visas for relatives will rise to 480,000 minus the number of visas allocated for immediate relatives in 1994. In another nod to the principle of family unity, and in an effort to reduce backlogs for visas for Mexican nationals, the act made available at least 77 percent of second-preference visas (allocated to the spouses and minor children of legal residents) on a first come/first served basis, eliminating the per country ceiling (*Interpreter Releases* 1990).

One major change in the new law is an expansion in the proportion of visas set aside to be awarded specifically on economic grounds. The number of such "economic" visas will almost triple, rising from 54,000 under previous immigration law to 140,000 under this act. In addition to this quantitative change, the law substantially modifies qualification procedures and administrative mechanisms. First, it instructs the U.S. Department of Labor to set up a pilot program to determine if it is feasible to identify occupations where there are labor shortages and issue categorical certifications for the immigration and employment of workers in those occupations, to replace the ad hoc, case-by-case approach currently used. Second, it stipulates that employers must inform their workers of their intention to import foreign workers. As Papademetriou (1992: 26) describes these provisions, "They offer employers easier and more predictable access to foreign workers . . . while creating additional requirements which employers must meet if they wish to employ foreign workers."

These employment-based visas will be issued according to a new preference system. In the first preference, 40,000 visas will go to people of "extraordinary ability" (such as scientists, artists, and athletes), "outstanding" researchers and academics, and executives of U.S. multinationals. In the second preference, another 40,000 visas are allocated for immigrants with advanced degrees or "exceptional ability" *and* concrete offers of employment, after certification from the Department of Labor that a labor shortage exists in their respective fields. An additional 40,000 visas will go to third-preference immigrants—an assortment of skilled workers, professionals, and "other workers." The "other workers" category includes unskilled workers and is limited to 10,000 visas annually. Finally, fourth and fifth preferences provide 10,000 visas each for "special immigrants" (religious workers, those with foreign medical degrees, U.S. government employees, etc.) and investors (in cases in which their investment would create at least ten U.S. jobs).

Overall, the Immigration Act of 1990 will raise legal immigration from a current annual level of approximately 534,000 to a fixed ceiling of 700,000 annually in 1992–1994 and 685,000 beginning in 1995. Despite the introduction of a cap on legal immigration—which does not include the separate categories of refugees and asylees—this ceiling may be exceeded beginning in 1995, depending on the amount of growth in the numerically unlimited "immediate relative" class. While this quantitative change is important, perhaps more significant is the act's emphasis on shaping immigration flows to perceived economic needs—a principle that has often driven U.S. immigration but has rarely been so explicitly pronounced in the legislative process.

Peter Schuck (1992: 91) concludes his discussion of the Immigration Act of 1990:

> The restrictionist road, along which U.S. immigration law had traveled for over six decades, well into the 1980s, again beckoned [in 1990], yet this time it was not taken. Many Americans believed that the 1965 and 1980 reforms had opened the front door too wide and that the immigrants passing through it added relatively little economic value to society. A recession had begun and the Persian Gulf war impended. In the end, however, those who wanted fewer and similar immigrants lost while those who sought more and different ones won.

Although Schuck frames his analysis of recent reforms in terms of competing special interests, his detailed documentation of the policy debates is consistent with the structural model presented here. Against a backdrop of restrictionist sentiment and an escalating recession, congressional lawmakers passed the expansionist Immigration Act of 1990, increasing the size of the immigrant flow and tailoring it to perceived economic imperatives.

Discussion

Beginning with the first federal immigration laws in the nineteenth century and continuing through the Immigration Act of 1990, U.S. immigration policies have exhibited a pronounced gap between their purported intent and their practical effects. Some analysts have suggested that this gap is due to the difficulty of controlling through legislation what is essentially an economically driven phenomenon (Bach 1978; López 1981). Others have postulated that it indicates the incompetence of the Immigration and Naturalization Service and the failure of its enforcement policies (Crewdson 1983; U.S. Congress, House 1972; U.S. Congress, Senate 1980). Still others have indicated that this gap stems from the difficulties of balancing competing, and equally compelling, exigencies—"right versus right" (Teitelbaum 1980).

It seems unlikely that this gap is the product of a single set of factors or underlying dynamics. Rather, it is proposed here that a number of tensions, or "paired oppositions," taken together help explain the pattern of apparent failure of immigration policies to achieve their purported intent, recreating what is often referred to as the immigration "problem." First, there is the opposition of employer and worker interests on the issue of immigration, making a "national" economic interest difficult to identify, much less to pursue. In the late nineteenth century, industrialists praised the stream of immigrants from Europe because these workers provided the cheap labor that fueled the burgeoning factories of the Industrial Revolution. Domestic labor was far less enthusiastic, *precisely because* the new immigrants allowed employers to stabilize wages and break the grip of union labor. As the vice president of a Jersey City local put it in 1884 when his union was defeated in its strike efforts, "It's that . . . Castle Garden [where the bulk of European immigrants landed] that's killing us" (New Jersey Bureau of Industry and Labor 1884). In 1885, Congress responded to organized labor's demands to curtail immigration from Europe with the Anti-Alien Contract Labor Law. This law—touted as the "salvation" of American labor against impoverished immigrant labor and the "greedy capitalists" who imported it (*Congressional Record* 1884: 5349)—was carefully crafted not to interrupt the "golden stream" that was so appreciated by Carnegie and his fellow industrialists. Pronounced a "sham" and a "sop to Cerberus" by opponents in Congress (*Congressional Record* 1885: 1839), the law was a symbolic measure, meant to appease workers but not to interfere with the labor supply.

A century later, IRCA's employer sanctions provision repeats the pattern. Pressed to do something to control illegal immigration but reluctant to "harass" employers, Congress passed a symbolic measure with little meaningful potential. The point here is not so much that illegal immigration is difficult to control through legislative measures (although it is), nor that Congress is somehow inept or incapable of designing effective policies. Rather, the far more fundamental issue relates to the very nature of the immigration "problem." Specifically, the inability of Congress to respond effectively has less to do with the difficulties of finding a *solution* than it does with arriving at a consensus on what is the *problem*.

Second, the structure and composition of labor force needs are clearly economic in nature, but they have profound political implications. Furthermore, a tension often exists between the real needs of the economic structure at a given point in time, and the political ability or willingness to recognize those needs. It is proposed here that the gap between official immigration policies and de facto policies may reflect this discrepancy. Since the 1950s, illegal immigration to the United States has been high, as undocumented immigrants have provided much of the low-wage labor in sectors of the economy such as agriculture, construction, hotels, and restaurants. Wages and working conditions in these sectors are often insufficient to attract U.S. workers to these jobs. Policy makers have been unwilling to improve enforcement of labor standards as a strategy for reducing the appeal of undocumented workers. But neither are they prepared to send the message that the U.S. economy systematically produces jobs that only Third World workers find attractive, by officially endorsing the importation of workers to fill those jobs. The result is a clandestine movement—illegal immigration—that satisfies the economy but whose margins are politically unpalatable.

Finally, it may be that the liberal democratic principles upon which Western democracies are grounded are at odds with the police functions necessary to control and regulate immigration and refugee flows. Even in the absence of the political ambiguities and class divisions described above, it may be that controlling the movement of the economically destitute and politically persecuted requires measures antithetical to basic constitutional and human rights. While it is true, for example, that "Operation Wetback" in 1954 succeeded in deporting many of the illegal Mexican immigrants in the Southwest, it also resulted in the deportation of a not insignificant number of U.S. citizens and legal residents (Morgan 1954). The Clinton administration's difficulties in devising a policy for handling the Haitian refugee problem is a further illustration of this tension. Having stated in his electoral campaign that he would not violate Haitians' right to apply for asylum, President Clinton now faces the very real tension between human rights, on one hand, and border control on the other.

It is suggested here that the notable discrepancy between the stated purpose of U.S. immigration policies over time and their practical consequences is at least in part the product of those three sets of tensions or "paired oppositions." To the extent that the political economies of the other developed industrial countries included in this study share certain fundamental commonalities, it is likely that some variety of these paired oppositions will be found elsewhere, as will their consequences for immigration policy.

References

Bach, Robert L. 1978. "Mexican Immigration and U.S. Immigration Reforms in the 1960s," *Kapitalistate* 7:73–80.

Bailey, Eric, and Dan Morain. 1993. "Anti-Immigration Bills Flood Legislature," *Los Angeles Times*, May 3.

Baker, Susan González. 1990. *The Cautious Welcome: The Legalization Programs of the Immigration Reform and Control Act*. Santa Monica, Calif.: Rand Corporation.

Bauder, Don. 1993. "Corporate Profits Increase despite Tough Times," *San Diego Union-Tribune*, April 3.

Bean, Frank D., Georges Vernez, and Charles B. Keely. 1989. *Opening and Closing the Doors: Evaluating Immigration Reform and Control*. Lanham, Md.: University Press of America.

Brossy, Julie. 1990. "Aliens Entering without Papers Show Sharp Rise," *San Diego Tribune*, March 12.

Calavita, Kitty. 1982. *California's "Employer Sanctions": The Case of the Disappearing Law*. Research Report Series, no. 39. La Jolla: Center for U.S.-Mexican Studies, University of California, San Diego.

———. 1984. *U.S. Immigration Law and the Control of Labor: 1820–1924*. London: Academic Press.

———. 1990. "Employer Sanctions Violations: Toward a Dialectical Model of White-Collar Crime," *Law and Society Review* 24:4:1041–69.

———. 1992. *Inside the State: The Bracero Program, Immigration and the INS*. New York: Routledge.

Carnegie, Andrew. 1886. *Triumphant Democracy, or Fifty Years' March of the Republic*. New York: Charles Scribner's Sons.

Congressional Record. 1882. 47th Congress, 1st Session.

———. 1884. 48th Congress, 1st Session.

———. 1885. 48th Congress, 2nd Session.

———. 1902. 57th Congress, 1st Session.

———. 1921. 66th Congress, 3rd Session.

———. 1954. 83rd Congress. 2nd Session.

Congressional Research Service. 1980. *History of the Immigration and Naturalization Service*. A Report Prepared for the Use of the Select Commission on Immigration and Refugee Policy. Washington, D.C.: U.S. Government Printing Office.

Cornelius, Wayne A. 1982. *America in the Era of Limits: Nativist Reactions to the "New" Immigration*. Research Report Series, no. 3. La Jolla: Center for U.S.-Mexican Studies, University of California, San Diego.

Crane, Keith, Beth Asch, Joanna Zorn Heilbrunn, and Danielle C. Cullinane. 1990. *The Effect of Employer Sanctions on the Flow of Undocumented Immigrants to the United States*. Lanham, Md.: University Press of America.

Crewdson, John. 1983. *The Tarnished Door: The New Immigrants and the Transformation of America*. New York: Times Books.

Dillin, John. 1989a. "Illegal Immigration Surges in '89," *Christian Science Monitor*, December 27.

———. 1989b. "Stalking Illegal Immigrants," *Christian Science Monitor*, November 30.

Fix, Michael. 1991. *The Paper Curtain: Employer Sanctions' Implementation, Impact, and Reform*. Washington, D.C.: Urban Institute Press.

Fix, Michael, and Paul T. Hill. 1990. *Enforcing Employer Sanctions: Challenges and Strategies*. Santa Monica, Calif.: Rand Corporation, and Washington, D.C.: Urban Institute.

Fuchs, Lawrence. 1990. "The Corpse That Would Not Die: The Immigration Reform and Control Act of 1986," *Revue Européenne des Migrations Internationales* 6:1:111–27.

Galarza, Ernesto. 1964. *Merchants of Labor: The Mexican Bracero Story*. Sage Yearbook in Politics and Public Policy. Santa Barbara, Calif.: McNally & Loftin.

Greene, Sheldon L. 1972. "Public Agency Distortion of Congressional Will: Federal Policy toward Non-Resident Alien Labor," *George Washington Law Review* 40:3 (March): 440–63.

Hadley, Eleanor. 1956. "A Critical Analysis of the Wetback Problem," *Law and Contemporary Problems* 21:334–57.

Hamilton, Alexander. 1791. *Report on Manufacturing*. American State Papers, Finance I.

Harwood, Edwin. 1983. "Can Immigration Law Be Enforced?" *Public Interest* 72 (Summer): 107–23.

Higham, John. 1955. *Strangers in the Land: Patterns of American Nativism, 1860–1925*. New Brunswick, N.J.: Rutgers University Press.

Hourwich, I.A. 1912. *Immigration and Labor*. New York: G.P. Putnam and Sons.

Ingwerson, Marshall. 1993. "Workers Brave New Job Frontiers," *Christian Science Monitor*, March 24.

Interpreter Releases. 1990. "Recent Developments: Congress Approves Major Immigration Reform," vol. 67:41 (October 29).

Jenks, J.W. 1913. *The Immigration Problem*. New York: Funk & Wagnalls.

Kilborn, Peter T. 1993. "New Jobs Lack the Old Security in Time of 'Disposable Workers'," *New York Times*, March 15.

Kirstein, Peter Neil. 1973. "Anglo over Bracero: A History of the Mexican Workers in the United States from Roosevelt to Nixon." Ph.D. dissertation, Saint Louis University.

López, Gerald P. 1981. "Undocumented Mexican Migration: In Search of a Just Immigration Law and Policy," *UCLA Law Review* 28 (April): 615–714.

Los Angeles Times. 1987a. "Minimum Wage Hike's Real Payoff," May 12.

———. 1987b. "America's Dwindling Middle Class," May 26.

Montwieler, Nancy Humel. 1987. *The Immigration Reform Law of 1986*. Washington, D.C.: Bureau of National Affairs.

Morgan, Patricia. 1954. *Shame of a Nation: A Documented Story of Police-State Furor against Mexican-Americans in the U.S.A.* Los Angeles: Los Angeles Committee for the Protection of the Foreign Born.

New Jersey Bureau of Industry and Labor. 1884. *7th Annual Report*.

Papademetriou, Demetrios G. 1992. "International Migration in North America: Issues, Policies, Implications. Immigration Policy and Research." Working Paper No. 14. Washington, D.C.: Bureau of International Labor Affairs, U.S. Department of Labor.

President's Commission on Migratory Labor. 1951. *Migratory Labor in American Agriculture*. Report of the President's Commission on Migratory Labor. Washington, D.C.: U.S. Government Printing Office.

Reisler, Mark. 1976. *By the Sweat of Their Brow: Mexican Immigrant Labor in the United States, 1900–40*. Westport, Conn.: Greenwood Press.

Samora, Julián. 1971. *Los Mojados: The Wetback Story*. Notre Dame, Ind.: University of Notre Dame Press.

Schuck, Peter H. 1975. *The Judiciary Committees: A Study of the House and Senate Judiciary Committees*. The Ralph Nader Congress Project. New York: Grossman Publishers.

———. 1992. "The Politics of Rapid Legal Change: Immigration Policy in the 1980s," *Studies in American Political Development* 6 (Spring): 37–92.

Stewart, William, Mark Gascoigne, and R. Wayne Bannister. 1992. "Impact of Undocumented Persons and Other Immigrants on Costs, Revenues and Services in Los Angeles County." Report Prepared for Los Angeles County Board of Supervisors.

Teitelbaum, Michael S. 1980. "Right versus Right: Immigration and Refugee Policy—the United States," *Foreign Affairs* 59:1 (Fall): 21–59.

U.S. Commission on Agricultural Workers. 1992. *The Final Report of the Commission on Agricultural Workers.* Washington, D.C.: U.S. Government Printing Office.

U.S. Congress. House. 1972. *Illegal Aliens: Hearings before the Subcommittee on Immigration, Citizenship, and International Law of the House Committee on the Judiciary.* Parts 4–5. 92nd Congress, 2nd Session.

———. 1983. *The Immigration Reform and Control Act of 1983: Hearings before the Subcommittee on Immigration, Refugees, and International Law of the House Committee on the Judiciary.* 98th Congress, 1st Session.

U.S. Congress. Senate. 1864. *Senate Report.* 38th Congress, 1st Session, S. Report 15.

———. 1911. Senate Immigration Commission. *Immigration Commission Report.* Senate Document No. 747. 61st Congress, 3rd Session.

———. 1980. *Dept. of Justice Authorization and Oversight for Fiscal Year 1981. Hearings Before the Senate Committee on the Judiciary.* 96th Congress, 2nd Session.

———. 1981. *The Knowing Employment of Illegal Immigrants: Hearings before the Subcommittee on Immigration and Refugee Policy of the Senate Committee on the Judiciary.* 97th Congress, 1st Session.

———. 1985. *Senate Judiciary Committee Report on S. 1200.* Report 99-132, 99th Congress, 1st Session.

U.S. Department of Labor. Bureau of International Labor Affairs. 1991. "Employer Sanctions and U.S. Labor Markets: Second Report." Washington, D.C.: U.S. Government Printing Office.

U.S. GAO (General Accounting Office). 1982. "Information on the Enforcement of Laws regarding Employment of Aliens in Selected Countries." GAO/GGD-82-86. Washington, D.C.: U.S. Government Printing Office, August 31.

———. 1985. "Illegal Aliens: Information on Selected Countries' Employment Prohibition Laws." GAO/GGD-86-17BR. Washington, D.C.: U.S. Government Printing Office, October.

———. 1987. "Immigration Reform: Status of Implementing Employer Sanctions after One Year." GAO/GGD-88-14. Washington, D.C.: U.S. Government Printing Office, November.

———. 1990. "Immigration Reform: Employer Sanctions and the Question of Discrimination." GAO/GGD-90-62. Washington, D.C.: U.S. Government Printing Office, March.

U.S. INS (Immigration and Naturalization Service). 1959. *Annual Report.* Washington, D.C.

———. 1987. "Implementation of the Immigration Reform and Control Act: Final Rules," *52 Federal Register* 84, May 1.

———. 1988. "Employer Activity Report through October 31, 1988." Unpublished internal report.

U.S. Select Commission on Immigration and Refugee Policy. 1981. "U.S. Immigration Policy and the National Interest." Final Report and Recommendations of the Select Commission on Immigration and Refugee Policy to the Congress and the President of the United States. Washington, D.C.: U.S. Government Printing Office, March 1.

U.S. Statutes at Large. 13 U.S. Stat. at Large, pp. 385–387.

Van Vleck, W.C. 1932. *The Administrative Control of Aliens: A Study in Administrative Law and Procedure*. New York: Commonwealth Fund.

3

The United States:
Benign Neglect toward Immigration

Philip L. Martin

The United States is engaged in a historic experiment. More immigrants are arriving than ever before—about 3,000 per day. These immigrants differ from natives in education, income, and prospects for success. The United States and most other industrial countries have fostered diamond-shaped income distributions, with most of the population in the middle classes. The income distribution for immigrants, by contrast, has an hourglass shape, since they tend to be bunched at the extremes of the education and income spectrum; many are college-educated professionals, and even more are unskilled workers without high school educations.

There is no consensus among politicians, researchers, or Americans in general whether the immigrants arriving today will be assets or millstones tomorrow. The tea leaves involving the success of some immigrants in business and education can be read to suggest that the nation will reap an economic windfall tomorrow due to today's immigration. But other income, education, and public assistance data can be interpreted to suggest that the United States may be adding directly and indirectly to its underclass via immigration.

The United States has the world's most wide-open front door for immigrants, with the admission of about 850,000 immigrants annually.[1] In addition, the United States gets large numbers of "unwanted immigrants," including an estimated gross 2 million illegal entries each year, of whom 200,000–300,000 settle, plus asylum applicants whose claims are denied but who nonetheless remain, plus aliens who are granted "in-

[1]The United States anticipates the admission of at least 700,000 family and economic immigrants annually, plus refugees, estimated at about 140,000 for 1993.

between" legal statuses such as "family fairness," under which they are neither illegal aliens nor legal immigrants. As in other industrial countries, there is a growing gap in the United States between the announced goals of immigration policy, such as having newcomers enter through the front door of legal immigration, and the reality that many immigrants continue to enter through the side door open to asylum seekers or the backdoor of illegal immigration.

Other industrial countries are also experiencing rising levels of immigration, as well as a growing gap between immigration policy goals and outcomes. What makes the United States unique is its seeming policy of benign neglect toward this gap.[2] Such neglect—despite heated rhetoric—is remarkable because, as registered by opinion polls, most Americans want legal and illegal immigration reduced. Politicians in California and elsewhere have struck a responsive chord by campaigning on platforms that call for "securing" the U.S.-Mexican border and denying social services to illegal immigrants.

There are at least three reasons why the United States, although it is experiencing the same unwanted immigration as is Europe, nonetheless appears to be less concerned about high levels of immigration than are France and Germany. First, the United States celebrates its immigration history. The motto *e pluribus unum* (from many, one) helps explain the American confidence that people of diverse origins have and can continue to forge an American identity.

Second, there are many special interest groups and thinkers who believe that the United States should accept more immigrants. From farmers to ethnic advocates to a few demographers and economists, there are Americans who argue that the United States can continue to benefit from immigration, as in the past. All of the arguments used against immigration today were raised against past immigrants, they note, and these arguments were proved groundless by past immigrants' success.

The third reason for benign neglect is more subtle; the American economic and social system, in contrast to similar systems in other industrial democracies, permits immigrants to generate fairly immediate and visible economic benefits. However, any costs of immigration tend to be deferred, often until the immigrants organize and demand catch-up assistance. In Europe, by contrast, new arrivals are more likely to gain immediate access to more readily available public housing, social welfare benefits, and other public services, making integration costs apparent soon after their arrival. For these reasons, it is harder in the United States than in Europe to argue for immigration

---

[2] Benign neglect is defined in William Safire's *Political Dictionary* as "a suggestion to allow tensions to ease." Daniel Patrick Moynihan used the term in a 1970 memo to urge President Nixon to treat race issues with "benign neglect" in order to deny fuel to the extremists on both sides.

restrictions on the grounds that the costs of immigration outweigh the benefits.

A Global Perspective

The United States is not alone in facing rising immigration pressures, and there are few prospects that pressures to enter industrial countries will subside on their own during the 1990s. The reasons are apparent in demographic and economic data. The world's population is almost 5.5 billion, the world's workforce is 2.5 billion, and both numbers are increasing by over 90 million annually.

About 90 percent of the world's population and workforce growth occurs in developing nations, which create "real" jobs for perhaps half of their annual new crop of workers. In addition to having to create more jobs for the youth who join the workforce each year, developing nations face three daunting catch-up job creation tasks: they must find nonfarm jobs for ex-farmers, as some of the world's 1 billion farmers seek nonfarm jobs; they must create jobs for adults who are not now in the workforce, such as urban women;[3] and they must reduce currently high levels of unemployment and underemployment. There is little prospect for reducing unemployment and underemployment in emigration countries, from Algeria to Yugoslavia, during the 1990s.

Despite widespread unemployment and underemployment in developing nations, and wages and incomes that are ten to twenty times higher in industrial than in developing countries, most poor people do not even try to "go north" to share in the industrial countries' wealth. Most of the world's people will live and die within a few kilometers of where they were born. Far fewer people migrate to industrial countries than would like to, indicating that governments are not powerless to control migration. But even a small migrant percentage of the huge world's workforce can translate into large numbers of migrants: if just 2 percent of the annual *increase* in the world's workforce migrates, there are 2 million additional migrants each year.

There are about 100 million immigrants—refugees and asylees, and legal and unauthorized workers—living outside their countries of citizenship (Martin 1992). This "nation of migrants" is equivalent in size to the world's tenth most populous country. Only about half of the world's migrants are in industrial countries: 15 to 20 million are in Western Europe; 15 to 20 million are in North America; and 2 to 3 million are in the industrial nations of Asia, including Japan, Taiwan, and Singapore.

---

[3]In most OECD industrial nations, half of the population is in the labor force. However, in high-emigration developing nations such as Turkey and Mexico, only one-third of the population is employed or looking for work. These low labor force participation rates reflect both higher population growth rates (and thus a higher proportion of young people) and too few formal-sector jobs, especially for women in urban areas.

Some of these immigrants have been invited to live and work legally in their host societies, perceived to be fellow citizens and future leaders. Some migrants are present illegally. And many have a gray-area legal status—they are legally tolerated in the country but in theory are not immigrants, such as the Croatians in Germany and the Salvadorans in the United States, allowed to remain until conditions improve in their home countries.

Industrial countries create categories or doors through which new-comers enter. The most familiar door is the front door for settler immigrants, the welcome door that was opened for Europeans who migrated to North and South America and Australia during the nine-teenth and early twentieth centuries. Immigration policies in these countries went through three phases. They first welcomed or facilitated practically all newcomers, then imposed *qualitative restrictions* on who could enter (in the 1870s and 1880s in the United States), and finally established quantitative restrictions or annual quotas on immigration (in the 1920s in the United States).

Today side doors and backdoors have become the most important ports of entry into industrial nations. Western European nations opened their front doors to the return of their nationals displaced by World War II and to citizens in newly freed colonies, and then developed the guestworker side door for migrant workers who were expected to depart after one to two years of high-wage employment. Many guestworkers became unwanted immigrants in the sense that, instead of returning to their countries of origin, they settled and sent for their families. The guestworker side door of the 1960s has since been joined by a side door through which applicants for asylum pour into Western Europe, as well as by the backdoor to illegal immigration.

Opening side doors to newcomers has frequently been associated with backdoor illegal immigration. Indeed, in several instances a side-door migrant worker program was developed as an alternative to back-door illegal immigration. But there is an iron law of labor immigration: there is nothing more permanent than temporary workers. Employers are loathe to do without the migrant workers to whom they have become accustomed, and once migrants are in an industrial country, it is very difficult to force out those who wish to stay. Migrants who wish to settle can generally keep their cases in the legal system long enough to develop an equity stake in the country that makes their deportation difficult.

Industrial Country Reactions

Immigrants are entering industrial countries through front, side, and back doors, but there has been a surprising diversity of responses to rising immigration pressures. The twenty-four Organization of Economic Cooperation and Development (OECD) countries have a population of about 775 million, or 15 percent of the world total, and a GNP of U.S.$15 trillion, three-fourths of world GNP. These countries have slowly growing populations; by 2000, their projected population of 814 million will be only 13 percent of the world's 6.2 billion people.[4]

How are these industrial countries reacting to today's immigrants? In much of Western Europe, controlling immigration is a top domestic priority. If voters there cannot be convinced that immigration is under control, political parties that have been in power since World War II fear that they may be dislodged or forced to share power with anti-immigrant parties.

The immigration crisis in Europe is connected closely with the issue of how to deal with the escalating cost of the social welfare state. Economic restructuring and demographic trends have produced a relatively large number of older and often immobile and inflexible workers, so that European nations must cope with both high levels of unemployment and labor shortages. Immigrants, many officially unwanted, sometimes fill these labor market niches, where they are joined in this quasi-underground economy by some native workers who draw social welfare benefits while they work for cash wages.

The escalating cost of the social welfare state and the fact that racially and ethnically distinct immigrants may be "needed but not wanted" have given rise in many European countries to the sense that the immigration problem is intertwined with the problem of social welfare costs. If natives and settled foreigners could be encouraged or forced to fill the jobs in agriculture, construction, and services now taken by newly arrived immigrants, this argument runs, or if foreigners could fill these jobs under conditions in which they do not become residents and gain access to social welfare benefits, then the immigration issue could be treated with benign neglect. Governments would not feel pressured to act on immigration and thus could avoid taking actions that only fuel extremists on the spectrum between open and closed borders. Europeans have yet to find such a silver bullet for immigration policy.

The reaction to unwanted immigration in North America is different. In the United States and Canada, opinion polls report that most residents want immigration levels reduced, but controlling immigration generally ranks well below controlling taxes, crime, and health care costs in public priorities. In both countries, restrictionist symbols, such as the introduction of employer sanctions in the United States in 1986 and an annual cap on immigration in 1990 legislation,

---

[4]The population of the OECD countries is projected by the World Bank to increase by only 37 million during the 1990s. At current rates of immigration, this would mean that immigration offsets population declines in Western Europe and Japan and would account for about half of U.S. population growth in the 1990s.

have permitted front, side, and back immigration doors to remain fairly open to newcomers.

However, immigrants are concentrated in a few areas in the United States and Canada, and in these areas concern about out-of-control immigration is similar to levels of concern in Western Europe. Nevertheless, in North America the burden of proof lies with those who wish to restrict immigration. The history of both the United States and Canada is replete with assertions that a particular group of immigrants could not become productive citizens. These assertions proved to be false, raising a substantial hurdle to those who argue that too many of today's immigrants will be difficult to integrate tomorrow.

Asian island countries such as Japan have been noted as exceptions to the tendency of industrial countries, visible since the 1950s and 1960s, to rely on migrant workers to fill undesirable jobs. However, these islands seem to have reached their limit in terms of taking jobs to workers rather than importing workers to fill jobs. Japan has at least 500,000 legal and illegal migrant workers, and South Korea, Taiwan, and Singapore are initiating or expanding guestworker programs to legalize growing influxes of illegal migrant workers (Martin 1991).

In Western Europe, then, immigration is a crisis. It is treated with benign neglect in North America. And in Asia immigration is seen as an economic policy instrument that requires proper management. These different perceptions of the immigration problem, as well as differential policy responses to it, may not persist. During the 1950s, for example, analysts predicted that labor relations systems in industrial countries would converge despite very different labor histories, because all industrial countries faced the common challenge of coping with assembly-line production systems (Kerr et al. 1960). In all the industrial democracies, traditional industrial unions are in retreat, and the locus of union power is increasingly in the public sector.

Will industrial country policies toward labor migration eventually converge? It seems likely that they will. The different responses to immigration today in Western Europe, North America, and Asia probably reflect the fact that each area is at a different point on the experience-with-migration spectrum, rather than reflecting fundamental differences in how they will ultimately respond to this common challenge. What is not yet clear is whether the European crisis response or the U.S. benign neglect policy typifies what industrial country reactions will be early in the twenty-first century.[5]

---

[5]The Asian policy of treating labor migration as another economic policy will probably give way to a more comprehensive policy toward labor migration as employers become dependent on migrant workers and some of these workers settle.

Why Migration?

Migration occurs because of demand-pull factors that draw migrants into industrial countries, supply-push factors that push them out of their own countries, and intervening variables such as networks of friends and relatives already in industrial societies, who serve as anchor communities for newcomers. Although most of today's migration streams have their origins in the colonial or labor recruitment policies of industrial countries, it appears that government-approved demand-pull factors are of waning importance in explaining current immigration levels, while supply-push and network factors are becoming more important. The fact that supply-push and network factors are not under the direct control of industrial country governments does much to explain these countries' sense that they have lost control over immigration.

Industrial countries could reduce unwanted immigration by curtailing the demand-pull factors that attract migrants, by relieving the supply-push factors that encourage migrants to leave their countries, or by breaking the networks that link immigration and emigration areas. The G-7 leaders in July 1991 embraced the response of reducing supply-push pressures by accelerating economic growth in emigration nations, noting that today's unpredictable waves of migrants have the potential to be economically and politically destabilizing. International organizations such as the OECD and World Bank have been asked to redouble their efforts to promote what has been termed "stay-at-home" development.

Free trade, more investment, and increased aid may be desirable, but they are not a magic bullet for resolving supply-push emigration in the 1990s. Indeed, it is more likely that the economic and social restructuring that is often necessary to accelerate economic growth may initially *increase* supply-push emigration. Development is the eventual remedy for supply-push emigration, but in the short term, development tends to cause a migration hump, or more, rather than less, pressure to emigrate (U.S. Commission 1990).

Although reducing supply-push factors by accelerating development is a laudable goal, it represents the industrial nations' attempt to solve the problem of unwanted immigration by fixing problems in other countries' backyards. Interior and immigration ministers responsible for preventing unwanted immigration often discuss ways to break networks that link areas of origin and destination. They sometimes decry the middlemen who bring migrants into a country unlawfully for a fee, and they occasionally join in the calls to restrict family unification rights or to deny social service benefits to newcomers.

Industrial countries' attempts to break migrant networks are usually too little, too late. Tamper-proof identification cards can easily be forged, policies to return asylum seekers to the countries through which they arrived can prompt migrants to "forget" how they came, and tough border controls in one area can push illegal entries elsewhere.

The most effective remedies for "out-of-control" immigration are likely to be found in industrial countries' attempts to deal effectively with unofficial demand-pull factors in their own backyards (Straubhaar 1992). In today's deregulated economies and labor markets, there are more and more job niches for immigrant workers in industries that range from seasonal agriculture to construction to hotels and restaurants. Labor markets are flexible, and a supply of willing immigrants can quickly create a demand for these workers to tend children, lawns, or the elderly.

Demand-pull is not just hiring the unauthorized workers who are already present. Demand-pull factors are also at work when an industrial country protects from international trade its industries that depend on immigrant workers (Weintraub 1990). As President Carlos Salinas of Mexico frequently reminded audiences, the United States seems to prefer Mexican tomato pickers to Mexican tomatoes, since the United States does a much better job keeping out Mexican tomatoes than Mexican workers. One result is that Mexican tomato growers complain of labor shortages, while competing Florida growers report surpluses of workers as well as tomato production costs below those of Mexico. Similarly, European Community policies that restrict imports of Polish pork but accept Polish workers add to demand-pull factors that encourage Polish immigration into Western Europe.

Demand-pull and supply-push factors are like battery poles; both are necessary to start a car or a migration stream. Once started, intervening variables such as networks influence who migrates where (Massey et al. 1987). Most migrants arrive in industrial countries with contacts in the anchor community of previous immigrants; friends and relatives already in the receiving country can provide information that the migrant can readily understand regarding jobs and housing for newcomers, and in some cases the financing and expertise needed for illegal entry.

A network can be based on family or job. Individuals and families settled in an industrial country often serve as anchors for the numerically more important migration of their relatives. Immigration countries can encourage families to queue up for a turn to enter legally, but many relatives ignore the queues and enter immediately—illegally. In the United States these immigrants often travel from their illegal U.S. residences to the U.S. embassy in their respective home countries to pursue their applications for legal immigration status.

Networks include more than helpful friends and relatives. Some of the most troublesome unwanted migration results from the activities of "middlemen," labor brokers or contractors who promise to place a migrant worker in an industrial country job for a fee, which can be one-fourth to four times the immigrant's first year earnings. The human exploitation involved in such labor brokering can be enormous, and migrants without language skills, local contacts, or knowledge of their rights are especially vulnerable to labor brokers and to their employers.

The family and labor-brokering networks that bring immigrants into industrial countries have been likened to highways; what were once winding paths have become freeways as a result of the communications revolution, which helped to raise expectations in emigration areas; the transportation revolution, which increased access to and lowered the cost of migrating; and the so-called rights revolution, which makes it hard for industrial countries to deport migrants who want to stay (Hollifield 1992).

Researchers know that demand-pull, supply-push, and network factors explain much of today's migration, but they do not know how to assign weights to these factors, nor can they link a policy measure that affects one of the factors with a specific level of reduction in immigration pressure. However, disaggregating the factors that motivate migration permits two generalizations. First, even if demand and network factors each contribute one-third to overall migration pressure, it is clear that immigration into industrial countries will remain high during the 1990s. Even if industrial countries could eliminate the demand-pull factors over which they have direct control, two of the three factors that stimulate immigration would remain unchecked.

The second generalization is that the most important variables influencing migration tend to shift from government-approved demand-pull factors to supply-push and network factors. During the early stages of guestworker programs, analyses indicate that the number of newly admitted migrant workers can be perfectly explained by industrial-country labor market indicators (Böhning 1984; Piore 1979). But once migration "takes on a life of its own"—after supply-push and network factors become more important—governments and even mainstream businesses lament the apparent loss of immigration control.

This feeling of having lost control often results when governments play catch-up. In many cases, governments introduce employer sanctions to reduce demand-pull migration *after* a migration stream has matured and supply-push and network factors have come to the fore.

The U.S. Experience

The United States is a nation of immigrants in which most residents have traditionally opposed accepting later waves of newcomers. Only once, in 1953, did more than 10 percent of U.S. residents surveyed in an opinion poll favor increasing immigration levels (Martin and Midgley 1994). Most Americans concur with the position of the past five

U.S. presidents, all of whom expressed some version of the major conclusion of the U.S. Select Commission on Immigration and Refugee Policy: in order to keep open the front door to legal immigrants, the United States must close the backdoor to illegal aliens (U.S. Select Commission 1981).

The United States has been unable to close its immigration backdoor. Indeed, looking at immigration patterns since the Select Commission issued its report in 1981, (1) the front door to legal immigrants has opened wider; (2) new side doors have opened to grey-area migrants, most of whom will eventually be allowed to stay; and (3) illegal backdoor immigration remains at historically high levels.

The United States has recognized as legal about 9 million immigrants since 1982, including 3 million illegal aliens whose status was regularized. The United States expects to admit 800,000–900,000 legal immigrants and refugees each year throughout the 1990s, plus perhaps 100,000 side-door asylum seekers and 300,000 unauthorized immigrant settlers. These projected immigration flows suggest that, despite two centuries of experience, the United States has not been notably successful in closing the gap between immigration policy goals and outcomes. Immigration reforms in 1965 that gave Eastern Hemisphere countries equal annual immigration quotas were not expected to alter the predominantly European origins of most U.S. immigrants, yet this law unleashed the fourth immigration wave—of Hispanics and Asians—which continues today.

Other recent U.S. immigration reforms have also produced effects that were the opposite of what was intended. Efforts in 1986 to reduce illegal immigration failed. Reforms in 1990 to increase the number of professional immigrants admitted for economic reasons were accompanied by an overall increase in the annual immigration target so that over 80 percent of U.S. immigrants continue to be mostly unskilled persons admitted for family unification.

Recent U.S. immigration reforms have employed restrictionist symbols to cloak what were in fact expansionist measures. The restrictionist symbol of the 1986 reforms was employer sanctions; these sanctions failed to prevent unauthorized migrants from finding jobs because, as widely anticipated, migrants resorted to fraudulent documents to gain employment (Fix 1991). The restrictionist symbol of the 1990 legislation was an annual cap on immigration, but this cap can be exceeded if many close relatives of U.S. residents request entry, and the quota does not include refugee admissions.

What lessons does the American experience suggest? First, immigration is cumulative and self-perpetuating. A country that thinks it can admit an annual number of immigrants equivalent to, say, 0.5 percent of its population may wish to announce a target or quota of 0.4 percent, because immigration channels tend to widen over time.[6] Second, there is often a larger gap between policy goals and outcomes in immigration than in other areas, in part because managing flows of people is inherently difficult. Governments should be modest in their promises to manage immigration with any degree of precision.[7] Third, past waves of immigration to the United States have been followed by periods of little immigration. It is not clear how much time societies need to absorb a wave of newcomers, or whether the immigration pauses that the United States experienced in the past could be lengthened or shortened today in order to produce in 2050 the perception that today's immigration was in the national interest. In the past, two or three decades of rising immigration have been followed by several decades of little immigration. It is this last point—the breathing space that followed past waves of immigrants—that has become an issue today in areas such as California.

California—Wave of the Future?

California is often a bellwether for events that later appear throughout the United States and in other industrial nations. In California, the arrival of 3 million immigrants and refugees during the 1980s gave the state a population growth rate higher than that of Mexico and comparable to that of Morocco. If California continues to attract one-third of legal U.S. immigrants and one-half of illegal entries, then the state's current population of 31 million is projected to rise to between 38 and 40 million by the year 2000 (see table 3.1).

Most immigrants to California are Hispanics and Asians. Some are professionals, but most are unskilled. During the 1980s, their arrival demonstrated the extraordinary economic and job growth that can be achieved with a First World infrastructure and a Third World labor force (Muller and Espenshade 1985). Los Angeles, for example, emerged as the nation's largest manufacturing center for both high-tech aerospace and related defense industries, and for the low-wage garment, shoes, and furniture industries. What was remarkable about this economic growth was that Mexican shoemakers who could not find jobs in Mexico

---

[6]Immigration is in this sense different from trade. Trade channels tend to narrow over time as special interests seek protection from imports, so periodic rounds of trade negotiations seem necessary to keep trade channels open and widening. Immigration channels, by contrast, seem to widen and deepen over time if (1) demand-pull and supply-push reasons to migrate persist and (2) government efforts to restrict immigration are insufficient.

[7]Experience should make one cautious about embracing expert systems that ostensibly can select immigrants on the basis of their economic promise to the United States. It is agreed that young, well-educated, English-speaking immigrants are most likely to be economically successful in the United States. However, the nature of immigration point systems is to award the maximum number of points for fairly rudimentary knowledge of English, so that a points-for-English system designed to ease entry for Irish immigrants may in fact help Indian and Pakistani immigrants gain admission.

TABLE 3.1
CALIFORNIA'S POPULATION: GROWTH AND CHANGE

	1970	(%)	1980	(%)	1990	(%)	2000[1]	(%)	2010[1]	(%)	2020[1]	(%)
Anglo	15,392	77	15,704	67	17,489	57	18,131	48	18,716	41	22,221	41
Afro-American	1,400	7	1,784	8	2,199	7	2,644	7	3,127	7	3,712	7
Hispanic	2,369	12	4,544	19	8,111	26	12,087	32	16,450	36	19,531	36
Asian and other	792	4	1,575	7	3,077	10	4,910	13	7,024	16	8,340	16
Total	19,953	100	23,608	100	30,826	100	37,772	100	45,316	100	53,804	100

[1] Medium projection. Fertility rates are projected to fall linearly from their 1989 levels to 2.0 for Asians and Afro-Americans, and to 2.5 for Hispanics, by 2020. The Anglo rate is projected to rise to 1.8 by 2020. Life expectancy is expected to converge for all Californians to 80 for females and 76 for males by 2030.

Net migration into California was assumed to be 330,000 annually. These foreign and domestic migrants are projected to be 45 percent Hispanic, 40 percent Asian, 10 percent Anglo, and 5 percent Afro-American.

Sources: U.S. Bureau of the Census; Leon Bouvier, *Fifty Million Californians?* (Washington, D.C.: CIS, 1991).

were crowding into expensive apartments in Los Angeles in order to make shoes there. A logical question would have been why low-wage industries such as shoemaking did not move to the areas of low living costs whence the workers came.

California and the United States have diamond-shaped workforces. About one-fourth of U.S. adult workers are college-educated professionals and managers; one-half are high-school-educated skilled and semiskilled operatives, craftsmen, and clerks; and one-fourth have less than a high school education and often work as laborers, maids, and janitors. Immigrants, by contrast, have more of an hourglass or barbell education and skill distribution; they tend to be either more or less educated than American workers. About 30 percent of all U.S. immigrants are college-educated professionals, 20 percent are high-school-educated operatives, and 50 percent have less than a high school education (Borjas 1990).

The hourglass shape of immigrant education and skills means that immigration reinforces the other factors that are promoting economic inequality by adding workers at the top and bottom of the labor force. At the top, immigrant scientists and engineers fuel the growth of California's well-paid education and high-tech industries. At the bottom, immigrant farmworkers and laborers help to hold down wages, and thus prices, for fruits and vegetables and for gardening services. The result is growing economic inequality which, given the state's budget shortages, cannot be offset by California's shrinking social service programs. Indeed, the gap between the priorities of the older white population (which casts most votes in elections) and young minority immigrants (who often do not vote) has been described as an important factor in making California a unique laboratory in which to test whether the world's first "universal" nation can function effectively (Hayes-Bautista, Schink, and Chapa 1988).

There are many reasons to believe that California can be prosperous with high levels of immigration. California is an export-oriented producer of products and services that immigrants can sell to their countries of origin. The Asians and Latinos who comprise 80 percent of all U.S. immigrants serve as natural bridges to fast-growing Pacific Rim and Latin American economies, and they undoubtedly have played an important role in expanding California's trade with countries in both regions.

But California is also fraying around the edges. The older white population that supported a high-tax, high-service model of government during the 1960s and 1970s no longer seems willing to pay high taxes for services now perceived to be ineffective. Despite three decades of federal, state, and private antipoverty programs, the problems of underclass Americans seem to be as severe as ever. With fewer untried options left, compassion fatigue has replaced a willingness to mount new efforts to uplift needy Americans and immigrants. Increasingly, immigrants and needy Americans must vie with each other for scarce resources. As one example, during the fall of 1993 the U.S. Congress lengthened from three to five years the period after their arrival that needy immigrants can be denied access to federally paid supplemental security income in order to provide more than the usual twenty-six weeks of unemployment insurance benefits to unemployed workers.

The link between large-scale immigration and the problems of the underclass has not and probably never can be established conclusively. However, in the aftermath of the May 1992 riots in Los Angeles, there has been a great deal of speculation about this linkage. Some analysts suggest that the availability of eager immigrant workers makes it harder for disadvantaged American workers to climb the job ladder. Or, perhaps more accurately, if immigrants are readily available, American employers do not have to recruit and train disadvantaged U.S. citizens, and these citizens develop into a hard-core underclass (Briggs 1992).

A Grand Bargain?

What is to be done? The middle-of-the road position in immigration matters was perhaps best expressed by Father Theodore Hesburgh, chair of the Select Commission on Immigration and Refugee Policy. He argued that the United States must "close the back door of illegal immigration in order to keep open the front door of legal immigration." Hesburgh's metaphor pictured only two doors for newcomers: a front door for family unification, refugees, and migrants needed for economic reasons, and a backdoor through which illegal or unwanted immigrants entered. Hesburgh and the Select Commission recommended against a large-scale side-door guestworker program, arguing that there is nothing more permanent than temporary workers.

The middle-of-the-road response was repeated by President Clinton on July 27, 1993: "We must say 'no' to illegal immigration so that we can continue to say 'yes' to legal immigration." In February 1994, the administration announced plans to increase the budget of the Immigration and Naturalization Service by 30 percent, to $2.1 billion, to step up the effort to reduce backdoor illegal immigration.

U.S. efforts to close the backdoor in order to keep open the front door represent a "grand bargain" between advocates for restricting immigration and those who favor more immigrants. The often-intense negotiating that precedes U.S. immigration reforms reflects the reluctance of a nation of immigrants to take the uncomfortable step of "pulling up the gangplank." However, recent grand bargains have been only half successful, with the "admissionist" element usually succeeding and the "restrictionist" element usually failing. The legalization program in 1987–1988, for example, regularized the status of almost 3 million illegal aliens, while employer sanctions failed to deter illegal entries.

The United States is searching for another grand bargain to cope with continuing illegal immigration. The restrictionists now seem to have the upper hand: California is in recession, and the state's politicians are pointing to the federal government's failure to keep illegal immigrants out of the country as the cause for state and local governments' ballooning education, health, and criminal justice costs.

At the same time, pro-immigration and pro-immigrant groups worry that recent newcomers, many of whom are unskilled and unlikely to ascend the American job ladder, need more government assistance to learn English, acquire job skills, and gain a chance for themselves and their children to achieve the American Dream. This suggests the basis for a 1990s grand bargain: stepped-up efforts to reduce illegal immigration, coupled with an expanded effort to help newcomers integrate into American society. If such a grand bargain were negotiated, admissionists would get additional integration help for newcomers, while restrictionists would see immigration flows reduced.

There is as yet very little dialogue between admissionists and restrictionists that might lead to such a grand bargain. Instead, restrictionists hope to reduce unwanted immigration without having to spend large sums to integrate the newcomers whom they had warned would be difficult to bring into the American mainstream.

Some admissionists, who want both more immigrants and better conditions for them, believe that the status quo is preferable to a grand bargain that includes fewer immigrants. They argue that aging industrial societies must eventually do more to integrate immigrants in order to prevent population and economic stagnation. These admissionists have persuaded courts to provide immigrants with rights and access to services.

Restrictionists, on the other hand, remember that past waves of immigration were followed by periods when the doors to immigration almost closed. The longer the United States vacillates, some restrictionists reason, the more drastic will be the immigration restrictions eventually adopted.

Representatives from the extremes of the immigration spectrum have in many cases drowned out the voices of moderation. This is unfortunate; the making of immigration policy should involve thoughtful discussions of the probable consequences of alternative immigration policies for the society in general, instead of being dominated by unprovable assertions by spokespersons for narrow special interests.[8]

Special interests may prefer the immigration status quo, but in many ways the status quo represents the worst of all worlds; mostly unskilled immigrants arrive, find niches in the economy that offer high wages relative to home country standards, and then begin to climb the American job ladder. But many immigrants and the Americans who lobby on their behalf no longer seem willing to wait the three generations that past immigrant flows required for full economic and social integration. At the turn of the century, first-generation immigrants mostly remained unskilled, non-English-speaking workers; second-generation immigrants were often bilingual and, with U.S. educations, better prepared to move up in the American labor market; and third-generation immigrants were usually indistinguishable within the population at large.

---

[8]The debate over immigration during the 1980s was largely conducted along economic or labor market lines, with partisans arguing that (especially illegal) immigrants did or did not displace U.S. workers and depress their wages. This debate was never resolved. The data and models used to look for job displacement and wage depression could not find much, but they also could not answer the counterfactual question of what would have happened to technology or employer efforts to recruit and train underclass American workers if immigrants had not been available.

It appears that the U.S. debate over immigration in the 1990s will be framed by public finance concerns; that is, do young immigrants contribute more in tax revenues than they cost in public services, both today and in the future? The literature is clear on one point: the taxes that young immigrants contribute flow disproportionately to the federal government, while the public costs occasioned by their presence tend to be borne by state and especially local governments.

However, just as with the 1980s debates over the labor market effects of immigrants, the debate over their public finance effects is being framed by the extremes. Governor Pete Wilson of California was accused of "immigrant bashing" when he suggested that almost 10 percent of California's $51 billion state budget goes to cover the education, health services, and other costs of legal and illegal immigrants. Admissionists argue that more public funds should be available to help immigrants, but they see such expenditures as investments in the nation's future workforce rather than a cost argument against current immigration flows.

The ethnic accounting that is common in industrial democracies today makes it hard to wait sixty years for full integration. Population shares are the benchmarks against which everything from job shares to political representation is judged. Furthermore, many of the institutions that successfully integrated immigrants in the past—schools, churches, the military, labor unions, and political parties—are now smaller and less sure of their ability to deal with newcomers.

The challenge is how to deal fairly on both immigration control and integration. Admissionist-minded groups, which want to get as many immigrants as possible inside the country before the drawbridge goes up, have blocked restrictionist groups' efforts to take extreme steps to stop all immigration or persuade some current immigrants to leave. If the status quo continues, large numbers of unskilled immigrants are poised to arrive, while compassion-fatigued publics may support policies antithetical to integrating newcomer immigrants or helping disadvantaged natives. Such a political gridlock would yield yet another deficit to be passed on to later generations, the deficit of uplifting those left behind.

References

Böhning, W.R. 1984. *Studies in International Labor Migration*. London: Macmillan.

Borjas, George J. 1990. *Friends or Strangers: The Impact of Immigrants on the U.S. Economy*. New York: Basic Books.

Briggs, Vernon, Jr. 1992. *Mass Immigration and the National Interest*. Armonk, N.Y.: M.E. Sharpe.

Fix, Michael. 1991. *The Paper Curtain: Employer Sanctions' Implementation, Impact, and Reform*. Washington, D.C.: Urban Institute Press.

Hayes-Bautista, David, Werner Schink, and Jorge Chapa. 1988. *The Burden of Support: Young Latinos in an Aging Society*. Stanford, Calif.: Stanford University Press.

Hollifield, James. 1992. *Immigrants, Markets, and States: The Political Economy of Immigration in Postwar Europe and the U.S.* Cambridge, Mass.: Harvard University Press.

Kerr, Clark, John Dunlop, Fredrick Harbison, and Charles Myers. 1960. *Industrialism and Industrial Man*. Cambridge, Mass.: Harvard University Press.

Martin, Philip. 1991. "Labor Migration in Asia," *International Migration Review* 25:1 (Spring).

———. 1992. "International Migration: A New Challenge," *International Economic Insights* 3:2 (March–April).

Martin, Philip, and Elizabeth Midgley. 1994. *Immigration to the United States: Journey to an Uncertain Destination*. Washington, D.C.: Population Reference Bureau.

Massey, Douglas, Rafael Alarcón, Jorge Durand, and Humberto Gonzales. 1987. *Return to Aztlan: The Social Process of International Migration from Western Mexico*. Berkeley: University of California Press.

Muller, Thomas, and Thomas Espenshade. 1985. *The Fourth Wave: California's Newest Immigrants*. Washington, D.C.: Urban Institute Press.

Piore, Michael J. 1979. *Birds of Passage: Migrant Labor and Industrial Societies*. New York: Cambridge University Press.

Straubhaar, Thomas. 1992. "Allocational and Distributional Aspects of Future Immigration to Western Europe," *International Migration Review* 26:2 (Summer).

U.S. Commission for the Study of International Migration and Cooperative Economic Development. 1990. *Unauthorized Migration: An Economic Development Response*. Washington, D.C.: The Commission.

U.S. Select Commission on Immigration and Refugee Policy. 1981. *Final Report*. Washington, D.C.: The Commission.

Weintraub, Sidney. 1990. *A Marriage of Convenience: Relations between Mexico and the United States*. New York: Oxford University Press.

Commentary

Disentangling the Strands of U.S. Immigration Policy Reform

David A. Martin

Some of the discussion regarding U.S. immigration policy seems to suggest that the immigration law reform efforts of the last two decades, especially those that seek more effective enforcement of laws against unauthorized migration, represent a new form of nativism. This is a discouraging misreading of recent efforts to deal with growing migration pressures. If we are beset with nativism, where are the mass roundups of people who look foreign? Where are the scientists proving that foreign stock is polluting native blood, that sloping craniums reveal inferior mentality? How could multiculturalism become such a powerful mantra? How could antidiscrimination have been a key element in the new enforcement package adopted in 1986? How could major increases in immigration quotas, including new "diversity" visas, pass the U.S. Congress in 1990?

Nativists have not disappeared, of course, but they have been a fringe element in the national-level policy controversies of the last two decades. The congressional hearings and debates on the Immigration Reform and Control Act of 1986 (IRCA) were remarkably free of the Americanism-style breast-beating that had marked some earlier reform movements. We debase the linguistic currency if we call recent enforcement efforts "nativist." More importantly, we make it far more difficult to understand the real challenges facing this nation (and others) in controlling migration when we use labels that seem to suggest a basic illegitimacy or futility in all enforcement measures.

Recent enforcement initiatives, including enactment of employer sanctions, reflect a more complex set of motivations. One important strand is simple frustration at law-breaking and concern about the networks of organizers, document counterfeiters, and other manipulators who spring up when law-breaking is widespread. These worries have not been a major preoccupation; they have not yet crystallized in a way that would energize government action.[1]. If they had, enforcement would surely have been better funded, more sure of itself, more determined. They tend instead to burst forth unexpectedly and then subside. But respect for the law is a deep-rooted strand in American tradition, and it behooves us to sustain it rather than disparage it. Many countries now beset by corruption, extortion, or outright brigandage would love to cultivate such a tradition, yet they hardly know where to start. Once lost, the habit is hard to reclaim.

The last two decades have been marked by efforts to tighten enforcement against *undocumented* migration. These efforts began in the early 1970s, not long after we had finally purged our immigration laws of the national origins quotas. It is as though we finally had a set of legal admission provisions of which we could be relatively proud. If the basic provisions are, at long last, generally sound and fair, then why not ask that affected persons honor them? This is, at least, one plausible way of reading the key question that drove policy debates through the 1970s and 1980s.

If I am right about this, then the "apparent irony" noted in Calavita's chapter is no puzzle at all: "The apparent irony of today's restrictionism is that . . . its heightened pitch in the mid-1980s occurred at a time of *declining* unemployment." The changes in the mid-1980s were not nativist phenomena, lashing out at the foreigners among us and blaming them falsely for other sufferings or misfortunes so as to avoid confronting the real sources of the problems. The changes instead were focused on illegal migration, not all migrants nor all foreigners. This is not scapegoating; it defines a certain problem and then focuses on it as such. Insistence on law observance can quite easily coexist with, even reach a peak during, times of economic prosperity.[2]

---

[1]The priority attached to new enforcement efforts may be rising, however. A growing backlash against what have been portrayed as blatant immigration scams has generated high-level interest in enforcement reforms once again. In an October 1993 press briefing featuring remarks by the president, the vice president, and the attorney general, and attended by several key members of Congress, the Clinton administration announced a get-tough package, providing heightened penalties for smuggling, expedited procedures for resolving asylum claims in certain port-of-entry cases, increased funding of the Border Patrol, and other steps. Whether these initiatives will take the steam out of efforts to adopt more sweeping reforms remains to be seen, but the personal involvement of government officials at the highest level suggests something more enduring.

[2]A historical perspective on these developments was offered by Doris Meissner, Commissioner of the U.S. Immigration and Naturalization Service, in her first meeting with reporters since assuming her job on October 18, 1993. Noting that the United States is "in a period of historically high immigration," she also pointed out that immigrants account for proportionately less of the U.S. population (7–8 percent) than they did in the peak decade of immigration, 1900–1910, when they represented 14–15 percent of total population. "Things like immigration are very wonderful—in retrospect," Meissner

It is quite true, however, that IRCA's chief enforcement device, employer sanctions, has proven highly deficient in practice, for all the reasons that Calavita describes. Truly shrewd, effective, and determined policy making has indeed been defeated in the immigration area, many times over many years, by operation of the paired oppositions or contradictions identified. Rather than choosing one side or the other of the pair, Congress and the public tend to retreat into symbolic efforts that temporarily satisfy the drive for reform but eventually prove ineffective. But perhaps the shelf life of such symbolic solutions is growing shorter; the interval leading to a new disillusionment and new pressure for action is shrinking.

If so, I am not convinced that employer sanctions can never work—a conclusion that Calavita's chapter seems to suggest. If a clear-cut decision for the enforcement side of the paired oppositions were made, employer sanctions could make a significant dent in illegal migration. In fact, the last six years have implanted certain behaviors that could serve well as a foundation for such enforcement, given a few adjustments in the approach. Most U.S. employers and employees are now quite accustomed to going through the ritual of completing an I-9 form upon hiring, empty ceremony though it may sometimes be because of the availability of false documents. That entrenched routine counts for something. If, let us hypothesize, Congress now mandated a single, hard-to-counterfeit employment authorization document to be carried by all U.S. workers, citizen and alien alike, and if it multiplied INS and Department of Labor enforcement resources so that all employers perceived a real chance that they would get audited (and, as long as we're hypothesizing, let's also stipulate an attention-getting increase in the fines), then I-9 verification would grow real teeth and probably shut off significant parts of the labor market to the undocumented. It would still be "pragmatically easy" for employers to collect I-9s, but these relatively minor changes in the process and the follow-up could mean major gains in effective enforcement.

Under current conditions, of course, the complicated politics of immigration makes such a scenario unlikely. It is an odd politics, especially in the United States, where, in contrast to many other countries, disparagement of enforcement against unlawful migration or against employment of unauthorized migrants is thought to be a liberal stance. Calavita rightly notes the role of symbolic (and hence empty) policy initiatives in this area. But other symbols are also important—

---

observed. "When it happened a hundred years ago and it all worked out and we're glad [now] to have these connections to other countries—lovely. But it's never been wonderful and easy when it's happening. It's extraordinarily difficult. . . . In the 1890–1910 period, people killed each other over these kinds of antipathies" (quoted in Ronald J. Ostrow, "Foreigners Come to U.S. to Survive, INS Chief Says," *Los Angeles Times*, October 30, 1993).—*Editors' note.*

negative symbols that are often hastily attached to what are meant as serious proposals for law enforcement. A single uniform document that all would-be workers must produce at the time of employment can be immediately "sound-bited" as equivalent to the hated South African pass laws. A proposal to build a more businesslike barrier along the southern border is immediately likened to the late Berlin Wall.

My reaction to such proposals was the same, swift negative the first time I heard them; I don't want my country even remotely associated with those despised (and now defeated) regimes. But perhaps it is time for a phase of sober second thoughts. The power of those negative symbols should be more closely examined. If a ragged fence between here and Mexico is legitimate (and it is hard not to concede this point), then why not a soundly constructed, cleverly engineered barrier? And every time I am asked to produce my driver's license or my credit card, I question whether uniform document-production schemes have to lead to a police state.

If the underlying laws that these devices would enforce are unjust, then the analogies to Berlin and South Africa might hold. But the best response in that case would be to change the laws rather than simply to undermine enforcement. In fact, the United States hasn't done too badly in the law-changing business over the past three decades. We have repealed national origins quotas, eliminated the most objectionable exclusion grounds, improved the refugee and asylum provisions, and even increased admission quotas. If measured, sober, careful enforcement of the laws cannot be implemented in times of relative calm, however, then we risk an exaggerated, extreme, heedless rush into enforcement when matters have built to a crisis. Then perhaps we would learn what real nativism looks like.

In this vein, one other policy realm deserves more attention than the Calavita chapter gives it: the system for bestowing or denying political asylum. Asylum can provide a flash point for backlash or exaggerated reactions to all types of migration or to the presence of foreigners. Germany's recent headlines come to mind, but we don't need distant examples. The Mariel boatlift in 1980 generated an ugly negative response, one that fortunately subsided when the boat flow was controlled within a few months of its commencement. More recently, an impending Haitian boatlift turned president-elect Clinton into a surprising convert supporting what had been, until then, a Republican interdiction policy. Suddenly we witnessed our political system displaying the political will to regulate immigration flows resolutely—by virtually shutting off an entire migration stream.

But even as this went forward, there were signs of a new impending crisis in the mainland asylum system. Despite important reforms under regulations adopted in 1990—which according to most accounts greatly improved the quality of political asylum determinations by the INS—it has become apparent that the current system cannot keep pace with the rising intake of claims, now exceeding 100,000 per year (far more if we also count the claims filed separately with immigration judges).

Refugee advocates and representatives of the United Nations High Commissioner for Refugees tend to roll their eyes when commentators speak of asylum in the context of controlling illegal migration. "Control" smacks of restrictions and crackdowns, whereas asylum, in this important view, should be about generosity and welcome—a humanitarian institution, not a control regime. In fact, in the 1990s a political asylum system must be both. It must afford a vehicle for humanitarian protection, and it must also be a system capable of enforcement and control—because today's asylum claimants represent a very mixed population. They include brave activists who barely escaped, past victims still bearing the physical and psychological scars of brutality, other sympathetic cases that must be judged marginal at best under accepted UN treaty standards, persons fleeing poverty, and finally outright abusers and scam artists.

Unfortunately these last have been in the public eye lately. In 1993 the television program "Sixty Minutes" reported (and perhaps exaggerated) the problem of asylum claimants arriving at New York's JFK airport having lost or destroyed their documents sometime after gaining clearance to board at the foreign airport. Owing to a lack of detention space, a great many are released, with work authorization. In succeeding weeks, the appearance at U.S. shores of boats bearing hundreds of Chinese, apparently part of organized smuggling efforts, compounded the negative public reaction. And asylum applicants who had been released for months or years pending consideration of their claims were implicated in terrorist acts, including the bombing of the World Trade Center in New York City.

The challenge for future policy will be to preserve a solid core of humanitarian protection, while moving more effectively and far more expeditiously against those claimants who are not qualified for asylum. This will prove more difficult than tightening other parts of the control scheme (such as the I-9 process). For it is not just a question of resources, though undoubtedly more resources will be required. The government, and ultimately the citizenry, will have to come to grips with certain basic and unpleasant decisions that we have generally evaded up to now. We will have to decide about the exact standards marking out just who deserves protection, about the level of assurance that we will settle for concerning the facts about events that took place in distant countries (in an adjudicative arena where the facts are often quite elusive), and ultimately about due process protections that are reflective of the sensitivity of the claims, yet practical in the face of the large migrations that future decades are likely to bring. In short, analyses of American immigration policy have to consider political asylum as a matter of priority. It is not just an issue for Europe.

Commentary

Introducing the Critical Transparency School of Immigration Analysis

Mark J. Miller

In the 1980s a school of immigration policy analysis arose which, for lack of an agreed-upon designation, can be dubbed the critical transparency approach. Its hallmarks include the assumption that the key dynamic behind modern international migration is employer demand for labor. International migration, both legal and illegal, is primarily a labor market-driven phenomenon. Hence the necessary condition for it is found within industrial democracies, while the sufficient conditions are mainly found without. Government regulation of international migration fails or succeeds to the extent that it recognizes and is in or out of sync with the underlying dynamic.

From this perspective, problems of regulation commonly include a transparency gap between official and unofficial policies. Official policies, almost always considered restrictionist, are typically found to be symbolic rather than effective, repressive, misguided, giving rise to racism, or prone to producing unanticipated, untoward, or perverse effects. The exceptions to this rule are guestworker and seasonal worker policies, which while perhaps criticized for certain moral, legal, and administrative shortcomings, have the merit of responding to otherwise unmet employer demands for foreign labor. Analysts of this school evidence diverse normative presuppositions ranging from Marxism to ultraliberalism. What unites them is a deep skepticism about the capacity and the will of Western democracies to regulate international migration according to stated policy. The approach is critical in that it finds fault with the immigration policy status quo. It advocates transparency, which would require governments to admit to the apparent intractability of international migration and to the growing disjuncture between official policies aimed at curbing immigration and a putative reality of mushrooming migration.

Calavita's chapter exemplifies this approach, its merits and its limitations. Her major contentions can be summarized as follows: (1) Employer and worker interests are contradictory, hence a national interest in U.S. immigration policy is mythical or fanciful. Underneath the myth there is the reality of immigration serving employer interests. The symbolic nature of the 1885 anti-contract labor law and of the Immigration Reform and Control Act of 1986 (IRCA) attests to the reality of government regulation serving employer interests. Both laws responded to a perceived need to restrict and limit entry of aliens without affecting the continuity of such entry. (2) There is a persistent tension between the employment needs of the U.S. economy and a willingness to publicly recognize those needs. Currently the U.S. economy produces labor demand that can only be met by foreign labor. Yet the U.S. government fails to recognize the necessity of a foreign labor recruitment policy. (3) Regulation of international migration by the United States is increasingly inconsistent with liberal democratic principles. Hence immigration control efforts are limited and ineffective. Only draconian steps, like Operation Wetback in 1954, could alter immigration realities, driven as they are by labor market demand.

Calavita is brutally accurate about certain aspects that frequently are overlooked by U.S., and particularly foreign, students of U.S. immigration history. There is merit in recalling the historical role that the U.S. government and U.S. employers played in Mexican labor recruitment. Calavita accurately notes that, during the bracero period, the Mexican government requested imposition of laws penalizing illicit employment of aliens because many U.S. employers, with the connivance of U.S. government authorities, circumvented official procedures intended to protect Mexicans against exploitation. Post facto legalization served to undermine bracero recruitment procedures authorized by bilateral U.S.-Mexican agreements. The so-called Texas Proviso stripped the 1952 immigration law of any means of punishing illegal employment of aliens. That would remain the case until 1986. One consequence of the Texas Proviso perhaps was Operation Wetback, which resulted in a massive deportation of illegally resident Mexicans and some U.S. citizens of Mexican background.

Calavita appears to be more critical of bracero-like policies than some other adherents of the critical transparency approach, who as a general rule are not wont to subject guestworker or seasonal labor recruitment policies to the same critical standards they apply to other dimensions of immigration policy. There was a gaping disjuncture between official and unofficial policy during the bracero period, and this was one of the reasons contributing to the unilateral U.S. decision to discontinue the program in 1964, during a period of social reform. In light of the bracero experience, it is not altogether clear that it would be enlightened for the U.S. government to, in effect, legalize recurrent employer recourse to unauthorized alien employment through a new labor recruitment program.

The bulk of Calavita's analysis is devoted to IRCA, a law that is difficult to analyze satisfactorily in a few pages. The author, in my view, attributes too little importance to the influence exerted by adherents of the critical transparency approach in weakening the 1986 law. In some respects, the critique they made of key provisions of the legislation became self-fulfilling prophecy. Calavita correctly sees the proof of employment eligibility as the key flaw in the employer sanctions provision. She also notes the insufficient personnel resources devoted to enforcement. It is not as if advocates of employer sanctions were unaware of the possibility that widespread document fraud would thwart employer sanctions enforcement. Most proponents wanted a secure identification requirement, but they encountered strong, sometimes irrational, opposition. Some of this opposition was doubtlessly sincere and stemmed from unwarranted concerns that employment identification documents would threaten civil liberties and undercut the quality of democratic life in the United States. The opposition was also driven by the presumption, unwarranted in my eyes, that employer sanctions were a draconian, racism-tinged measure likely to engender additional employment discrimination against Hispanics.[1] The ferocity of the opposition to employer sanctions was telling, even if a large majority of Americans supported their enactment. U.S. Hispanics were about evenly split between opponents and supporters. Key proponents of employer sanctions, like Senator Alan Simpson, evidenced a willingness to compromise. Eventually IRCA was adopted with a provision calling for, in effect, review of the employee identification document requirement and possible corrective action if warranted. It remains a distinct possibility that this provision of the 1986 law will be revisited.

Calavita is probably correct in concluding that enforcement of employer sanctions has had a less-than-hoped-for effect on illegal immigration and illegal alien employment. However, scholars must be mindful of the limits to knowledge in this area. Calavita terms the 1986 law symbolic in the sense that it masks the reality of continuing illegal

---

[1] A 1990 report by the U.S. General Accounting Office, based on a nationwide employer survey and other investigative activities, concluded that the employer sanctions mandated in the 1986 Immigration Reform and Control Act had caused a "widespread pattern of discrimination" against foreign-looking and sounding applicants, including U.S. citizens, who were in fact eligible to work in the country (U.S. GAO, "Immigration Reform, Employer Sanctions, and the Question of Discrimination" [Washington, D.C., Report GAO/GGD 90-62, March 1990]). An independent audit of 360 hiring decisions in two cities, San Diego and Chicago, conducted in 1989 by the Urban Institute produced results consistent with the GAO's findings (Michael Fix, ed., *The Paper Curtain: Employer Sanctions' Implementation, Impact, and Reform* [Washington, D.C.: Urban Institute Press, 1991]: 267–70). — *Editors' note.*

migration while appearing to respond to calls to curb it. There is a grain of truth in this. But law is supposed to be symbolic in another sense. As Jacqueline Costa-Lascoux has pointed out with reference to employer sanctions, laws are educational. One of their primary functions is to discourage behavior viewed as harmful or unwanted. It does not seem unreasonable to presume that some, if not many, employers do comply with the law. It is true that the current ease of document fraud and the requirements of the I-9 form permit easy circumvention of the intent of the 1986 law (punishment of knowing illicit employment of aliens), but meaningful reform in democratic settings often occurs over decades, not years. At least IRCA went a big step beyond the Texas Proviso. One suspects that employer sanctions have had some deterrent effect. Some fines are meted out, and inspections, insufficient as they might be, presumably do have some limited effects discouraging illegal employment of aliens.

Calavita brands the 1986 law as restrictionist, although she notes that it featured fairly generous legalization provisions. IRCA, of course, was a legislative compromise and featured both restrictive and relatively generous provisions. That legal immigration jumped as a result of IRCA came as no surprise. Calavita is correct that the magnitude of Special Agricultural Workers (SAW) legalizations was unforeseen. Fairly rampant document fraud and questionable administration of the program contributed to this outcome. The SAW provision was undebated, unplanned, and proposed in extremis as a way to enable IRCA's adoption. Its inclusion did testify to the inordinate clout of certain employer interest groups in the legislative process. But evidence such as this does not warrant the conclusion that U.S. immigration policy is driven by employer interests. Clearly, employer interests are always influential and sometimes decisive, but they also can be contradictory. Monistic explanation oversimplifies a tremendously complex reality.

One of the principal contributions of the critical transparency approach has been to shed light on persistent employer demand for foreign labor, even in periods of high unemployment and economic distress. Some employers prefer to hire illegal foreign workers and some feel that they have no alternative. Calavita sees such employment practices as real needs dictated by the economic situation. However, the reality of such employer demand does not make it socioeconomically or politically desirable. Efforts to curb illegal migration and illegal alien employment through employer sanctions and related control policies seek to alter these practices. Calavita is very skeptical that this can be done, in part due to employer influence over Congress and the INS. The mediocre results of employer sanctions enforcement to date might seem to confirm this insight, but in my eyes it is too early to tell. One cannot rule out refinement and reinforcement of employer sanctions enforcement in the future. There is enormous grassroots support for enforcement of employers sanctions. My hunch is that incremental refinement and reinforcement of employer sanctions is more likely than their repeal or the maintenance of the status quo in coming years. Employer sanctions are not a panacea, but they appear to be an indispensable component of any comprehensive strategy to curb unauthorized immigration.

Calavita correctly notes a certain tension between liberal, democratic values and efforts to control international migration. While she does discuss the Immigration Act of 1990, one should never lose sight of the fact that the United States has a fairly generous legal immigration policy. The putative restrictionist quality of the 1986 law needs to be viewed in this light. The U.S. legal immigration tradition has helped legitimize alien entry and, due to its preference for family reunification, facilitates immigrant incorporation. The legal immigration system is an expression of U.S. democracy, even if most Americans would like to see reductions in legal immigration, not the increases authorized by the 1990 law. The Immigration Act of 1990 was remarkable because of the narrow bounds of debate over it. Its adoption was a testament to the influence of classical liberal ideas, particularly those of Julian Simon, as applied to international migration (see Simon 1989).[2] Migration was viewed above all from an economic perspective and as a marginal but net benefit to the U.S. economy.

The paradox behind the Immigration Act of 1990 is that it came at a time of mounting evidence that the nature of immigration and the socioeconomic effects of legal immigration to the United States were changing. Scholars as methodologically diverse as George Borjas and Alejandro Portes have documented important changes that make it appear less likely that the historical pattern of immigrant upward mobility in U.S. society will continue for many post-1965 immigrants (see Borjas 1990; Portes and Rumbaut 1990). Increasingly, there are calls for European-style immigrants policies to replace the U.S. government's traditional benign neglect of all legal immigrants except refugees.

Mounting evidence of integration problems may contribute to a future politicization of U.S. immigration policy. Democratic states are constrained by democratic and human rights considerations in their regulation of international migration. This does prevent recourse to draconian measures, and it virtually ensures that some illegal immigration will persist. At present there is no reason to anticipate that misgivings over legal and illegal immigration policy will lead to political controversies in the United States over immigration such as witnessed recently in Western Europe; yet public disquiet grew in the wake of the Los Angeles riots. There is indeed a disjuncture between public opinion

---

[2]For a restatement of Simon's ideas supported by more recent empirical data, see Stephen Moore, "The Economic Case for More Immigrants," in Vernon M. Briggs, Jr. and Stephen Moore, *Still an Open Door? — U.S. Immigration and the American Economy* (Washington, D.C.: American University Press, 1994): 75–155. — *Editors' note.*

and the expressed sentiments of U.S. lawmakers, on the one hand, which are generally hostile to illegal immigration, and its persistence in fact, on the other. Calavita sheds some light on this key paradox of modern democracy.

References

Borjas, George J. 1990. *Friends or Strangers: The Impact of Immigration on the U.S. Economy*. New York: Basic Books.

Portes, Alejandro, and Rubén G. Rumbaut. 1990. *Immigrant America: A Portrait*. Berkeley: University of California Press.

Simon, Julian. 1989. *The Economic Consequences of Immigration*. Oxford: Basil Blackwell.

Commentary

Illegal Migration to the United States—
The Demographic Context

Jeffrey S. Passel

Kitty Calavita traces the long history of interaction between the economy of rural Mexico and that of the United States, particularly the agricultural economy of the Southwest. However, I think we must look to more recent periods and to changes in the Mexican economy to explain the contemporary situation. The demographic dimensions of the interaction between the two countries have changed both quantitatively and qualitatively. Specifically, the number of persons born in Mexico and living in the United States has increased by more than a factor of five since 1960; between 1980 and 1990 alone, the number increased from 2.5 million to almost 4.5 million, according to decennial census data.

Contemporary illegal immigration has its origins in the mid-1960s. The end of the Bracero Program left in place a system of interaction between the U.S. labor market (especially in agriculture) and the economy of rural Mexico. Changes in Mexican agriculture led to a surplus of agricultural manpower. Undocumented Mexican immigrants continued to fill the demand for labor in the United States which had been met by the braceros. Over time, the undocumented agricultural workers branched out and filled a demand for low-wage, unskilled labor in other sectors of the U.S. labor market. As the migration networks matured, more immigrants came to U.S. cities; and as the economy of Mexico faltered in the 1970s and 1980s, more settled.

We can also look for the roots of illegal migration in legal immigration, especially from countries other than Mexico. The changes put in place by the 1965 immigration legislation opened up immigration from countries that had previously been excluded, notably Asian and Latin American countries. With more *legal* immigrants coming, friends and relatives of the immigrants came to visit. International travel became easier and new networks were created. Many of the friends and relatives wanted to stay but faced long backlogs for admission as permanent legal residents. They ended up staying illegally, and thus new streams of illegal immigration began.

The rhetorical and policy debates over illegal immigration of the 1970s and beyond have been driven principally by two concerns: the perceived adverse economic impacts of undocumented immigrants and a concern over the sheer numbers of people coming to the United States. In both areas there has been a gap between perceptions and research results; the conventional wisdom has simply not been supported by research findings.

One of the first official assertions about the illegal alien population was probably the best. In 1972, INS Commissioner Farrell conjectured that there were about 1 million undocumented aliens in the country, a number consistent with subsequent empirical efforts. By 1976 the INS was saying 4–12 million, and it settled on a range of 6–8 million illegal immigrants shortly thereafter. With the transition to the Carter administration the "guesstimates" got somewhat lower. Commissioner Castillo's guess in 1978 was 3–6 million, figures more in line with the limited empirical evidence that could be brought to bear at the time. All of these estimates turned out to be too high for the *resident* illegal population. The best available estimates imply that in 1980 there were 2 million undocumented aliens counted in the census, with perhaps another million uncounted, or *3 million* total. At the same time, the rate of growth was also overstated. Citing figures showing more than 1 million apprehensions per year along the U.S.-Mexico border, the INS and others claimed annual increases of 500,000 to 1 million per year in the undocumented population. Empirical research in the 1980s, however, suggested that 100,000–300,000 net growth per year was more accurate. The IRCA legalizations of the late 1980s reinforced the validity of the lower numbers.

Why the confusion? Certainly there is a lack of reliable data. Furthermore, a general inability on the part of most observers to appreciate what size population it takes to be noticed in an urban setting contributes to the confusion. Several demographic trends exacerbate these perceptual problems. First, by 1980 large-scale *legal* immigration from Latin America and Asia had led to greater visibility of foreigners for the first time in two generations. After declining for forty years, the foreign-born population grew by 46 percent between 1970 and 1980, largely due to *legal*, not illegal, immigration, and by another 40 percent between 1980 and 1990, again principally from legal immigration. The result is a tendency on the part of much of the public and media to equate *immigrants* with *illegal immigrants*.

A second problem is the failure to differentiate the large-scale movement of *temporary* labor between the United States and Mexico from *permanent* immigration to the United States. This difficulty is best illustrated by the widespread concern over changes (usually increases) in the number of apprehensions of illegal aliens that occur along the U.S.-Mexican border. Apprehensions mostly tap into the flow of temporary labor between the two countries. They are a function of many things other than the number of illegals coming to live in the United States—such things as the demand for agricultural labor, the relative values of the peso and the dollar, the number of Border Patrol agents and their deployment, the quality of Border Patrol equipment, the time of year, and so on. The INS and many others have often claimed that for every adult Mexican male that the INS catches, two or three actually come to the United States to *live*. If this were true, the migration over the last twenty years would have led to an acute shortage of males in Mexico. This has clearly not happened. The rate of permanent settlement has been much, much less than hypothesized.

So how many illegals are there in the United States? Based on available evidence, my best estimates are as follows. The number grew gradually from between 2.5 and 3.5 million in 1980 to between 3 and 5 million by 1986. At that time, the two legalization programs under IRCA reduced the resident illegal population by more than 2 million. There is some disagreement over how much (or whether) the flow of illegals into the country decreased immediately after IRCA's passage in late 1986, but there is widespread agreement that the flow is again approaching pre-IRCA levels. As a result of the Immigration Act of 1990 and some INS policy changes, there have also been a number of de facto legalization processes. At the same time, the normal progression from illegal status to legal status that has been occurring for decades continued. The result of all of these programs and policies is that by 1990 (and probably still today) the number of illegal aliens residing in the United States was about the same as it was in 1980 (in round numbers, about 3 million).

This is not a small number. But it *is* small in relation to inflammatory estimates of 6, 12, or 15 million illegal aliens. If 3 million undocumented aliens were spread evenly throughout the country, I doubt they would be a major concern, constituting only about 1–2 percent of the population. However, they are highly concentrated geographically. The largest numbers (possibly half or more) are in California, especially Los Angeles. Texas, New York, Illinois, Florida, and the District of Columbia also have large concentrations. However, with the possible exception of Los Angeles, even the large, highly visible concentrations of illegals tend to be substantially smaller than conventional wisdom or rhetorical guesstimates would suggest.

We must also take care not to *understate* the importance of the demographic context of current undocumented immigration. The 1980s saw between 9 and 10 million immigrants (legal and illegal) come to the United States. This figure exceeds the 1901–10 decade and approaches the ten-year high of more than 10 million (legal) immigrants for 1905–14. However, in terms of *net* immigration, the 1980s far exceeds the earlier period. More than 3 million immigrants emigrated during each of the first two decades of this century, while less than 2 million did so in the 1980s. As a consequence, the 1980s clearly exceeds earlier periods as the decade with the largest net immigration in the nation's history. (In fact, the second largest is the 1970s.) Also, net immigration from all sources now accounts for an extremely large share of total population growth in the United States. For the 1980s, my work suggests that about 37 percent of growth came from net immigration and almost 20 percent more from births to immigrants in this country. These percentages are likely to remain about the same for the next several decades.

Coupled with this increase in the absolute and relative importance of immigration is the contemporary shift in origins of the immigrants. In the 1950s, two-thirds of immigrants came from Europe and Canada, the traditional sources for the United States. By the 1980s, however, about 85 percent of the immigrants were coming from Latin America and Asia. The result has been a dramatic change in the composition of the American population. In little more than a generation, the United States has been transformed from an overwhelmingly white majority population with an almost entirely black minority to a population that is now only three-quarters white majority, with a minority population split equally between African Americans and other minorities. These trends will continue. In fifteen years, Latinos will pass blacks to become the nation's largest minority population. Within fifty years (under current trends), about one-quarter of the U.S. population will be of Asian or Latino descent, up from about one-eighth today. In addition, about one-seventh of the population will be foreign-born, attaining levels last reached in 1870–1920 (see Edmonston and Passel 1994: 1–71). Such rapid compositional changes have led to increased anxiety regarding immigration policy.

The economic impacts of immigrants, both legal and undocumented, have long been a matter of debate, as Calavita has shown. In recent years, a new area of concern has arisen. With increased immigration, increased governmental budgetary deficits, and the shifting of programmatic expenses from the federal government to states and localities, the debate over costs attributable to immigrants has intensified. Recent studies of Los Angeles and San Diego counties suggest that undocumented immigrants as a group are, on balance, a net burden to the counties in which they live because recent immigrants receive more in benefits than they pay in local taxes. However, these and other studies also show that *total revenues* (federal, state, and local) from immigrants exceed the costs of benefits and services received by them.[1] Perhaps the most egregious example of immigrant bashing comes from California, where Governor Pete Wilson has demanded a $1.5 billion reimbursement from the federal government for the estimated annual impacts of illegal and legalized immigrants on the state. He has targeted specific programs for cuts if the aid is not forthcoming, thus using the immigrants, at least implicitly, as political cover for program reductions affecting the general population.

The gap between perceptions and reality seems to be widening. Reactions against immigrants are increasing, while at the same time the Immigration Act of 1990 has opened the door to even greater numbers of legal immigrants. The economic benefits of immigrants are used to justify the increased levels of immigration, while state and local governments complain about the costs they must incur. Legislation to curb undocumented immigration has failed, while policy makers hesitate to embrace new approaches (see below) to controlling the illegal flow. Where does all this leave us? Awash in ambiguities and tensions, as Calavita points out. We are left, I think, in the uncomfortable position of not having any quick-fix remedies available purely through immigration law or policy. There continues to be a strong demand for the labor of undocumented immigrants. The United States is an attractive destination for potential migrants because even the low-wage jobs available to unskilled undocumented aliens pay a great deal more than whatever employment can be obtained in the sending countries. Employers can still use the services offered by undocumented aliens, particularly given that the risks to employers appear to be small. And the public, which remains sympathetic to the plight of individual immigrants, still desires the goods and services made available by the presence of undocumented immigrants.

The potential methods for controlling illegal immigration include: a national identification card or some sort of counterfeit-proof employment credential; an on-line employment verification system; increased liability for employers' failure to verify the authenticity of documents presented; more severe barriers to entry; and higher penalties (including imprisonment) for aliens attempting repeated unauthorized entry into the United States. The political will has not been present to provide the resources and enforcement activities necessary to impose these more drastic solutions. On the other hand, eliminating employer sanctions altogether is unacceptable to policy makers and the general public because of the message it would send to employers and to potential undocumented immigrants.

---

[1]For a compilation and critique of these studies, see Michael Fix and Jeffrey S. Passel, *Immigration and Immigrants: Setting the Record Straight* (Washington, D.C.: Urban Institute Press): 57–67. —*Editors' note.*

Ultimately the answer lies in reducing the pressure to come to the United States. This means economic development and job creation on a massive scale, especially in Mexico and other parts of Latin America. Even this is likely to lead to increased, not decreased, migration to the United States in the short run.[2] My guess is that we will continue to "muddle along." Enforcement will be increased, but not to the levels required to stop illegal migration. Some undocumented immigrants will continue to come to the United States and fill the economic niches where there is a demand for their labor. Perhaps an economic crisis of the magnitude of the Great Depression will force Americans to confront the issue head-on, or perhaps trade and economic development in sending countries will cure the situation. We still have many tough choices to make; not making them leaves us at the mercy of world events.

Reference

Edmonston, Barry, and Jeffrey S. Passel, eds. 1994. *Immigration and Ethnicity: The Integration of America's Newest Arrivals*. Washington, D.C.: Urban Institute Press.

---

[2]According to one study, economic development and restructuring stimulated by implementation of the North American Free Trade Agreement (NAFTA) may increase Mexican migration to the United States by as many as 100,000 persons annually before beginning to reduce the flow (Philip L. Martin, *Trade and Migration: NAFTA and Agriculture* [Washington, D.C.: Institute for International Economics, 1993]). See also Wayne A. Cornelius and Philip L. Martin, "The Uncertain Connection: Free Trade and Rural Mexican Migration to the United States," *International Migration Review* 27:3 (Fall 1993): 484–512.

4

Canada: Flexibility and Control in Immigration and Refugee Policy

Manuel García y Griego

Introduction

Canada is a country with an unusually strong immigration tradition, and it has obtained remarkable results by applying mostly liberal or moderate immigration control policies. During the postwar era Canada has probably received more immigrants per capita, virtually every year, than any other country except perhaps Israel and Australia. Though Canada has adopted somewhat stricter policies since 1989, it has not been especially stringent in enforcing its immigration prohibitions. Its control policies are unexceptional. Nevertheless, Canada today does not have a massive problem of illegal entries or an enormous number of foreigners coming in and seeking first asylum.

Indeed, Canada prepares an annual plan that targets the number of immigrants (and refugees) that it will accept, by category. By comparative standards it comes close to meeting government objectives. A recent analysis of immigrant landings during the 1991 calendar year notes that the target for landings from abroad (185,000) was missed—only 161,000 were admitted. Landings processed from within Canada exceeded by 9,000 the 1991 target of 35,000 (EIC 1992a: 11). Immigration centers receive a small but steady stream of people who are out of status and seek regularization; investigations locates a few thousand others every year who are ordered to depart. It is striking that a country with so long a history of relatively large-scale immigration and so large a foreign-

Grateful acknowledgment is made to several government officials, academics, immigration practitioners, and attorneys who consented to be interviewed anonymously for this project and who supplied the author with documentary information and suggestions.

born population does not have a sizable deportable population within its borders and has not experienced massive and widespread abuse of its immigration procedures.

Canada *does* have significant problems in the administration of its immigration policies, and at times there has been a public perception that foreigners have abused Canada's immigration system. The Canadian government's probing for ways to respond to refugee claimants, who arrived in increasing numbers during the 1980s, reveals many of the difficulties that other liberal democratic states experience when responding to unwanted newcomers. Immigration policies have flip-flopped awkwardly several times since 1967, and on occasion Canadian governments have found themselves caught up in responding to short-term crises of their own making. Several policy changes have produced unintended and undesirable results and required embarrassing reversals or politically painful choices. Prodded by litigation and adverse court decisions, Canadian governments have opened the appeals process for foreigners denied permanent residency by immigration officials. Lengthy adjudication processes have become common, unresolved cases frequently accumulate in embarrassingly large backlogs, and both the process of refugee determination and the removal of immigrants have become expensive. Canada has never lost control of its borders, but it has, on more than one occasion, lost control of its own admission process.

The implementation of immigration and refugee policy in Canada thus reveals many of the weaknesses present in other liberal democratic states that have found it difficult to keep out unwanted newcomers. However, Canada has not had to pay the political price of having to cope with the presence of a large unauthorized foreign population. Where does Canada's apparent success lie? Why do we not find, as we might in the United States and in several European countries, clear evidence of large gaps between immigration policy goals and outcomes? Is this narrow gap in the Canadian case an illusion? And what of the less dramatic but no less important failures of Canadian policy—especially the awkward management of refugee flows in the 1980s? Are these the Canadian equivalent of the wide gaps between policy goals and consequences that we find so evident in other industrial democracies? To what extent does the Canadian experience with the administration of immigration and refugee policy suggest a trend toward convergence with the experience of other industrial democracies, and to what extent do Canada's unique history, politics, and special circumstances account for what appears to be an anomalous (and relatively happy) outcome?

Although this chapter cannot address these questions completely, it will sketch the outlines of an argument that advances three claims. First, a number of fortuitous and unique circumstances have insulated Canada from the more difficult challenges that the United States has faced or those confronting the European industrial democracies otherwise comparable to

Canada. The pressures of unwanted immigration have been much weaker in Canada than in her sister industrial democracies. Canada has faced similar pressures but under more favorable circumstances. At the same time, Canada's long experience with immigration has given it the self-confidence to address these challenges and to accept or even promote large-scale immigration as a desirable end. Canadian willingness to embrace a relatively high level of immigration has contributed to a situation where immigration policy was frequently perceived to be functioning well in most cases, despite occasional policy errors, some of which were not minor. Finally, Canada's painful experience with the politics of two founding nationalities and its tentative and early steps toward multiculturalism have facilitated the absorption of a growing Third World population within the framework of a liberal democratic society.

Second, though Canada's immigration policy-making apparatus has demonstrated its capacity to make significant mistakes (a trait evident in other countries as well), it has also demonstrated unusual *flexibility* and agility. Canadian governments have proved to be quite capable of getting legislation through quickly and setting up the administrative machinery to implement it. There have been painful hitches in specific areas almost every time that a major policy change has been made since 1967, but the government has responded flexibly and in a relatively timely fashion.

Third, it is clear that the Canadian government's immigration policy making and implementation suffer from many of the same weaknesses that other liberal democratic societies have exhibited in a more dramatic fashion, even though we do not see massive flows of undocumented immigrants or large numbers of foreigners seeking first asylum. Once we strip away Canada's unique circumstances and account for the flexibility in the administration of immigration policies, we are left, in fact, with a liberal democratic state that cannot, because of its liberal and democratic character, respond effectively to potentially large flows of unwanted immigrants. Many Canadian officials recognize this, and this may account in part for what in recent years have appeared to be overreactions to some policy challenges (such as the Sikhs in 1987) and a bias toward quick, but not always fortuitous, policy responses. Canada also exhibits the all-too-familiar difficulties that other liberal industrial democracies face with respect to unwanted newcomers. Although Canada has managed relatively well during the past three decades, it is not immune to the difficulties that surface in other developed countries regarding immigration control.

Canada's Immigration Experience and Policy Framework

Since Canada's confederation in 1867, approximately 13 million immigrants have landed, though not all have stayed. Canada has a vast territory (even if much of it is inhospitable), and immigration was initially viewed as promoting colonization. Large-scale immigration began at the turn of the century. Between 1895 and 1913 over 2.5 million immigrants arrived in Canada—an enormous number relative to Canada's 1911 population of only 7.2 million. The vast majority of these new Canadians were English-speaking immigrants from the British Isles or the United States, or other Europeans, chiefly Germans, Dutch, and Scandinavians. The composition of the immigrant flows was primarily the result of a racist immigration administration, which largely kept out nonwhite immigrants, especially the Chinese. Following the devastation of World War II, Canada received newcomers from Poland, Ukraine, Italy, Germany, and the Netherlands.

Canada did not have a formal immigration policy until it adopted a comprehensive immigration act in 1952, although it had established a practice of administration that promoted immigration for national economic ends and excluded social undesirables, especially from Asia. In 1947 Prime Minister MacKenzie King articulated a rationalization for the existing practice and defended it against critics who objected to the high levels of immigration or to its racial biases. "The policy of the government," the prime minister declared, "is to foster the growth of the population of Canada by the encouragement of immigration . . . and permanent settlement of such numbers of immigrants as can advantageously be absorbed in our national economy" (Canada, House of Commons 1947: 2644). King dismissed fears that Canada could no longer absorb large flows, relative to its population, without suffering a reduction in the standard of living of its citizens.

> This need not be the case. *If immigration is properly planned*, the result will be the reverse. A larger population will help to develop our resources. By providing a larger number of consumers, in other words a larger domestic market, it will reduce the present dependence of Canada on the export of primary products. The essential thing is that immigrants be selected with care, and that their numbers be adjusted to the absorptive capacity of the country (Canada, House of Commons 1947: 2645, emphasis added).

In response to criticism that Canadian policy was discriminatory, King articulated the nationalist view that no foreigner had a fundamental human right to enter Canada and that Canada was "perfectly within her rights in selecting the persons whom we regard as desirable future citizens." The people of Canada did not wish to make "a fundamental alteration in the character" of the population, he declared, and "large-scale immigration from the orient would change the fundamental composition of the Canadian population" (Canada, House of Commons 1947: 2646).

The 1960s witnessed a turning point in Canadian immigration policy. In 1962 Canada abandoned its racist exclusionary policy without legislation by amending immigration regulations. The new immigration system provided for universal admission based on skills, family unification, and humanitarian considerations. Also in 1962 Canada adopted its first legalization program—one designed specifically for Chinese long-term out-of-status residents.

In 1966 Canada created the Department of Manpower and Immigration and began to focus explicitly on how immigrant workers could strengthen the Canadian labor force, which was then perceived to be lagging in skills by comparison with other industrial nations. In 1967 a new set of immigration regulations were adopted that established Canada's famous point system for immigrant selection. Immigrants were admitted according to three broad categories: independent applicants, sponsored dependents, and nominated relatives. Also in 1967 the Immigration Appeal Board was created to hear cases where applicants could appeal refusals, and in 1969 Canada acceded to the 1951 Geneva Convention Relating to the Status of Refugees.

Between 1962 and 1969, then, Canada moved away from a discretionary administrative system to one with more clearly established rules and procedures, though it did so through regulatory change and not parliamentary legislation. It also embraced the liberal principle of racial nondiscrimination in the selection of immigrants and recognized an international obligation to provide refuge, while it simultaneously reaffirmed its traditional goals of providing for family unification and promoting national economic advancement via the admission of skilled workers. Immigrant admissions started to rise in the mid-1960s and have fluctuated mostly between 100,000 and 200,000 per year since that time (see table 4.1).

These early changes in immigration policy were not made in a manner to encourage public debate, nor were they the products of obvious public pressure. Canadian policy making has tended to be developed in a rather closed fashion through state initiative and relatively insulated from public scrutiny or pressure. Immigration has been perhaps more closed than other issue areas. "Immigration," wrote Freda Hawkins in 1975, "has always been and continues to be managed by Cabinet and a very small group of senior officials" (Hawkins 1976: 56). Changes in immigration policy prior to 1976 were effected largely through regulatory reform and characterized by case-by-case decision making, sometimes by the minister for immigration himself. A 1975 Canadian government document explained this approach by noting:

TABLE 4.1
IMMIGRATION TO CANADA, 1944–1991

Year	Immigrants Landed	Year	Immigrants Landed
1944	12,801	1968	183,974
1945	22,722	1969	161,531
1946	71,719	1970	147,713
1947	64,127	1971	121,900
1948	125,414	1972	122,006
1949	95,217	1973	184,200
1950	73,912	1974	218,465
1951	194,391	1975	187,881
1952	164,498	1976	149,429
1953	168,868	1977	114,914
1954	154,227	1978	86,313
1955	109,946	1979	112,096
1956	164,857	1980	143,117
1957	282,164	1981	128,618
1958	124,851	1982	121,147
1959	106,928	1983	89,157
1960	104,111	1984	88,239
1961	71,698	1985	77,510
1962	74,586	1986	92,590
1963	93,151	1987	152,751
1964	112,606	1988	161,929
1965	146,758	1989	192,001
1966	194,743	1990	214,230
1967	222,876	1991	229,730

Source: Canada Employment and Immigration Commission.

Governments have preferred to use regulations rather than statutes for expressing policies respect what classes of people might be admitted to Canada. Regulations can be changed relatively easily and quickly, and thus new policy can be implemented with a minimum of delay. The result has been a steady flow of new regulations over the years (from the government's "Green Paper" on immigration, quoted in Greenbaum 1976: 96).

The report might have added that the government occasionally worried about the Canadian public's reactions to what the government saw as necessary but politically controversial changes, and that regulatory reform offered a quiet way of introducing substantive changes in policy.

Starting in 1976 Canadian governments have made several legislative changes in immigration policy. The 1976 Immigration Act (which took effect in 1978) constituted a major overhaul of the illiberal 1952 act and established in law the principles of nondiscrimination and universality that had been introduced by regulation in 1967. The 1976 act's provisions for landed immigrants remained essentially intact until the adoption of Bill C-86 in 1992. The 1976 act reaffirmed Canada's role as a country of immigration and sought four analytically distinct but somewhat overlapping goals: economic growth, demographic growth, family unification, and humanitarianism.

The 1976 act did not set a limit on the number of immigrants or refugees who could be landed in Canada, so immigration officials were obliged to land all foreigners who met the selection criteria. The act did establish, however, that the Ministry of Immigration would set targets for the number of immigrants to be landed, and these should be made with demographic considerations in mind. As required since the act became law in 1978, the minister for immigration has tabled an "Annual Report to Parliament on Immigration Levels," which is the federal government's target after a consultative process that has involved provincial governments and interested parties. Table 4.2 summarizes the selection criteria presently employed by Canada for independent immigrants (Quebec's selection system, which operates under the Canada-Quebec Accord, has some differences though the objectives and outcomes are similar) (EIC 1992b: 12). Six of the characteristics appearing in table 4.2 (education, specific vocational preparation, experience, occupation, arranged employment, and knowledge of official languages) directly relate to Canada's labor force needs. One other (age) underscores Canada's interest in young workers. (A potential immigrant between the ages of twenty-one and forty-four received 10 points maximum; 2 points were deducted for each year under twenty-one and over forty-four.) From among these seven characteristics a young educated and skilled immigrant applicant with some experience and a knowledge of English or French could obtain a maximum of 80 points (70 constituting a pass mark for independent immigrants). Zero units in experience or occupation, moreover, would constitute an automatic processing bar except under unusual circumstances. The remaining 20 points were more directly related to administrative discretion by the immigration officer: 10 points assigned on the basis of personal suitability and 10 for levels control.

The selection criteria described in table 4.2 underwent some change between 1967 and 1985, including the addition and subtraction of additional economic considerations and changes in the weights assigned to each criterion. The 1976 act, for example, dropped the category of "nominated relative," which constituted a more distant relative of a Canadian resident who obtained admission at a lower pass mark for

TABLE 4.2
THE POINT SYSTEM FOR INDEPENDENT IMMIGRANTS

Factor	Units of Assessment	Notes
Education	12 maximum	
Specific vocational preparation	15 maximum	
Experience	8 maximum	0 units is an automatic processing bar unless (1) applicant has arranged employment and (2) employer accepts lack of experience
Occupation	10 maximum	0 units is an automatic processing bar unless applicant has arranged employment
Arranged employment	10	
Age	10 maximum	10 units if aged 21 to 44; 2 units deducted for each year under 21 or over 44
Knowledge of official language(s)	15 maximum	
Personal suitability	10 maximum	
Levels control	10 maximum	
Total	100	
Pass Mark	70	

economic criteria on the basis of family relations. In its place the act created the category of "assisted relatives"—persons who were not immediate relatives of Canadian residents and who also met labor force criteria. For example, under the 1976 act, brothers or sisters of Canadians and unmarried children over age twenty-one of parents in Canada could not become landed immigrants unless they met economic criteria (Hawkins 1988: 388; Matas 1989: 102).

Bill C-86 introduced one important new element in the admission of immigrants: an administrative "ceiling" for certain immigrant categories. The 1976 Immigration Act did not allow for much flexibility in adjusting the immigrant flow to planned levels. The law required the government to consider and process all immigrant applications received, regardless of the number already accepted in any given year (EIC 1992b: 15).

The new act created three streams for the differential treatment of applications depending on category and domestic circumstances (EIC 1992b: 16). Stream 1 will be processed on demand without limit; these include immediate family members of Canadian residents (spouses, dependent children, etc.), people found to be convention refugees by the Immigration and Refugee Board (IRB), and certain investors who could be expected to contribute significantly to Canada's economy. Stream 2 will be processed on a first-come, first-served basis with the total number set out in the annual immigration plan. Stream 2 applicants—such as parents, grandparents, and government- and privately sponsored refugee applicants for resettlement—will no longer be accepted once enough have been admitted to meet the annual target. People who have arranged employment or are self-employed, among others, would similarly not be accepted once target levels were reached. (As the C-86 "Briefing Book" explains, the intent of this section "is to be able to cut off authorizations once the domestic labour market becomes saturated" [Canada, House of Commons 1992].) Stream 3 will also be limited according to an annual plan. Stream 3 applicants include persons applying as independent immigrants, persons qualified in designated occupations (assuming no Canadian is available for the job), and entrepreneurs with business experience.

The 1976 act created a cumbersome procedure for refugee status determination. In the 1980s, as increasing numbers of refugee claimants began to arrive and petition for refugee status from within the country, the process broke down. A good many of these cases were considered to be "manifestly unfounded claims," i.e., persons who had not even a remote claim to refugee status and were abusing Canada's relatively open system for temporary admission of pending refugee claimants and taking advantage of its slow administrative procedures so as to remain in the country without a departure order. It is noteworthy that Canada has an adjudicative model of refugee determination. No person can be prevented from entering or be removed by a simple executive order; the claimant must remove himself or herself voluntarily or the claim must be adjudicated. Claimants had two opportunities to establish that they were refugees: at "determination" and at "redetermination." An adversarial process and long delays in status determination characterized the refugee process in the 1980s. By 1986 there was a backlog of 18,000 cases, and the number was growing rapidly. In 1986 the government established a number of special measures to clear the backlog, including a fast-track system of case review, a minister's permit system, and an administrative adjustment system that served as a quasi legalization (Hawkins 1988: 388; Matas 1989; 98, 140; author interviews with the Immigration and Refugee Board, September 1992).

In 1987 the government formally introduced legislation to address this problem, in the form of Bill C-55. The bill obtained royal assent in 1988 and went into effect as the Refugee Reform Act on January 1, 1989. In the meantime the refugee backlog had reached 95,000 cases by the end of 1988. Processing of backlogs was expected to be completed by the end of 1992 (author interviews, September 1992).

The Refugee Reform Act created a new institution—the Immigration Refugee Board—and a complex, multistage process of refugee determination that was somewhat modified in 1992 by C-86. In response to the perception that many refugee claimants were "manifestly unfounded," a claimant first went through a process to determine whether he or she had violated the Immigration Act. Next the claimant appeared at an initial hearing before a two-person panel, a "hearing within a hearing within a hearing" designed to screen out manifestly ineligible claimants. If determined to be ineligible, the applicant was ordered deported or given a departure notice; if either panelist approved, the applicant proceeded to a credible-basis hearing. Again the claimant appeared before a two-person panel; a positive ruling by one would be sufficient to establish that the applicant had a credible basis for claiming persecution in the convention refugee sense. A successful claimant proceeded to a full hearing, where two IRB members examined the claim; if one member approved, the person was accepted as a convention refugee and would then be required to apply for landed immigrant status. If both panelists rejected the claim, the applicant faced a departure or deportation order but could apply for leave to the Federal Court of Appeal. The court must give its permission before the appeal can be heard, and review could not address the merits but only matters of law and procedure (Matas 1989: 99–101; author interviews, September and November 1992).

Bill C-86, adopted in December 1992, removed the screening hearing because, by 1991, 95 percent of the applications were not manifestly unfounded claims. It also altered the balance so that, under some circumstances, two votes, rather than one, would be required to succeed to the next stage.

The final legislative change to be discussed is also the most curious. In July 1987 174 Sikhs arrived in Nova Scotia by boat after having been refused asylum in Europe. The government called Parliament into emergency session and enacted Bill C-84, the Refugee Deterrents and Detention Act. Bill C-84 was designed to give the government authority to detain refugees for seven days without review, to keep undocumented refugees in detention indefinitely, to turn back boatloads of refugees in Canadian waters, and to conduct forcible searches for evidence that a person in the country planned to help refugees come to Canada. Airlines could also be required to hold passports of would-be refugees (Matas 1989: 98, 140; author interviews, September and November 1992). By responding to the arrival of the Sikhs in this manner, the Canadian government clearly demonstrated that it—not unlike some European countries at the time—feared the arrival of an overwhelming number of undocumented refugee claimants.

Notwithstanding this particular illiberal response and the difficulties the government has had with in-country processing of refugee claims, Canada's immigration control problems have not been comparatively large. Moreover, though Canada has not demonstrated an unqualified acceptance of refugee claimants, it has remained relatively open to immigrants and refugees. Landings dropped during the 1970s and early 1980s below the levels recorded in the 1950s, but throughout the postwar period Canada has admitted between 0.5 percent and 1.0 percent of its population as immigrants and refugees (see table 4.3). This is especially remarkable considering that, since the 1960s, immigration (and refugee) streams have shifted from Europe and the United States to Asia and the rest of the Third World. This shift was evident as early as the mid-1970s, when Freda Hawkins noted that "Canada is already a multiracial society and becoming more of one" (1976: 56). In 1956–1961 Europeans comprised 86 percent of the immigrants admitted, and Asians 2.7 percent. By 1972 the proportions were 42 percent and 21 percent, respectively (Boyd 1976: 89). By 1991, 97,000 immigrant landings (42 percent of total) originated in Asia and the Pacific region, 18 percent in Africa and the Middle East, and 16 percent in Central and South America. Europe and the United States provided the remaining 24 percent (EIC 1992a: 5). Given these relatively high levels of immigration and Canada's declining fertility, it is not surprising that the population of English or French ethnic origin has also been in steady decline.

TABLE 4.3
IMMIGRANT FLOWS AND STOCKS RELATIVE TO
CANADA'S TOTAL POPULATION

Flow Interval	Landed Immigrants (Annual Average) (1)	Population at Mid-interval ('000s)		Foreign-born as % Pop. $(4) = (3) \times 100 / (2)$	Immigrants Landed as % Pop. $(5) = (1) \times 100 / (2)$
		Total (2)	Foreign-born (3)		
1944–48	59,357	12,292			0.5
1949–53	139,377	14,009	2,060	15	1.0
1954–58	167,209	16,081			1.0
1959–63	90,095	18,238	2,844	16	0.5
1964–68	172,191	20,015			0.9
1969–73	147,470	21,569	3,295	15	0.7
1974–78	151,400	22,993			0.7
1979–83	118,827	24,343	3,867	16	0.5
1984–88	114,604	25,309			0.5
1989–91	211,987	27,297			0.8

Sources: Employment and Immigration Canada; Statistics Canada.

Notes: Population at mid-interval corresponds to the census year in the middle of the five-year interval or end of single three-year interval (1989–91).

Newfoundland included in population totals starting in 1951; in 1951 Newfoundland's population was 361,000.

The 1991–1995 Immigration Plan proposed specific targets by immigrant category by year, for a total number of 250,000 planned landings for each year between 1992 and 1995 (see table 4.4). The plan envisions an initial rise in family class immigrants in 1992 and then a decline to an annual level similar to that experienced in 1991. It also envisions higher levels of refugee resettlement than actually experienced in 1991, though lower than initially planned for that year. It also plans for 25,000 refugees landed in Canada each year—nearly 15,000 more than actually landed in 1991. The plan reflects an expectation of moderate growth in the number of independent immigrants, assisted relatives, and business immigrants. Canada, therefore, expects continuing high levels of immigration and only moderate growth in some immigrant categories.

TABLE 4.4
THE 1991–1995 IMMIGRATION PLAN

Component	Planned 1991	Actual 1991	Planned 1992	1993	1994	1995
Family Class	80,000	84,123	100,000	95,000	85,000	85,000
Refugees						
Government-assisted refugees and members of designated classes (selected abroad)	13,000	7,666	13,000	13,000	13,000	13,000
Privately sponsored refugees and members of designated classes (selected abroad)	23,500	17,335	20,000	20,000	15,000	15,000
Refugees landed in Canada (after Jan. 1, 1989)	10,000	10,354	25,000	25,000	25,000	25,000
Independent Immigrants						
Principal applicants	20,000	24,283	21,500	22,500	29,000	29,000
Spouses and other accompanying dependents	21,000	18,872	20,000	25,000	33,000	33,000
Assisted Relatives						
Principal applicants	7,000	7,896	7,000	8,500	11,500	11,500
Spouses and other accompanying dependents	12,500	13,961	12,500	15,000	19,000	19,000
Business Immigrants						
Principal applicants	7,000	4,293	7,000	6,500	5,000	5,000
Spouses and other accompanying dependents	21,000	12,707	21,000	19,500	14,500	14,500
Retirees	5,000	4,204	3,000	0	0	0
Total	220,000	205,694	250,000	250,000	250,000	250,000

Flexible Responses toward "Illegal Immigration"

For much of the past two decades Canadians have wondered whether they had a problem of "illegal immigrants." They have not been immune to the debates in the United States, reproduced in the Canadian media, over how to respond to the massive influx across the U.S.-Mexican border and, more recently, over the interdiction of Haitians arriving on U.S. shores by boat. Canadian officials have been quite aware that some illegal entrants to the United States actually have entered across the land border from Canadian territory. Not surprisingly, some public reactions to the presence of unauthorized immigrants living in Canada have sounded like echoes from the United States: complaints about immigrants taking away jobs or obtaining access to Canada's generous social welfare system, for example. Similarly, Canadian officials have followed U.S. developments closely. The government adopted a legalization program in 1973 and an employer sanctions law that penalizes the knowing employment of unauthorized foreigners, and it has tried to anticipate the possibility that large numbers of "illegal immigrants" might be present. As one astute observer noted, any country that experienced so high a level of legal immigration "is bound to experience a certain level of illegal migration." This observer added: "However, it appears that Canada has not experienced the degree of seriousness of illegal immigration which other immigrant-receiving countries have" (Robinson 1983: 29).

Canada's first postwar experience with the large-scale arrival of foreigners out of status occurred quite openly in the early 1970s and escalated rapidly until brought under control by the Trudeau government. This was a direct result of a feature of the 1967 regulatory reforms and the functioning of the new Immigration Appeal Board. Section 34 of the 1967 immigration regulations permitted temporary visitors to apply for landed immigrant status after their arrival in Canada and, if denied, to invoke broad grounds of appeal.

> Word spread out that the best way to get into Canada was simply to come, apply for landed immigrant status, and, if refused, submit an appeal to the new Immigration Appeal Board. An appeal would take time, particularly if many visitors were applying, and this would give a would-be immigrant time to settle in, find a job, and perhaps start a family, which would lessen the chances of deportation (Hawkins 1988: 387).

In 1970, 45,000 visitors arrived in Canada and applied for landed immigrant status; the number increased steadily through 1972. In November 1972 Section 34 of the 1967 Immigration Regulations was revoked by the Liberal government. By the end of May 1973 the

Immigration Appeal Board had a backlog of 17,472 cases and was handling only about 100 cases a month. That summer, the minister of manpower and immigration announced a sixty-day "adjustment of status programme," which would allow migrants to regularize who had been in Canada continuously since November 30, 1972. When Project 97, as the program came to be known, ended in October 1973, about 39,000 persons from more than 150 countries had obtained landed immigrant status. When one adds the number of cases adjudicated by the board and those regularized through earlier administrative measures, Canada legalized about 52,000 immigrants (Hawkins 1988: 387–88).

The events that culminated in Project 97 underscore several features characteristic of Canada's immigration crises, when these have occurred. First, the crisis itself was the unintended consequence of a Canadian policy change—of government error—and not obviously the result of structural labor market forces or an expanding underground economy. Second, it was possible to resolve the crisis with a new administrative procedure. Third, it was the ready availability of a broad appeals procedure and the inability of the Canadian system, utilizing rules of due process, to adjudicate cases quickly that contributed directly to the crisis. Fourth, although the public and government both perceived this to constitute a "crisis" situation, the number of people involved—a demographic measure of the dimensions of the crisis—suggests that in 1973 Canada still had a broad range of possible policy options available. Even though fewer applicants for legalization came forward than had been anticipated, a relatively open amnesty program of the type implemented in 1973 would not have been so easy to adopt if the potential number of out-of-status migrants had been a million or more. Finally, though the adjudicative machinery was slow and cumbersome, the political administration was able to respond in a manner that was widely perceived to be flexible, rapid, and effective.

In the summer of 1982 the Canadian government again asked itself whether there might not be a significant illegal immigrant population residing in the country. In December it announced policy proposals to establish a new legalization program and to strengthen employer sanctions by making penalties applicable even when an employer would have *unknowingly* hired an unauthorized foreigner. Also in December, Minister of Employment and Immigration Lloyd Axworthy appointed W.G. Robinson, a barrister and solicitor from Vancouver, to prepare a report on illegal migrants. Robinson held extensive consultations with Canadian immigrant groups, lawyers, public officials, employers, and ordinary citizens with opinions to share regarding the government's proposals. His report, issued six months later (Robinson 1983; see also Robinson 1984), approached the problem in a manner not unlike that of the U.S. Select Commission on Immigration and Refugee Policy, which had focused its attention on illegal migration to the United States in a report completed in 1981. Robinson's report, however, concluded that the problem of illegal migrants in Canada was not one "of serious proportions" (p. xiii). Accordingly, he recommended against "unconditional amnesty" (advocating instead that the Ministry of Employment and Immigration handle claims on a case-by-case basis) and against any change in the employer sanctions law.

Even if one accepts as plausible Robinson's conclusion that Canada did not have an illegal migrant problem of crisis proportions, the analysis contained in this report is worth discussing because it underscores some of the potential difficulties that Canada has in controlling unwanted immigration. Though Canada has not experienced a massive influx of illegal entrants, this is not because Canada's immigration control system is illiberal or draconian. Robinson discovered in preparing his report that most unauthorized immigrants in Canada did not come across the land border with the United States—in large part, perhaps, because such immigrants are more likely to remain in the United States than to seek to enter Canada. The vast majority of deportable foreigners in Canada entered as visitors, and the government therefore has a record of their arrivals and destinations. Monitoring the departure of visitors to ascertain who might have overstayed, however, was (and is) a surprisingly difficult proposition. The volume of traffic across the land border with the United States would cause extraordinary delays if border crossers were required to document their departures as well as their entries. Moreover, even if this practice were instituted, given that the number of persons entering without inspection into the United States from Canada is assumed to be larger than the number entering Canada without inspection, a significant number of the apparent overstayers would in fact have departed and would have been illegally in the United States, not Canada. Robinson did recommend testing different border control procedures, but his lack of enthusiasm was palpable.

Similarly, obstacles arose to the idea that immigration enforcement should become more aggressive and "proactive." Robinson noted that the investigation of foreigners for removal is conducted in a "reactive" fashion—in response to tips from informers and from local police agencies. The random searching of places where illegal migrants might work or congregate was considered by many of those consulted to be discriminatory, problematic, and possibly illegal. Immigration officers, Robinson noted, do not have powers of search and seizure. Individuals have no legal obligation to cooperate with immigration officers, nor can immigration officers compel employers to produce personnel records of employees. "In weighing possible legislative encroachments upon the freedom of individual Canadians," Robinson wrote, "it is customary to ask whether the evil is so great as to warrant such a far-reaching response" (1983: 91).

Canada's employer sanctions law was recognized to be ineffective, but Robinson did not recommend that it be changed. Section 97 of the Immigration Act makes it unlawful for an employer to *knowingly engage* in the employment of any person other than Canadian citizens or permanent residents or other foreigners authorized to work. Employers are considered to have knowledge where "exercise of reasonable diligence" would have provided it. The maximum penalty for violating these sanctions was Can$5,000 and a two-year term of imprisonment. In practice, however, courts imposed fines of Can$75–$500. In any given year between 1979 and 1982 no more than sixty cases were prosecuted. The low frequency of prosecutions has several explanations: (1) it was difficult to demonstrate employer knowledge; (2) there was difficulty getting witnesses (the unauthorized foreign worker was usually the most important witness at the trial); and (3) the minimal sentences applied led prosecutors to conclude that "the deterrent effect is not worth the time, cost and effort" (Robinson 1983: 94).

These difficulties appeared notwithstanding the use of Canada's social insurance number (SIN), which in principle should have allowed employers to screen unauthorized workers. A card beginning with a "9" was meant to alert employers that there could be restrictions on the holder's authority to be employed. Many unauthorized workers, however, were found to have used their own cards, others used fictitious numbers, and still others obtained employment without ever having to show a card or provide a number (Robinson 1983: 97).

It is tempting to argue that in 1983 the government responded to the problem of illegal immigration simply by declaring that it did not exist. Some, like the Canadian Bar Association (CBA), argued in their brief to Robinson that "illegal immigration indeed represents a serious problem." However, what the CBA meant by a serious problem was not what had moved the minister to launch the study and entertain proposals for mass legalization and strengthened employer sanctions. The CBA noted that immigration offices had difficulty in coping with the number of persons out of status who came forward voluntarily and who "routinely wait months before an inquiry is scheduled" (CBA 1983: A17). But although adjudicative inquiries seem to be a major weakness in the Canadian immigration system for out-of-status applicants as well as for refugee claimants, it is clear that Canadian enforcement had not uncovered evidence of a large population of deportable foreigners, nor has it since then (author interviews, September 1992).

Canada, however, does not yet have the means to determine the size of its out-of-status population. Several indicators suggest that it is small and not problematic. Many out-of-status persons detected in 1983, for example, were long-term residents; some would have qualified for the

1973 legalization but had not applied. A large proportion of detected migrants had long-standing relations with relatives in Canada. Indeed, the major cause cited for unauthorized immigration was not employer demand for an exploitable labor force; it was the obstacles that Canadian law places on relatives who are not members of a Canadian resident's immediate family. This appeared to be the major explanation for foreigners being out of status in Canada, notwithstanding evidence that some illegal migrants are employed in exploitative conditions (Robinson 1983: 18).

The possible characterization of Canada's illegal immigrant problem as serious depends to an inordinate degree, therefore, upon informed speculation rather than data. Perception constitutes the basis for determining whether the matter is serious enough to warrant a policy response. What is at stake is evidently something other than the dimensions of a problem in some objective sense, measurable in numbers of migrants or a magnitude of impact. The government's concern with the legitimacy of public institutions was articulated as a source of worry over illegal migration. Robinson noted that the problem may not be of crisis proportions, but "if a 'tolerable limit' is exceeded, our laws will be in danger of losing general public acceptance and respect" (Robinson 1983: 18).

Toward Refugee Control

"Illegal immigration" of the type found in modern industrial societies—associated with a growing labor demand for unskilled workers and an underground economy—has not been a significant issue in Canada. And while this perhaps has facilitated rapidity and flexibility in Canada's policy responses, the opposite has been the case in the realm of refugee determination. The problem has not been with refugee resettlement, in which would-be refugees who meet both refugee and immigration criteria are selected abroad. The area in which Canada's immigration control problems most resemble those of other liberal democratic states is in the inland asylum processing of refugee claimants.

Refugees have been a small but always present component of immigration flows to Canada. Canada landed about 400,000 refugees under special programs between 1947 and 1988, and over 100,000 as part of its ongoing admissions process between 1960 and 1988 (Adelman 1990: 41). The most notable of these flows were displaced Europeans (1947–1952), Hungarians (1956–1957), Czechs (1968–1969), Chileans (1973), Vietnamese and Cambodians (1975–1978), Indochinese (1979–1982), and Poles (1982–1985). Inland processing of asylum claimants was virtually unheard of before 1980. Canada only received 500 such claims in 1977, but the number grew quickly to 6,100 in 1983 (Hawkins 1988:

388). In part due to the cumbersome nature of the refugee determination process, the number of pending claims began to accumulate and the number of refugee claimants arriving, some of them without foundation, rose steadily. By the mid-1980s the refugee admission system had become a matter of political controversy. When a boatload of Sikhs arrived in 1987, the stage was set for the illiberal response that followed (Bill C-84, the Refugee Deterrents and Detention Act).

A detailed examination of the sources of the backlogs and of the breakdown of the Canadian refugee processing system during the 1980s is not warranted here. It is important to note, however, that whatever the shortcomings of the Canadian processing system, it was designed with liberal principles in mind. It reflects vividly how, in James Hollifield's phrase, "simple constitutional protections [such] as equality before the law and due process act as constraints on the capacity of liberal states to regulate migration" (1992: 575). This is not to argue that the Canadian system is too generous to refugee claimants. Nor is it to suggest that the crisis was entirely of the government's own making—though David Matas and others have shown how the abuse of the minister's permit system may have encouraged a flow of unfounded claimants (Matas 1989: 94–96). In large part, it is Canada's self-definition as a liberal democratic state that has made it inflexible in responding to refugee flows. Two different aspects of the Canadian context—a case-by-case adjudicative model of refugee claims processing, and a changing rights regime within Canada resulting from the adoption of the Charter of Rights and Freedoms in 1982—have made it difficult for Canada to cope with inland refugee claims.

The adjudicative process was created as an extension of immigration appeals established with the Immigration Appeal Board in 1967. Tom Kent, one of the founders of this change who was deputy minister of immigration at the time, later conceded that in practice the appeal procedure had turned out to be "extremely clumsy." But the motivation for moving away from a discretionary procedure in which individual cases were handled by the Ministry was clear. An appeals procedure was completely absent until 1967, Kent recalled. "We civilized the process" (Kent 1988: 9).

In 1985 the Canadian Supreme Court declared unconstitutional the "redetermination" provisions of the 1976 Immigration Act in a landmark case known as *Singh et al. v. Minister of Employment and Immigration* (Hathaway 1991: 83). The case was decided on both Charter and Bill of Rights dimensions, and it linked a procedural protection—the right to an oral hearing—to a substantive right—a refugee cannot lawfully be removed from Canada to a country where his or her life or freedom would be threatened. One of the justices argued that "fundamental justice requires an oral hearing, 'where a serious issue of credibility is involved'; and, by implication, where there is a direct connection between that issue and a decision affecting life, liberty and the security of the person, within the meaning of section 7 [of the Charter]" (Law Reform Commission 1991: 27). Another justice cited the Canadian Bill of Rights and agreed with the outcome on the basis of a right to a fair hearing "in accordance with the principles of fundamental justice" (Law Reform Commission 1991: 27).

The practical effects of this were that the procedures for adjudicating claims had to be amended, and Bill C-55 was in part promoted for this purpose. One empirical study of the adjudication of claims after Bill C-55 went into effect noted that the practical influence of the *Singh* decision and a quasi-judicial process could be observed "at *every* level of determination" (Law Reform Commission 1991: 28–29, emphasis in original). Moreover, quite apart from the effects of *Singh*, the process was designed to open opportunities for appeals at several points, although leave for appeal is discretionary and in principle is granted only when there is a serious possibility of error. Nevertheless, "in practice refugee cases appear to hold a fatal attraction for review courts, and their differences with decision-making panels turn frequently on subtle variations in inference" (Law Reform Commission 1991: 28–29).

It was noted earlier that the procedure employed under the 1976 Immigration Act had resulted in 95,000 backlogged cases by the time Bill C-55 took effect on January 1, 1989. The new procedure administered by the IRB has not avoided creating additional backlogs. During the first two years of the new procedure's implementation (1989–1990), 58,000 inland claims for refugee determination were received. Only 34,000 of these had gotten as far as the initial hearing by January 1991, and 21,000 (or about one-third) had completed the full hearing stage (author interviews, September 1992).

The recognition that the new procedure resulted in a costly process led in part to the reforms sought in Bill C-86. Typically, refugee claim-ants receive welfare and assistance from provincial social services until they obtain permission to work, which often occurs after the credible-basis hearing has been completed successfully. Rapidly processed claims took six–twelve months to complete; some claimants have waited as long as twenty-four months to be landed, "provided the case does not run into complications" (EIC 1992b: 22–23). The cost of each rejected refugee claim—which are the ones that get protracted the longest—is estimated at Can$30,000–$50,000 (EIC 1992b: 18).

Other aspects of the C-86 reform bill relating to refugees sought to reduce access to certain categories of refugee claimants. The bill strengthened provisions that had been adopted in C-55, but not yet implemented, regarding the return of claimants to what are known as "safe third countries." If a claimant traversed or sojourned in a "safe" country en route to Canada—as is often the case, given Canada's geographic location—Canada could send the claimant back to that country and deny the individual access to the refugee system. As Howard Adelman notes, "[the] provision is intended to place the total refugee burden on those countries that are most accessible to refugees in flight" (1992: 2). One of the key issues here is whether the United States is a "safe country" for Salvadorans, for example, or the United Kingdom for Sri Lankans (Matas 1989: 294–95). Another aspect was the seeking of bilateral agreements with other refugee-receiving countries to share the responsibility for assessing refugee claims and to reduce "asylum shopping"—the tendency of individuals to file a claim for asylum in more than one country at a time. Canada sought and recently obtained such an agreement with the United States. This has been of particular interest to the Canadians because almost one-third of those claiming refugee status in Canada arrive through the United States, some with bona fide U.S. visitor visas (EIC 1992b: 22).

Though Canada's refugee system is relatively open by global standards and its refugee acceptance rates are among the world's highest, like the rest of the world Canada has been moving in the direction of narrowing the door through which refugee claimants can enter. Some observers have criticized this as an abandonment of Canada's international obligations. Others have noted that Canada's refugee policy seems to be "an expensive and elaborate process for those few that make it past the barriers, and a refusal [to consider a refugee application] for the rest" (author interviews, September and November 1992). Given that about half of Canada's refugees in the 1990s are expected to be inland asylum seekers, the issues posed by an inflexible administration and the perceived need for control are only likely to become more acute.

Conclusions

Canada's postwar immigration and refugee policies reveal a fluctuating pattern of opening and closing. On the one hand, overall levels of immigration have risen somewhat, though they have not surpassed the 1 percent immigration intake per population level established in the 1950s. Simultaneously, Canada has become much more open to immigration from parts of the world other than Europe and the United States. And although its acceptance of asylum applicants is not as high in per capita terms as some European countries, Canada has remained relatively open to refugees. On the other hand, procedures for getting access to Canada as an asylee have tightened, and some government pronouncements (and legislation, such as C-84) have conveyed to the Canadian public the impression that there is widespread abuse in the refugee determination system and an urgent need to scrutinize each new refugee claimant more strictly.

For the most part immigration policy changes since 1962 have strongly reaffirmed Canada's commitment to principles of non-discrimination, due process, natural justice, and the rule of law. This commitment has not always been made easily, and both litigation and adverse court decisions have played important roles. Moreover, Canada's relative openness to immigration usually has been accompanied by an interest in selecting immigrants in a manner that serves national economic and demographic purposes. In the one area where newcomers are landed as a matter of right—convention refugees—the process is adjudicative and complex. Canada thus has tried to steer a middle course in which a relatively large number of immigrants and refugees are admitted—but in a manner consistent with the principles of a liberal democratic state and the political realities imposed by immigration controversies.

Canada's geography and economy have been helpful. Except for those instances, such as during the Vietnam War, when the United States itself has generated a significant number of persons seeking to escape violence, Canada has been isolated from principal sources of refugee flows. Many illegal immigrants who arrive in Canadian territory are motivated to go to the United States rather than to remain in Canada. The relatively large flows of landed immigrants, including lower-skilled assisted relatives and refugees, have apparently been sufficient to meet Canada's demand for low-skilled labor. Its population of out-of-status foreigners has rarely been large enough to cause concern, even though Canada's procedures to reduce access to the labor market are inadequate. An examination of the difficulties with employer sanctions in Canada suggests that, were it to attract a large number of illegal immigrants, Canada would face political and administrative difficulties not unlike those prevailing in the United States, even if most of the flow still consisted of visitors who overstayed their permits.

The Canadian government has characterized its own initiatives to control the access of refugees as an attempt to "manage" immigration. This is one way that a liberal democratic state may seek to justify its need to exercise control. Though some of those initiatives suggest that Canada is backing away from liberal principles, it is noteworthy that the burden of the argument still seems to fall on those who would close the system to newcomers, rather than on those who would seek to keep it relatively open.

References

Adelman, Howard. 1990. *A Survey of Post War Refugee Intakes and Developments in Canadian Refugee Policy*. Toronto: Center for Refugee Studies, York University.
———. 1992. "Processing Bill C-86," *Refuge* 12 (July): 1–2.

Boyd, Monica. 1976. "Immigration Policy and Trends: A Comparison of Canada and the United States," *Demography* 13 (February): 83–104.

Canada. House of Commons. 1947. *Official Report of the Debates.* 3rd sess., 20th Parliament, vol. 3. Ottawa: Controller of Stationery.

———. 1992. "Clause by Clause Briefing Book; Bill C-86: An Act to Amend the Immigration Act and Other Acts in Consequence Thereof." 2 vols. Ottawa: Controller of Stationery. Mimeo.

CBA (Canadian Bar Association). 1983. "Submission to W.G. Robinson." In *Illegal Migrants in Canada; A Report to the Honourable Lloyd Axworthy, Minister of Employment and Immigration.* Ottawa: Employment and Immigration Canada.

EIC (Employment and Immigration Canada). 1992a. "Analysis of Immigrant Landings; January–December 1989, 1990, 1991." Ottawa: Strategic Analysis, Strategic Planning and Research Directorate, EIC, July. Mimeo.

———. 1992b. *Managing Immigration: A Framework for the 1990s.* Ottawa: EIC, June.

Greenbaum, Donald M. 1976. "Selection and Control." In *Immigration: Policy-making Process and Results; Processus d'élaboration de la politique et résultats,* edited by Bernard Bonin. Toronto: Institute of Public Administration of Canada.

Hathaway, James C. 1991. *The Law of Refugee Status.* Toronto: Butterworths.

Hawkins, Freda. 1976. "Dilemmas in Immigration Policy-making: The Problems of Choice, Political Will and Administrative Capacity." In *Immigration: Policy-making Process and Results; Processus d'élaboration de la politique et résultats,* edited by Bernard Bonin. Toronto: Institute of Public Administration of Canada.

———. 1988. *Canada and Immigration; Public Policy and Public Concern.* 2d ed. Kingston: McGill-Queen's University Press.

Hollifield, James F. 1992. "Migration and International Relations: Cooperation and Control in the European Community," *International Migration Review* 26 (Summer): 568–95.

Kent, Tom. 1988. "Immigration Issues: A Personal Perspective." In *Policy Forum on the Role of Immigration in Canada's Future.* Kingston: John Deutsch Institute for the Study of Economic Policy.

Law Reform Commission of Canada. 1991. "The Determination of Refugee Status in Canada: A Review of the Procedure." Ottawa: The Commission, February. Mimeo.

Matas, David (with Ilana Simon). 1989. *Closing the Doors: The Failure of Refugee Protection.* Toronto: Summerhill.

Robinson, W. G. 1983. *Illegal Migrants in Canada; A Report to the Honourable Lloyd Axworthy, Minister of Employment and Immigration.* Ottawa: Employment and Immigration Canada.

———. 1984. "Illegal Immigrants in Canada: Recent Developments," *International Migration Review* 18 (Fall): 474–85.

PART III

RELUCTANT COUNTRIES
OF IMMIGRATION:
FRANCE, GERMANY, BELGIUM,
AND BRITAIN

5

Immigration and Republicanism in France: The Hidden Consensus

James F. Hollifield

Introduction

From the perspective of the 1980s, which saw the rise in France of a powerful anti-immigrant political movement, the "Front National," immigration in postwar France might appear to be raging out of control. It is true that French immigration policy has undergone many twists and turns—especially since 1974, when France (like many of her European neighbors) attempted to stop immigration—and immigration has become a focal point of social conflict and partisan politics. Yet the underlying principles, as well as the outcomes, of immigration policy have shown remarkable consistency. Despite the suspension of legal worker immigration in 1974, the xenophobic rhetoric of politicians like Jean-Marie Le Pen, and the restrictionist policies adopted by various governments in the 1980s and 1990s, France has remained relatively open to immigration, a tradition that dates to the middle of the last century. Annual levels of immigration have not fallen below 100,000 per year since the early 1950s, and the right to asylum has been respected by every postwar government. In addition, France has maintained one of the most liberal naturalization policies in Western Europe despite repeated assaults during the last two decades, especially since May 1993, when the government of Edouard Balladur launched a series of reforms to roll back some of the rights of foreigners and to tighten naturalization policy.

The author wishes to acknowledge the support of the Centre d'Études et de Recherches Internationales of the FNSP in Paris. Comments on an earlier version of this paper by Miriam Feldblum, Mark Miller, Martin Schain, Georges Tapinos, Claude-Valentin Marie, and Patrick Weil are greatly appreciated.

How can we explain the continuity of France's immigration policy and outcomes in the midst of controversy and almost constant crisis? Has France in the past thirty years lost control over the entry of foreign nationals into its territory, as many politicians and pundits suggest? Is there a crisis of immigration control in France today? The continuity in both the principles and the results of French immigration policy is closely linked to the power of what some historians and other analysts have referred to as the "republican synthesis."[1] This is a reference to a particular phase of French political development, most closely associated with the twenty years or so preceding World War I, when many of the universalist and republican principles of the French Revolution gained the legitimacy they had lacked in previous periods of French history. The last decade of the nineteenth century saw the victory of republicans over royalists; the final separation of church and state and the triumph of secular authority; and, most importantly, the application of the principles of due process and equality before the law, with the vindication of Captain Dreyfus. Republicanism became a powerful political ideology, linking key elements of the liberal Catholic right and the radical (or radical socialist) left, in effect forging a new consensus among political elites. Although these forces for political change quarreled and fell into disrepute during the turbulent interwar years (leading historians to their first diagnosis of *le mal français*), the republican synthesis (and the elite consensus that it spawned) remained strong enough to carry France through the dark years of the 1930s and 1940s.

Throughout this crucial period of modern French history (roughly 1890 to 1940), France was rapidly becoming a *country* (if not a *nation*) of immigrants. The distinction between a country and a nation of immigrants is crucial, because state building and nationhood in France preceded the intensive periods of immigration (the French nation-state was formed in the crucible of absolutism during the ancien régime, at the time of the French kings, eventuating in the French Revolution in 1789). Immigration did not play a significant role in the historical process of building the French nation-state, as it did, for example, in the United States, Canada, and Australia—all clearly nations of immigrants. In the case of the United States, immigration constitutes what Alexis de Tocqueville referred to as a "founding myth" of the nation, despite the numerous episodes of nativism and restrictionist politics that occurred in the course of American history. By comparison with the United States, immigration has not played the

---

[1] Perhaps one of the best accounts of the impact of republicanism on French political development is the introductory essay in Hoffman 1963. On the triumph of republicanism, see Cobban 1961: 225–59. For a powerful account of the impact of the republican model on French immigration policy, see Patrick Weil's seminal work (1991).

role of "founding myth" in the history of the French nation.[2] This relationship between immigration and nation building is absolutely crucial in enabling liberal democratic and republican states to control immigration and make immigration policy. The argument made here is that the more closely associated immigration is with the political myths that legitimate and give life to the regime, the easier it is for the state to justify its immigration and refugee policies and to manage the ethnic or distributional conflicts that often arise as a result of immigration.

As a cornerstone of French political and legal culture, republicanism has played a vital role in the country's history of immigration and refugee policy. Immigration accelerated in France during the latter decades of the nineteenth century. It was associated not only with the triumph of republicanism—a form of left-wing, rights-based politics—but also with the takeoff of French capitalism, which was late and slow by comparison with the cases of Britain or Germany. To sustain the surge in economic growth during the belle époque (or, as Hobsbawm called it, "the age of capital"), French industrialists needed access to additional supplies of labor, which they had great difficulty finding at home. The reasons for labor shortages in the early decades of twentieth-century France relate primarily to sociodemographic patterns of development. French population growth slowed dramatically during the first half of the nineteenth century and never really recovered until the post-World War II period (see Spengler 1979; Sauvy 1950). This anemic population growth—together with the sedentary nature of French peasant farmers, who resisted market pressures to leave their relatively comfortable family farms—created labor shortages in such important industrial sectors as mining and steel. These shortages set the stage for a rise in immigration in the late nineteenth and early twentieth centuries.

The Demographic and Republican Nexus

Immigration in modern France is closely linked to three factors: slow population growth, the pattern and timing of industrialization, and political changes associated with the rise of republicanism and colonialism. Immigration started in earnest following the revolutions of 1848 and rose steadily during the Second Empire, intensifying during the early republican period (1870–1890) and on toward the turn of the century and the belle époque. France did not experience a rural exodus, such as occurred in England at the time of the enclosure movements in the eighteenth century, or in nineteenth-century Germany with the libera-

---

[2]On the role of immigration in French history, see Noiriel 1988; Noiriel and Horowitz 1992. For a discussion of the relationship between immigration and American political myths, see Fuchs 1990. And for an excellent historical account of the role of immigration in the creation of an American identity, see Archdeacon 1983.

tion of the serfs in East Prussia and a westward movement of German labor into the industrial regions of the Rhineland. French capitalists were therefore forced to invent a working class. While there were many misgivings about the influx of foreign labor in France during the Third Republic, most of these immigrants were coming from culturally compatible neighboring countries, two of which—Belgium and Switzerland—were in part French speaking. By 1900, the bulk of foreign labor was coming from Belgium and Germany; but by the 1920s the primary sending countries were Italy and Poland (see Bonnet 1976; Schor 1985).

The pattern of private recruitment of immigrant labor by industry, with very little state control, was repeated during the interwar and postwar years. The historical pattern of immigration in France has been for the private sector to organize the recruitment of foreign labor, which then accelerates to the point that the state is compelled to step in to try to regain control. Immigration during the early decades of the twentieth century was *organized but uncontrolled*, and the republican model served primarily to integrate newcomers, turning immigrant workers from neighboring European countries into French citizens, just as French peasants had been socialized into a modern, republican culture (via public schools and the army) two or three generations earlier (see Braudel 1986; Berger 1972).

During World War I, the French state took the first halting steps to assert control over the immigrant population, through the establishment of national identity cards. The historian Gérard Noiriel attaches great importance to this period, which saw the beginning of a French system of immigration and population control. The state tried to create a national/legal identity for vast segments of the population, native as well as foreign (Noiriel 1988).

Immediately following World War I, however, French industry once again faced labor shortages because of the war's crippling effects on the French population. In the early 1920s two major forces emerged that would influence thinking about French immigration policy—and especially issues of control—well into the post-World War II period. The first force was French business, or employers, who created the General Immigration Society (SGI), a private organization which, with the blessings of the divided and stalemated governments of the 1920s, took as its mission to organize the recruitment and placement of immigrant (primarily Italian) labor. The second force in French immigration policy, which was less noticeable but no less powerful in its influence, was the National Alliance for Increasing the French Population, basically a pronatalist lobbying group, long active in Third Republic politics. This organization's influence extended well beyond its rather narrow focus on French birthrates and family and population issues. While employers were interested in securing an unlimited supply of cheap, foreign labor, the pronatalists were inspired by nationalist, political motives.

We should not underestimate the strength of the demographic, pronatalist lobby in the history of French immigration policy. The pronatalism of the Third Republic (which was discredited somewhat when some members collaborated with the racist and ethno-nationalist policies of the Vichy regime) was rather easily transformed into the *populationnisme* of the Fourth and Fifth Republics (see Teitelbaum and Winter 1985; Weil 1991; Hollifield 1992: 51–58). The pronatalist movement emerged relatively unscathed from the experiences of defeat, occupation, and liberation, and its members embraced the new nationalist/ republican ideals of the postwar leaders. Beginning with the provisional Tripartite Government, the *populationnistes* took immigration as one of their primary concerns. Immigration also provided a new rallying cry during the 1945–1950 period, when population policies were still viewed with suspicion because of their association with eugenics, *pétainisme*, and fascism. The thrust of the populationists' immigration policies was outlined in the first issue of the French demographic journal *Population*, by its founder, Alfred Sauvy (1950). Sauvy made a case for the large-scale recruitment of immigrant workers and their families from the culturally compatible Southern European, Catholic populations of Italy, Spain, and Portugal. Sauvy argued that such a strategy would give the French population (and by extension the economy) a fighting chance to catch up with more powerful European competitors and adversaries, primarily Germany and Britain. By imposing a kind of national origins quota to select for culturally compatible immigrants, the injection of a new stock of foreign population (and human capital) could be accomplished with minimal impact on French society and culture. Moreover, the French already had considerable experience with the importation of Italian labor, and Spain was viewed as a logical partner in this enterprise because of the long-standing traditions of exchange between the two Catholic countries.

In Charles de Gaulle the *populationnistes* gained a powerful ally in their attempts to shape postwar French immigration policy. De Gaulle took a personal interest in the problems of population decline and thereby helped to rehabilitate the old Third Republic lobby. As leader of the Tripartite Government, de Gaulle promoted national reconciliation in order to move quickly to reconstruct the French economy and set in motion the large-scale industrialization that powerful political and economic factions had blocked during the Third Republic. The thinking of the Gaullist reformers (including Jean Monnet, who was to head the newly created National Planning Agency) was that all necessary resources should be mobilized to set the economy on a new path, and that this should be done quickly to take advantage of the political honeymoon between business and government in the wake of liberation. The social and political stalemate of the Third Republic was broken, at least temporarily, and the old obstructionist, anti-industrial, and anticapitalist French right was discredited by virtue of the Vichy experience. Now was the time for "liberal" and republican reformers to strike. The important point in this discussion of the reconstruction of French political economy is that the recruitment of immigrant labor was emerging in the aftermath of World War II as a key element in a new consensus, supported by major segments of the republican right (especially the Gaullists) oriented toward big business and rapid economic growth, and by segments of the old republican left (the radicals, socialists, and eventually the communists as well).

It is important to keep in mind that the emerging consensus for a new immigration policy, based on expansive (i.e., anti-Malthusian) demographic and economic principles, was firmly anchored in the universalist, republican ideals discussed above. Republicanism in postwar France included a profound respect for the civil and human rights of foreigners, especially refugees whose plight was easily recognizable following the devastation of World War II. For example, France was quick to ratify the Geneva Convention, and the French left was eager to return to the Republican policies of the interwar period, when France was a haven for those fleeing fascist persecution in Italy, Spain, Germany, and beyond. Adopting liberal refugee and asylum policies also was a way for the new French regime to repudiate the sins of Vichy—a situation reminiscent of the founding of the Federal Republic of Germany, where a constitutional guarantee of the right to asylum was viewed as a way to overcome the horrors of the Nazi regime (and to quickly assimilate ethnic German refugees from East Central Europe). One of the least noticed innovations of the Tripartite Government—and a great accomplishment of the early Gaullist reformers—was the creation of a full-blown welfare state, built upon republican and Catholic, rather than social democratic, principles (see Ashford 1991). Newly arriving immigrants would benefit from the social rights associated with the construction of a French welfare state. If we combine these civil, human, and social rights of foreigners with the liberal naturalization and citizenship policies of the Fourth Republic, we can see the emergence of an expansive and "liberal" immigration policy in the years following liberation. The policy was built on the pragmatic assessments of economic planners, the nationalist aspirations of some demographers and politicians, and the edifice of a revitalized republican synthesis.

Even the criteria of ethnic selection (or a kind of national origins quota) promoted by Georges Mauco, Alfred Sauvy, and the *population-nistes* were rejected in the Ordonnances of 1945, which laid down the basic outline of immigration and naturalization policy in postwar France—or what Weil (1991: 61) has called "the rules of the game." Unfortunately, as Weil goes on to point out, the rosy liberal-republican scenario and the process of political and economic reconstruction were disrupted (almost before they got off the ground) by the wrenching process of decolonization. French immigration policy in the 1950s and 1960s must be understood in terms of the demographic and republican nexus, which helped forge a consensus for the recruitment of foreign workers. But the crises and controversies surrounding immigration *control* in the 1970s and 1980s stem in large part from the turbulence of decolonization and the dismantling of the French Empire, which was itself, ironically, a creation of nationalist and republican aspirations. The liberal-republican side of the history of immigration in postwar France cannot be told without reference to the legacy of colonialism, decolonization, and especially the Algerian War, which created new fault lines in French society along ethnic and racial divisions. The reshaping of a republican consensus and the crisis of decolonization are like two sides of a coin; together they give us a complete picture of the history of immigration and immigration policy in postwar France.

A brief look at the size and evolution of France's foreign population will help round out the historical picture. Table 5.1 presents the changes in the foreign population in France as measured by various censuses taken from 1921 to 1990. By 1931 France was statistically a country of immigration; 6.6 percent of the population was foreign, a figure that is comparable to other immigration countries such as the United States and Canada. The foreign population dropped slightly during the war years and the early period of reconstruction (falling to 4.1 percent in 1954), but it rose again with the successive waves of immigration in the 1950s and 1960s. The proportion of foreigners in the total population *never* falls below 6 percent in any subsequent census, including the one in 1990. The immigration waves in the 1950s and 1960s were settler (as opposed to temporary) in nature, albeit with a heavy labor component. They were also closely linked to the colonial legacy—that is, to a variety of population movements associated with decolonization. These facts—the permanent nature of immigration and the weight of the colonial legacy— mark an important difference between the French and German experiences, and they indicate some similarities with the British experience. Should we therefore conclude that France by the 1960s (unlike Germany) was a full-fledged country of immigration?

Looking only at the numbers, especially the size of the foreign population stocks, the argument can be made that France has been a country of immigration at least since the turn of the century. Yet despite the long and continuous history of immigration in modern France, immigration has *never* achieved the legitimacy that it has enjoyed in the United States or Canada. Apart from the fact that immigration did not play the role of a "founding myth" in any of France's various political regimes (republican or otherwise) in the nineteenth or twentieth centuries, some of the policies pursued by postwar French governments, especially in the late 1970s and early 1990s, were/are designed to discourage settler immigration and encourage some nationalities, particularly Algerians, to return to their countries of origin. In fact, from the beginning of the postwar period until roughly 1981, there was a sort of guestworker or rotation policy embedded within French thinking about immigration (similar to the German guestworker policies), which helps to explain why governments in the 1970s and 1990s could seriously contemplate a halt to all types of immigration. The zero immigration option was espoused by Minister of the Interior Charles Pasqua in 1993. But in order to understand these rather abrupt shifts from recruitment to suspension in the 1970s and to "zero immigration" in the 1990s, we must take a closer look at the origins of postwar immigration policy in the 1950s and 1960s, which defined problems of immigration control in the highly statist and nationalist terms of economic and demographic planning.

Economic Planning and Population Policy

The postwar French system of immigration control was created in a very short period of time after liberation. The two principal agencies for managing immigration and refugee flows—the National Immigration Office (ONI) and the French Office for the Protection of Refugees and Stateless Persons (OFPRA)—were established in 1946, and population/ family policies in general were given a boost by the creation of the National Institute for Demographic Studies (INED). The ONI was touted (by Gaullists on the right and Communists on the left) as a model agency for the recruitment and placement of foreign workers in various sectors of the French economy. Trade unions were especially pleased to have a "neutral" state agency to oversee foreign worker and immigration policy. The unions had lobbied hard to avoid a return to the interwar system of the SGI, where business organized and controlled immigration. Business associations, such as the National Council of French Employers (CNPF) were not yet sufficiently well organized to have any formal influence on the creation of this system of immigration control. They offered little resistance to the new directions in immigrant worker policy, except, ironically, to question the wisdom of importing large numbers of immigrant workers at a time of high unemployment, when many French laborers and veterans were returning from Germany.

The two groups that were most influential in setting the agenda for postwar French immigration policy were economic planners, on the one hand, and demographers on the other. Two individuals stand out among the policy elite during this period: Jean Monnet, who would coordinate economic, and eventually European, policy as head of the National Planning Agency (CGP), and Alfred Sauvy, who was to become a principal spokesperson and adviser on economic and population issues for various Fourth Republic governments. Sauvy (unlike Monnet) was

TABLE 5.1
EVOLUTION OF THE FOREIGN POPULATION IN FRANCE, 1921–1990
(CENSUS DATA)*

Year	1921	1931	1954	1975	1982	1990
Total population	38,797,540	41,228,466	42,781,370	52,599,430	54,273,200	56,625,000
Total foreign population	1,532,024	2,714,697	1,765,298	3,442,415	3,680,100	3,607,600
% of foreigners in the total	3.9	6.6	4.1	6.5	6.8	6.4
European nationalities (including USSR)	1,435,976	2,457,649	1,431,219	2,102,685	1,760,000	1,453,360
African nationalities	37,666	105,059	229,505	1,192,300	1,573,820	1,652,870
Algerians			211,675[1]	710,690	795,920	619,923
Moroccans	36,277	82,568	10,734	260,025	431,120	584,708
Tunisians			4,800[2]	139,753	189,400	207,496
French West Africans		16,401		70,320	138,080	178,133
American nationalities	22,402	32,120	49,129	41,560	50,900	77,554
Asian nationalities (not including USSR)	28,972	86,063	40,687	104,465	293,780	417,020
Turks	5,040	36,119	5,273	50,860	123,540	201,480

[1]French Muslim Algerians.
[2]Individuals from within the French Empire (l'Union française) are counted as French, except French Muslim Algerians, who were counted as foreign during this period.
Source: J. Costa-Lascoux, *De l'immigré au citoyen* (Paris: Documentation Française, 1989), p. 19; INSEE; Ministère des Affaires Sociales et de la Solidarité Nationale.

not a member of the Gaullist inner circle; he was, nonetheless, closely connected to it through Robert and Michel Debré, two staunch pronatalists (see Debré and Sauvy 1946). Other academics and public figures (such as Georges Mauco and Alexandre Parodi) were influential in helping to shape French immigration policy, but *planning* was very much the spirit of the age and immigration came to be viewed in terms of input-output tables (see Tapinos 1975; Weil 1991: 54–75). Foreign labor was considered an essential factor of production—to be managed as such—and it was seen as a way of stimulating employment and economic growth.

Throughout the "thirty glorious years" of virtually uninterrupted high economic growth from the mid-1940s to the mid-1970s, each economic plan published by the CGP contained specific targets for the importation of foreign labor, ranging from 430,000 in the First (Monnet) Plan of 1946–1947 to 325,000 for the Fifth Plan, 1966–1970. These figures, while not irrelevant, had little bearing on the actual levels of immigration in the 1950s and 1960s because the system of immigration control during this period of very high growth rates and rapid decolonization quickly slipped into private hands (see table 5.2). The ONI became little more than a clearinghouse for various businesses, which took it upon themselves to go directly to the sending countries (Italy had given way to Spain, Portugal, and former colonies of North Africa, especially

TABLE 5.2
IMMIGRATION IN FRANCE, 1946–1990
(THOUSANDS)

Year	1946–55	1956–67	1968–73	1974–80	1981–87	1988–90
Permanent workers	325.2	1205.9	801.3	192.9	195.1	50.7
	(32.5)[1]	(109.6)	(133.6)	(27.6)	(27.9)	(16.9)
	(48.94)[2]	(44.06)	(39.16)	(13.77)	(17.42)	(14.8)
Seasonal workers	247.6	1126.9	821.9	857.3	664.2	190.7
	(24.8)	(102.4)	(137.0)	(122.5)	(94.9)	(63.6)
	(37.26)	(41.17)	(40.16)	(61.18)	(59.30)	(55.7)
Family members	91.7	404.2	423.2	351.0	260.6	100.9
	(9.2)	(36.7)	(70.5)	(50.1)	(37.2)	(33.6)
	(13.80)	(14.77)	(20.68)	(25.05)	(23.27)	(29.5)
Total	664.4	2737.1	2046.5	1401.2	1120.0	342.3
	(66.4)	(248.8)	(341.1)	(200.2)	(160.0)	(114.1)
	(100.0)	(100.0)	(100.0)	(100.0)	(100.0)	(100.0)

Note: Numbers in parentheses are:
[1]The average annual rate of immigration and
[2]The percentage of total immigration for each type of immigration for a given period.
Source: Office des Migrations Internationales (OMI).

Algeria, as the principal recruiting grounds for foreign workers—see table 5.3), find the labor they needed, bring the workers to France, get them integrated into the workforce, and *then* seek an adjustment of status. This practice of bypassing the institutions created to manage immigration flows came to be known as "immigration from within," and the legalization rate was the most important statistic for measuring the state's ability or inability to control immigration. By the late 1960s, according to this measure, almost 90 percent of new immigrant workers were coming to France, finding a job, and then requesting an adjustment of status (see Hollifield 1992: 45–73). During this period, immigration policy was as expansive and liberal as in any industrial democracy, and the French state and society were having little trouble assimilating the new arrivals, who were still largely coming from Spain and Portugal.

But it was also during this period that the ambiguous status of citizens from the former colonies of North and West Africa began to pose a crucial problem of control. Following the Evian Agreements and the granting of independence to Algeria in 1962, the status of these former "citizens" remained virtually unchanged: they had the right to move freely between the *métropole* and their home country. The continued arrival of hundreds of thousands of Algerians, which accelerated in the latter part of the 1960s, led the French government into a series of attempts to renegotiate the freedom of movement clause of the Evian Agreements. Even though the French state was reluctant to unilaterally impose restrictions on the comings and goings of Algerian nationals (which in effect would have abrogated bilateral treaties), in 1968 the

TABLE 5.3
IMMIGRATION OF WORKERS AND FAMILY MEMBERS BY NATIONALITY

Nationality	1946–55	1956–67	1968–73	1974–81	1982–87
Italians	27,838	36.813	9,359	4,529	1,367
	66.8	27.4	4.6	5.1	2.5
Spaniards	1,490	49,785	24,240	2,714	804
	3.6	37.1	11.9	3.1	1.5
Portuguese	424	26,359	91,413	17,082	4,991
	1.0	19.6	44.8	19.3	9.3
Moroccans	600	7,994	27,383	19,576	12,288
	1.4	6.0	13.4	22.1	22.8
Tunisians	—	2,418	15,852	5,912	5,314
	—	1.8	7.8	6.7	9.9
Turks	—	279	8,505	10,157	5,528
	—	0.2	4.2	11.5	10.3
Yugoslavs	29	3,125	11,208	1,820	693
	0.1	2.3	5.5	2.1	1.3
Others	11,302	7,407	16,131	26,624	22,841
	27.1	5.5	7.9	30.1	42.4
Total	41,683	134,179	204,090	88,414	53,825
	100.0	100.0	100.0	100.0	100.0

Note: Figures are annual averages. The second row of numbers represents the percentage of total immigration for each nationality for a given period.
Source: Office des Migrations Internationales.

government of Georges Pompidou succeeded in convincing the Algerian government to allow somewhat greater French control over the movement of Algerian nationals, although the principle of no restriction on tourist visas for Algerians was maintained. Morocco and Tunisia, which became major sending countries in the 1968–1973 period (see table 5.3), also kept their relatively privileged status as ex-colonies. The same was true of the states of West Africa, even though immigration from Senegal, the Ivory Coast, and so on, remained very low until the late 1980s and 1990s, by comparison with North Africa (see table 5.1 for a breakdown of the foreign population by nationality as of 1990). In effect the process of decolonization—which created a special category of protected immigrants who were quasi-citizens of France—together with high economic growth rates made a mockery of French control policies in the 1960s. The legacy of decolonization has continued to play havoc (well into the 1990s) with attempts by French governments to control immigration, because individuals in former African colonies who were born during French rule still have the legal right to ask for "reintegration" into the French nation, thus guaranteeing a right to naturalization for a cohort of former French nationals (most of them thirty years old or older) who constitute a latent reservoir of African immigration to France. Much of the 1993 debate surrounding the reform of the Nationality Code turned on the issue of the naturalization and citizenship of "Franco-Algerians" and their children.[3]

As immigration soared to over a quarter of a million a year between 1956 and 1967 (see table 5.2), French governments began to take concrete administrative steps to reassert control over immigration. Attempts to renegotiate the free movement of Algerian nationals represented only one among many initiatives, most of which came not from the Foreign Ministry but from the Ministry of the Interior and the Ministry of Labor. A series of administrative memoranda having the force of law were drafted in the early 1970s to enforce immigration and labor laws by requiring employers, in particular, to meet stringent requirements for the housing and care of foreign workers before bringing immigrants into the labor force. These administrative orders were met with strong resistance from certain sectors, such as construction, mining, and some manufacturing industries, who feared the impact that such a tightening on the recruitment and hiring of foreign workers might have on wages. The situation in the labor market was further complicated by the settlement of the general strike following the May revolt in 1968. The Grenelle Accords, negotiated by then prime minister Pompidou, granted large wage concessions to French workers (25 percent increases in wages), making a cheap, tractable supply of foreign labor even more vital to employers facing a heated economy and increasing demand for their products. Finally, it is important to note that the major steps were taken in 1968 to implement the "freedom of movement clause" of the Treaty of Rome, allowing citizens of the European Economic Community member states to move freely in search of employment. This clause effectively removed French control over Italian immigration. Other major European sending countries (Spain and Portugal) were not yet members of the EEC. Their nationals would not benefit from freedom of movement until the 1980s, following their transition to democracy and the takeoff of their economies, which dramatically reduced the propensity for emigration from these states to France.

The fact that the French economy had come to rely so heavily on immigrant labor by the early 1970s (foreign workers were to be found in substantial numbers in almost every sector) meant that employers were successful in getting the government to ease restrictions on immigration. While the rate of status adjustments declined slightly to around 50 percent in 1972, it rose again to 60 percent the following year. Thus the first real

---

[3]The reform of the Nationality Code proposed in May 1993 by the Balladur government, spearheaded by Minister of the Interior Charles Pasqua, seeks to limit the automaticity of citizenship for second-generation Franco-Algerians by imposing a residency requirement (of five years) on the parents and requiring proof of the "adhesion" of these individuals to the French nation. See Weil 1993; see also Costa-Lascoux 1993.

attempts by the French government to assert control over immigration (workers, families, seasonals, and the like) ended in failure, unlike the German experience with guestworkers, where immigration of Turks was stopped and many were convinced to return home at the first shallow postwar recession in 1967–1968 (see Martin on Germany, this volume). Even though the levels of immigration and stocks of foreign labor continued to be calculated as part of France's planning process, the national plans ceased to have any real importance for guiding French economic, labor, or manpower policies. The combination of high demand for labor (and goods and services), the ambiguous status of citizens of the former colonies (especially Algerians), and respect for the civil and human rights of foreigners (grounded in the republican synthesis) helped to keep the immigration valve wide open in France right up until the first major economic recession of the postwar period, beginning in 1973 with the Yom Kippur War and the Arab oil embargo.

This abrupt change in the economic climate brought an end to the "thirty glorious years" and gave the French political and administrative authorities the ammunition they needed to attempt to stop immigration. The use of the term *arrêt de l'immigration* (total halt to immigration) is very controversial because some observers question the seriousness of the French government's desire to halt all immigration following the first deep postwar recession in 1973–1974. Also there is considerable dispute as to whether the intention of the Giscard-Chirac government (1974–1976) was to stop all forms of immigration, or just worker immigration. Clearly, however, the change in French immigration policy in 1974 marked a seachange in the thinking about immigration in France. Suddenly immigrants were viewed more as guests than settlers, more as a liability than an asset. The French government also began to back carefully away from official ties to former colonies in North and West Africa. Whereas the various Gaullist governments of the 1960s had taken great pains to maintain close political and economic ties with France's former African colonies, even if this meant continued high levels of immigration, the administration of Valéry Giscard d'Estaing was willing to sacrifice the special relationship between France and its former colonies if this could help put an end to further immigration.[4]

An administrative or statist reflex was building to stop immigration and force as many undesirable foreign residents as possible to return to their countries of origin (see Hollifield 1991). Algerians were an especially tempting target. As it turns out, however, the Algerian government

---

[4]The best account of this turbulent period of change in French immigration policy is to be found in Weil 1991. Weil documents carefully the frantic efforts by the Giscard governments, headed first by Jacques Chirac and then Raymond Barre, to stop all forms of immigration, including family reunification. Regardless of semantics concerning the use of the term *arrêt de l'immigration*, it seems clear that the French state was committed to a major shift in policy.

already had taken the initiative in September 1973 to suspend immigration unilaterally in protest over the increasing attacks on its nationals in France. The French government (under the young prime minister Jacques Chirac) was pleased to see the Algerians moving in this direction, but further measures were deemed necessary to stop all forms of immigration and force the return of a substantial segment of the resident alien population. It was during this period of the mid- to late 1970s that a new system of immigration control began to evolve (through a process of trial and error). It laid down the parameters not only for immigration policy (what is possible and what will or will not work) but also for partisan debates over immigration and integration in the 1980s and 1990s.

By trying to respond to increasingly hostile public opinion and by attempting to use foreign workers and their families to solve rising problems of unemployment, the governments of Valéry Giscard d'Estaing (headed first by Jacques Chirac and then Raymond Barre) began to chip away at the foundations of the republican consensus in the areas of immigration and naturalization. In so doing, they fanned the flames of conflict between citizen (i.e., French) and immigrant workers that had been growing in the wake of rent strikes in 1975. For the first time in the postwar period, local working-class organizations, especially in Communist-controlled towns, succumbed to xenophobia. Tensions ran high, and immigrant workers were targeted as scapegoats for the deteriorating economic situation. The governments of the day tried to seize upon the changed political-economic climate to impose a new system of immigration control. All further immigration of workers would be halted, and new return policies would use carrots (economic incentives) and sticks (refusal to renew residency permits) to lower the resident foreign population. In addition, as Weil (1991) has so clearly documented, the governments attempted to prevent family reunification. These policies were to constitute a crucial test of the republican model.[5]

Rule of Law and the Council of State

As happened in many of the labor-importing countries of Western Europe, especially the Federal Republic of Germany, enforcing rotation of guestworkers turned out to be extremely difficult because of legal and constitutional constraints that prevented governments from acting to undermine the civil and human rights of resident aliens. Nowhere were these constraints more evident than in France in the late 1970s. As the policies of no immigration and forced return seemed to be failing, the

---

[5]The author has written about this shift in policy and its implications for immigration control in several other works. See, for example, Hollifield 1992: chaps. 4, 6, and 8. But by far the best account of the role of French institutions, especially the Council of State, in transforming and shaping these policies is in Weil 1991. On the impact of return policies, see Lebon 1979: 37–46.

French government took some fairly dramatic steps to ensure that they would succeed.

Worker immigration was slowed (see table 5.2) but not stopped. However, family and seasonal immigration proved much more difficult to manage. By freezing worker immigration, French administrative authorities inadvertently stimulated other forms of immigration, particularly family, seasonal, and clandestine immigration (primarily in the form of false tourism). When the government of Raymond Barre began to realize that family immigration remained high, the first reaction was to try to prevent family members from entering the labor market, in the hope that this would discourage individual workers from bringing their families to join them in France. This policy of limiting family reunification was tried in West Germany as well, but, as in France, it was reversed in the courts. The second administrative reaction was to attempt a forced repatriation, primarily of Algerian workers.

But in each instance the judiciary, particularly the Council of State, acted as an internal check on the legality (if not the constitutionality) of these policies.[6] Early in the reform process, the Council of State moved to limit the government's capacity to administer what were still considered to be foreign worker programs. The Marcellin, Fontanet, and Gorse administrative/executive orders, issued early in the 1970s to stop unauthorized recruitment of immigrant workers, were declared null by the Council, which pointed out that the administration (i.e., the executive) could not unilaterally make decisions to suspend worker immigration. Such a dramatic shift in immigration policy would require parliamentary approval—something the government did not pursue during the 1970s because a full-dress debate over immigration policy could have proved politically divisive and embarrassing to the government. Likewise, the Council of State debated the government's attempts to organize the forced return of North African workers and to deny "rights" of family reunification. The Council cautioned the government that it was once again on shaky legal and constitutional ground. More than once the government was forced to back down from its hard-line, restrictionist positions in the

---

[6]The Council of State is perhaps one of the more mysterious and misunderstood French political institutions. It has basically two functions: to act as an advisory body for the government (i.e., the president and the Council of Ministers) on legal and political matters, and to serve as the highest administrative court of appeal in the French judiciary. It does not (strictly speaking) have constitutional powers of judicial review, but its advisory opinions have traditionally carried great weight, making it difficult for a government to go against its rulings. The most recent evidence of the power of this body with respect to immigration and refugee policies came in September 1993, when the president and prime minister sought a ruling from the Council of State on the implementation of the Schengen Agreement and its implications for the French Constitution. See *Le Monde*, September 9, 1993, and the section of this chapter on the "Return to Power of the 'Republican' Right."

face of a possibly embarrassing public confrontation with the Council of State.[7]

The Council of State functions as an important arbiter of relationships between the state and the individual in France. By virtue of its elite status and long history as the guardian of liberal and republican principles—especially the equality of individuals before the law—the Council of State is able to function as a check on the administrative and executive powers of the state. Governments, while not constitutionally bound to abide by the decisions of the Council, have traditionally deferred to its judgment in matters concerning the legality of government actions, the wording of bills, and whether a particular decree or piece of legislation is likely to stand the test of French (constitutional and administrative) jurisprudence. In the case of immigration policy, no matter how badly the government wanted to reduce the range of rights and entitlements for resident aliens (especially Algerians), it was simply unwilling to challenge the republican consensus or the rule of law. These values were deemed too important to risk for the sake of stopping immigration and reducing the size of the foreign population. A similar constitutional debate was initiated in France in 1993, with the adoption by Parliament of more restrictionist immigration and refugee laws (see below).

The Algerian government, for its part, proved to be unwilling to go along with the forced repatriation of its nationals. Only voluntary repatriation was deemed acceptable. Even France's strategy of paying foreign workers to return to their countries of origin was a failure; only 80,000 or so workers took advantage of these economic incentives, and most of the beneficiaries were Spanish and Portuguese. Only a few years later they would gain freedom of movement into French territory by virtue of Spain's and Portugal's admission in the 1980s as full members of the European Community. Thus immigration in France continued well after the cutoff date of 1974, and it remained at historically high levels for family and seasonal immigration (see table 5.2). The practice of legalization continued, although at a reduced rate; the primary beneficiaries of this process were nationals from EC member states, who constituted an increasingly large percentage of *legal* immigration flows by the end of the 1970s. Meanwhile, the foreign population (and the stock of immigrant

---

[7]See Weil 1991 for a detailed story of the Council of State and its crucial role in the making of French immigration policy. At least one French scholar and jurist, Daniele Lochak, disputes Weil's account of the Council's impact on the decision-making process. Lochak pointed out that the Council was merely ratifying changes of policy that already had been decided by the government of the day, after furious internal debates (author interview). Lochak has written extensively about the rights of foreigners in France and about the role of Council of State in French administrative law and civil liberties. See, for example, Lochak 1985. Through her activities as a founding member of the GISTI, Lochak has been an activist on behalf of foreigners' rights and an "insider" with respect to the judicial administration of immigration and refugee policies.

labor) continued to grow, although the foreign population stock stabilized during the 1980s at around 6.5 percent of the total population (see table 5.1).

Even though demand-pull was slowly giving way to supply-push immigration in the early 1980s, as the countries of the Maghreb and West Africa became ever more populous and economically desperate, the primary reason for the continuation of immigration in France (as in the Federal Republic of Germany) was the republican consensus and the power of rights-based politics, which prevented the state from acting to halt all forms of immigration. This rights-based political and humanitarian dynamic reinforced the economic factors that continued to draw Africans into the French labor market, despite the fact that unemployment rates in France hovered around 10 percent throughout the 1980s and into the 1990s.

Republicanism, Control, and Integration in the 1980s

In 1981, French immigration policy took another turn with the election of France's first left-wing government since the Popular Front of 1936. François Mitterrand and the Socialist Party promised to make life easier (and more secure) for the millions of foreigners living in France, while at the same time asserting greater control over illegal immigration in order to protect French workers from unfair foreign competition. This has been the general policy response of "liberal" governments to immigration in most of the industrial democracies in the 1980s. In France, however, the failure of the policies to stop immigration that had been promoted by the governments of the 1970s—combined with rapidly deteriorating economic conditions in the early 1980s, economic restructuring and rising unemployment in manufacturing, and the election of the first purely left-wing government since 1936—led to a highly charged partisan debate over a range of public policy issues, but especially over the issues of immigration, ethnicity, and religious versus secular authority. Immigration control was inextricably linked with problems of integration and religion, as French authorities started to come to grips with the permanent settlement of millions of Muslim North Africans and the arrival of an increasing number of sub-Saharan Africans, many of whom were entering as asylum seekers. By 1990 almost half (45.8 percent) of the legally resident foreign population in France was of African origin (see tables 5.1 and 5.3).

The problem of assimilation was seriously compounded by the fact that the French economy was undergoing its deepest restructuring since the reconstruction effort of the 1950s to address the devastation of World War II. Gaullist policies of economic and political grandeur during the 1960s had created a number of "national champions" in manufacturing, which were to lead the "modernization" of the French economy. But no sooner had these national champions (in steel, automobiles, etc.) begun to flourish in the 1960s than the global move away from rust-belt industries (heavy manufacturing) and toward high-tech information-based industries in the 1970s rendered the national champions obsolete. Steel, mining, and shipbuilding industries became lame ducks virtually overnight, and the automobile industry was severely weakened. The French state (particularly in the nationalized sectors) was left holding the bag, and the first socialist governments (Mauroy I and II) under Mitterrand faced the task of shoring up (or continuing to dismantle) these core manufacturing industries. Since foreign workers were heavily concentrated in these sectors, they would be among the first casualties in this process of industrial restructuring. Many foreigners and newly arrived immigrants were able to shift to the more dynamic service sector, even though second-generation immigrants (especially women) were hit hard by unemployment, which for the total foreign population rose from 4.6 percent in 1975 to 14 percent in 1982 and almost 20 percent by 1990.[8] The rates vary considerably from one economic sector to another, especially when we control for age (first versus second generation) and gender.

The economic strategy of the socialist government (Mauroy I, from 1981 to 1983) was to nationalize even more sectors of the economy and to reflate as a way of solving the unemployment problem. These policies ran directly counter to trends in the European and the world economies, which were being swept by deregulation, denationalization, a new monetarism, and policies to spur competition and trade. As a result, the first Mauroy government quickly found itself facing double-digit inflation and a growing current account deficit. At the urging of Finance Minister Jacques Delors, the government decided to reverse course, launching a program of economic austerity and keeping the French franc anchored in the European exchange rate mechanism. These moves further aggravated the employment picture, and subsequent restructuring in the manufacturing sector led to layoffs of large numbers of unskilled (mostly second-generation) immigrant workers. Unemployment among foreigners soared in the early to mid-1980s to around 15 percent, with the French workforce not far behind (at around 10 percent). Unemployment among young foreigners fluctuated between 30 and 40 percent in the immediate aftermath of the 1982–1983 recession. It was during this crucial period, which saw a liberalization of immigrant rights and the adoption of economic austerity policies, that political

---

[8]For a sectoral analysis of immigrant employment in France until 1981, see Hollifield 1992: 141–66. These most recent figures on unemployment among foreigners were taken from Lebon 1992: 22. For more on immigration and the French labor market, see Tribalat 1991. On the crisis and restructuring of the French economy in the 1980s, see Lipietz 1991: 17–42.

activity among unemployed and disaffected second-generation immigrants accelerated, injecting a new "ethnic" dimension into French politics (in the form of such pro-immigrant groups as S.O.S. Racisme and France Plus). The period also saw the rise of the anti-immigrant Front National, headed by Jean-Marie Le Pen (see Wihtol de Wenden 1988; Taguieff 1988). In effect, a polarization of the electorate over the issues of immigration and unemployment was concomitant with increases in the political mobilization and participation of second-generation immigrants.

Thus the first socialist governments of the 1980s confronted a large and growing immigrant population that was having increasing difficulty finding employment and was becoming more politically and culturally militant. Islamic militancy was on the rise throughout the Middle East and North Africa in the wake of the 1979 Iranian Revolution, and a fringe group of second-generation North Africans (mostly Algerians) in France were returning to their Islamic roots, partly out of a sense of loss of identity (having been born and reared in France by foreign parents, but not yet or only recently having obtained French nationality) and partly out of a sense of frustration at being unable to find gainful employment (see Kepel 1988). Still, there were many success stories in the political, economic, and sociocultural integration of immigrants during the 1980s, for what was coming to be known *overtly* as the French "republican model" emphasized immigrants' acceptance of such fundamental republican values as equality before the law and the primacy of secular authority.[9]

From a labor market standpoint, many foreign workers were successful at moving out of declining manufacturing sectors and into the more dynamic service sectors. The internal labor market continued to function as a mechanism for allocating immigrant labor despite the economic crises and high unemployment that caused many distributional problems and contributed to social inequalities. To combat the socioeconomic problems associated with immigration, socialist governments (headed by Pierre Mauroy from 1981 to 1984 and Laurent Fabius from 1984 to 1985) made good on election promises to ease the insecurities of the resident foreign population, first by enacting a generous amnesty for illegals. Anyone who had entered France prior to January 1981 was eligible for a temporary residency permit, valid for three months, which would allow the individual to complete an application process for an adjustment of status. By the end of the operation, which lasted well into 1983, over 145,000 amnesty claims had been made. This amnesty gave the French government its first empirical look at the

---

[9]Perhaps one of the best presentations of the French republican model is to be found in Schnapper 1991. The same principles are enunciated, albeit in a more subtle form, in the semi-official report of the High Council on Immigration (Haut Conseil 1992), especially pp. 35–50.

clandestine/illegal population in France. The results of the amnesty, analyzed at the Ministry of Labor by a team headed by Claude-Valentin Marie, revealed a young, single population, largely of North African origin. Most of the "illegal" immigrants had entered France as tourists and overstayed their visas (Marie 1985; see also Garson et al. 1986).

Since proof of employment was one of the conditions of the amnesty, it is not surprising that over 95 percent of those foreigners who came forward to request amnesty had jobs at the time they made their requests. Most of them worked either in construction (30 percent) or in some tertiary/service sector, such as restaurants, hotels, domestic service, and so on, while only 10 percent of those granted amnesty worked in the agricultural sector. The overwhelming majority (66 percent) worked in small firms with fewer than nine employees, further evidence of the shift in foreign employment away from manufacturing and toward the more dynamic service/small business sectors. What the survey of amnestied "illegals" revealed was a clandestine population that had grown since the 1974 cutoff in legal worker immigration. It also demonstrated that new flows of foreign labor had emerged to fill a demand in construction and service industries as a result of the suspension of legal worker immigration (Marie 1987).

Along with the amnesty (which incidentally included amnesty for employers of illegal immigrants, to encourage them to continue providing work for those who came forward), the government of Pierre Mauroy set in motion a series of reforms of residency and work permits, designed to make it easier for foreigners to get the papers necessary to live and work in France. These reforms aimed to create a single ten-year residency and work permit (a sort of French green card) that would greatly facilitate the integration of the resident foreign population. However, the card was never fully developed. An increasing number of restrictions limited the card to only a minority of the resident alien population. Much more important from the standpoint of integration were the expansion of rights of association for foreigners and the suppression of certain police powers, such as arbitrary identity checks. These reforms in the area of civil rights and civil liberties did more than anything else to stimulate a new political activism among immigrants in France, helping to promote such groups as S.O.S. Racisme. Gradually at first, but with increasing speed as we move further into the 1980s, immigrants (especially those from the Maghreb) were emboldened to participate in politics and make new claims to rights and entitlements.

This new activism took the form of ethnic and civil rights politics, which was not exactly what many of the socialist reformers had in mind when they set the process of political reform in motion. According to one of Mitterrand's closest advisers on immigration issues, Mitterrand was nonetheless pleased to see immigrant politics take a multicultural turn in the 1980s—a development that many observers have equated with the

American model of ethnic pluralism. But many "republicans" of the left (such as Jean-Pierre Chevenement) and the right (such as Dominique Schnapper and Philippe Seguin) were horrified to see individuals making political demands on the basis of their ethnicity.[10]

The change in the political-economic climate and the greater assertiveness of immigrants fueled a partisan backlash against immigration, which took the form of the Front National, headed by Jean-Marie Le Pen. The reasons for the rise of this anti-immigrant and xenophobic political movement are many, but the common thread that united an otherwise volatile and inchoate electorate was opposition to socialist policies on immigration and fear of unemployment (see Mayer and Perrineau 1989; Ehrmann and Schain 1992: 272–76). This new anti-immigrant and xenophobic politics (tinged with racist and anti-Semitic discourse) was to constitute another crucial test of the elite republican consensus on immigration. Perhaps not surprisingly, some segments of the traditional Gaullist and Christian Democratic right were quick to take up the agenda of the Front National, calling for a tightening of immigration controls and a more stringent naturalization policy. In the run-up to the 1986 legislative elections, immigration became a focal point of campaign debates as politicians of the right scrambled to avoid losing any more votes to Le Pen. The right won the legislative elections of 1986, and a new government under (a now older) Jacques Chirac placed reform of immigration and naturalization policy high on the agenda. Under the rules of weighted proportional representation by which the election had been fought, the Front National managed to win its own parliamentary bloc, with thirty-three of its members elected to the new Assembly. Le Pen's electoral success ensured that immigration would remain on the national agenda well into the 1990s, and that the problem of immigration control would be redefined in terms of citizenship and national identity.

The Front National fired the first salvos in the battle over citizenship and integration in the 1980s with the clarion call to keep France for the French. The response from the left, especially Mitterrand and the socialists, was to propose giving resident aliens the right to vote in local elections, a proposal that was calculated to sow discord among the parties of the right. The first coalition government, led by Jacques Chirac from 1986 to 1988, weighed into the debate over control, citizenship, and integration by pushing for a reform of the Nationality Code and placing a new emphasis on the security and police aspects of immigration control. Concerning the latter, police powers were reinforced via a new law that made it easier for police to arrest and expel any foreigner deemed to be a threat to public order or security. But the measure also gave new life to civil rights and civil liberties groups, such as S.O.S. Racisme and the

---

[10]These comments are based on author interviews. For one reaction to the rise in ethnic politics in the 1980s, see the controversial book by Barreau (1992), the former director of the Office of International Migration. See also Schnapper 1992.

GISTI Immigration Rights Association. The latter organization is the most important private group working and lobbying for the protection of foreigners' rights. The GISTI became increasingly vigilant in the late 1980s in its efforts to combat administrative and police actions against foreigners, especially at the prefecture level, where many decisions are made concerning the rights of residency and employment of foreigners.

Another serious challenge to the republican consensus on immigration and naturalization policy came during the first coalition government, when the Chirac government proposed a change in Article 23 of the Nationality Code, to scale back the automaticity of the attribution of citizenship to second-generation foreigners. Rather than automatically granting citizenship at age eighteen to individuals born in France of foreign parents, the proposed reform would have forced these individuals to make a positive choice for French citizenship and to take a sort of oath of allegiance to the French nation. Even though the principal group targeted by this legislation—second-generation Franco-Algerians—was unaffected, this largely symbolic reform provoked a firestorm of protest from the republican left and right, forcing the government to withdraw the bill and create a commission of experts to study the reform. The commission, which came to be known as the Commission of Sages, fell back on the republican consensus in its hearings and deliberations, reaffirming the liberal aspects of French jurisprudence in the area of naturalization and nationality laws (see Long 1988). In effect, no changes were made to French law, and the naturalization process remained a relatively open one in comparison with other European states, especially the Federal Republic of Germany, where stringent naturalization procedures have been a principal obstacle to the integration of the large foreign population and a point of heated political debate in the 1990s. Naturalization rates in France (see table 5.4) were not extraordinarily high in the 1980s, nor were they particularly low. The French state and society continued to absorb and assimilate the foreign population during the 1980s despite the turmoil and controversy surrounding the issues of citizenship and nationality.

Notwithstanding the many twists and turns in French immigration policy following the attempt to stop immigration in 1974, the republican consensus has remained intact, and a new politics of ethnicity and civil rights arose in the 1980s and 1990s (see Wieviorka 1992; Taguieff 1991). The re-election of François Mitterrand to a second presidential term in 1988 and the return to power of the socialists in a minority government headed by Michel Rocard did not, however, lay to rest the issues of immigration control, integration, and citizenship. Le Pen received 14.5 percent of the vote in the first round of the 1988 presidential election, confirming the importance of immigration for the electorate, especially in a period of great economic uncertainty and insecurity. Opinion polls taken in the late 1980s and early 1990s showed nearly one-third of voters

TABLE 5.4

NATURALIZATIONS

(THOUSANDS)

Year	By decree	By declaration	Total
1986	33.4	22.6	56.0
1987	25.7	16.7	41.8
1988	26.9	27.3	54.2
1989	33.0	26.5	59.5
1990	34.9	30.1	65.0

Source: André Lebon, *Immigration et presence étrangère en France 1990/1991—les données, les faits* (Paris: La Documentation Française, 1991).

to be sympathetic to the Front National's positions on this issue. But Le Pen and his movement were eclipsed to some degree by the momentous changes in the European political landscape beginning in 1989. The push for a single European market by 1993 and the debates over European political and economic union introduced a new element into immigration and citizenship debates. The collapse of communism in East Central Europe and the breakup of the Soviet Union in 1989–1990 fundamentally altered immigration debates throughout Europe, shifting attention away from the demographically expansive states of North and West Africa and toward the East, where there was a fear that economic and political collapse would be followed by civil war and waves of refugees. This fear turned out to be justified in what was Yugoslavia, but the refugee picture was further complicated by the conflict in Algeria between Islamic fundamentalists and a more secular military government.

European Union and the Crisis of Republican Identity

The republican consensus on immigration has survived many internal assaults since 1974, but perhaps the greatest challenge of all has come from the outside in the form of the European Union. As the face of Europe was changing in 1989–1990 with the fall of the Berlin Wall, the collapse of the Soviet Union, and the end of the Cold War, the French political and intellectual class were transfixed by a debate over three Moroccan high school girls who in 1989 chose to wear traditional Islamic headscarves into a public school classroom. This episode, more than any other, exposed the fault lines in the republican model. It reopened debates over secular authority and the separation of church and state (reminiscent of crucial moments in the development of the Third Republic around the turn of the century) and brought to the fore the problems of integrating a large Muslim population. Issues of immigration control temporarily took a backseat to the problems of integration and ethnic relations. The specter of multiculturalism seemed to loom on the horizon, and a fear of Americanization (or of the "American model") replaced fears of being overwhelmed by Third World immigration. Not since the heady days of the 1950s has there been such rampant (and virulent) anti-Americanism in France.

After a heated public debate over the issue of the scarves—which split the political (and intellectual) class between liberals (who favored greater freedom of expression for ethnic minorities) and republicans (who favored strict adherence to the Third Republic principles of secular authority)—the government of Michel Rocard opted for a compromise that allowed the Moroccan girls to wear their scarves in the classroom so long as they did not disrupt school activities or proselytize fellow students. This (pluralist) compromise drew criticism from left-wing and right-wing republicans, who felt betrayed by public authorities. Two left-leaning republican newspapers (*Libération* and *Nouvel Observateur*) inveighed against the decision, which was nonetheless endorsed by the Council of State. The tenor of editorials in these and other newspapers was that French authorities had sold out the republican model in favor of the dreaded "American model" of multiculturalism. The whole issue, however, became moot when Morocco's King Hassan II ordered the girls to remove the offending scarves.

The symbolic importance of the scarf controversy should not be underestimated. Issues of immigration and ethnicity touched one of the founding myths of the republic—the separation of church and state. The irony is that the republican consensus, which was so important in helping France maintain relatively open immigration and naturalization policies, was turned on its head. Issues of immigrants' assimilation and integration brought to the fore the more nationalist and particularist dimension of the republican model, and the ongoing process of European integration further exacerbated tensions between the universalistic (human and civil rights) dimension of French republicanism and its particularist (nationalist) dimension.[11]

Three developments in the process of European integration have helped create a crisis of the republican model: first is the attempt by a core group of European states, known as the Schengen Group, to regulate immigration in the EC through the establishment of a border-free area with common visa and asylum policies. This group originally comprised France, Germany, and the Benelux countries. The second

---

[11]The Rocard government created an interministerial group to monitor problems of integration in the wake of the scarf controversy. This High Council on Immigration has published two reports on the progress of immigrant assimilation (Haut Conseil 1991, 1992). These two reports represent a good review of the French republican model and the ambitions of the French government for the integration of ethnic and cultural minorities. For an excellent rendition of the relationship between French republicanism and the construction of Europe, see Todd 1990.

development that has directly challenged the republican model is the Maastricht Treaty's provision for a European Union, which proposes giving the vote to EC nationals in local and European elections. In other words, a German citizen living in France would be eligible to vote in local and European elections in France. The third and final development that challenges the republican model is the refugee and asylum crisis that has resulted from ethnic conflict and civil wars in East Central Europe, especially in the former Yugoslavia.

Attempts to formulate a European immigration and refugee policy (among the Schengen Group) have challenged key aspects of the republican consensus. Establishing a common visa policy, for example, would require French authorities to accept a type of quota system that would exclude certain ethnic and national groups from eligibility for tourist visas. The former French colonies of North and West Africa would be the first to see limits placed on the mobility of their nationals as a result of France's participation in such a European immigration policy. Hence, France would be forced to renegotiate visa restrictions with its former colonies. A national origins quota system, which seems to be favored by German authorities in particular, would run against the grain of the republican model in France. Likewise, creating gradational citizenship for European Community nationals would violate the republican model's egalitarian and nationalist principles. Setting up a special category of citizenship for EC nationals would open the way for greater discrimination against third country nationals, and the tight bond between citizenship, nationality, and the right to vote would be broken. For this and other reasons relating to the election of members of the French Senate, the Maastricht Treaty on European Union, which is concerned first and foremost with creating a single European market and currency, poses special constitutional problems for France. Even though immigration control and citizenship issues are not the treaty's primary objectives, they were hotly debated during the referendum over Maastricht, which passed in September 1992 by the narrowest of margins.

Finally, the biggest crisis in immigration control in the 1990s in Europe is not related so much to illegal immigration as to the surge in refugees and asylum seekers, which threatens to undermine the stability of post-Cold War Europe, especially Germany. While Germany has been overwhelmed by asylum seekers from East Central Europe, especially from the former Yugoslavia, Romania, and Turkey, France has managed to control and limit the influx of refugees relatively well. As reflected in table 5.5, the number of asylum seekers in France rose steadily but not dramatically in the late 1980s, from roughly 30,000 in 1985 to around 55,000 in 1990. As in other West European states, the rate of rejection of asylum requests has been high, reaching almost 85 percent in 1990. But French authorities have little control over those

TABLE 5.5
ASYLUM SEEKERS

Year	Number	Rate of rejection (%)
1985	28,809	56.8
1986	26,196	61.2
1987	27,568	67.5
1988	34,253	65.6
1989	61,372	71.9
1990	54,717	84.3

Source: André Lebon, *Immigration et présence étrangère en France 1990/1991 — les données, les faits* (Paris: La Documentation Française, 1991).

whose claims to asylum are rejected. In fact, the tens of thousands who are rejected each year have joined false tourists as one of the principal groups of illegal immigrants in France and throughout Western Europe today.

Nevertheless, the crises of European integration and the changes in East Central Europe do not seem to have altered the French system of immigration control in its fundamental aspects. In fact, France seems to be managing the immigration and refugee crises better than most of its European neighbors, with the possible exception of Switzerland. Recent control data indicate a rise in the number of foreigners refused admission at the French border, from roughly 50,000 in 1986 to over 65,000 in 1990; and the number of infractions of French labor laws (including employment of illegal aliens) has been rising (Lebon 1991; Marie 1992). But nothing dramatic has occurred. The levels of legal immigration have remained at a little over 100,000 per year, and rates of naturalization (see above) have remained the same for over a decade.

The Return to Power of the "Republican" Right

As the French economy slipped slowly into deep recession in 1992–1993, the left began to lose its nearly decade-long grip on power. The battle over immigration control and assimilation took a new turn in the spring of 1993 with the crushing defeat of a badly divided Socialist Party in the parliamentary elections. The "republican" right, under the new leadership of Edouard Balladur, returned to power determined to implement its anti-immigrant platform and thereby eliminate, once and for all, the electoral threat of the Front National. The victory of the right (the RPR and UDF received over 80 percent of the seats) was the largest in any parliamentary election since 1815, so the new majority's mandate to govern was clear. It wasted little time in introducing restrictionist measures to reform immigration, naturalization, and refugee policy.

As in the first coalition government, in the Balladur cabinet Charles Pasqua was again named to head the Ministry of the Interior. He took charge of the reform efforts, which amounted to a broadside attack on the civil and social rights of foreigners. The reform, referred to here as Pasqua's second law, undermines some aspects of the republican model, as spelled out in the Ordonnances of 1945. The first target of reform was naturalization. The new government dusted off the 1986 bill to change the Nationality Code, softened it a bit (but proposed no radical change in the basis of French citizenship law from *jus soli* to *jus sanguinis*), and proposed to eliminate the automatic and involuntary way in which citizenship was attributed to second-generation immigrants. The law requires that children born of foreigners in France file a formal request for naturalization between the ages of sixteen and twenty-one, and that they take an oath to the republic in an official ceremony similar to the American process of naturalization. Presumably this new mechanism for acquiring French nationality will reinforce the French identity of naturalized citizens.

But more important than the reform of the Nationality Code—which essentially implements the recommendations of the Commission of Sages outlined above—is the reinforcement of police powers and the restriction of civil liberties for foreigners or foreign-looking individuals in France. In effect, Pasqua's second law attempted to reinforce immigration control measures, some of which (such as employer sanctions) were already on the books. But among its innovations is a bill designed to prevent illegal immigrants from benefiting from French social security, especially health care. This bill opened a rift in the cabinet between hard-line Minister of the Interior Pasqua and the more liberal-republican Minister of Social Affairs Simone Weil, who argued successfully that emergency medical care should not be denied to foreigners. Such disputes among political elites over the social rights of immigrants and the public finance dimensions of uncontrolled migration ran parallel to similar debates in the United States, where the governors of California and Florida have brought suits against the federal government to receive compensation for the costs to their states of illegal immigration.

In addition to modifying naturalization procedures and social rights, Pasqua's second law also sought to reform and limit the civil rights of immigrants and asylum seekers by increasing the powers of the police and the administration to detain and deport unwanted migrants. This policy gave the police much wider powers to check the identity of "suspicious persons." Race was not supposed to be sufficient grounds for stopping an individual, but any immigrant (legal or otherwise) who threatened "public order" could be arrested and deported. Immigrant workers and foreign students were obliged to wait two years, rather than one, before being allowed to bring family members to join them in France, and an illegal immigrant could not be legalized simply by marrying a French citizen. Mayors were to hold the authority to nullify any suspicious marriage, and anyone deported for any reason would automatically be denied reentry into France for one year.

These restrictionist measures, designed to roll back civil and social rights for foreigners and "tighten" naturalization procedures, immediately drew fire from immigrant rights' groups (especially the GISTI) and from those institutions of the liberal and republican state that were created to protect the rights of individuals. The Council of State, as it had done several times before, warned the government that it was on shaky legal ground, especially with respect to the "rights" of family reunification and political asylum. But the rulings of the Council of State are advisory, and no matter how much weight they may carry (morally, politically, or legally), the government can choose to ignore them, especially when it has such a comfortable working majority in the National Assembly. The Council of State's rulings can, however, presage binding decisions of the Constitutional Council, which has limited powers of judicial review and can be invoked by the opposition in Parliament. This is what happened in August 1993, when the Constitutional Council ruled that several provisions of the new policy were unconstitutional. Specifically, the one-year exclusion from French territory of anyone deported for whatever reason, the new restrictions on family reunification, and the tighter controls on marriages between French nationals and foreigners were declared unconstitutional. Key republican principles (both universalist and nationalist) enshrined in the Declaration of the Rights of Man and the Citizen—such as equality before the law—were cited in the ruling as grounds for rejecting certain provisions of the new immigration and refugee policies. The ruling also raised questions about asylum policy and the constitutionality of France's participation in the Schengen Agreement because the Preamble of the 1946 French Constitution requires the government to consider all requests for political asylum (at minimum to ensure due process for asylum seekers). This aspect of French constitutional law presumably would prohibit French authorities from summarily deporting individuals who had been refused asylum in another EC country (as both the Schengen and Dublin agreements stipulate).

These political and legal maneuverings in 1993 led inexorably to a full-dress, constitutional debate over immigration and refugee policy in France. President Mitterrand, who had considerable constitutional (as well as political and moral) authority, remained for the most part on the sidelines, having been severely weakened by the magnitude of the right-wing victory in Parliament. Mitterrand chose not to contest these changes in immigration and refugee policy, to which he was opposed. Minister of the Interior Pasqua continued doggedly to pursue more restrictionist immigration and naturalization policies, at both the symbolic level and the level of electoral politics. All victories on this issue would come at the electoral expense of the principal rivals of the RPR, namely the Front National on the right and the Socialist Party on the left. At Pasqua's urging and with the assent of the

Council of State, the government decided to force the constitutional issue by calling for a constitutional amendment to clarify the legality of France's participation in Schengen—that is, the authority of the government to refuse to hear asylum cases already decided or under consideration in other EC states. An amendment was passed by a special Congress of the Assembly and the Senate at Versailles in November 1993, demonstrating the power of the right-wing majority in the legislature to change some aspects of the republican model, if necessary, to control immigration. Pasqua denounced the Constitutional Council's interference with the government's immigration policy as "government by judges," and he pointed out that such meddling was an affront to the principle of popular sovereignty and the power of Parliament.

It is too early to tell whether these measures will be sufficient to stop immigration (the so-called zero immigration policy enunciated by Pasqua) or whether this policy spells the end of the republican consensus, which has been the driving force in French immigration policy for almost a century. But if previous attempts by governments in France to stop immigration are any guide to the future, these recently adopted measures are unlikely to halt all forms of immigration. Pasqua, the man behind these new policies, admitted as much, but he reiterated that stopping immigration is the policy of the conservative government in France. He stated that France "has been a country of immigration, but it no longer wishes to be." These policy and political responses constitute a tacit recognition that there is only so much that a state can do to alter push-pull forces, and that a "roll back" of civil and social rights for foreigners is the most effective way to control and stop immigration. But in France, as in other liberal republics such as the United States and Germany, administrative and executive authorities are confronted with a range of constitutional obstacles to such policy shifts. The French republican model, with its universalist and egalitarian principles, remains essentially intact despite repeated assaults from the right and a clear lack of popular support. Taking into account the recent changes in French immigration and refugee law, France still has the most expansive naturalization policies of any state in Western Europe, and the country has preserved the principle of *jus soli*, as well as due process and equality before the law. The republican model and the elite consensus have been weakened but not destroyed.

Conclusion: Continuity in the Midst of Crisis

Four points should be made in conclusion. The first is that France has long been a country of immigration, even though immigration has not achieved the status of a founding myth as in the United States, Canada, or Australia. Despite this ambiguity, there is an implicit recognition in French immigration policies of the contribution that immigrants have

made to the construction of French society and the economy, and there is
not the same crisis atmosphere in France that prevails today in Germany.
The reason for the legitimacy that is (implicitly if not explicitly) accorded
to legal immigration in France is the republican consensus, which is
both universalist and nationalist. This is not an oxymoron, because the
thrust of French political development in the postwar period has been to
promote the cosmopolitan and universalist ideals of the French Revolution, especially in their civil and human rights aspect, while cultivating
French nationalism. This is the essence of Gaullism, for example.
Immigrants in the 1950s and 1960s benefited from this republican,
nationalist consensus insofar as immigration was a major feature of
policies for economic and social reconstruction. French immigration
policy was based as much on economic and demographic planning as on
the old republican consensus, but both were crucial to maintaining an
open society.

The second point concerns the politicization of immigration and the
rise of a new politics of citizenship and integration. As in Germany, the
use of foreign labor (or guestworkers) to sustain high rates of economic
growth turned out not to be sufficient to justify continued high levels of
legal immigration. Unlike Germany, however, when French authorities
attempted to enforce policies of foreign worker rotation to solve problems of unemployment, a whole range of republican values came into
play and the Council of State quickly acted to check the power of the
administrative state. In Germany, a similar institutional and constitutional dynamic was at work, but without the same impact on the
legitimacy of legal immigration. German elites continue to insist that
Germany is not a country of immigration, despite the reality of millions
of permanent resident aliens.

Thus, in spite of the politicization of immigration policy, the republican model in France has remained strong enough to sustain a legal
immigration policy. The same may also be true of Germany, but the fact
remains that the French have lost the illusion of temporary or guestworker policies, whereas the Germans have clung to this illusion much
longer; and many segments of the political elite, as well as public
opinion, refuse to recognize that Germany has become a country of
immigration.[12]

The third point is that European integration has led to a crisis of the
French republican model. Since the French are losing their political grip
on Western Europe—partly as a result of German unification and partly
as a result of the end of the Cold War—the republican vision of France
(and of Europe) has come under pressure. Nowhere is this more evident
than in the areas of immigration and citizenship policy. But France, like

---

[12]For a more complete comparison of French and German immigration policy, see
Hollifield 1992; Thranhardt 1992: 15–74.

other European immigration countries, is caught in a dilemma. The French are being pushed—especially by their German partners—to cooperate in the construction of a European Union, which means losing some of their own national specificities, especially in the areas of immigration and citizenship policy. A national origins quota system and gradational citizenship (for EC nationals) are but two areas in which the republican model is under pressure.

The final point is that debates over immigration control in France have given way to debates over integration, multiculturalism, and nationality, with some anti-American overtones. Here there seems to be greater consensus between right-wing and left-wing republicans on the need to avoid encouraging American-style ethnic or civil rights politics. This fear of multiculturalism is driven in large part by a fear of Islamic fundamentalism and a fear of being overwhelmed by immigration from the Third World. Yet there is every reason to believe that the republican model will survive these fears and crises, as it has survived for over forty years. The current crisis, for example, pales by comparison with the crises of defeat and occupation (Vichy) or decolonization (Algeria). It remains to be seen whether Muslim North Africans can be assimilated in the same way as Italians or Poles in earlier periods of French immigration history (this is a popular republican argument), especially since the schools, the army, the trade unions, and even political parties no longer have the power to assimilate outsiders as they once did. Still there is reason for optimism. The republican model and the hidden consensus that it has generated among political and administrative elites have proved in the past to be far more flexible and resilient than one might expect.

The conclusion, therefore, is that France does not have a crisis of immigration control in the 1990s, and policies that were designed decades ago have stood the test of time. It is entirely possible that France and Europe could see a spurt in economic growth in the 1990s as a result of European economic and political union, and foreign/immigrant labor may prove once again to be essential in these societies with declining populations. The 1990s could repeat some of the history of the 1950s. Clearly, however, the political climate has changed, and it is unlikely to be favorable to a renewal of large-scale legal immigration. It is likely that France will continue to muddle through, with immigration and naturalization policies that do not move too far away from the hidden republican consensus.

References

Archdeacon, Thomas. 1983. *Becoming American: An Ethnic History*. New York: Free Press.

Ashford, Douglas E. 1991. "In Search of the État Providence." In *Searching for the New France*, edited by James F. Hollifield and George Ross. New York: Routledge.

Barreau, Jean-Claude. 1992. *De l'immigration en particulier et de la nation française en général*. Paris: Pré aux clercs.

Berger, Suzanne. 1972. *Peasants against Politics*. Cambridge, Mass.: Harvard University Press.

Bonnet, J.C. 1976. *Les pouvoirs publics français et l'immigration dans l'entre-deux-guerres*. Lyon: Centre d'Histoire Économique et Social de la Région Lyonnaise.

Braudel, Fernand. 1986. *L'Identité de la France*. Paris: Flammarion.

Cobban, Alfred. 1961. *A History of Modern France, Vol. 2: 1799–1945*. Baltimore: Penguin.

Costa-Lascoux, Jacqueline. 1993. "Continuité ou rupture dans la politique française de l'immigration: les lois de 1993," *Revue Européenne des Migrations Internationales* 9:3:233–61.

Debré, R., and A. Sauvy. 1946. *Des français pour la France, le problème de la population*. Paris: Gallimard.

Ehrmann, H.W., and M.A. Schain. 1992. *Politics in France*. New York: Harper Collins.

Fuchs, Lawrence. 1990. *The American Kaleidoscope*. New London, Conn.: Wesleyan/University Press of New England.

Garson, Jean-Pierre, et al. 1986. *Economie politique des migrations clandestines de main-d'oeuvre*. Paris: Publisud.

Haut Conseil a l'Intégration. 1991. *La connaissance de l'immigration et de l'intégration*. Paris: La Documentation Française.

———. 1992. *Conditions juridiques et culturelles de l'intégration*. Paris: La Documentation Française, March.

Hoffman, Stanley, ed. 1963. *In Search of France*. Cambridge, Mass.: Harvard University Press.

Hollifield, James F. 1991. "Immigration and Modernization." In *Searching for the New France*, edited by J.F. Hollifield and George Ross. New York: Routledge.

———. 1992. *Immigrants, Markets, and States*. Cambridge, Mass.: Harvard University Press.

Kepel, Gilles. 1988. *Les banlieus de l'Islam*. Paris: Seuil.

Lebon, André. 1979. "Sur une politique d'aide au retour," *Economie et Statistique*, July.

———. 1991. *Immigration et présence étrangère en France 1990/1991*. Paris: La Documentation Française.

———. 1992. "L'immigration en France, données, perspectives," *Revue Française des Affaires Sociales*, December.

Lipietz, Alain. 1991. "Governing the Economy in the Face of International Challenge." In *Searching for the New France*, edited by James F. Hollifield and George Ross. New York: Routledge.

Lochak, Daniele. 1985. *Étrangers: de quels droits?* Paris: PUF.

Long, Marceau. 1988. *Etre français aujourd'hui et demain*. 2 vols. Paris: La Documentation Française.

Marie, Claude-Valentin. 1985. *La régularisation des étrangers "sans papiers" de 1981–82: resultats d'enquete*. Internal report of the Ministére des Affaires Sociales et de la Solidarité Nationale.

————. 1987. "Immigration clandestine, la régularisation des travailleurs 'sans papier' (1981–1982)," *Bulletin Mensuel des Statistiques du Travail*, supplement no. 106.

————. 1992. "Le travail clandestin: Des condamnations pénales en forte croissance," *Infostat Justice* 29 (September): 1–6.

Mayer, Nonna, and Pascal Perrineau. 1989. *Le Front National à découvert*. Paris: Presses de la FNSP.

Noiriel, Gérard. 1988. *Le creuset français*. Paris: Seuil.

Noiriel, Gérard, and D. Horowitz. 1992. *Immigrants in Two Democracies: French and American Experience*. New York: New York University Press.

Sauvy, A. 1950. "Besoins et possibilités de l'immigration en France," *Population* 2–3:209–34.

Schnapper, Dominique. 1991. *La France de l'intégration*. Paris: Gallimard.

————. 1992. *L'Europe des immigrés*. Paris: F. Bourin.

Schor, R. 1985. *L'Opinion française et les étrangers, 1919–1939*. Paris: Publications de la Sorbonne.

Spengler, J.J. 1979. *France Faces Depopulation*. Durham, N.C.: Duke University Press.

Taguieff, Pierre-André. 1988. *La Force du préjugé*. Paris: La Découverte.

————. 1991. *Face au racisme*. Paris: La Découverte.

Tapinos, Georges. 1975. *L'Immigration étrangère en France*. Paris: Presses Universitaires de France.

Teitelbaum, M.S., and J.M. Winter. 1985. *Fear of Population Decline*. Orlando, Fla.: Academic Press.

Thranhardt, Dietrich, ed. 1992. *Europe: A New Immigration Continent*. Münster: Verlag.

Todd, Emmanuel. 1990. *L'invention de l'Europe*. Paris: Seuil.

Tribalat, Michele, ed. 1991. *Cent ans d'immigration, étrangers d'hier français d'aujourd'hui*. Paris: Presses Universitaires de France/INED.

Weil, Patrick. 1991. *La France et ses étrangers*. Paris: Calmann-Lévy.

————. 1993. "La réforme du code de la nationalité: intégration ou suspicion?" *Le Monde*, May 13.

Wieviorka, M. 1992. *La France raciste*. Paris: Fayard.

Wihtol de Wenden, Catherine. 1988. *Les Immigrés et la politique*. Paris: Presses de la FNSP.

Commentary

Reconsidering the "Republican" Model

Miriam Feldblum

As part of an approach to French politics, the republican model recently has acquired new currency in French immigration and citizenship studies. James Hollifield's wide-ranging analysis of French immigration policy demonstrates the usefulness of the approach. Relying on two features usually identified in the French republican model—the combination of universalistic and assimilationist state strategies, and the fusion of political and cultural ideologies of membership—Hollifield builds a historical explanation of the evolution of postwar French immigration policy. According to Hollifield, the republican model provides an accounting of both the incentives and the constraints operating in the French case.

But there are several problems with the current usage of republicanism as a key explanatory factor. Above all, republicanism is a political tool, not an analytical one. Reliance on the republican model as a premise of an analytical approach often has the consequence of distinguishing France from other countries on the basis of a national exceptionalism. The approach cannot adequately treat the proliferation of republicanist rhetoric as part and parcel of French political discourse; republicanism always has been part of the ideological medium in France. Finally, it is not evident to what degree republicanist features actually account for key moments in the evolution of French policy.

Comparative studies of immigration policy, such as the present endeavor, are attempts to construct analytical frameworks that examine variation and/or convergence across states. Often the goal is to identify common factors or series of factors at work. At the same time, there is no doubt that some degree of national exceptionalism always operates. On the one hand, the approach that identifies republican ideologies and strategies as an independent variable in the evolution of French immigration policy appears quite reasonable. French republicanism is grounded both in ideologies originating in the French Revolution and in specific historical junctures. As one example of the approach, Hollifield asserts that republicanist influence in immigration policy explains France's "remarkable consistency" and "continuity" in the postwar period. This understanding of republicanism, however, does not contextualize immigration policy in its historical evolution. Rather, it reifies various historical and ideological strands into a more or less static "French model" to be juxtaposed against other national models. In counterpoint to the comparative undertaking, locating the republican model in the nexus of the analytical framework only succeeds in setting up a series of national exceptionalisms to be identified.

This said, it is evident that a French republican model has gained currency not only in scholarly studies of immigration, but also with the makers of French immigration policy and with popular commentators. A republican, national integrationist model of immigration arguably has become the national paradigm in France. Nevertheless, comparativists must assume a critical approach to these national paradigms and myths. As in other countries, there is a great deal of interdependence and overlap in France between the scholarly and policy-making communities. From this perspective, the usefulness of the so-called French republican model lies not in its analytical power but in its diverse appeal to policy makers, intellectuals, political elites, activists, and others.

Situating the republican model as part of an analytical framework detracts from any substantive examination of republicanist rhetoric and myths in French political discourse. Republicanism, in the approach I have outlined here, is often depicted as a multifaceted model. As in the characterization of the (hidden) "republican consensus" found in Hollifield's chapter, the model is at once universalist and particularist, nationalist and guardian of individual and human rights, conservative and progressive, expansive and constrictive. What this list points to is not simply tensions in the republican model, as may be suggested by the approach. What it reflects is the manipulation of republicanist discourse by those across the political spectrum, from immigrant associations to the far-right National Front.

From Le Pen's nativism, which can be seen as a subtext to republicanist strands in French history, to the calls by France Plus and S.O.S. Racisme (two immigrant associations) to rediscover true French republicanism, republicanism has been a political tool in French politics. The contemporary politics of immigration has reinforced the ambiguities of French republican and nationalist traditions. It would be a mistake either to conflate a "republican consensus" with humanist, expansive politics or to contrast it to a constrictive, racial politics. Given the competing interpretations of republicanism, it may be useful to delimit the extent to which, historically, republicanist ideologies and practices in

France have operated as parameters in politics. But for my purposes it is important to underscore that the frameworks in which republicanism has operated, the ways people have referred to it, and the meanings they have attached to it have not remained constant.

What can the republican model explain in the evolution of French immigration policy? To identify the causal forces in the French case requires in part a careful dissection of the political process of immigration policy making and its institutional, structural context. The republican model itself does not explain how and why specific courses of action were taken. Furthermore, a full understanding of the causal factors at work also requires a sustained examination of the international environment. Questions about trends in domestic immigration policy, whether in France or elsewhere, must be situated within the context of global and transnational changes in the postwar period.

In sum, there are major difficulties with the argument that the French republican model has determined—either greatly or partially—French policy responses to immigration in the postwar period. The argument tends to reduce French policy evolution to an example of national exceptionalism. This approach does not deal with the usage of the republican model as a political tool. It too often ignores the determinative role of international, economic, structural, or institutional factors. These weaknesses point to the need to reconsider, and adopt a more critical stance toward, the analytical value of the model.

Commentary

From Hidden Consensus to Hidden Divergence

Patrick Weil

France, with the longest history of immigration in Europe, has long been proud of its ability to assimilate immigrants into its "republican" society. According to the republican model, immigrants' ethnic or national origins are erased by the second generation. Thus the French-born child of an Italian, Polish, Spanish, or British foreigner cannot be distinguished from a child with French ancestors. There is therefore no social basis for discrimination: structural or institutional racism, in the British sense, is inconceivable.

But if the republican model remains generally legitimate and effective in French politics, it works less perfectly than Hollifield seems to believe. The model rests on an ambiguity, and it is this ambiguity that explains the fierce political battle that took place over immigration between 1974 and 1984. It also helps explain the rise of the National Front. The model is a synthesis, full of tensions between egalitarian rights legally guaranteed to any immigrant by the rule of law, and ethnic preferences that affect the recruitment process in the labor market. This synthesis functioned adequately during the 1945–1974 period of economic boom. However, in the subsequent years of economic crisis, defenders of the right of any legal resident to settle in France, regardless of nationality, clashed with groups who held that immigrants from certain ethnic backgrounds cannot be assimilated and should therefore be deported. Efforts in the late 1970s to deport North Africans failed, and egalitarian republican law prevailed. Even today, the central immigration issue in France is not one of border control but of nationality law.

When French immigration policy was endowed with its first coherent juridical structure, it appeared to be an egalitarian and liberal one.

The ordinance of November 2, 1945, ratified a system of issuing permits that progressively guaranteed security of settlement. It did not include any provision for ethnic preferences, nor the means for the government to implement such selectivity. But we should not forget that France's foremost immigration policy expert, Georges Mauco, had defended a regime of ethnic selectivity based on the "interwar" model. Because immigration to France was viewed as permanent, European workers were preferred to North Africans in the international labor market.

Thus the National Immigration Office in charge of recruiting immigrant workers was located in Milan rather than Istanbul. And in 1946 French authorities refused an offer from the governor of Algeria to transfer 100,000 workers from Algeria to France. Nevertheless, these Algerian workers later gained entry to France, for economic, not political, reasons. During the later stages of French colonial rule in Algeria, Algerians gained the right to French citizenship and, consequently, freedom of movement between Algeria and France.

Immigration policy makers reacted by changing the labor recruitment process. As Hollifield notes, in 1956 the French state implemented the "practice of bypassing the institutions created to manage immigration flows" in order to favor the entry of Italians, Spanish, and Portuguese immigrants over Algerians. The result was a marked decline in Algerian immigration—180,000 arrived between 1949 and 1956, but only 120,000 between 1956 and 1962—while immigrants of other nationalities rose from 160,000 in the former period to 430,000 in the latter. This demonstrated the ability of the state to implement ethnic preferences. Through the 1962 Evian Accords, France's new Algerian citizens gained the right to travel and settle freely in France; this created a new concern for the French civil servants and politicians who were defenders of ethnic selectivity.

Another battle occurred between 1974 and 1984, when, for economic reasons, worker immigration was first interrupted and then halted definitively. The question then became: Will legal migrants be allowed to settle permanently in French territory and society? For many policy makers the question read differently: Can we accept the permanent settlement of (undesirable) North African immigrants? A broad acceptance policy would contradict the implicit intent of most postwar policy makers, such as Valéry Giscard d'Estaing, who tried to implement a policy of forced returns, including the deportation of 500,000 Algerians. Giscard d'Estaing's policy of selectivity by ethnicity failed under opposition from labor unions, religious groups, and left-wing political parties, as well as Gaullist and Christian Democratic right-wing parties. The Council of State also played an important role in immigration policy, helping to implement the egalitarian "republican" rule of law.

In July 1984 a new "green card" law reasserted the primacy of the legal principles of the 1945 ordinance that guaranteed 90 percent of foreign residents a renewable ten-year residence permit, thus ensuring the right of immigrants and their families to settle in France. Yet for many opponents to the settlement of North African immigrants, the watershed date is neither 1980 (the year that Giscard d'Estaing's deportation effort failed) nor 1984 (the date of the "green card" law). It is 1975, when Jacques Chirac issued a decree to legalize family unification. Supporters of selectivity by ethnicity envision this decree as opening the door to the settlement of North African families. But they are incorrect on two counts: first, family unification has been a key component of French immigration policy since the beginning; and second, North African family immigration commenced long before 1975.

I disagree with Hollifield's statement that "attempts to formulate a European immigration and refugee policy (among the Schengen Group) have challenged key aspects of the republican consensus." France already had implemented a quota system that excludes certain ethnic and national groups from tourist visas. American, Canadian, European, and Japanese tourists can easily enter France. However, since 1984 such entry has been increasingly difficult for Algerians and Moroccans, and not because of the Schengen Agreement or the Maastricht Treaty.

On the refugee issue, France has demonstrated that it can implement an effective national policy, as Hollifield notes. Administrative reform of the asylum-seeking process has had a real impact: the number of asylum seekers decreased from 61,000 in 1989 to 27,000 in 1992 (this compares to 438,000 in Germany in 1992).

As for illegal immigration, the number of illegal immigrants in France has been consistently overstated. The French police are quite efficient at keeping illegal immigrants out. Moreover, the Schengen Agreement gave the French an additional advantage. Within that configuration, with Spain and Italy to the south, Germany to the east, and Belgium to the north, these states all serve as buffers protecting France against illegal immigration. More and more illegal North African workers are now going to Spain or Italy rather than to France.

The debate over settlement has in fact concluded, even if some prominent right-wing politicians are still prepared to lend their voices to Le Pen's call for the departure of non-European immigrants. The real issue is nationality. French law automatically awards French citizenship at age eighteen to all French-born foreign residents, regardless of parents' national origin. For specific historical reasons, many French-born Algerians are in fact French. This egalitarian openness is seen as a key element of the French liberal tradition, but it is now under attack. Conferring French nationality on "undesirable" or "unassimilable" foreigners is sometimes judged to be ill conceived. At one end of the debate, Giscard d'Estaing argued for France to endorse the German tradition of citizenship exclusively by descent. Some experts have focused more subtle attacks on dual nationality and on the "instrumental" use of French nationality by some applicants, thereby supposedly proving the weakness of these individuals' allegiance to France.

The status of the European system of citizenship today favors such views. Depending on his or her birthplace, a child educated in the European Community may or may not become a citizen. A French-born child of a Moroccan immigrant will become a French citizen at age eighteen, while such a child born in Germany or Spain would retain Moroccan citizenship. Foreigners from non-EC countries who live within the EC also face discrimination. A Canadian or Pole who has lived in Paris for twenty years will have fewer rights than a recently arrived Greek or Irish immigrant. The Maastricht Treaty runs the risk of accentuating the marginalization of non-EC residents that began with the crisis in France's "republican" institutions and the intensely political nature of the French debate over immigration. In this context, integration has become a crucial watchword for the antiracist movement. It is an effective weapon in the heated debate about the right to be a French and a European citizen.

Commentary

Questioning the Hidden Consensus

Georges Tapinos

Hollifield presents the French case as a sustained, positive stand in favor of immigration and suggests further that the recent challenge to this stand should not be construed as a shift in policy. In other words, France holds a *stable* view of what migration should be, this view translates into policy, and this policy reflects what Hollifield terms the "republican synthesis." I would like to offer a different reading of these three elements and then suggest two major aspects that Hollifield's chapter neglects: the radical changes in the characteristics of France's foreign population and, partly as a result, the increasing importance of migration in the country's public debate.

Is there indeed a hidden consensus—a coherent, continuous policy toward immigration in France? It is generally agreed that the management of immigration issues has been based partly on demographic considerations but also, and more importantly, on economic factors. What we have, in fact, is the state's definition of general rules of recruitment. Can one really identify in this a continuous migration policy? There are three missing elements that preclude a positive answer to this question.

There is, in fact, a legal framework, established in 1945, that conditions entry and work on having a work contract prior to entering France. However, holding this legal framework constant, the administrative practices that have alternately permitted or prevented the regularization of illegal migrants, without changing the law, have induced radical changes, in both directions, in the de facto immigration regime. Thus policy continuity appears as an ex post facto reconstruction.

A second consideration is the fact that—absent an immigration policy determined at the governmental level, with clear objectives and guidelines for its implementation—immigration policy became the ob-

ject of conflicting interests between the government departments involved. Some departments were concerned exclusively with meeting the
needs of the labor market and had no settlement or assimilation dimensions in their policy. Others sought to place labor migration in the
broader perspective of international relations with emigration countries.
Tensions between the Ministry of Labor, the Ministry of the Interior, and
the Ministry of Foreign Affairs regarding Algerian migration in the
mid-1960s are a case in point.

Finally, in the total absence of parliamentary debate on immigration
issues, immigration policies—or, more precisely, migration management—lacked legitimacy. The implicit assumption was that, since migration was an adjustment to labor market shortages, the market contained
the appropriate and fair mechanism for achieving equilibrium, to the
benefit of all concerned. The dynamics of international migration demonstrate that this was not the case. Some groups benefited more than
others. Some effects—both positive and negative—were felt with different lags after entry. For these reasons, different procedures, mediated
through the political system, were needed to balance conflicting interests. Undoubtedly the fact that political institutions—Parliament and
political parties—neglected immigration issues goes far to explain the
success of the extreme right, which large segments of the public viewed
as the only group addressing these issues.

Hollifield seems too quick to accept the notion that economic and
social regulation is fully in the hands of the French state. I am not
suggesting that the state is absent from the immigration arena. However,
I am proposing that we incorporate into the analysis the behavior of the
actors involved: migrants and firms. The history of French migration
over the last forty years is the history of individuals seeking work and
employers seeking labor. To understand the fluctuations in migrant
flows, the impact of border closure, and the role of return incentives, we
must look to the micro level. Labor agreements are not policy; they did
not initiate the flows, only consolidate them.

To view the French case as characterized by a sustained, positive
stand on immigration, one has to relate this position to some implicit
fundamental ideology in French society; that is what Hollifield does by
referring to the republican synthesis. This synthesis stems, according to
Hollifield, from "the universalist and republican principles of the French
Revolution." What do these principles imply for immigration policy?

A distinction should be made between the openness of the country
(that is, the degree to which France will accept incoming immigrants)
and the openness of the society (that is, the opportunities available to
immigrants already present and part of the society). As far as the
openness of French society is concerned, a case can be made that the so-
called republican synthesis has unambiguous implications for the people already there, whatever their national origin. Indeed, it could be

conceived as the ideological basis of an idealized French model that views foreigners as individuals, not as members of an ethnic community—individuals who should be able to find their own way in the society without facing legal discrimination but also without the benefit of any specific positive action in their favor. In concrete terms, this translates into a very low, nearly nonexistent level of legal discrimination, the right to family unification, the possibility of gaining French citizenship through marriage, naturalization, or (for the children of immigrants) birth in France, but it excludes any political rights. An example is the family allowance; foreigners receive allowances for all of their children, but the amount is smaller for those of their children who remain in the home country.

Does this republican synthesis imply anything specific regarding entry policy? That is a very different question. True, the republican synthesis has some implications for the acceptance of *political* refugees, and French immigration history can recall in this respect the admission of Russians after 1917, of Spaniards (from both sides of the Spanish civil conflict) after 1936, of Iranians before and after Khomeini, of Khomeini himself, of the Vietnamese, and so on. Beyond that, I see absolutely no implications as far as admission of immigrants is concerned. Further, one could make the case that this universal message translates rather into the export of these principles beyond France's borders, which in the best case might translate into specific schemes of colonization (such as the Département d'Outremer), and in the worst case into ideological and colonial expansion. In fact, it is hazardous to assume that French immigration policy has been based on universalist principles. Such a position contradicts a century of immigration practice, in which demographic concerns and economic necessities have always provided the (only) rationale for admission. There is more realpolitik than universalist principles at work.

Two points might be added to Hollifield's analysis. First, the characteristics of France's foreign population have changed as a result of the maturation of the migration process and the legal closing of the French border in 1974. As a result of these two factors, the duration of migrants' stays has increased and migrants' expectations of returning home have changed. As compared to nationals, migrants are more diverse in their ethnic composition, and there is an overall increase in the share of non-Europeans in the migrant population. During the years of high migration from the late 1950s through the mid-1970s, typical migrants to France were men, generally employed in the industrial sector, with a lower level of unemployment than natives, often living without their families, and frequently residing in institutionalized housing. In contrast, the last censuses show a feminization of the migrant population, an extension in the age structure at both ends, a decrease in the economic participation rate, a dramatic increase in unemployment, an increase in tertiary activities, an increase in small business employment, and a decrease in fertility differentials. The distribution of foreigners by country of citizenship has also been dramatically altered. These changes are at the root of present debates about increased job competition between natives and foreigners, the concern that the French will lose their national identity as a consequence of increased ethnic, cultural, and religious differences between newcomers and the native-born.

The changes introduced by the process of European integration constitute the second major element missing from Hollifield's analysis. European integration has in fact weakened the incentive to move within the European Community, partly as a result of decreasing wage and labor cost differentials between countries. But there has been a sharp increase in the number of migrants from non-EC countries. The dismantling of internal barriers to mobility, combined with the potential for large migration flows from the east—and, more importantly, from the south—call for a common policy for dealing with non-EC nationals, an idea that has met with strong resistance. Whether such a policy evolution involves strengthening entry restrictions, a change in citizenship laws, or a greater openness to trade and aid, the applicability of national models—and the French model in particular—is being called into question.

6

Germany: Reluctant Land of Immigration

Philip L. Martin

The German Immigration Dilemma

Germany's leaders have declared that "the Federal Republic of Germany is not, nor shall it become, a country of immigration." The German government has asserted that "restricting non-EC immigration is necessary to safeguard social peace and to integrate the aliens already in Germany." Nonetheless, these immigration policy goals have not been achieved. In the early 1990s, over 1 million newcomers—ethnic Germans, family unification immigrants, applicants for asylum, and legal and illegal alien workers— entered the country each year. Almost all were from non-European Community countries. This gap between immigration goals and results has led to considerable dissatisfaction among Germans.

There are many signs of discontent. Public opinion polls indicate that over 60 percent of all Germans want immigration reduced or stopped,[1] and many cling to the hope that some of the foreigners living in Germany will return home. Germans dissatisfied with the inability of the major political parties to close the gap between immigration goals and outcomes have given anti-foreigner political parties 5–15 percent of the vote in state and local elections. Most tragic have been the attacks on foreigners in Germany in 1992 and 1993. The police reported an average of fifty to one hundred anti-foreigner incidents daily, including arson attacks in Mölln, near Hamburg, and Solingen, near Cologne, that left eight Turks dead.

The author is indebted to Elmar Hönekopp, Gunter Bierbrauer, Elizabeth Midgley, and participants in the conference on "Controlling Illegal Immigration" for helpful comments.

[1]The *Guardian*, September 1, 1992. Seventy-eight percent of those polled agreed that immigration was Germany's most pressing problem, compared with 21 percent who cited unification.

Immigration has become perhaps the major social issue in Germany. There are almost 7 million foreigners in Germany, of whom 2 million are in the workforce, making foreigners 8 percent of Germany's unified population of 81 million and 5 percent of its workforce. These foreigners are likely to stay in Germany. Children under age eighteen account for one-fourth of the foreign population. Two-thirds of these children were born in Germany and are unlikely to migrate to their countries of citizenship after being educated in Germany. Yet German immigration policy still strives toward goals announced in 1981: reducing immigration, promoting voluntary returns, and integrating the foreigners who choose to remain.

The gap between immigration policy goals and outcomes, and the attacks on foreigners, have moved immigration into the limelight. In the wake of the attacks on Turks settled in Germany, political leaders announced crackdowns on the so-called skinhead youths who receive at least moral support from anti-immigrant political parties, and the German public responded in large numbers to calls for demonstrations against xenophobia.[2] The major political parties tried to reduce the ostensible reasons for the anti-foreigner violence by agreeing in 1992 to limit the annual influx of ethnic Germans, and in mid-1993 to restrict the entry of applicants for asylum.

But neither demonstrations in support of foreigners nor efforts to restrict some entries have resolved the issue of whether Germany should be an immigration country. Nor has Germany been able to decide how to integrate the foreigners living there. The options under discussion include offering noncitizen foreigners local voting rights, offering dual citizenship, and simplifying the process through which foreigners become naturalized citizens. As Germany searches for durable immigration and integration policies, ostensibly nonimmigrant foreign workers continue to arrive.

Flawed Policies That Worked

Germany arrived at today's disjuncture between immigration policy goals and actual outcomes by several paths. Germany had the unusual experience of pursuing guestworker and open asylum policies that were fundamentally flawed but nevertheless worked the first time they were tested, helping to silence critics of these policies. For example, the employment of guestworkers fell by 25 percent from 1966 to 1967 (see table 6.1), while German employment fell only 3 percent, suggesting that guestworkers could be rotated in and out of the labor market as needed. Similarly, when the number of applicants for asylum exceeded 100,000 in 1980, Germany required Turks (who accounted for half the appli-

---

[2]Kostede (1993: 3) reports that over 3 million Germans have demonstrated against anti-foreigner sentiment in Germany since November 1992.

TABLE 6.1
FOREIGNERS AND FOREIGN WORKERS IN GERMANY: 1950–1993

Year	Foreign Population (000s)	Percent of Total Population	Foreign Workers (000s)	Remittances (DM mil)	Turks' Remittances (DM mil)
1950	567.9				
1951	506.0				
1952	466.2				
1953	489.7				
1954	481.9		72		
1955	484.8		80		
1956			99		
1957			108		
1958			127		
1959			167		
1960	686.2	1.2	279	300	0
1961	686.1		549		
1962			711		
1963			829		
1964			986		
1965			1,217		
1966			1,314		
1967	1806.7		991		
1968	1924.2	3.2	1,090	2,150	350
1969	2381.1	3.9	1,372	3,300	700
1970	2976.5	4.9	1,949	5,000	1,250
1971	3438.7	5.6	2,241	6,450	1,900
1972	3526.6	5.7	2,352	7,450	2,300
1973	3966.2	6.4	2,595	8,200	2,600
1974	4127.4	6.7	2,287	7,700	2,650
1975	4089.6	6.6	2,039	7,400	2,500
1976	3948.3	6.4	1,921	6,700	2,150
1977	3948.3	6.4	1,869	6,100	1,800
1978	3981.1	6.5	1,864	6,250	1,900
1979	4146.8	6.7	1,937	6,950	2,600
1980	4453.3	7.2	2,013	7,450	2,950
1981	4629.8	7.5	1,900	7,650	3,200
1982	4666.9	7.6	1,771	7,650	3,150
1983	4534.9	7.4	1,709	7,700	3,100
1984	4363.6	7.1	1,608	8,300	3,400
1985	4378.9	7.1	1,536	7,800	3,250
1986	4512.7	7.4	1,545	7,450	2,800
1987	4240.5	6.9	1,624	7,350	2,350
1988	4489.1	7.3	1,607	7,450	2,500
1989	4845.9	7.7	1,684	7,500	2,500
1990	5342.5	8.4	1,793	7,060	2,400
1991	5882.3	7.3	1,981	6,429	2,300
1992	6495.8	8.0	2,120	6,825	2,600
1993	6878.1	8.5	2,184	6,838	

Source: Bericht der Beauftragten der Bundesregierung für die Belange der Ausländer die Lage der Ausländer in der BRD: 1994 (March). Population data for 1987 through 1989 were corrected with 1987 census data; data after 1990 refer to unified Germany. In 1993, 97 percent of the foreigners lived in the former West Germany, which has a population of about 60 million. Foreign workers are those in the German social insurance system—about 5 percent, or an additional 110,000 foreigners in Germany are self-employed.

TABLE 6.2
ASYLUM SEEKERS IN THE FEDERAL REPUBLIC OF GERMANY: 1980–1994

Year	Asylum Seekers	Decisions Made	Persons Approved	Percent Approved	Persons Rejected	Percent Rejected
1980	107,818		12,783	12		
1981	49,391		8,531	17		
1982	37,423		6,209	17		
1983	19,737		5,032	25		
1984	35,278		6,566	19		
1985	73,832		11,224	15		
1986	99,650		8,853	9		
1987	57,379		8,231	14		
1988	103,076		7,621	7		
1989	121,318		5,991	5		
1990	193,063	148,842	6,518	4	116,268	78
1991	256,112	168,023	11,597	7	128,820	77
1992	438,191	216,356	9,189	4	163,637	76
1993	322,599	513,561	16,396	3	347,991	68
1994	50,353	167,730	14,615	9	122,873	73

Source: Federal Office for the Recognition of Asylum Applications, Nuremberg. Asylum data for 1994 are for January–May. Approval and rejection data for years before 1989 are not strictly comparable, and the asylum law changed effective July 1, 1993.

cants) to obtain entry visas. Three years later the number of applicants for asylum fell to less than 20,000 (see table 6.2). Neither rotation nor visas were long-run solutions to underlying guestworker and asylum issues, but the first time these policies were tried they solved the immediate problem and slowed the search for durable solutions.

Most of the foreigners living in Germany are the legacy of the failed guestworker policies of the 1950s and 1960s. Guestworkers from Southern Europe helped sustain Germany's "economic miracle," but they did not follow the plan and leave their manufacturing, mining, and construction jobs to make room for fresh temporary workers. It suited their employers to keep them, and it suited the foreign workers to stay and to bring their families to Germany. As Max Frisch noted, Germany recruited workers but got human beings, and the settlement of probationary migrant workers in Germany transformed a narrow labor market policy into a much wider immigration phenomenon.

The origins of the asylum issue are different. Some of the framers of Germany's 1949 Basic Law had sought refuge outside Germany during the 1930s and 1940s, and their recollection of the difficulty of finding countries willing to accept them gave impetus to the provision of Article 16: "Persons persecuted for political reasons shall enjoy the right of asylum." There are no numerical limits or quotas on those seeking or obtaining asylum in Germany; and because asylum is a constitutionally guaranteed right, applicants are entitled to public assistance and accommodations until their applications are resolved.

Two facts stand out regarding the 1 million applicants for asylum who have arrived since 1989 and led Germany to revise its asylum system in July 1993 (Hailbronner 1994). First, about 95 percent were judged to be economic rather than political refugees and thus had their claims for asylum rejected.[3] Second, state and local governments paid an average $10,000 per year to house, feed, and clothe each asylum applicant during the two to four years that were often required to process a claim.[4] Disaffected youths as well as many other Germans resent the visible reminder that foreigners who do not face political persecution are abusing a humanitarian provision of the German Constitution. However, achieving a political consensus on how to change Germany's asylum law proved to be controversial. The conservative governing coalition wanted to amend the Constitution to remove the absolute right to apply for asylum, while the opposition parties believed that it was possible to solve the asylum crisis without amending the Constitution.

The asylum reform that went into effect on July 1, 1993, left unchanged the constitutional right to asylum. But it added another clause that requires asylum applicants who arrive in Germany through neighboring countries that also provide asylum to make their claims in those countries. Applicants can still fly into Germany and request asylum, but visa requirements and fines on airlines are expected to close this port of entry. Applicants arriving from a list of countries deemed to be "safe" have the burden of proving that they have been singled out for persecution; such applicants are allowed to apply for asylum in Germany, and then they are returned to Turkey or Romania while their applications are considered.

Searching for Durable Policies

Germany's immigration problem is that an officially nonimmigrant country is in fact one of the world's major destinations for immigrants. Today's unwanted immigration has its roots in guestworker and asylum policies that reflect the circumstances of the era in which they were made. Because these policies initially appeared to be working, they slowed the search for durable policies.

With unwanted immigration rising, the gap between policy goals and outcomes has become so wide that Germany is now embarked on a quest for durable immigration policies. Achieving a durable policy

---

[3]On appeal, up to 20 percent of all asylum applicants are allowed to remain legally in Germany. These include persons from Serb-occupied portions of Croatia.

[4]Parkes (1992: 9) puts the cost of accommodating asylum applicants at DM 1,400 monthly, or about $840 per month and $10,080 per year.

requires resolving both domestic and international issues. Germany may have to reexamine who is a German and how a foreigner becomes a German in order to deal with the immigration of ethnic Germans now living in Eastern Europe and the former USSR, as well as to integrate foreigners living in Germany.

However, perhaps the most intriguing development during the past five years is the reemergence of the labor shortages and foreign worker programs that first led Germany down the immigration path. Germany responded to recent domestic labor shortage complaints and joblessness in its restructuring Eastern European neighbors with a series of avowedly nonimmigrant migrant worker programs.

Since 1989 Germany has developed seasonal worker, work-and-learn, firm-to-firm subcontracting, and frontier worker programs; in 1992 over 300,000 foreign workers participated in these programs. The programs' design, as well as a 1990 change in Germany's immigration law, are meant to prevent these foreign workers from settling in Germany.

Illegal Immigration

In Germany and most other European nations, there is not much U.S.-style illegal immigration of millions of persons slipping surreptitiously across borders. European nations are fairly open to Eastern and Southern Europeans, so most unauthorized workers enter legally and become unauthorized only when they violate the terms of their entry by going to work. Some employers prefer to hire these unauthorized workers in order to avoid payroll taxes that finance Europe's social safety net (and can add 50 percent to the hourly wage the employer pays). Some foreign workers also prefer to work off the books, thereby saving the 20–30 percent of their wages that are typically deducted for pension, unemployment, and health programs.

Since Germans also engage in off-the-books employment, the labor inspectors responsible for limiting the size of the underground economy see illegal alien employment in construction and janitorial services as just another part of the underground economy. The Ministry of Labor's method of cutting down on the black labor market has been to develop a social welfare card and database, and to require that the card be shown when a worker is hired and that it be carried by workers in construction and other industries where abuses are common.

The German Ministry of Labor is gaining 700 additional inspectors to combat the underground economy (former intra-German border guards are being retrained as labor inspectors), but officials nonetheless are only guardedly optimistic about their ability to prevent unauthorized workers from finding jobs in Germany. These officials would like to see more changes in German labor laws, such as lowering from the current U.S.$300 level the monthly wage that exempts employers from reporting their workers to the pension system. However, their major plea is for prosecutors and judges to treat unauthorized employment as a serious crime.

Future Immigration Policies

Germany is likely to accept at least several hundred thousand newcomers every year during the 1990s, adding the equivalent of 2 million residents, or 1 million workers, during the decade. Some of these newcomers will be ethnic Germans, some will be applicants for asylum, some will be family members and relatives of immigrants settled in Germany and of German citizens, and some will be migrant workers. Although the government will be able to draw legal distinctions between ethnic Germans, asylum applicants, family unification immigrants, and migrant workers, these distinctions cannot be set forth plainly if the country's leaders continue to announce that Germany is closed to immigrants.

Four types of responses have been discussed regarding the prospect of several hundred thousand newcomers arriving annually during this decade. First, Germany could reduce the number of persons eligible to enter by redefining who is entitled to automatic entry as a German, or by restricting family unification in Germany. This so-called British option would preserve a wide-open door for selected immigrants, but it would restrict entries by reducing the number of persons eligible to enter.

Second, Germany could adopt a U.S.-type immigration queue system that leaves unchanged the definition of ethnic German and family member but establishes an annual entry level or quota that has the effect of requiring those persons wishing to enter Germany to wait in queue. An annual immigration quota, combined with an entry priority system, might permit Germany to manage the annual influx in a manner that reflects its own, rather than the migrants', priorities.

Third, development and other assistance could be provided to those eligible to immigrate into Germany, or to the areas in which they live, so that they choose to remain at home. Accelerating development—especially in Eastern Europe and the former USSR, where 3 to 5 million "ethnic Germans" live—is desirable for its own sake. However, it is unlikely to stem emigration pressures soon.

Fourth, Germany could try to divert newcomers from immigrant into nonimmigrant channels. Instead of coming to Germany as asylum applicants or ethnic Germans, some newcomers might be persuaded to arrive as migrant workers who, it is hoped, would leave after two or three years.

From an outsider's point of view, it seems inevitable that Germany will reluctantly acknowledge that it has become a land of immigration. This acknowledgment may be tied to the development of an immigration system that reflects entry priorities between the four major immigration strands:

ethnic Germans, refugees accepted on humanitarian grounds, family unification immigrants, and imported migrant workers.

The acknowledgment that Germany takes immigrants, and the consequent establishment of priorities for their entry, may also lead to a change in policy toward foreigners currently in the country. The government now has a three-point foreigners policy—no additional non-EC immigration, the promotion of voluntary returns to the immigrants' countries of origin, and the integration of foreigners and their families who wish to stay. The latter two points appear to contradict each other since policies that promote returns may impede integration.

Germany is engaged in a debate over the meaning of integration, over naturalization procedures, and over the country's future as a multicultural society. Integration was described in 1991 as a "stepwise accommodation to our [German] living relationships and the peaceful coexistence of people with different backgrounds, with mutual respect for each other's nation, culture, and religion" (Liselotte Funke, in Herrmann 1992: 29). This has generally meant that foreigners who are integrated are expected to respect German culture and the constitutional separation of state and church, to learn German, and to send their children to German schools.

Some analysts argue that integration would come sooner if more foreigners became naturalized German citizens. Fewer than 20,000 foreigners a year became naturalized Germans during the 1980s, in part because Germany has fairly restrictive and expensive naturalization procedures which require, among other requisites, fifteen years of residence. Children of foreigners are not accorded German citizenship by virtue of German birth, but Germany has simplified naturalization procedures for those between seventeen and twenty-three years of age who have lived in Germany for at least eight years. Some argue that this liberalization is insufficient, that Germany should make German citizenship more attractive by permitting naturalization after five years of residence and offering dual citizenship.

A third issue in Germany is whether the country should become a multicultural society. Practically everyone who favors or opposes "multicultural society" has a different definition of what is envisioned, ranging from tolerance of ethnic differences to state support for maintaining such differences. The debate is at an early stage, with an as yet uncertain outcome.

Phase 1: From Emigration to Guestworkers

Germany was primarily a country of emigration until the 1950s. Of the 45 million immigrants who arrived in the United States between 1820 and 1960, about 7 million, or approximately one in six, were from Germany. Germans constituted one-third of the immigrants arriving in the United States during the 1850s and 1890s, and one-fourth of the immigrants arriving during the 1830s, 1840s, 1870s, 1880s, and 1950s. Over 90 percent of all German emigrants came to the United States, and some 60 million Americans, or one in four, reported in the 1980 population census that they had German roots.

As Germany was transformed from an agricultural into an industrial nation in the late 1800s and early 1900s, internal migration became more important than transatlantic migration. Most movement was east to west, from East Prussia to the central German cities of Berlin, Leipzig, and Dresden, and later to the western German Rhineland (Bade 1984: 62). When ethnically Polish Prussian/German citizens arrived in the Ruhr as a result of employer recruitment and cheap rail fares, they were termed "Ruhr Poles." Italians were also imported to work on Ruhr-area farms and in mines and factories.

Migrant workers from Poland replaced some of those moving west on Prussian estates. In theory, these nonimmigrant seasonal workers were required to depart when their jobs ended. Even though many of them settled and most of the Poles who moved west integrated successfully, Germany's early experience with foreign workers did not lead to a sense that "leakage into settlement" was a serious consequence of migrant worker programs (Bade 1992).

The number of foreigners in Germany during this time was significant. The 1900 population census recorded almost 800,000 foreigners, and the 1910 census recorded almost 1.3 million, making them 2 percent of the population. In both years, half of the foreigners were considered to be Austrians, and the 10 percent from the Netherlands outnumbered the 9 percent from Italy. About one-third worked in agriculture. The 1926 census reported almost 1 million foreigners, including 25 percent each from Poland and Austrian-controlled Czechoslovakia.

Like France, Germany had considerable experience with migrant workers and foreign residents before World War II. However, unlike France, Germany did not derive from this experience a belief that further immigration could serve useful national purposes. Instead, Germany seems to have emerged from its prewar experience with immigration believing that rotational guestworker programs could be made to work as designed.

Hitler came to power in 1933, and Germany expanded its industrial capacity enormously. During World War II, Germany relied on prisoners of war and forced labor in its factories rather than enlisting German women to join the workforce. The 7.7 million prisoners of war and workers from occupied countries in Germany in summer 1944 provided German managers with considerable experience in dealing with a foreign workforce (Mehrländer and Schultze 1992a: 7). In the opinion of at least a few Germans, when labor shortages appeared in the 1950s, some of these managers were confident that they could once again manage a multinational workforce.

When the Federal Republic of Germany was founded in 1949, there was initially massive unemployment as 8.3 million refugees and displaced persons arrived between the end of the war and 1950. Many were pessimistic about their future in Germany; according to contemporary opinion polls, up to half of the German population wanted to emigrate (author interview with Friedrich Heckmann, June 1993). Even after currency reform, Marshall Plan aid, and the development of the "social market economy" put Germany on the path to sustained economic growth, unemployment persisted as West Germany absorbed more refugees and displaced persons (they accounted for 90 percent of Germany's population growth in the 1950s).[5]

The economic miracle that began in the 1950s absorbed these immigrants, and their availability permitted Germany to expand its economic output without raising wages, thus making German exports competitive. There was competition between "natives" and "refugees" for housing and jobs in the 1950s, but the newcomers had German citizenship and spoke German, they knew they had little chance of returning to their homes in the east, and the German government and political parties actively tried to integrate them.

The guestworker story turned out differently. Germany's unemployment rate fell sharply in the early 1950s, and some German employers threatened to move their factories abroad if they could not obtain additional workers. Foreign workers were trickling into Germany; there were 80,000 in July 1955, including 10 percent from Italy (Mehrländer and Schultze 1992a: 10). Italy was not opposed to having its citizens work in Germany, but it wanted them to be recruited under the terms of a bilateral agreement. With German farmers requesting Italian workers to harvest their crops and Italy insisting on an agreement, the stage was set for the German-Italian labor recruitment agreement of December 1955.

Guestworker Recruitment

The number of foreign workers in Germany rose to 280,000 by 1960, including 44 percent from Italy.[6] In 1960, the number of vacant jobs for the first time exceeded the number of unemployed workers. As a result, German employers who were producing cars, machine tools, and appliances for booming domestic and export markets began to

[5]The former West Germany absorbed large number of Germans who moved west: one writer called the westward movement of 8 million Germans between 1944 and 1946 "the greatest migratory movement of modern times" (Ardaugh 1987: 13). Estimates of the number of Germans who moved west between the end of World War II and the construction of the Berlin Wall in 1961 range from 9 million to 13 million.

[6]Unless otherwise specified, the data in this chapter refer to West Germany.

employ Greek, Spanish, and Yugoslav workers. German employers wanted the government to put guestworker recruitment and employment on a firm legal basis; after negotiations with unions guaranteed foreigners equal wages, Germany signed labor recruitment agreements with Spain and Greece in 1960, Turkey in 1961, and Portugal in 1964.[7]

There was no serious discussion in the early 1960s of pursuing alternatives to the importation of foreign workers (Schiller et al. 1976). There were four reasons why importing foreign workers seemed to be the right thing to do. First, the German labor force was shrinking for demographic and related reasons, such as a delayed baby boom, the spread of education, and better pensions which prompted earlier retirements. Second, there was a reluctance to risk what was still perceived to be a fragile economic recovery on what were thought to be risky mechanization and rationalization alternatives to importing foreign workers. Third, Europe was unifying anyway, and Germany had agreed that Italians and other EC nationals would have freedom of movement rights after January 1, 1968. With Italians soon able to come as they wished, Germany thought it was simply regulating unilaterally the rate at which EC workers would soon arrive in any event. Fourth, the early 1960s provided Western Europe with a peculiar international economic environment. Germany in the 1960s had an undervalued currency in a world of fixed exchange rates, so that local and foreign capital was invested in Germany to produce goods for export markets. The incentive to invest and create jobs in Germany was significant: if the exchange rate was U.S.\$1 = DM 5 when it "should" have been \$1 = DM 4, then a \$100 investment in Germany was worth DM 500 to the investor rather than its "true" DM 400 value. For this reason, American multinationals poured so many dollars into Europe that a French writer warned of "the American challenge." Germans had little incentive to invest and create jobs abroad in this era.[8]

The 1957 Treaty of Rome established the European Economic Community (EEC) and guaranteed citizens of member states the right to work in any EEC nation after 1968.[9] The Berlin Wall closed the door from East to West Germany in 1961, encouraging labor-short German manufacturers to cast a wider net for additional labor: hence Ger-

[7] A treaty was signed with Tunisia in 1965, and most Moroccan workers were recruited under a 1966 revision of the 1963 agreement. A Yugoslav-German labor recruitment agreement was signed in 1968.

[8] For discussions of why importing guestworkers seemed the rational policy, and thus spurred little serious debate in Germany, see Martin 1980; Miller and Martin 1982; Kindleberger 1967; Schiller et al. 1976.

[9] Freedom of movement within the EEC means that a worker from any member state may enter another and remain for up to three months in search of a job. If the migrant finds employment, the host country must grant any necessary work and residence permits.

many's labor agreements with Greece, Spain, Yugoslavia, and Turkey in the early 1960s.[10]

German employers recruited "guestworkers." Many were farmers between ages eighteen and thirty-five, although there were significant numbers of semiskilled construction workers, miners, skilled workers, and even schoolteachers who migrated to Germany to work on assembly lines. News spread rapidly of jobs that paid in one month the equivalent of a year's earnings at home, and there were soon long lists of Turks and Yugoslavs signed up with government authorities, waiting for their chance to go abroad.

The recruitment system was well organized (see Miller and Martin 1982). German employers who had vacant jobs asked local employment offices for more workers, and the latter made only a pro forma search for local workers in a time when there were ten vacant jobs for each unemployed worker. An employer's request for, say, 1,000 unskilled workers was sent to German recruitment offices in Istanbul, Belgrade, and Rome, where workers who had registered to work in Germany were screened for health and skills and then awarded one-year work and residence permits.

Only a day or two after arrival, a migrant would be at work on an assembly line or at a construction site. With ten Turks wanting to work in Germany for each one needed, the Germans could be selective, and they were. The result was that many workers considered to be skilled in their home countries worked as unskilled workers in Germany. For example, some 30–40 percent of the Turks recruited to work in Germany were considered skilled workers in Turkey, and an estimated 40 percent of Turkey's carpenters and stonemasons were employed in Germany in 1970.

Most migrant workers were not recruited by name, but German employers could request particular workers, creating an incentive for workers wishing to migrate to persuade their friends and relatives already abroad to have German employers request them. Migrants sometimes traveled to Germany as tourists, found employers who would hire them, and then got their employers to request them by name in order to legalize their status. By some estimates, 20–30 percent of the Turks employed in Germany during the peak recruitment years went originally as "tourists."

The number of migrant workers soon swelled far beyond original expectations. Most of the migrant workers in the 1960s were recruited by

---

[10]Germany recruited workers during the 1960s from EC-member Italy and from seven non-EC recruitment countries: Greece, Morocco, Portugal, Spain, Tunisia, Turkey, and Yugoslavia. Greece became a member of the EC in 1981, and Spain and Portugal became members in 1986. Greece had to wait until 1988 before its citizens got full freedom of movement rights, and Spain and Portugal, scheduled to have freedom of movement rights in 1993, got mobility rights one year early, in 1992.

major manufacturers such as Siemens, Volkswagen, and Mercedes-Benz. At Opel's major auto assembly plant, for example, the number of migrant workers increased from 2,200 in 1968 to 9,300 in 1972, when migrants were one-third of all Opel workers.

The peak recruitment years were 1968 to 1972, when the migrant workforce rose from 1 million to 2.6 million, or from 5 to 12 percent of the German workforce. Trains and planes were chartered to bring 500–1,000 workers to Germany every day; and despite the migrants' increased visibility in German workplaces and around train stations, German politicians, employers, unions, and the migrants themselves continued to proclaim that the foreign workers were only guests and that labor migration itself would soon be ended by automation at home and economic growth in lower-wage countries abroad. Many migrants continued to leave after one or two years in Germany, but few Germans were prepared for the settlement of migrant workers in their country in the early 1970s.

Settlement

The guestworker policy had been trumpeted in Germany and abroad as a worker rotation program. It was convenient for policy makers, employers, and the migrants themselves to believe that, after one or two years, most of the guests would leave with their savings and be replaced by fresh recruits. However, a rotation policy was not in the interest of either the migrants or their employers. Migrant workers earned high wages, but they soon learned that the instant wealth they hoped to achieve was rooted in the false belief that they could earn German wages at Turkish living costs. Migrants had to stay abroad longer than planned to realize their savings goals, and some sent for their families. German employers did not discourage such family unification. Wives of the guestworkers could also work, and their presence persuaded trained and experienced migrants to remain, saving employers the cost of recruiting and training new migrants.

Instead of enforcing rotation strictly, the German government—at the urging of Southern European governments, German unions, migrant assistance groups, and international organizations—relaxed rules on prolonging stays and on family unification. As a result, the number of nonworking migrants rose. In 1968, there were about 1.9 million foreign residents and 1 million foreign workers in Germany (table 6.1). Five years later, there were 4 million foreign residents and 2.6 million foreign workers. After 1973, the foreign population rose while the number of foreign workers fell. The number of foreign workers in the old West Germany was 1.8 million in 1990, and the foreign population was 5.2 million, meaning that there were almost two nonworking dependents for every foreigner in the workforce.

The growing number of foreigners, and their increased visibility outside the workplace, was noticeable by the early 1970s. In parts of many German cities, including Frankfurt and Berlin, foreigners soon outnumbered Germans. The presence of Yugoslav and Turkish children in German schools revealed that many "guests" had decided to stay. The reaction of most Germans was negative. Politicians told xenophobic Germans that the migrant workers were necessary to assure economic growth, but many Germans believed that "over-foreignization" was too high a price to pay for economic success. Some Germans were influenced by xenophobia in neighboring Switzerland, and the slogan "Foreigners out! Germany for the Germans" became a major rallying cry of rightist and nationalist politicians.

A few economists warned that Germany's famed industrial engine was becoming calcified because, with migrant labor so readily available, employers did not aggressively develop new technologies. These Cassandras warned that while the Japanese auto industry in the early 1970s had begun to experiment with robots to assemble cars, the Germans hired Turks (Schiller et al. 1976; Martin 1977). Thoughtful Germans wondered whether migrant children should be integrated into German schools and society, or whether they should be taught in Italian or Turkish classrooms so that they could fit into their home societies when their parents returned.

By 1973 it was clear that many of the temporary guests had become more or less permanent residents, and that most Germans were opposed to the unanticipated settlement of Turks and Yugoslavs in Germany. The German government reacted by restricting immigration. First the government announced a tripling of the employer-paid recruitment fee in February 1973 to discourage employers from requesting migrants. A wave of wildcat strikes that summer, which involved a significant number of migrant workers, convinced the government that foreign worker recruitment must be stopped. The government used the October 1973 oil embargo to announce a ban on the further recruitment of guestworkers. The November 1973 recruitment ban was justified in terms of the OPEC oil embargo which allegedly threatened to provoke an economic recession and rising unemployment throughout the industrial countries, making additional migrants unnecessary. However, German employers whose requests for new migrants were thus blocked thought that the government had simply found a convenient excuse to halt the immigration that was troubling German voters.

The fist of "no more recruitment" was wrapped in the glove of new measures to improve the status of migrants in Germany. No migrant could be forced by unemployment to leave Germany, although unemployed migrants were encouraged to return home voluntarily to jobs created with German-financed development projects. Spouses and dependents could continue to join migrants who had valid work and residence permits and proof of suitable housing, but they had to wait one or two years before being allowed to work.

Phase 2: From Guestworkers to Foreign Residents

If the failure of guestworkers to rotate in and out of the German labor market marked the first significant gap between migration policies and outcomes, several subsequent German policies seemed to compound the sense that the government could not predict accurately the effects of migration policy changes (Heckmann 1981; Böhning 1984). The first gap followed the 1973 recruitment stop, which was intended to prevent the number of foreigners in Germany from rising. It did not; instead, migrant workers who feared that they could not return to Germany if they went home brought their families, increasing the foreign population from 4 million in 1973 to 4.5 million in 1980. The foreign population rose despite the recruitment ban, but the foreign workforce fell from 2.6 million to 2 million. Foreign workers, who had been trumpeted as additions to the workforce but not additions to the dependent population, soon had a higher dependency rate than Germans.

Other German attempts to regulate the foreign population also backfired. In an attempt to discourage family unification, Germany announced that foreigners could not move into cities that were already "overburdened" (defined as cities where foreigners represented 12 percent or more of the population). This hard-to-enforce measure simply reduced the mobility and flexibility that had made migrants attractive in the first place.

Financial incentives to influence migrant behavior also backfired. A mid-1970s change in the children's allowance program paid full children's allowances only to children living in Germany, a response in part to newspaper stories of Turkish parents getting allowances for their real and/or fictitious children living in Turkey. The desire to save tax monies by paying a lower allowance to children abroad encouraged parents to bring all their children to Germany, frustrating the goal of limiting the growth of the foreign population.

The fourth German policy that backfired was the departure bonus program of 1983 and 1984. The 1982 election campaign had been won by the current government of the Christian Democratic Union (CDP), Christian Social Union (CSU), and Free Democratic Party (FDP) in part on the grounds that it would "do something" about immigration. The preceding government of the Social Democratic Party (SPD) had "solved" the asylum crisis of 1980 by imposing visa requirements on Turks, but the "foreigners out" slogans of anti-immigrant parties forced the mainstream parties to promise to reduce the growing number of foreigners as well.

The newly elected Kohl government introduced the French system of payments to induce foreigners to leave Germany, a proposal that had been discussed during the previous SPD government. A migrant family that gave up its work and residence permits could get a departure bonus of up to $5,000, and departing workers could get their share of social security contributions refunded immediately upon arrival back home. The foreign population fell from 4.7 million in 1982 to 4.4 million in 1984 and 1985 but then rebounded to 4.5 million in 1986. Studies showed that most of the foreigners who returned home would have left in any event, so Germany merely bunched normal returns during the nine-month program.

Foreigners Today

The 7 million foreigners living in Germany are mostly long-term residents from non-EC nations. The foreign population, which rose by 10 percent from 1992 to 1993, is located (97 percent) in the former West Germany. Detailed data are available only through December 31, 1992, when there were 6.5 million foreigners in Germany (*Bericht* 1994). Almost three-fourths of the foreigners are from non-EC nations; Turks are the largest single group of foreigners, numbering 1.9 million, followed by Yugoslavs (900,000), Italians (560,000), and Greeks (350,000). Over three-fourths of these foreigners have been in Germany more than four years, and 60 percent have lived in Germany for more than ten years. About one-eighth of the annual 800,000 births in Germany have been "foreigners" (*Bericht* 1994).

Almost all foreigners in Germany live in urban areas. Foreigners comprise 8 percent of the population, but they are almost 26 percent of Frankfurt's population, 24 percent of Munich residents, and 10–20 percent of the population in cities such as Cologne, Berlin, and Stuttgart. In most cases, foreigners live in older apartments in neighborhoods with both German and foreign residents; there is less residential segregation than in most American cities.

There have been numerous surveys of Germans and foreigners to establish integration parameters. Most conclude that, for older foreign workers, there is far more workplace than residential integration. However, the situation of foreign youths is different: foreign children go to school with German children, but their paths often diverge during their teenage years in ways that some fear will produce an ethnic underclass in Germany (Mehrländer 1974, 1983, 1987).

Most of the almost 2 million foreign workers arrived before 1973 as twenty- to thirty-year-olds. Now between the ages of forty and sixty, they are usually well integrated at their workplaces. Most foreign workers are still unskilled or semiskilled workers employed in cyclical manufacturing industries; but because Germany pays very high manufacturing wages and provides extensive fringe benefits, many of these foreign workers are part of the blue-collar elite. However, foreigners who lose their jobs often have a hard time finding new ones: like the 2:1 ratio between black and white unemployment rates in the United States, the unemployment rate for foreign workers in Germany is about double that of Germans in the former West Germany, where practically all settled guestworkers live (Engelen-Kefer 1990).

Foreign workers remain concentrated in the industries that recruited guestworkers three decades ago. Half of the foreign workers are employed in manufacturing, and their share of unskilled employment in iron and steel, textiles and plastics, and auto assembly is often 15–30 percent of the workforce. Large manufacturers that recruited guestworkers during the 1960s have workforces today that are one-third foreign, but few foreigners have become supervisors or even skilled workers. Instead, these firms contend that the unskilled and semiskilled migrants are comfortable where they are and that many are unwilling or unable to learn how to operate the new machines now being introduced.

Services employ about one-fifth of Germany's foreign workers, and one-fifth of the restaurant workforce are foreigners. Trade and construction each employ 8 percent of foreign workers; foreigners represent 10 percent of the construction workforce but only 5 percent of the workforce in retail trade. In national data, foreign workers are not the majority of the workforce in even narrowly defined industries and occupations; that is, there seems to be no German occupation or industry comparable to U.S. domestic service or seasonal farmwork in which the majority of workers are immigrants (Buttler and Dietz 1990).

Migrant workers have always had some opportunities to participate in German society. Migrant workers join and participate in German unions, and one-third were members of German unions in 1989 (Mehrländer and Schultze 1992b: 47), although most studies conclude that German unions favor the interests of German workers when these interests conflict with those of migrants. Migrant workers have been elected to posts in German unions, and they have also been elected to the independent plant-based works councils that negotiate with management over issues such as layoffs.

Phase 3: Integration, Ethnic Germans, and Migrant Workers

Policies for Settled Guestworkers

Settled guestworkers and their families account for most of the foreigners living and working in Germany. In 1981 the government announced the policies referred to previously that were directed toward guestworkers: Germany would reduce further non-EC immigration and promote the voluntary return of settled foreigners and the integration of those wishing to remain in Germany. Non-EC immigration has been increasing as applicants for asylum and migrant workers from Eastern Europe enter Germany, but there is less and less hope that settled foreigners can be persuaded to depart voluntarily; in most surveys, fewer than 20 percent plan to leave.[11]

Integrating settled guestworkers has been a top domestic priority throughout the 1980s, but the tension between promoting returns and integrating the migrant workers and their families who have settled in Germany has precluded the development of a policy that seems likely to promote successful integration.

Former chancellor Helmut Schmidt's statements about foreigners illustrate this ambivalence. After his October 1980 re-election, Schmidt made the integration of foreigners his government's top domestic priority. Schmidt argued that Germany had no choice but to integrate the migrants who had made economic contributions during the 1960s, but he then added that "4 million is enough." He announced new programs to help foreign youths with language problems become apprentices in the occupational training system. But this integration program was offset by a new restriction to discourage older children from coming to Germany: they would have to wait one or two years before they could work. Appealing to popular sentiment, Schmidt acknowledged the sacrifices Germans would have to make to integrate foreigners: "It's not easy for Germans who live in an apartment house and don't like the smell of garlic to have to put up with it and even to have a lamb slaughtered in the hallway." Such statements made it clear that integration was envisioned as something of a more equal but still separate process; there was little hint that politicians in the early 1980s envisioned a melting-pot blending of the German and Turkish cultures in Germany.

Turks are of special concern because they were the last, poorest, and most visible migrants to arrive in Germany. Almost one-fourth of Germany's foreigners are Turks, and Turkey has made no secret of its desire to join the EC. If Turkey were to become an EC member country, Turks would have the free migration right that goes with full membership, and more might migrate to Germany. Turkey was not a significant emigration country until the early 1960s, but during the 1970s some 2 million Turks migrated abroad for employment. One study estimated that almost one-fifth of Turkey's men between the ages of twenty and thirty-five (some 700,000 in total) emigrated from Turkey during the late 1960s and early 1970s. Further, despite rapid economic growth in Turkey during the 1980s, up to one-third, or 2.5 million, might emigrate today if they could (Martin 1991: 94).

---

[11] Faruk Sen, of the Center for Turkish Studies in Essen, estimates that the proportion of Turks in Germany who plan to return home fell from 60 percent in the early 1980s to 15 percent today (*Die Welt*, June 6, 1993).

Many Germans view Turks as the most difficult foreigners to integrate into German society because of their relative lack of education and skills, the importance of the Islamic religion in their daily lives, and political divisions within Turkish society that are reflected in the migrant population abroad. Islamic fundamentalists, for example, sometimes extract money from Turkish workers and businesses in Germany to finance the building of mosques there and to promote fundamentalist views in Turkey. Fundamentalist Turkish and leftist Turkish youths clashed violently after protests of anti-foreigner violence in 1993. Observers have noted that many second- and third-generation Turks in Germany seem to be more nationalistic and religious than Turkish youths in Turkey, a possible reflection of their foreign status in Germany.

German fears about the Turks' ability to integrate were reflected in the (mostly unstated) German opposition to Turkey's 1987 application to join the EC. Turkey's admission would give its citizens the right to migrate freely to Germany and seek jobs there (as Italians, Greeks, Spaniards, and Portuguese do today). But many Germans feared that economic integration would, in the case of Turkey, be accompanied by *massive* immigration. Germans note that Turkey's population (62 million in 1994) is growing by 2.2 percent, or 1.4 million, annually, while Germany's population of 81 million would be shrinking were it not for immigration. Turkey today has a larger population than West Germany and would have been the most populous country in the EC (Hönekopp 1990; Hönekopp and Werner 1979).

A growing and poor Turkey within the EC might unleash a new wave of migration to Germany. Per capita income differentials are substantial: 12:1 between Germany and Turkey in 1992, versus 7:1 between the United States and Mexico.[12] German fears of additional Turkish migration are not stilled by arguments that, even if a wave of Turks were to come to Germany to seek jobs, they would not remain unless they could find jobs. Germany projects a decrease in the number of jobs that unskilled Turkish workers could easily fill, so there should be few unwanted Turkish migrants languishing in Germany's projected high-tech and high-skill economy. But German fears that Turks would find niches in Germany's partially deregulated economy and labor market led most Germans to oppose Turkey's application to join the EC; the EC refused Turkey's application in 1989 (Sen 1990).

Many Germans worry that not enough is being done to integrate Turks and other foreigners living in Germany. Most of the focus is on foreign youths. The majority of twenty-year-old foreign youths in Germany today have neither a high school diploma nor certification that they have learned an occupation. The fear is that these 10 percent

[12]The World Bank's *Atlas 1994* (pp. 18–19) puts former German GNP per capita at $23,030 in 1992, versus $1,950 in Turkey. The U.S. GNP per capita was $23,120, versus $3,470 in Mexico.

of all youths in Germany could turn into an ethnically distinct underclass. Germany has made numerous efforts to integrate foreign youths in the apprenticeship system, which provides training for 400 occupations. In this employer co-financed training system, sixteen- to nineteen-year-olds both study in the classroom and learn an occupation under supervision in a workplace. This dual classroom and on-the-job training system provides certification and status to occupations ranging from mechanic to hairdresser, and it is considered a key to Germany's manufacturing and export prowess (Schober and Stegmann 1987).

Without immigration, Germany's population and workforce are expected to shrink. The 1993 labor force of 41 million, for example, is expected to shrink to 39 million in 2000 and 37 million in 2010 if fertility and mortality rates remain at 1990 levels and there is no immigration.[13] The effects of low fertility are felt first among the younger age groups: the number of fifteen- to thirty-year-olds, for example, is projected to fall from 18 million in 1990 to 15 million in 2000 and 13 million in 2010 (Hof 1992: 21).

Some analysts argue that Germany needs 300,000 to 400,000 immigrants annually in order to staff German factories with skilled workers (Hof 1992). German youths, they note, have been favoring university preparation over apprenticeship, and many foreign youths in Germany drop out of school instead of becoming apprentices in fast-growing computer, banking, and insurance occupations. The result is that Germany is producing fewer skilled workers than needed, and unemployed foreign youths are not prepared to fill the skilled jobs that remain vacant. Immigration and a revised integration policy, it is hoped, would permit the apprenticeship system to turn out skilled workers.

But there is no agreement on what constitutes a successful integration policy. Like the United States, Germany has a decentralized administrative system under which each state develops its own educational policies. During the 1970s, schooling for foreign children reflected the range of expectations of West Germany's sixteen state governments, so that foreign children in Berlin were taught in German to promote their integration, while children in Bavaria were taught in Turkish or Serbish to encourage their return home. Although there is a growing recognition that most foreigners are in Germany to stay, so that children are now taught primarily in German, there are vigorous debates over how to overcome the segregation of foreign schoolchildren that results from housing patterns.

---

[13]The 1990 birth rate was 1.3; men lived an average 71.4 years, and women an average 77.7 years.

Opinions differ on whether the challenge of integrating especially the Turkish youths living in Germany is a half-full or half-empty glass. Interviews with some policy makers and researchers turned up evidence that more foreigners are switching from training for sunset occupations (as mechanics or hairdressers, for example) to growth occupations such as computer programming and health care. There is also evidence that the language skills of foreign youths born in Germany are improving, reinforcing the perception that the most difficult integration challenges may already have been overcome. However, other experts begin their assessment by noting that, despite recent progress, half of all foreign youths still have no training certificate at age twenty, making them equivalent to U.S. high school dropouts. Those closest to foreign youths, such as teachers in apprenticeship programs, seem most pessimistic, while those most familiar with first-generation foreign workers, such as union officials, seem most optimistic about integration (Martin 1991: chap. 4).

Integrating foreign youths is perhaps the most hotly debated legacy of Germany's guestworker programs, but there seems to be little agreement on exactly what Germany should do to accelerate integration. Many Germans define integration as participation in those things they find important, so that politicians who are worried about the right of second- and third-generation foreigners to participate in Germany's political life want to make it easier for foreign residents to acquire German citizenship and/or vote in local elections.

Germany has a relatively difficult and, for the intending citizen, uncertain process to naturalization (Schmalz-Jacobsen, Hinte, and Tsapanos 1993; Brubaker 1992). Most foreigners must live in Germany at least ten years, give up their current citizenship, know the German language, be employed or employable, have adequate accommodations for themselves and their families, and pay a $300 application fee, and then their applications to become naturalized Germans are weighed by local authorities who determine whether their naturalization is "in the interest of Germany." German law gives considerable discretion to officials to interpret each of these requirements, and there are allegations that these officials frequently reject applications without explanation. This situation discourages aliens from undertaking the lengthy and expensive effort to naturalize.[14]

Germany has 7 million foreign residents, including over 1 million children born in Germany who must, a age sixteen, obtain, for example,

---

[14]Immigration reforms in 1990 and 1993 introduced the *right* of some foreigners to become naturalized Germans. For example, foreign youths between the ages of sixteen and twenty-three who have lived in Germany for at least eight years, and other foreigners who have lived in Germany for at least fifteen years, have the right, under certain circumstances, to become naturalized German citizens upon the payment of a reduced $60 fee.

Turkish or Yugoslav passports and then German residence and work permits. However, in 1991, only 27,000 foreigners applied to become naturalized Germans.[15] Germany's Commissioner for Aliens Affairs Cornelia Schmalz-Jacobsen argues that Germany should offer "double citizenship" to foreigners born in Germany, so that a second- or third-generation Turk born in Germany could become primarily a German citizen but also retain Turkish citizenship for personal and practical reasons.[16] Others argue that the way to expedite naturalization is to simplify the naturalization process, not complicate it with a primary and a secondary citizenship. Germany has recently simplified naturalization for young people who have lived in Germany for at least eight years. As of 1991, foreigners between ages sixteen and twenty-three are entitled to German citizenship practically automatically if they apply for it; they no longer have to first prove that they are not collecting social assistance payments and that they have adequate living quarters. However, immigration reforms also make it more difficult for newly arrived foreigners to secure the residence right that is a prerequisite to an application for naturalization.

Several European countries have extended rights to vote in local elections to long-term noncitizen residents. Some German politicians favor this Swedish and Dutch method of encouraging political participation, and the Maastricht Treaty to deepen EC integration calls on member states to permit nationals of EC countries who have lived in another member state for three or more years to vote in local elections. If noncitizen voting rights are made available to European Union countries, some German politicians believe that it will be impossible to permit Dutch nationals, for example, who are living in Germany as students, to vote in local German elections, but not Turkish nationals who have been residents for thirty years.

Asylum

Germany included a liberal asylum clause in its 1949 Basic Law. Its authors included persons who had difficulty finding refuge abroad during the Nazi era (1933–1945), and Article 16 states that "persons persecuted for political reasons" shall have the right to asylum in

---

[15]German data distinguish between those with a right to naturalization and those who are permitted to apply to become naturalized Germans. These data refer to those permitted to apply.

[16]Non-Turks have difficulty inheriting Turkish property and do not obtain the advantages of being a Turkish citizen while investing German savings in Turkey. Under current circumstances, a Turk born in Germany who does not naturalize owes loyalty and military service to Turkey. This means that every year at least 10,000 Turkish youths—many of whom speak no Turkish—are expected to report for military service in Turkey. Since it is difficult to integrate them into Turkey's military system, Turkish youths living abroad return to Turkey for two months and pay a fee of $8,000–10,000 to satisfy their military service obligation.

Germany. Under this asylum provision, individuals escaping from Communist nations in Eastern Europe were offered accommodations and permission to work in Germany while their claims that they faced persecution at home, and thus deserved immigrant status in Germany, were considered.

The number of asylum applicants was initially small: about 70,000 persons applied for asylum between 1953 and 1968, and 116,000 applied between 1968 and 1978. The number of asylum applicants rose to 51,000 in 1979 and to 108,000 in 1980 as a consequence of a military coup in Turkey, the absence of a visa requirement for Turks, and the German practice of giving asylum applicants a work permit while their cases were under consideration (see table 6.2). Turkish newspapers reproduced the German asylum application, and word soon spread that asylum was the easiest way to get the German work permits that the Turks really wanted.

A few experts suggested that Germany needed to reevaluate its policy of providing a lengthy appeal procedure for each applicant and its practice of providing work permits to asylum applicants. However, Germany never conducted such a reevaluation because it discovered a quick fix: Germany began requiring Turks wishing to enter the country to obtain visas before leaving Turkey. The number of Turks applying for asylum dropped sharply: there were only 49,000 applications in 1981 despite side doors such as traveling to East Berlin, crossing into West Berlin (where there were no entry inspections), and then applying for asylum. After West and East German authorities negotiated a partial closure of this side door, the number of asylum applicants dropped to 20,000 in 1983.

Germany was unprepared for the upsurge in asylum applications that occurred in the mid-1980s. In 1986, almost 100,000 aliens applied for asylum, and in 1988 there were over 100,000 applications. Applications almost doubled to 193,000 in 1990, and then doubled again to 438,000 in 1992 (see figure 6.1). However, only about 10,000 applicants per year were recognized as refugees, so that as the number of applicants rose, the percentage who were approved fell to less than 5 percent. In 1991, over half of the asylum applicants came from Romania, Bulgaria, the former Yugoslavia, the former Soviet Union, and Poland. During the first quarter of 1993, over one-third of the average 12,000 asylum seekers each month were from the former Yugoslavia, one-eighth were from Turkey, and one-half were from Romania.

The German government managed the upsurge in asylum applications badly. The federal government employs the hearing officers who determine whether an applicant's claim of political persecution at home has merit. The state governments are responsible for housing, feeding, and approving work permits for applicants, and states are assigned applicants roughly in proportion to their population shares. Thus

Figure 6.1

Asylum Seekers and Asylum Granted in Germany

1980-1994

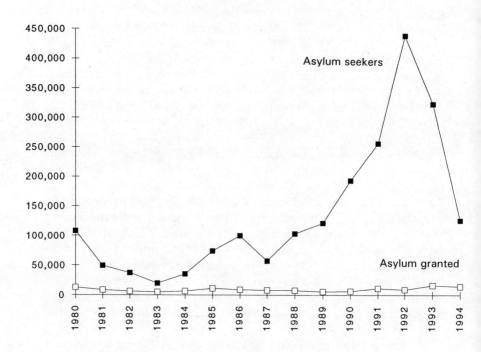

Note: 1994 applications are projected on the basis of January-June.

Bavaria must take 14 percent of asylum applicants, and the five states of the former East Germany must take 20 percent. State governments, in turn, assign applicants to their cities and towns, and so it is local governments that ultimately foot the $10,000 annual bill for each asylum applicant awaiting a decision on whether he or she will be granted safe haven in Germany.

The popular response was predictable. Widely distributing asylum applicants (95 percent of whose claims would be rejected) and requiring local taxpayers to foot the bill contributed to anti-foreigner sentiment everywhere. Especially in the former East German states, the cost of caring for thousands of asylum applicants at a time of economic depression made the population open to the messages of anti-foreigner movements. Ad hoc federal policy changes often inflamed anti-foreigner sentiments further: in order to discourage asylum applicants from coming to Germany, as of 1989 they were prohibited from working while their cases were being considered, but their forced idleness made these visibly unoccupied foreigners an even more inviting target for anti-foreigner sentiments (Werner 1992). The work ban was canceled in 1991, and today each state decides how long an asylum applicant must wait before being issued a work permit.

As the number of asylum applicants rose, so did German attacks on foreigners. Four of the over 4,000 incidents since mid-1991 have been well publicized: the September 1991 and August 1992 attacks on for-eigners in Hoyerswerda and Rostock, respectively, in the former East Germany, in which police and Germans did little to protect foreigners being attacked by German youths, and the arson attacks in November 1992 and May 1993 in the West German cities of Mölln and Solingen, in which eight Turks died.[17] Most Germans roundly condemned these attacks on foreigners: many marched in candlelight processions, and German politicians called on Germans to respect their foreign neigh-bors. Numerous studies of young "skinheads" reported that 70 percent of the estimated 65,000 "organized right-wing extremists" were under age twenty-one, poorly educated, and pessimistic about the future.

The arson attack in Solingen produced the now familiar responses: Germans marching in outrage, and political leaders calling for swift and tough justice. But two new elements were added to the discussion. First, during the funeral marches there were several clashes between right- and left-wing Turkish youths, and between Turkish and German youths. Second- and third-generation Turks in Germany are, according to most studies, more likely to be "fundamentalist Moslems" than are youths in Turkey, provoking fears of further intra-Turkish clashes in Germany in the future.

The second issue raised by the Solingen arson attack is whether and how to integrate Germany's 1.9 million Turks and thus head off future Turkish-German clashes. German politicians, who have yet to acknowl-edge that Germany has become a reluctant land of immigration, have been debating proposals to offer dual citizenship and local voting rights to resident foreigners. Ex-German president Weizacker and Commis-sioner for Aliens Affairs Schmalz-Jacobsen have announced their sup-port for dual citizenship, and a poll taken in June 1993 found that 53 percent of all Germans supported dual citizenship and 62 percent would extend local voting rights to foreigners (*Der Spiegel*, June 7, 1993, p. 21). While it is not clear that dual citizenship and the right to vote in local elections are the top priorities of foreigners in Germany, adopting these measures, proponents argue, might help convince Germans that the

---

[17]Blanke (1993) includes a chronology of events leading up to the German asylum compromise.

foreigners among them should be considered fellow citizens rather than merely fellow residents.

However, the ruling CDU-CSU-FDP government is not willing to support dual citizenship and local voting rights, especially given the wave of elections in 1994.[18] Threatening to resign if the coalition government continues to block the dual citizenship proposal of its own aliens commissioner, Schmalz-Jacobsen expresses frustration that many Germans and political representatives harbor the hope that foreign residents can somehow be persuaded to leave. Schmalz-Jacobsen has used her position to argue that most foreigners are in Germany to stay, that more will be coming for economic and demographic reasons, for family unification, and to seek asylum, and that Germany should have an active immigration policy with annual immigration targets or quotas, rather than permit the individual decisions of foreigners to determine the flow of immigrants.

Asylum and violence against foreigners continue to be major domestic issues in Germany. Politicians thought that they had solved both problems with a reform of the asylum law that went into effect on July 1, 1993. After an emotional debate, two-thirds of the German Parliament agreed to a compromise in which the Article 16 guarantee of asylum remained unchanged, but a new article permitted Germany to turn back without a hearing asylum applicants who arrived through safe third countries that also offer asylum. Germany is surrounded by such countries, so that Romanians, for example, who acknowledge that they entered Germany through Poland are returned to Poland.[19] Since Poland's accommodations and work opportunities are less attractive than Germany's, the hope is that this approach will reduce the number of economic migrants trying to enter Germany as asylum seekers.

Foreigners who fly to Germany or who slip across borders clandestinely are separated into two groups. Those from countries in which there is political persecution enter Germany's current system, which permits lengthy appeals. Those from so-called safe countries have shortened hearings during which the burden of proof is on the individual applicant to prove that, despite the general absence of political

---

[18]Dual citizenship is not necessarily welcomed by the migrants' countries of origin. In April 1994 President Demirel of Turkey urged Turks to become naturalized German citizens—and not delay in hopes of securing dual citizenship—so that they can become a more effective "lobby for Turkey" in Germany (*Süddeutsche Zeitung*, April 18, 1994).

[19]Under the Agreement on the Effects of Migratory Movements signed on May 7, 1993, Poland agreed to accept all asylum applicants who transited through Poland en route to Germany. Germany in turn agreed to provide Poland with DM 120 million ($75 million) in 1993 and 1994 so that Poland could accommodate the asylum seekers returned by Germany. The agreement applies only to asylum applicants who entered Germany after July 1, 1993, and Germany was limited in 1993 to returning no more than 10,000 aliens to Poland. Relatively few asylum seekers who entered Germany through Poland were returned there; as of October 1993, only 20 returned asylum seekers had sought asylum in Poland.

persecution in the home country (Ghana and Romania, for example), the applicant was persecuted (Hailbronner 1994).

Germany has developed perhaps the most complicated and least effective system for determining who needs asylum protection. It is not clear whether the magic bullet solution of returning asylum applicants to the country through which they entered Germany will prove any more durable than the earlier "required visa" solution. Some observers predict that the 1993 asylum compromise will simply lead to an upsurge in clandestine border entries.

Germany has almost 1,400 miles of border with its eastern and southern neighbors, and the 30,000 aliens caught near these borders in 1992 have been estimated to be only 10 percent of those who attempted illegal entry (author interview with Roland Schilling, June 1993). If legal entry leads to rapid deportation, Germany could develop a U.S.-Mexico-style border problem.[20] Furthermore, if an Iranian or Sri Lankan who slips into Germany is caught and then asks for asylum but "does not remember" or refuses to report the country through which he entered Germany, the asylum applicant may be difficult to deport.

Ethnic Germans

The years 1989 and 1990 witnessed two revolutions in Europe. The fall of the Berlin Wall in 1989 marked the end of Communism, permitting previously captive East Germans to emigrate freely, and 1990 was the year of German unification, accomplished in a quick and costly manner to avert further east-to-west migration. Germany is now having to deal with the migration aftermath of World War II. It is investing heavily in the former East Germany in hopes of keeping the 16 million former East Germans where they are. Germany is also searching for a durable solution for the 3 to 5 million ethnic Germans living in Eastern Europe and the former USSR who have the right to enter Germany as citizens.

Between the August 1961 construction of the Berlin Wall and the end of 1988, some 616,000 East Germans moved west. In 1989, thousands of East Germans took "vacations" in Hungary and Czechoslovakia and, once there, sought refuge in German embassies in Budapest and Prague. Eventually East Germany permitted these "refugees" to travel by train across East Germany into West Germany. Then, in November 1989, the Berlin Wall was opened. Over 340,000 East Germans moved west in 1989, and they continued to migrate west at the rate of 40,000 a month during the first six months of 1990.

Germany moved to halt "unification in West Germany" in a costly unification process that took "the deutsche mark to migrants, rather

---

[20]This did not appear to be the case in 1993. During the first six months of that year, 35,000 illegal aliens were apprehended at Germany's borders; during the second six months, there were 19,200 (Hailbronner 1994: 6).

than migrants to the deutsche mark." However, east-west internal migration continues because wages in the east are just two-thirds of western levels and eastern unemployment rates are twice western rates. An estimated 180,000 easterners moved west in 1991, and about 275,000 commute daily or weekly from the former East Germany (Mehrländer and Schultze 1992a: 19). Unification has made the former East Germany somewhat akin to Appalachia in the 1960s: a source of potential internal migrants who can be persuaded to stay where they are but only through government assistance and economic development.

The East Germans were considered German nationals as soon as they arrived in West Germany; they immediately received German passports, work permits, and voting rights. After unification, all former East German passports were replaced by West German passports.

East Germans were not the only German citizens moving into Germany. So-called ethnic Germans also trickled west throughout the 1980s, although fewer than 50,000 arrived annually before 1986. Ethnic Germans are persons whose German parents or grandparents lived in the German Reich on December 31, 1937. Under Article 116 of the German Basic Law and Germany's 1913 naturalization law, they and their children remained German citizens even though many became Polish or Soviet citizens when some German territories were occupied after World War II. Millions of these ethnic Germans moved west after the war, but an estimated 4 million remained in 1950 (Mehrländer and Schultze 1992b: 19).

In 1988 the number of ethnic Germans resettling in Germany rose sharply (to 200,000), and it approached 400,000 in both 1989 and 1990. Until 1990 most of the ethnic Germans arrived from Poland, but in 1990 over two-thirds were from the former USSR and Romania. The ethnic Germans arriving in Germany produced mixed reactions. When their numbers were small, they were welcomed by the still influential expatriate organizations in Germany and by most Germans. But as emigration from Eastern Europe and the former USSR became less restricted, Germans fearful of a mass migration from east to west began to resent the young immigrants with (often dubious) German credentials. During the early 1990s, news stories shifted their focus from individuals making daring escapes from persecution in the east to cover stories of the widespread sale of documents that "proved" one's ancestors had served in the German army during World War I. Germans began to complain about the cost of housing and supporting (often large) families of ethnic Germans while they learned the German language. Even organizations committed to helping ethnic Germans argued in 1990 that annual quotas were needed to minimize social tensions and keep the door to Germany open.

In January 1993 Germany implemented a new law on ethnic German repatriates that restricts to 225,000 the number of ethnic Germans who may move into Germany annually, limits the cash payments they receive upon arrival and the duration of their language training,[21] and provides funds for both development and cultural assistance to discourage emigration.[22] The federal government also expanded its effort to educate Germans about the ethnic Germans, explaining, for example, that the new arrivals are the descendants of Germans who were made to suffer in their adoptive countries during and after World War II. A major provision of the 1993 law declared that only ethnic Germans living in the former USSR still suffer the consequences of World War II, a finding that makes it easier for ethnic Germans from Russia, but harder for ethnic Germans in Eastern European countries, to migrate to Germany.

Only 2 million persons in the former USSR have "German" stamped in their passports (half of them live in Kazakhstan). But there could be as many as 5 million people in the former USSR who might be able to take advantage of Germany's "law of return" and emigrate; 650,000 applications to emigrate have been filed with German consulates in the former USSR, and 100,000 ethnic Germans have received permission to emigrate but have not yet done so. Germany is reducing the demand-pull attractions by requiring that paperwork be completed in the former USSR, by restricting benefits in Germany, and finally by imposing a quota on annual entries. There is a simultaneous effort to accelerate development and guarantee political freedom in the countries sending migrants so that emigration is unnecessary.

The decision to restrict the entry of ethnic Germans to 225,000 annually suggests that Germany may be moving toward an immigration policy with an annual quota or target number for newcomers and a set of entry priorities. The government's new policy toward ethnic Germans includes all four elements of the likely responses to unwanted immigration noted earlier: reducing the pool of those eligible to enter, establishing an immigration queue, providing development assistance so that those eligible to immigrate do not, and providing opportunities for those who qualify as immigrants to enter as easily as nonimmigrants.

Migrant Workers in the 1990s

Ethnic and East Germans trickled westward during the 1980s for political freedom and economic opportunity. After EC-92 measures stimulated economic and job growth in the former West Germany, and Eastern European nations eased their emigration restrictions, economic motiva-

---

[21] Under the 1993 law, ethnic Germans are entitled to six months of German language training and then up to nine months of "integration pay," which is equal to the average unemployment insurance payment.

[22] Germany spent DM 180 million ($112 million) in 1992 in Eastern Europe and the former USSR to improve conditions in areas where ethnic Germans live. Expenditures of DM 250 million were planned for 1993.

tions predominated among the Poles and others arriving in West Germany (Martin, Hönekopp, and Ulmann 1990).

Germany tried to cope with economic in-migration by developing a series of migrant worker programs designed to prevent the worker settlement of the guestworker era. The first such migrant worker programs were subcontracting agreements between German and foreign firms. Under these agreements, which were initiated in the early 1980s, a Czech or Polish firm, for example, would agree to do the brickwork on a German building, and the firm would supply both the construction workers and the supervisory engineers to direct their work. Draft subcontracting agreements are submitted to the German Employment Service for approval, which verifies that the agreement provides for the payment of prevailing wages and offers acceptable working conditions. The migrant workers who come to Germany—without their families—can stay for a maximum of two years (about half of these workers are from Poland). While they are in Germany they are paid partly in German marks and partly in their home currencies, and some of these wages remain with the subcontracting firm until the workers return home. There are no firm-specific quotas on the number of subcontracted foreign workers who can be employed, but there are industry-by-industry quotas and a countrywide quota, which in 1992 was 100,000.

The number of subcontracted foreign workers exploded from 6,600 at the beginning of 1990 to 90,000 in the summer of 1992, with over three-quarters employed in construction. German unions, firms, and the Ministry of Labor complained that subcontracts were being used to pay less-than-prevailing wages to construction workers, and that they permitted illegal workers to be employed in Germany. The construction industry council complained that "every legal foreign worker is accompanied by two illegal workers," and that the failure of foreign firms to pay stipulated wages gives them an unfair competitive advantage (Kieselbach 1993). As a result of these complaints, unions, employers, and the Ministry of Labor agreed in June 1993 that German firms employing foreign workers under subcontracting arrangements must specify the following in the subcontracting agreement: (1) what wage will be paid to foreign workers, (2) that the German firm will pay this wage directly to the worker, and (3) that the German firm will be liable for any labor law violations committed by the foreign firms. In 1993 German firms also began paying recruitment fees to the Ministry of Labor: DM 1,200 ($750) for each subcontracted foreign worker spending six months in Germany, and DM 2,000 ($1,250) for workers in Germany for more than nine months.

A second type of migrant worker program includes the various work-and-learn programs that Germany has instituted with most European countries. These reciprocal programs permit trainees between the ages of eighteen and forty to live and work in Germany for up to eighteen months; they also give young Germans the opportunity to live and train in Poland,

Russia, Romania, and so on. German employers submit work-and-learn offers to their local employment offices, which, without testing the German labor market to determine whether young Germans or settled foreigners are available, transmit the offers to employment offices in Eastern Europe. There are quotas on the number of persons from each Eastern European country who can take part in work-and-learn programs in Germany; in 1991, these quotas totaled 8,100, but only 2,200 trainees were actually in Germany.

The largest of the 1990s migrant worker programs is the seasonal worker program. This program was begun in 1991, when the November 1973 guestworker recruitment stop was modified to permit non-EC foreign workers to be employed in Germany for ninety days or less; that is, the two-decades-old recruitment stop applies only to jobs that last ninety-one days or more. Under the seasonal worker programs in effect with most of the Eastern European countries, German employers submit to their local employment offices signed bilingual contracts that describe the job, name the worksite, specify the pay and the start and stop dates, and spell out provisions for (required) housing, meals, and transportation. The local employment office reviews the contracts and tests the local labor market before issuing seasonal work permits to the workers who, in 90 percent of the cases, are requested by name by German employers. Both German employers and foreign workers make required payroll tax contributions (which add about 35 percent to the hourly agricultural wage of DM 6–10 [U.S.$3.50–$5.90]).[23]

The seasonal worker program was begun at the behest of farmers and hotel and restaurant operators in areas where there is a seasonal demand for labor. The program began in 1991, arguably as an effort to legalize the previously illegal seasonal employment of East Europeans in Germany. It was initially small—as of May 1991, for example, German employers requested only 35,000 workers, even though estimates of the number of Poles and other East Europeans who had worked illegally in Germany in 1989 and 1990 ranged up to 1 million. By the end of 1991, however, over 128,000 foreign workers had been employed in Germany sometime during the year. In 1992 and 1993 the number of seasonal workers employed in Germany was about 200,000 each year.

The seasonal worker program appears ripe for abuse. Recruiting workers by name gives them an incentive to get to know an employer by first working illegally. Some employers have tried to stretch the letter of the seasonal worker regulations by hiring three seasonal workers for three or four sequential ninety-day periods, thus sidestepping the ban on recruiting foreign workers for more permanent jobs. In an attempt to encourage unemployed German workers to fill jobs that might otherwise go to

---

[23] As of May 1, 1993, German employers pay a recruitment fee of DM 100 ($62) to the Ministry of Labor for each seasonal worker.

seasonal foreign workers, Germany revised its Employment Promotion Act in April 1994 to require unemployed workers—14 percent of whom were foreigners in March 1994—to accept seasonal jobs in agriculture as a condition of receiving unemployment insurance benefits, which replace up to 70–90 percent of unemployed workers' earnings. Recipients of unemployment insurance benefits who do seasonal farmwork receive an additional DM 25 ($15) daily.

The fourth new migrant worker program is for frontier workers. Frontier workers are foreigners who reside in the countries bordering Germany but commute to jobs up to fifty kilometers inside Germany. German employers can request frontier workers by asking their local employment offices to issue them work permits, and frontier workers can visit German employment offices in search of jobs. German employment offices issue work permits to frontier workers only after testing local labor markets to ensure that German workers are unavailable. Daily cross-border commuting is encouraged, but frontier workers are permitted to remain overnight in Germany for up to two days each week.

Can these migrant worker programs deter the employment of unauthorized workers, provide a safety valve for Eastern Europe, but not become an immigration side door to Germany? Many politicians answer in the affirmative. In their opinion, Germany's new migrant worker programs are far less burdensome than dealing with asylum seekers, ethnic Germans, and settled foreigners and their families. But some observers are far more cautious; they note the explosive growth in the number of foreign workers employed under these programs—over 300,000 in 1992. Some add that the complaints of worker abuses in the seasonal and subcontractor programs indicate that migrant workers today have far fewer rights than did the guestworkers of the 1960s.

Can legal nonimmigrant workers become effective substitutes for unauthorized workers? Germany did not begin fining employers who hired illegal alien workers until 1972. Since then the government has increased these fines several times, so that employers can now be fined up to DM 100,000 ($62,000) per illegal alien hired. However, labor inspectors acknowledge that the prospect of such fines has not prevented the hiring of several hundred thousand illegal aliens despite the existence of legal channels through which migrant workers can be hired.[24]

---

[24]German enforcement of employer sanctions depends largely on complaints from employers, unions, and workers, and on a computer comparison of two employee lists. The employers of "dependent" employees (those who earn more than DM 500 [$312] monthly) must register them with one of the health insurance programs. This list is then compared with the list of work permits issued, in order to spot persons who appear on one list but not on the other. Fines are stiffer for evading social insurance taxes, which add 20–40 percent to wages, than for hiring unauthorized workers, and this requirement to register for social insurance is believed to minimize the employment of aliens who do not have work permits. However, if an employer does not register employees for social insurance, this computer matching process fails to detect illegal aliens.

Lessons from Germany

Germany illustrates how a nonimmigration country can become a major destination for immigrants if it pursues flawed policies that initially work as intended (Unger 1980). Germany became a reluctant land of immigration when the guestworkers it recruited did not rotate in and out of the labor market as planned. When guestworkers settled in Germany and brought their families, they created a "foreign" population that is reproducing itself in the bottom half of the income distribution.

The major lesson from Germany is that guestworker or probationary immigrant programs begun for narrow labor market reasons are far easier to start than to stop. However, Germany's asylum and ethnic German experiences also illustrate how open-ended promises made under different circumstances can produce unexpected results. The German experience suggests that countries should be cautious in making blanket immigration promises.

The German immigration dilemma for the 1990s is to balance competing demands for immigration via the front, side, and back doors, while simultaneously accelerating the integration of settled foreigners (Apel 1992; Schmalz-Jacobsen, Hinte, and Tsapanos 1993). Germany's front door remains open to ethnic Germans and the close relatives of settled foreigners; until 1993 there were no annual quotas or limits on the entry of such immigrants. Germany closed the side door to probationary immigrant guestworkers in 1973, but it recently began to reopen side doors to presumably nonimmigrant foreign workers. Side-door foreign worker programs were begun in the late 1980s and early 1990s as a safety valve for Eastern Europe, in the hope that legal migrant workers could substitute for illegal workers, not because Germany felt that the experience gained during the guestworker era would diminish the gap between migration policy goals and outcomes.

As Germany grapples with the basic immigration questions of how many, from where, and in what status, it must also deal with the unfinished business of integrating its 7 million foreign residents. Incomplete integration was spotlighted in 1992 and 1993 by arson attacks on foreigners that resulted in the deaths of eight Turkish residents, some of whom had been born in Germany. The result has been confusion. A few Turkish and German activists, as well as some German politicians, used these attacks to press for double citizenship, local voting rights, and other rights for foreigners. However, the majority of politicians and Germans still cling to the belief that Germany is not a country of immigration. While they may deplore the violence against foreigners, they are likely to argue that violence against foreigners is a reason not to become an immigration country. A symbolic offer of double citizenship may send a signal to Germans that Turks and other foreigners are there to stay, but it is not likely to turn Germany into an acknowledged immigration destination.

Germany and most other nonimmigrant industrial democracies are likely to become reluctant lands of immigration during the 1990s (Massey et al. 1993; Ghosh 1991). International migration is, after all, spurred by demand-pull factors that attract migrants, supply-push factors that encourage emigration, and intervening variables such as networks and rights that expedite or impede cross-border movements. Only one of these three factors—the demand-pull attractions of jobs, high wages, a social welfare net,[25] and political freedom—is under the direct control of the industrial democracies. Furthermore, the industrial nations are striving to increase some of the factors that serve as magnets for migrants, such as economic and job growth, and better communications and transportation linkages.

Instead of reducing the demand-pull factors that attract migrant workers, many industrial democracies have embraced efforts to reduce supply-push emigration pressures in the countries that send immigrants (Körner 1990; Straubhaar 1986, 1988, 1992). Development is desirable for its own sake, but it is not a magic bullet remedy for emigration pressures. Indeed, most of the evidence suggests that the economic restructuring necessary to accelerate development temporarily increases emigration (U.S. Commission 1990).

Industrial democracies do not want to reduce the demand-pull factors that attract migrants, and they cannot reduce supply-push emigration pressures in the short term. Can they nonetheless sever the bridges that link emigration and immigration nations? Breaking these intervening variables appears to be getting harder rather than easier. Immigrant communities that have established themselves in the industrial democracies serve as anchors for additional arrivals; their capacity to provide information, shelter, and perhaps even financing for a legal or illegal entry is captured in analogies to networks or highways.

If immigrant networks are likened to highways, then what were once winding paths have become freeways, thanks to three revolutions. The communications revolution helped raise expectations in emigration areas as migrants abroad reported on life in immigrant countries and as television and movies exaggerated the wealth of industrial democracies. The transportation revolution increased access to and lowered the cost of migration; today even rural residents can get into a capital city and be en route to an industrial country in a matter of hours. Third, the rights revolution tied the hands of governments that wanted to tightly regulate migrant behavior. Courts and countries that have extended rights and special protections to women and minorities find it difficult to prevent

---

[25]Some observers assert that mass immigration is not compatible with a social welfare state, neither in Germany (Afheldt 1993) nor in the United States (Briggs 1992).

immigrants from also benefiting from these strictures on governmental discretion (Hollifield 1992).

Persisting demand-pull and supply-push forces have combined with stronger networks to widen the gap between the official goal of no immigration and the reality of mass immigration in Germany. The effect has been to convert Germany into a reluctant land of immigration, reluctant in the sense that immigration is still not anticipated or planned for, but it promises to continue nonetheless throughout the 1990s.

References

Afheldt, Horst. 1993. "Sozialstaat und Zuwanderung," *Aus Politik und Zietgeschichte* 7:42–52.

Apel, Günther. 1992. "Gedanken zu einem zuwanderungspolitischen Konzept," *Zeitschrift für Ausländerrecht und Ausländerpolitik* 3:99–107.

Ardaugh, John. 1987. *Germany and the Germans*. London: Hamish Hamilton.

Bade, Klaus J., ed. 1984. *Auswanderung-Wanderarbeiter-Gastarbeiter: Bevolkerung, Arbeitsmarkt and Wanderung in Deutschland seit des 19. Jahrhunderts*. Ostfildern: Scripta Verlag.

———. 1992. *Deutsche im Ausland-Fremde in Deutschland. Migration in Geschicte und Gegenwart*. Munich: Beck Verlag.

Bericht der Beauftragten der Bundesregierung für die Belange der Ausländer über die Lage der Ausländer in der BRD: 1993. 1994.

Blanke, Bernhard. 1993. *Zuwanderung und Asyl in Modernen Konkurrenzgesellchaften*. Opladen: Leske and Budrich.

Böhning, W.R. 1984. *Studies in International Labor Migration*. London: Macmillan.

Briggs, Vernon, Jr. 1992. *Mass Immigration and the National Interest*. Armonk, N.Y.: M.E. Sharpe.

Brubaker, Rogers. 1992. *Citizenship and Nationhood in France and Germany*. Cambridge, Mass.: Harvard University Press.

Buttler, Friedrich, and Frido Dietz. 1990. "Die Ausländer auf dem Arbeitsmarkt." In *Ausländer in der BRD*, edited by the Bundesinstitut für Bevolkerungsforschung. Boppart: Boldt.

Engelen-Kefer, Ursula. 1990. "Aspekte der Ausländerbeschäftigung." In *Bericht '90: Zur Situation der ausländischem Arbeitnehmer und ihrer Familien—Bestandsaufnahme und perspektiven für die 90er Jahre*. Bonn: Beauftragte der Bundesregierung für die Integration der ausländischen Arbeitnehmer und ihrer Familienangehorigen.

Ghosh, Bimal. 1991. "The Immigration Tide: European Countries—Both East and West—Are Scrambling to Manage the Immigration Problems of the Next Decade," *European Affairs* 5:6:78–82.

Hailbronner, Kay. 1994. *Ausländerrecht: Ein Handbuch*. Heidelberg: C.F. Muller.

Heckman, Friedrich. 1981. *Die Bundesrepublik: ein Einwanderungsland?* Stuttgart: Klett-Cotta.

Herrmann, Helga. 1992. *Ausländer: Vom Gastarbeiter zum Wirschaftsfaktor*. Cologne: Institut der deutschen Wirschaft, Beiträge zur Gesellschaft-sund Bildungspolitik.

Hof, Bernd. 1992. "Arbeitskräftebedarf der Wirschaft, Arbeitsmarktchancen für Zuwanderer." In *Zuwanderungspolitik der Zukunft, Gesprächskreis Arbeits und Soziales* (edited by Ursula Mehrländer) 3 (February).

Hollifield, James. 1992. *Immigrants, Markets, and States: The Political Economy of Immigration in Postwar Europe and the U.S.* Cambridge, Mass.: Harvard University Press.

Hönekopp, Elmar. 1990. *Zur beruflichen und sozialen reintegration türkischer Arbeitsmigranten in Zeitverlauf.* Nuremberg: IAB.

――――. 1993. "The Effects of Turkish Accession to the EC on Population and the Labour Market," *Intereconomics,* March–April, pp. 69–73.

Hönekopp, Elmar, and Heinz Werner. 1979. "Effects of the Southward Extension on the EC Labor Market," *Intereconomics,* September–October, pp. 243–47.

Kieselbach, Kurt. 1993. "Initiative gegen Schwarzarbeit," *Die Welt,* June 8.

Kindleberger, Charles P. 1967. *Europe's Postwar Growth: The Role of Labor Supply.* Cambridge, Mass.: Harvard University Press.

Körner, Heiko. 1990. *Internationale Mobilität der Arbeit: eine empirische und theoretische Analyse der internationalen Wirtschaftsmigration im 19. und 20. Jahrhundert.* Darmstadt: Wissenschaftliche Buchgesellschaft.

Kostede, Norbert. 1993. "Erleuchtung für die Politik," *Die Zeit,* February 5.

Martin, Philip. 1977. "Issues in the Evaluation of European Labor Flows," *Social Science Quarterly* 58 (September): 25–69.

――――. 1980. *Guestworker Programs: Lessons from Europe.* Washington, D.C.: International Labor Affairs Bureau, Department of Labor.

――――. 1991. *The Unfinished Story: Turkish Labor Migration to Western Europe.* Geneva: ILO.

Martin, Philip, Elmar Hönekopp, and Hans Ulmann. 1990. "Europe 1992: Effects on Labor Migration," *International Migration Review* 24:91 (Fall): 591–603.

Massey, Douglas S., et al. 1993. "Theories of International Migration: A Review and Appraisal," *Population and Development Review* 19:3:431–66.

Mehrländer, Ursula. 1974. *Soziale Aspekte der Ausländerbeschäftigung.* Bonn: Neve Gesellschaft.

――――. 1983. *Türkische Jugendliche—keine beruflichen Chancen in Deutschland?* Bonn: Neve Gesellschaft.

――――. 1987. *Aüslanderforschung 1965 bis 1980: Fragestellungen, theorefische ansätze, empirische Ergebnisse.* Bonn: Neve Gesellschaft.

Mehrländer, Ursula, and Günther Schultze. 1992a. *Einwanderungskonzept für die Bundesrepublik—Fakten, Argumente, Vorschläge.* Gesprächskreis Arbeits und Soziales, no. 7. Bonn: Friedrich Ebert Stiftung.

Mehrländer, Ursula, and Günther Schultze, eds. 1992b. *Einwanderungs Deutschland: Bisherige Ausländer-und Asylpolitik.* Gesprächskreis Arbeits und Soziales, no. 14. Bonn: Friedrich Ebert Stiftung.

Miller, Mark J., and Philip L. Martin. 1982. *Administering Foreign-worker Programs: Lessons from Europe.* Lexington, Mass.: Lexington Books.

Parkes, Christopher. 1992. "Tensions Rise as the Economy Weakens," *Financial Times,* October 6.

Schiller, Günter, et al. 1976. *Ausländische, Arbeitnehmer, und Arbeitsmarkt.* Nuremberg: IAB-BA.

Schmalz-Jacobsen, Cornelia, Holger Hinte, and Georgios Tsapanos. 1993. *Einwanderung-und dann?—Perspektiven einer neuen Ausländerpolitik*. Munich: Knaur.

Schober, Karen, and Heinz Stegmann. 1987. "Ausländische Jugendliche—Demographische Entwicklung sowie Ausbildungs-und Beschäftigungssituation." In *Aspekte der Ausländer beschäftigung in der BRD*, edited by Elmar Hönekopp. Nuremberg: IAB.

Sen, Faruk. 1990. "Die Türkei muss noch warten," *Europäische Zeitung*, March, p. 27.

Straubhaar, Thomas. 1986. "The Causes of International Migration—A Demand Determined Approach," *International Migration Review* 20:4.

——. 1988. *On the Economics of International Labor Migration*. Bern: Haupt.

——. 1992. "Allocational and Distributional Aspects of Future Immigration to Western Europe," *International Migration Review* 26:2 (Summer).

Unger, Klaus. 1980. *Ausländerpolitik in der BRD*. Saarbrücken: Breitenbach.

U.S. Commission for the Study of International Migration and Cooperative Economic Development. 1990. *Unauthorized Migration: An Economic Development Response*. Washington, D.C.: U.S. Government Printing Office.

Werner, Jan. 1992. *Die Invasion der Armen: Asylanten und illegalle Einwanderer*. Mainz: Von Hase/Koehler Verlag.

World Bank. 1994. *Atlas 1994*. Washington, D.C.: World Bank.

Commentary

Are Immigration Control Efforts
Really Failing?

Rogers Brubaker

Since my reservations are less concerned with Philip Martin's treatment of the German case than with the frame of reference that informs and structures this collective undertaking as a whole, I focus my comments on that frame of reference and on some problems that arise in applying it to the German case. There are clear intellectual benefits to applying a common grid to a series of case studies. But one problem with this procedure is that it may flatten out the distinctiveness of the individual cases. I will try to bring out the distinctiveness of the German case with respect to the overall problematic that informs this project: the problematic of failed control. I argue that Germany is not suffering, and does not perceive itself as suffering, from a generalized failure to control illegal or unwanted migration.

In line with the overall framing of the project, Martin's chapter diagnoses Germany as having a generalized immigration problem; it has this problem because its immigration control policies have failed; they have failed, in particular, to restrict non-EC immigration. As Martin sums it up: "Germany's immigration problem is that an officially nonimmigrant country is in fact one of the world's major destinations for immigrants." In the last few years Germany has been struggling with an acute crisis in its system of political asylum. By 1992, as the number of asylum seekers soared, ultimately reaching 438,000 for the year, virtually the entire political class had come to view the asylum system as having broken down. By contrast, the other components of migrant stocks and flows have not been perceived as acutely problematic. By contrast with France, for example, there has been relatively little public concern in Germany with illegal entry or illegal work, despite the fact that the latter, by all accounts, has increased sharply in the last few years. Similarly, the new legal temporary workers to whom Martin calls attention are largely invisible to the public eye. To be sure, there has been considerable public debate about ethnic German immigrants. But this reflects not a perceived generalized failure of immigration control but rather the anomalous and somewhat embarrassing system of ethnic preference that opens the door to immigration and automatic citizenship for ethnic Germans from Eastern Europe and the former Soviet Union.

Somewhat more surprisingly, there has been relatively little public concern with the former guestworkers. In summer 1993 Turkish (and German) protests in response to the deaths of five Turks in a firebombing attack suddenly focused attention on Turks—at 1.9 million by far the largest community of foreigners. But what is striking, in comparative perspective, is how invisible Turks have been in the immigration controversy during the last five years or so. The contrast with France, where North African immigrants have been at the center of political debate about immigration during the same period, is sharp. There are of course political entrepreneurs in Germany trying to focus on foreigners in general, including former guestworkers. But that is the nature of competitive democratic polities: there are always political entrepreneurs competing to define, promote, and galvanize attention on particular social and political problems. The fact that Germany (like other Western European countries) now has active and moderately successful far-right parties that target immigrants in general, not only asylum seekers, does not mean that public debate as a whole is framed in these same generalized terms. In fact, neither the large Turkish immigrant community nor the other components of the former guestworker population have been a major focus of public debate in recent years.

In sum, there has been acute concern in Germany about asylum seekers but not about other components of the foreign-born population. It is not at all clear that policies have failed in these other domains. True, they produced unintended consequences. People did not expect that the labor migrants recruited a generation ago would become the settlers of today. Nor did they expect a sudden upsurge in ethnic German resettlers in the late 1980s. But it is misleading to speak of policy failure here. Certainly one cannot say that a policy of rotation failed, for there never was a policy of rotation. There was an *expectation* of rotation, a so-called *principle* of rotation; but there never was a *policy* of rotation. There was, instead, a policy of open-ended, renewable work contracts, and a policy of permitting family unification. The policy governing temporary migration today is quite different; it is explicitly geared toward enforcing time limits on stays. Whether it will work is an open question. But no such policy was even tried in the guestworker era. Nor can one speak of policy failure in the case of the ethnic German migration. Here, too, there were unexpected outcomes, and to some extent unwanted outcomes, but there was no policy failure.

The policy was explicitly geared to facilitating the resettlement in Germany of ethnic Germans from Eastern Europe and the former Soviet Union, and to assuring the automatic civic incorporation of the resettlers. To be sure, nobody anticipated the sudden lifting of exit restrictions that enabled so many people to take advantage of this policy. But that does not make this a case of policy failure.

The case of asylum is strikingly different. Here there was a clear policy failure. At least since the mid-1980s, policies have been designed to deter what was widely perceived as misuse of the asylum system by persons without bona fide claims to asylum. In the near unanimous opinion of the German political class today, these policies of deterrence clearly failed; perceived misuse of the asylum system since the mid-1980s dramatically increased, rather than decreasing. Are we to conclude from this policy failure that the state lacks the capacity and/or the will to deter unwanted asylum claims? Quite the contrary. The recent constitutional and legislative changes, with the majority of Social Democrats joining the conservative parties of government in supporting the restrictive measures, suggested (at least to Germany's eastern neighbors, who feared that the burden of accommodating asylum seekers and processing asylum claims would be shifted onto them) that the German state possessed an all-too-clear will and an all-too-effective capacity to insulate itself from unwanted asylum claims.

The editors of this volume have posited a generally declining capacity and/or will to regulate immigration flows on the part of the major industrialized countries of immigration. I find this formulation problematic. In the first place, in some cases, including Canada and Germany, we see an *increasing* capacity and an *increasing* will to control unwanted flows—especially to deter unwanted asylum claimants.[1] More fundamentally, I have reservations about the concepts of declining will and capacity to regulate immigration. The notion of declining will implies an erosion over time in the will to control immigration. Yet no such generalized erosion is evident. We see rather an *intensifying* will to control immigration on the part of some political actors, but one that clashes with opposed commitments of other political actors. In other words, we see not a declining will to control immigration but an increasing *politicization* of issues of immigration control. For example, it is not a declining will to control immigration that keeps the United States from having a truly effective employer sanctions program, but rather sharp political disagreement about how vigorously employer sanctions should be enforced, disagreement that reflects conflicting interests, clashing ideologies, and differential power.

---

[1] Gary Freeman has also argued that the capacity to regulate migration is growing, not declining, over time in certain industrialized democracies, most notably Australia and Canada. See Gary P. Freeman, "Can Liberal States Control Unwanted Migration?" *Annals of the American Academy of Political and Social Science* 534 (July 1994): 17–30. —*Editors' note.*

The notion of declining capacity to control immigration is equally problematic. Consider two aspects of capacity. First, there is administrative/infrastructural capacity. If anything, this seems to be increasing in most states. It is, of course, conspicuously weak in some countries, notably those of Southern and Eastern Europe. But precisely those states are currently making heavy investments in their infrastructures of migration control. The second dimension of capacity is political capacity. The editors suggest that states are hemmed in by their liberal and democratic commitments. Clearly there is truth in this argument (although I would say it is liberal and humanitarian rather than liberal and democratic concerns that restrict states' freedom of action). The systems of family reunification in place in all Western countries of immigration, justified on humanitarian grounds, provide an important means for certain classes of potential immigrants to circumvent immigration controls. Liberal commitments inhibit, to varying degrees, the implementation of draconian systems of monitoring populations and deporting undocumented persons. One could easily list more examples. Yet important as these commitments are, the foundations of the inter-state system remain profoundly illiberal. In global perspective, the very institution of citizenship, tying particular persons to particular states by virtue of the morally arbitrary accidents of birth, serves as a powerful instrument of social closure and a profoundly illiberal determinant of life chances. True, states are open at the margins to citizens of other states—but only at the margins. Seen from the outside, the prosperous and peaceful states of the world remain powerfully exclusionary.

The liberal and humanitarian commitments of Western states do prevent them from establishing a hypothetically "perfect" system of immigration control, from fully shielding themselves from unwanted or illegal migration. But they do not prevent states from establishing systems of immigration control that, in global perspective, are very effective indeed—when effectiveness is measured *not* against some utterly unrealistic ideal of zero immigration, but rather against the extremely large and rapidly growing global demand for admission. Seen from the *inside*—that is, from the point of view of the citizens of favored countries—immigration control may be strikingly imperfect; but seen from the *outside*—from the perspective of those turned down for tourist visas, or those at the end of a twenty-year waiting list for admission, or those willing to pay large sums of money and undertake risky voyages in order to circumvent barriers to entry—immigration control appears all too effective. Of course, control is not absolute; but states do have the capacity, and the will, to influence the "price" of entry, including specifically the price of illegal entry. There will always be people willing to pay the price, even to the point of risking their lives. But through their ability to set the price (within broad and flexible limits determined inter alia by liberal and humanitarian commitments), states do have a substantial capacity to control migration, as well as the will to exercise that capacity.

Commentary

Germany's Need for Long-term Immigration Policies

Elmar Hönekopp

West Germany has received millions of immigrants since World War II—
refugees and displaced persons, ethnic Germans and their descendants,
Germans who migrated from East to West Germany, and foreign
workers and their families. The numbers tell the story: one-third of the
60 million people living in the former West Germany today were born, or
have parents who were born, in the former East Germany or beyond. In
many cases, the integration of these immigrants or their children is still
ongoing.

Since 1989, Germany has emerged as one of the world's major
destinations for immigrants: 4 million newcomers (net) have arrived in
Germany over the last four years. Many are ethnic Germans from
Poland and the former Soviet Union, but there is an increasing influx of
asylum applicants and other refugees from the former Yugoslavia, Asia,
and North Africa and sub-Saharan Africa. As Philip Martin puts it,
somewhat against her will, Germany has become an immigration country. The issue now is how Germany will respond to this state of affairs.

Most of the east-west migration to Germany is a result of the
socioeconomic reforms that began in the countries of Eastern Europe in
1989. These reforms led to a drastic decline in the production of goods
and services, a sharp and often delayed drop in employment, and a
consequent rise in unemployment. These impacts vary across regions.
The major urban areas of Eastern Europe are relatively less affected,
while remote rural areas and regions whose industries are particularly
threatened by the globalization of production are experiencing high
levels of unemployment. This unemployment generates internal migration. However, the rural unemployed cannot easily move to jobs in urban

areas because of labor market mismatches: internal migrants often lack the skills that are in demand; there is a shortage of urban housing; and there simply are not enough urban jobs for all of the unemployed.

Economic restructuring displaces workers selectively; the groups most affected are older workers, women, and less qualified or less productive workers. But because these workers lack skills, they are not in demand in urban areas or abroad. The workers who emigrate tend to be a country's youngest and best qualified workers. Their exodus from the domestic labor market can impede economic development. This yields a paradox: the same emigration that provides short-term relief for the domestic labor market in the sending country can slow economic development in the long term.

Although economic restructuring is the main cause of present east-west migration to Germany, the ethnic conflicts that erupted following the breakup of the Soviet Union and the East Bloc countries also influence migration—either directly, by pushing people across borders in search of sanctuary, or indirectly, as people relocate internally, exacerbating unemployment and stimulating emigration. These two factors often interact, with generalized economic distress aggravating ethnic conflicts.

South-north migration to Germany presents a different situation. It is propelled by many forces, but one stands out: rapid population growth. Annual population growth in many developing countries, especially in Africa, exceeds 3 percent (versus 0.1 percent in Germany). Even more decisive, however, is the fact that economic growth in these countries is not sufficient to provide employment for the many young people who are entering the workforce. For example, the Algerian and Egyptian economies would have to grow by 9–10 percent per year to fully employ youths entering the labor market.

Unemployment and underemployment in countries to the east and south of Europe are likely to increase in the future, while per capita incomes decrease, widening the economic gap between emigration and immigration areas. While increasing numbers of workers from these countries are seeking jobs at home, other trends, such as the mechanization of agriculture, are displacing large segments of the rural labor force. Eventually many of these unemployed workers will move to the cities, and some of them will move on to Europe.

Does Germany, and the rest of Europe for that matter, need these immigrants? Germany's population is aging. Without immigration, the population in Germany and in many other EC countries is projected to decline. For example, the population of West Germany is projected to decrease from 61.3 million in 1992 to 60.7 million in 2000 and 57.8 million in 2015. For united Germany, the population is projected to decrease from 77.6 million in 1992 to 76.9 million in 2000 and 73.9 million in 2015. Without immigration, population growth for the European Community is projected at a scant 0.1 percent per year between 1990 and 2000. A decrease in population would require numerous adjustments in growth-oriented industrial societies. Their economies, labor markets, and social security systems are based on the assumption that population growth will continue. If the rate of population growth stabilizes or declines, there will be fewer consumers purchasing goods and services in the domestic market.

Projections of the workforce potential of the former West Germany developed by the Institute for Labor Market and Occupational Research suggest that if labor participation rates remain unchanged and there is no net immigration, the German workforce will shrink. Even an increase in the participation rate would only postpone the shrinking of the workforce. However, an average net immigration of 215,000 persons per year, together with an above-average increase in labor force participation rates, would expand the potential workforce from 31.7 million in 1993 to 32.8 million by the year 2000 and 33.4 million by 2010.

It is hard to accept such projections when Germany and the European Community are experiencing high unemployment—over 9 percent in the former West Germany in 1993, projected to reach 10 percent in 1994 (with over 4 million jobless Germans). Nevertheless, despite high unemployment, immigrants continue to find jobs, suggesting structural rigidities in the labor market: either German workers are unwilling or unable to fill these jobs, or the availability of immigrants makes it unnecessary for employers to upgrade the jobs to make them attractive to native workers.

Do the projected stable or declining German workforce and coexisting labor shortages and surpluses demonstrate Germany's economic need for immigration? Without immigration, the German labor market clearly would have to adjust, placing an increased financial burden on workers as well as employers who pay into social security, health insurance, and other programs of the social safety net. Foreign workers will be needed, but at what rate? To keep the workforce from shrinking, Germany will need 200,000 immigrants per year after 2000, eventually increasing to up to 800,000 immigrants per year. However, these projections do not take recent and current immigration levels into account. The arrival of 4 million immigrants since 1989 and the continuing migrant flows into the country reduce somewhat the future need for additional foreign workers.

As Germany struggles to design an immigration policy for the 1990s and beyond, it must take the following considerations into account:

- Immigration pressures will remain high or increase, especially from the countries of North Africa and sub-Saharan Africa.

- Current high levels of unemployment should not obscure the fact that immigrants will be needed after 2000 to maintain a stable workforce.

However, current levels of immigration exceed what will be needed to maintain a stable population and workforce in the future.

- Temporary migrants become settlers. This has been the pattern in the past, and it will continue to be so, regardless of whether immigrants arrive as refugees or as temporary workers, or whether they come from the east or the south.

- Policies aimed at reducing immigration pressures must be multilateral.

Although most experts accept these realities, politicians do not. This situation explains the proliferation of calls to halt immigration and proposals to reduce settled immigrant populations. Germany is now an immigration country, and politicians must develop long-term immigration policies that address that fact. Such policies should include a ceiling on immigration, along with criteria for admitting certain types of immigrants. Once immigrants are admitted to Europe, eventually they will enjoy freedom of movement. For this reason, immigration ceilings and categories should be based on international agreements, possibly within the framework of the EC.

Politicians must prepare the German public for more or less permanent immigration, and studies must be undertaken on the effects that continuing immigration will have on various sectors of society: the labor market, the education system, housing, and social security. Immigration imposes both costs and benefits. The sooner Germany accepts that immigration is likely to continue, the sooner the country will be able to deal with the costs in a manner that reduces their negative impacts on affected social groups and institutions, especially workers and unions.

7

Anxious Neighbors:
Belgium and Its Immigrant Minorities

Marcelo M. Suárez-Orozco

On January 1, 1993, a new Europe was born, relinquishing old country boundaries in favor of joining in a single market. As the walls that once carved Europe into sometimes ferociously nationalistic states disappeared, a new sense of potential prevailed. Yet even before the festivities to celebrate the New Year—and the new continent—had ended, just-released unemployment figures injected a note of sobriety into the discussions of Europe's possibilities for 1993, as evident in the following report from Lille, France:

> Few towns are better placed than this northern industrial capital to benefit from Europe's push for unity. The Channel Tunnel and high-speed rail links will soon put Paris, Brussels and London within 90 minutes. Blue-and-gold European flags, a new train station conceived as a European hub and a massive conference center called EuroLille demonstrate this point. But in an example of the problems accompanying the establishment of

The author gratefully acknowledges the financial support provided by the John D. and Catherine T. MacArthur Foundation, the National Science Foundation, and the Center for German and European Studies, University of California, Berkeley for the completion of this project. Thanks are also due to my Belgian colleagues, Professor Eugeen Roosens, Chairman, Centre for Social and Cultural Anthropology, Catholic University of Leuven; Professor Johan Leman, of the Royal Commission for Immigration in Brussels; and Dr. Marie-Claire Foblets, of the Faculties of Law and Anthropology at the Catholic University of Leuven for their immeasurable generosity. Drs. P. Hermans and M. F. Cammaert, along with A. Martin, B. Sewieza, C. Stallaert, C. Timmerman, A. M. Van Broeck, and others at the Centre for Interculturalism and Migration Research were also extremely helpful.

a single European market on Jan. 1 [1993], all the fanfare
has left the four million inhabitants of the Lille region in
the cold. The billions of dollars spent on transport, the
relentless promotion of the European ideal and the
recent removal of border guards at the nearby Belgian
frontier have all been overshadowed by a single fact:
more and more people do not have jobs (Cohen 1993: 3).

There were some 438,000 unemployed workers in Belgium in January 1993. This trend is likely to continue; European Community figures
projected 16 million jobless people in the EC by the end of 1993 (Cohen
1993); and for those under twenty years of age, the unemployment rate is
already over 20 percent. Increasing pressure from the European Community's Executive Commission in Brussels to end state subsidies,
combined with the fact that large companies (such as IBM and Ford of
Europe) are likely to continue cutting back or risk losing out to less
expensive operations in Southeast Asia, almost ensure continued high
unemployment rates in the near future. Other industries such as coal,
textiles, and metalwork, which once recruited large numbers of legal
foreign workers from Southern Europe and North Africa, have suffered
severely since the 1970s.

The debate over the "immigrant problem" must be framed in the
context of these economic dynamics, as well as in the context of increasing waves of undocumented aliens and asylum seekers from the Third
World, the adaptation (sociocultural and economic) of earlier waves of
immigrants into Europe (particularly post-World War II, non-EC migrants from North Africa and Turkey), and the rise of ethno-nationalistic
feelings in some European countries.

In postwar Europe, large numbers of migrants, refugees, ex-colo-
nials, and others from the southern—and, more recently, eastern—
peripheries infiltrated the wealthier developed centers of the northwest
in search of a better future for themselves and their children (Nayer and
Nys 1992; Fassmann and Münz 1992; Wander 1990). Extra and Vallen
have estimated that by "the year 2000, one-third of the population under
the age of 35 in urban Europe will have an immigrant background"
(1989: 153). These large numbers of legal immigrants did not sneak in
overnight, unnoticed or unwelcome. Indeed, in many cases the immigrants were actively recruited by powerful sectors of the very Northern
European countries that now face an "immigrant problem" (Fassmann
and Münz 1992; Tomlinson 1989: 16; Roosens 1989b: 85). In the process,
these immigrants became "minorities." Along with newer waves of
undocumented immigrants and asylum seekers they have become the
object of public unease over the "foreign" presence in European cities.
There is concern that the future character of European society might
depend on what happens with the large legal and illegal immigrant

population (see *Cahiers Marxistes* 1988). Will Europe become what the Council of Europe has called a segregated, castelike society practicing "apartheid" (Alaluf 1982: 4; see also Roosens 1988)? Or will a better atmosphere of interethnic harmony and respect develop?

In Belgium it is clear that despite the formal end to legal worker immigration in 1974, the stream of low-skilled, undocumented workers and asylum seekers from the underdeveloped world continues (Nayer and Nys 1992; Fassmann and Münz 1992). According to some estimates, there may be as many as 100,000 undocumented workers in Belgium today (Johan Leman, personal communication), drawn by the substantial wage differentials between what is available in their home countries and what they can earn in the Belgian underground economy.

Thus we are facing an obvious paradox. On the one hand, unemployment among native workers and legal immigrants is relatively high, as is anti-immigrant sentiment; on the other, certain sectors of the economy have a continuing need for inexpensive, flexible, low-skilled workers, and their need draws more undocumented migrants. The following pages explore some of the central features in this paradox, as well as the specific regulations and formal and informal strategies for dealing with the problem of undocumented immigrants and asylum seekers. The chapter examines nativistic responses to the problem and explores some likely future scenarios. It concludes with an examination of how "non-policy" becomes policy when dealing with undocumented migrants and asylum seekers.

A Post-Industrial Paradox

In many Western European countries undocumented workers (from Africa, Eastern Europe, Asia, and South America) have become an explosive political issue: high unemployment rates in Belgium and elsewhere have raised public sentiment to a furious pitch (Cohen 1993; Kamm 1993; Fassmann and Münz 1992). In Antwerp, the extreme right-wing Vlaams Blok (Flemish Bloc), running on an anti-immigrant platform, won 24 percent of the vote in November 1991 (Havemann 1993). Sentiment is growing for action: "send the illegals home; all problems — unemployment, homelessness, delinquency, budget crises — will disappear with them."

Yet employers assert that without a reliable source of "disposable" undocumented workers willing to accept substandard wages, they simply could not get the job done (Kilborn 1993). In Japan the problem has a clear demographic angle: there are simply not enough native workers to do the work that needs to be done (see Cornelius on Japan, this volume). In Belgium, the issue is cost. Some Belgian business leaders see themselves in direct competition with Third World countries, where wages (hence production costs) are a fraction of Belgian rates. They view "black workers" as an integral component in their ability to compete in international markets. Others note that Belgian industries rely on undocumented foreign labor to produce cheaper products and thus attract larger domestic markets. For example, agricultural producers say that without undocumented workers they could not offer fruits and vegetables to the public at affordable prices (Johan Leman, personal communication). And the employment of "black workers" in the clothing industry means that Belgians can purchase designer clothes at a fraction of the price they would pay if the clothes were made by Belgian workers at official rates (C. Timmerman, personal communication).

Undocumented workers in Belgium sometimes work in substandard conditions. Willing to do the work local workers cannot or will not do (such as working with dangerous pesticides in agriculture or with dangerous chemicals in petrochemical industries), undocumented people are the most vulnerable of all workers.

Undocumented immigrants in Belgium find work in a limited number of economic sectors. Women typically work as maids, babysitters, or caretakers to the elderly; men work in the construction and petrochemical industries and in agriculture (Johan Leman, personal communication). Contrary to popular opinion, far from coming from the lowest socioeconomic and educational rungs of their societies, many undocumented persons have some education. In Brussels undocumented Latin American women, high school graduates and in some cases college graduates, often work as baby-sitters and maids (A.M. Van Broeck, personal communication).

Common Dilemma

Researchers concur that the problem of undocumented immigration in Belgium cannot be separated from the problem of undocumented immigration in Europe as a whole. For one thing, now that border controls within the European Community have been removed, once an undocumented worker gains entry into one member state, he or she gains entry into all the others.

Citizens of the European Community are free to work in any EC member country. However, massive numbers of EC workers are not expected to relocate within EC boundaries. Although specialized professionals might move from one country to another, local roots are deeper than the instrumental temptations to move to another country. In general, then, migration almost universally refers to non-EC citizens living within the European Community. Hence the significant numbers of Dutch nationals living in Belgium, just across the border from their home country (typically to pay lower taxes), are not seen as part of the immigration problem in contemporary Belgian society (Fassmann and Münz 1992: 474; Eugeen Roosens, personal communication).

Although EC citizens can move freely to work within the European Community, this right is not extended to non-EC immigrants. A non-EC country immigrant (a Moroccan immigrant residing legally in Paris, for example) cannot take up permanent residence in a second EC country with the intention of working. An estimated 7.5 million non-EC legal immigrants in Europe are affected by this policy. However, without borders the policy will be difficult to enforce. Once migrants gain entry into Europe, it will be extremely difficult to monitor their movements—and to enforce current laws.

As borders within the EC become increasingly irrelevant, control of the outer European border becomes more important. In northwestern Europe there is some anxiety that southern EC member countries (particularly Spain and Italy) will not be able to control entry effectively. Current policy makes the country of entry responsible for controlling the movement of immigrants; hence Spain will be responsible for keeping an eye on its migrants, Italy for keeping an eye on its migrants, and so forth. Another attempt to coordinate policy has been to allow refugees to apply to only one EC country at a time.

Many Belgians believe that there are already too many immigrants in their country (Roosens 1993). Others are bothered by the fact that immigrants tend to concentrate in certain areas, becoming even more visible to the majority Belgian population. Some natives are offended by the dress and behavior codes that are strategic markers of immigrants' differences (from European norms). Immigrant unemployment, crime, and use (and abuse) of the social security system are explosive issues. In addition, many Europeans fear an "invasion" from North Africa and Eastern Europe. They are concerned that the combination of European and non-European demographic patterns (low fertility rates and an aging population in Europe, versus high fertility rates and a younger population in North Africa) and economic dynamics (significant wage differentials between Europe and North Africa and Eastern Europe) will continue to create the conditions that attract undocumented immigrants.

Despite popular anxiety over the "immigrant problem," there is a continued need for foreign workers. According to some estimates, France will need to recruit between 160,000 and 360,000 foreign workers over the next two decades (Johan Leman, personal communication). Likewise, Belgium will continue to rely on cheaper foreign workers in labor-intensive manufacturing, leather working, the clothing industry, agriculture, and construction.

Employers of undocumented workers can realize enormous savings by not contributing to the social security system. For each BF 50,000 that a company pays a Belgian worker, it must pay a roughly equivalent amount into the social security system, pension fund, retirement fund, and so on (Marie-Claire Foblets, personal communication), giving employers another strong incentive to rely on "black workers."

Working-class natives and their unions counter that "black workers" take jobs and other resources from Belgians. Social security is a case in point. Not only does each "black worker" hired by a Belgian company take a job away from a Belgian; he or she also represents a loss to the social security system. Hence all Belgian workers lose resources. Legal non-EC migrants also resent "black workers" because they fan the winds of xenophobia against *all* foreigners, including those who are legally present.

Mainstream politicians have been reluctant to address the question of undocumented immigrants. Their past inaction left a vacuum that extreme right-wing anti-immigrant politicians have exploited. Although most mainstream politicians pay lip service to the notion that undocumented immigration "cannot be tolerated," there does not seem to be the political will to enforce current regulations. A double discourse (referred to below as "non-policy as policy") seems to be the resulting strategy.

Views from the Shadows

The most important groups of undocumented migrants in Belgium today are from Africa, Eastern Europe, Asia, and South America. Their exact numbers are either not known or not publicized by Belgian authorities. Researchers, operating in an atmosphere of increasing anti-immigrant sentiment, do not freely discuss numbers for fear of fanning the extreme right wing. Nevertheless, estimates from researchers working in the field suggest that Belgium has perhaps as many as 50,000 undocumented immigrants from Poland and another 50,000 from Morocco, Colombia, Peru, and various other countries in Africa and Asia (author interviews).

Undocumented immigrants tend to concentrate in Brussels, where Poles constitute the largest immigrant group. During 1989 as many as 3 million Poles became migrants (within Europe and to the United States and other parts of the world). While there has been a significant brain drain in Poland since the opening of 1989, most of the undocumented Poles in Belgium are low-skilled workers from rural backgrounds who are drawn by Belgium's relatively higher salaries.

Researchers working with Belgium's undocumented immigrants from Latin America estimate that there are about 5,000 Colombians and a smaller number of Peruvians residing in the country without proper documentation. Like the Poles, they are concentrated in Brussels. In general, the South Americans are of higher status than undocumented workers from Poland and other Eastern European countries. Most have a high school education, and many have done some university studies.

Latin American illegals apparently command higher wages and are more appreciated overall than the Eastern Europeans (A.M. Van Broeck, personal communication).

South Americans typically enter Belgium legally and then overstay. Because it is increasingly difficult to get a Belgian visa in Colombia and Peru, many Latin American immigrants enter Belgium through European countries that do not require them to have visas, such as Spain, and then move on to Belgium. As visa requirements become harmonized for all EC member countries, it may become increasingly difficult for undocumented Latin American migrants to enter Belgium.

Like the Poles, Latin American undocumented immigrants (primarily women) typically work as maids or baby-sitters or care for elderly people. Belgian employers say they prefer "black workers" from South America over Belgian workers for domestic jobs, asserting that South American "black workers" are more resourceful and have fewer problems than low-skilled Belgian workers (A.M. Van Broeck, personal communication).

Both Latin American and Polish workers face the worrisome prospect of being detained and sent home, but detention and deportation affect the two groups differently. A deported Polish worker can easily catch a bus back to Brussels; a worker deported back to a country in Latin America, on the other hand, would have to return to Brussels by plane (at a cost of around $1,000) and would also face the increasingly strict visa requirements to enter Europe.

Old Walls/New Walls: Controlling Europe in the Post-Cold War Era

In the 1950s, Belgian corporations, operating in conjunction with government authorities, organized the immigration of Italian and Spanish workers to Belgium (Roosens 1989a). In the early 1960s Belgium signed bilateral agreements with Turkey and Morocco to allow for additional labor migration. There was a quota system: certain numbers of people were allowed to enter Belgium to work in specific sectors, principally coal mines and chemical industries. Workers received permits to work legally for one year, and permits were automatically renewed for a second year. An immigrant worker's visa theoretically was linked to the contract for employment, but the connection was not well regulated. In fact, people who lost their jobs could usually remain (Marie-Claire Foblets, personal communication). In 1974 these bilateral agreements were terminated, but significant numbers of immigrants had already entered under these provisions and established themselves in Belgium. Today there are some 240,500 Italian, 138,500 Moroccan, 82,000 Turkish, and 52,000 Spanish immigrants in Belgium (see table 7.1).

TABLE 7.1
FOREIGN RESIDENTS BY NATIONALITY IN BELGIUM, 1990

Area	Residents	Area	Residents
EUR 12		AFRICA	
Belgium	—	Algeria	10,644
Denmark	2,371	Ivory Coast	337
Germany	26,673	Mauritius	630
Greece	20,718	Morocco	138,417
France	92,207	Tunisia	6,247
Ireland	2,016	Zaire	11,186
Italy	240,469	AMERICA	
Luxembourg	4,701	Brazil	915
Netherlands	62,397	Canada	1,559
Portugal	15,137	Chile	1,204
Spain	52,399	Colombia	576
United Kingdom	21,956	Haiti	248
EFTA		USA	11,489
Austria	1,032	ASIA	
Finland	516	China	2,168
Norway	778	India	2,473
Sweden	1,852	Indonesia	653
Switzerland	2,399	Iran	1,681
C & E EUROPE		Israel	1,729
Czechoslovakia	438	Japan	2,870
Hungary	745	Jordan	208
Poland	4,689	Lebanon	1,581
USSR	542	Pakistan	1,683
OTHER EUROPE		Vietnam	403
Turkey	81,776	AUSTRALIA & OCEANIA	
Yugoslavia	5,537	Australia	360
		STATELESS & UNKNOWN	
			1,116

There are two important aspects to immigration control: external controls (as individuals enter the country) and internal controls (once immigrants have gained entry). Belgium, like other EC countries, has specific documentation requirements for foreigners wishing to enter. In some cases, a foreign national wanting to enter Belgium for less than three months needs a visa. In other cases, because of bilateral or multilateral arrangements, citizens of specific countries (such as Poland) are not required to have visas. Persons legally entering the country for three months or less, with or without visas, typically do not have the right to work. Some undocumented workers enter the country this way, find illegal work, and remain, overstaying the three-month period.

In Belgium, the main control outside of international airports and seaports is the internal police. A policeman can stop anyone and demand to see his or her papers. This raises important questions that are currently being debated in Belgium: What means of control are acceptable in a democratic society? What methods are respectful of human rights and privacy and yet enable the state to control immigration?

Belgium has a system of identity cards for foreigners, and each one of these identity cards corresponds to a registration. These registrations were formerly held in the Ministry of Justice. The registration of immigrants was recently moved to the office in charge of public order (Marie-Claire Foblets, personal communication). Some observers argue that this transfer of responsibility from the minister of justice to the minister of public order is symptomatic of changing attitudes toward immigrants, since the minister of public order is also in charge of the criminal system. The fact that immigration policy is increasingly given a "police" angle concerns some immigrant rights attorneys. The government's argument is that this transfer of authority for registering immigrants will make immigration control more efficient. But turning immigrant affairs over to a police agency reinforces the popular perceptions that link immigrants and crime.

In the current atmosphere of anti-immigrant sentiment, the control of non-EC persons (Moroccans, Turks, and others) seems to be stricter than before—or so it appears to the immigrants (Hermans 1993: 51–76). A person without proper documents (passport, visa, identify card, or permit) may be "invited" to leave Belgium within ten days. Many undocumented workers who are asked to leave simply ignore the order, relocating to avoid a second detection. Should an undocumented immigrant be detected in a second "control," he or she may be detained up to a month pending deportation (Marie-Claire Foblets, personal communication). Detainees are put "at the disposition of the government." Even if not physically detained by the police, an immigrant without proper documentation can be forced to stay at a certain address pending deportation. The detention period lasts up to one month, within which period the government has the right to deport the person.

The authorities in Brussels recently proposed extending the detention period to two months, arguing that there are too many undocumented immigrants and too few resources to process individuals within the month required by law. There is a new ambassadorial appointee in Brussels whose job it is to encourage the embassies of the various home countries to speed up repatriations (and also to accept financial responsibility for repatriation costs). When all else fails (when the worker has no resources and the country of origin refuses to receive the person or to pay repatriation expenses), the undocumented worker is simply transported across the border into France or Holland. In post-1993 Europe, "dumping" undocumented workers across borders is of course meaningless. Some have proposed transporting them outside the EC borders but not back home (Marie-Claire Foblets, personal communication).

A new debate has arisen over whether the EC should assume control of immigration and asylum applications of non-EC nationals. According to some observers, the European Community should not be concerned with non-EC citizens, even if they are permanent residents of a member state. This raises the possibility that there will be a two-track Europe: one that enjoys the benefits of EC membership and one (composed of non-EC immigrants) that does not.

Family Reunification

Although the legal immigration of low-skilled workers into Belgium was halted in 1974, a policy for family unification kept the door open for certain groups of immigrants. Immigrant workers who had entered prior to 1974 and could demonstrate after one year in Belgium that they had adequate income and housing could ask family members to join them. The family members were limited to one wife (creating a problem with polygamists from Morocco) and children under the ages of twenty-one (for Morocco) or eighteen (for all other countries). (Recently proposed legislation would only admit children under the age of sixteen; lowering age limits illustrates the general tendency to restrict as much as possible the influx of legal immigrants under the laws of family reunion.)

Because the children and spouses of legal immigrants to Belgium can also immigrate, Belgian authorities have argued that this system could potentially encourage "backdoor" entries. For example, one strategy has been for a legal immigrant to marry a woman from his home village (at a considerable price to the woman's family), bring her to Belgium, divorce her, marry again, and so forth. In 1984 Belgium implemented new policies to gain control of reported abuses of the family unification law (to stop what Belgians were calling the "migration cascade"). A person who comes in through family reunion now has no right to open the door to someone else. If a person enters Belgium through marriage with a legal resident, he or she has no right, if divorced, to bring in a new spouse,[1] leading some legal scholars to argue that this policy is against the fundamental right of free choice in (re)marriage (Marie-Claire Foblets, personal communication). Proposals currently under consideration would not allow a new spouse of a legal immigrant to stay in Belgium if the couple divorced within a year of their marriage. Although family reunion remains a basic source of immigrant

---

[1] The bride-price for a woman who could gain entry for other men has fallen considerably now that the option is closed. Hence changes in Belgian laws have an impact on cultural patterns in remote African villages.

influx, the government continues its attempts to limit legal entry to the degree possible.

Asylum

Another mechanism that allows legal entry is the asylum laws. Asylum has gained a great deal of visibility in the current debate (Kamm 1993; Fassmann and Münz 1992). There is an increasing fear that Europe will be overwhelmed by people seeking asylum from wars, starvation, and natural disasters. During the last decade there has been a tenfold rise in the number of asylum seekers in Western Europe; a total of about 3 million asylum applications were submitted to Western European countries in the last ten years. Newly organized Moscow-based rings of "people smugglers" are bringing new tides of refugees into Northern Europe (mostly from Iraq, the former Yugoslavia, and Somalia) (Kamm 1993).

The process for applying for asylum in Belgium has traditionally taken up to three years. In the current climate of economic austerity and host anxiety about immigrant minorities, the high costs associated with housing and feeding asylum applicants while their applications are being processed (a reported $8.3 billion was the combined cost to Western European countries last year) contribute to a feeling that Europe simply cannot rescue all those who need rescuing.

Some observers note that the low acceptance rate for asylum applications (about 5 percent of all applications in Western Europe) confirms what right-wing politicians have been saying all along: the great majority of asylum seekers are really "economic migrants" in search of a better life. Belgian authorities contend that many economic migrants are abusing the asylum system by gaining entry into Belgium and then "disappearing" before their cases are resolved. On the other hand, human rights and refugee rights groups are alarmed by what they see as the erosion of asylum rights policies throughout Europe.

An important dimension of the asylum equation is that the provisions of many of Europe's asylum laws and policies were guided by the experience of Nazism and Communism—decidedly European crises. Large numbers of brown and black non-Europeans (often Muslims) are not, perhaps, what the laws were intended to deal with. Offering asylum to large numbers of non-Europeans raises questions regarding their future on European soil. Can these non-European populations, so different in culture and religion from earlier waves of refugees and migrants from within Europe, really be "assimilated"? Can there be a modern, European Islam? As we shall see below, these are some of the most controversial aspects of the debate over the immigrant and refugee problem in Europe.

In 1990, Belgium reported a total of nearly 13,000 asylum seekers (see table 7.2). The majority came from Africa (4,067 in 1990), mostly from Ghana and Zaire. Central and Eastern Europe sent some 3,300 asylum seekers, mostly from Romania and Poland. Asian countries produced nearly 3,000 asylum seekers in 1990, primarily from India and Pakistan.[2]

TABLE 7.2
ASYLUM SEEKERS IN BELGIUM, 1990

Area	Residents	Area	Residents
EUR 12	3	AFRICA (continued)	
EFTA	2	Somalia	22
		South Africa	7
C & E EUROPE	3,321	Sudan	13
Bulgaria	319	Togo	58
Czechoslovakia	27	Uganda	8
Hungary	58	Zaire	1,123
Poland	1,084		
Romania	1,751	AMERICA	102
USSR	82	Chile	47
		Colombia	30
OTHER EUROPE	2,195	Peru	22
Albania	50	Surinam	3
Turkey	1,673		
Yugoslavia	472	ASIA	2,929
		Afghanistan	24
AFRICA	4,067	Bangladesh	189
Algeria	29	China	73
Angola	287	India	1,032
Cape Verde	2	Iran	191
Egypt	3	Iraq	44
Ethiopia	55	Lebanon	292
Ghana	1,534	Pakistan	815
Guinea Bissau	3	Sri Lanka	82
Ivory Coast	46	Syria	77
Liberia	188	Vietnam	110
Morocco	117		
Nigeria	540	STATELESS	2
Senegal	32	TOTAL	12,621

Following the refugee experience of World War II, people from certain (Communist) countries could apply for asylum more easily than persons from other countries. However, Europe's liberal asylum laws of

[2]Under the terms of the Dublin Convention, the European Community proposes that the country of entry will take responsibility for processing the application for asylum. If asylum is approved or denied, the decision is binding for all member countries. An important issue now is harmonizing the process so that an applicant entering Spain and an applicant entering Holland undergo a similar process.

the Cold War era were never fully tested because the former Iron Curtain countries kept strict control over population movement. Now, without an Iron Curtain and with crises in the former Yugoslavia and elsewhere, European authorities must hurriedly formulate new laws and strategies to cope with increasing numbers of asylum seekers.

Many European countries, Belgium among them, have developed formal and informal strategies and policies for dealing with the sharp increase in asylum applications. One new approach being tried in Belgium and elsewhere is the controversial "safe country" formula. According to this formula, if in a given year 5 percent of all applications for asylum come from a single country and fewer than 5 percent of those applications are approved, then the country is designated a "safe country." Because residents of "safe countries" in theory should not need to seek asylum, all subsequent applications from citizens of countries already designated as "safe" are more easily rejected. Belgium's list of "safe countries" currently includes Ghana, Pakistan, India, Poland, and Romania. Asylum seekers from Zaire and China still have some chance of being received (Belgium has a tradition of offering asylum to the opposition in Zaire).

Human rights organizations have argued that some of these "safe countries" remain accused of systematic human rights violations (see Kamm 1993). Moreover, legal groups are challenging the "2 × 5%" rule by which governments determine whether or not a country is "safe," noting that reference to the percentage of application rejections from the previous year is arbitrary: political climates can change rapidly. They have also noted that the rule lacks flexibility. There is automatic discrimination against asylum seekers from "safe" countries. The challengers have taken their case to Belgium's high court, where a decision is pending. Legal experts predict that the "2 × 5%" rule will be struck down as unconstitutional. The government, knowing that it will likely lose on this point, is considering the possibility of declaring all countries "safe countries," in effect making everyone "safe" until proven otherwise. Such a move would radically shift the burden of proof to the applicants.

The unfolding crisis in the former Yugoslavia has seen the emergence in Europe of other policies and "non-policy" policies to deal with the new wave of asylum seekers. France, for example, has developed a formula to deal with asylum seekers from Bosnia: once asylum candidates agree to waive their right to petition for formal refugee status and they agree to return home once the danger is over, they are given a more limited right to stay in France. Those who have already formally applied for asylum, if they retract their applications, gain the provisional right to stay and work until peace makes it possible for them to return home.

Belgium has followed a similar course but in a more tentative, less organized fashion. Bosnian asylum seekers who withdraw their formal asylum applications have been given a conditional, carefully worded, temporary permit to stay. According to a legal scholar, these temporary permits amount to prohibiting the police from repatriating the bearers to their countries of origin (Marie-Claire Foblets, personal communication). In a limited number of cases, candidates have been given temporary right to work.

As we shall see in the discussion of "regularization" strategies, the current Belgian approach is to avoid setting precedents that could be perceived as general policies granting legal rights to large numbers of undocumented migrants or asylum seekers. In the current climate, there is a general retreat from previous mechanisms that generously provided for the permanent settlement of asylum seekers. In retrospect, it appears that the liberal asylum laws of 1951 flourished, in part, because of the Communist regimes' use of terror to control the movement of potential exiles. Had large numbers of people from the Eastern bloc been able to escape before the collapse of Communism, it is likely that many Western European countries would have been forced to reconsider their asylum policies sooner.

There is a growing concern that as wars and conflicts break out elsewhere in the world, others will rush to Europe claiming the same rights as those granted to the Bosnians. Many Europeans openly say, "We cannot become a last hope for all these troubled countries!" In Belgium, government actions in this sensitive field appear expedient, ad hoc, and purposefully vague: the main strategy appears to be policy by "non-policy." The objective is merely to control, to the extent possible, legal entry into the country.

Some European countries have dealt with asylum by setting quota systems that grant a limited number of applications per year to groups and countries that the authorities have designated as eligible to apply. Belgium has no such quota system.[3] In Belgium asylum seekers from certain countries who have been given injunctions to leave the country (their asylum applications having been formally denied) may be granted, ad hoc, the right to remain for additional but limited periods of time. According to some Belgian researchers, the asylum principle that a "well-founded fear of prosecution" should guarantee shelter has been undermined by politically inspired considerations. The fear that new conflicts have the potential to create an unbearable number of refugees has contributed to a more "instrumental" and "realistic" approach.

There is a general tendency on the part of various national governments to find creative strategies that make the asylum-seeking process more difficult and less open. Many European governments, for exam-

---

[3]In the past, Belgium offered asylum quotas, such as to the Vietnamese in the 1960s.

ple, require asylum seekers to present valid passports and even visas.[4] Many asylum seekers do not have such documents. Another strategy has been to turn part of the "policing" functions over to airline personnel. Airlines are to be fined if they embark passengers who lack proper passports and visas to enter an EC country. Under this policy, asylum seekers are to be weeded out by airline personnel in the country of origin, before they enter the country in which they intend to seek asylum.

There are additional strategies that make it difficult for asylum seekers to apply for consideration. Those who do make it into an international airport find that some governments, among them the French and Dutch, have "declared areas of their main airports 'international territory.' This permits them to circumvent obligations under international conventions to give applicants an asylum hearing when they arrive 'in the country'" (Kamm 1993: 1).[5]

At the Zaventem airport in Brussels another strategy has been to make it difficult for asylum seekers to meet human rights and refugee rights lawyers. Lawyers are in a struggle with the authorities for full and free access to potential asylum seekers at airports (the Bar of Brussels has lawyers at the airport to inform potential asylum applicants of their rights). Other government strategies to discourage asylum seekers include asking them for a local address or post office box where the notification for the hearing can be sent. A newly arrived asylum seeker often does not have a local address or post box. The government then automatically assigns him or her a post box in the office of the United Nations High Commissioner for Refugees in Brussels. Asylum seekers, often disoriented in the new setting, may fail to pick up the hearing notice and the case is automatically denied.

Lawyers working on behalf of asylum seekers argue that many, if not all, of these strategies may violate the fair hearing aspects of the Geneva Convention.

Regularization of Undocumented Immigrants

In the previous sections we established that a central aspect of current Belgian policy is to avoid setting precedents that would lead to further

---

[4] A human rights group in Germany recently said of the plan to require passports and visas from asylum seekers: "What this effectively means is that no refugee can come to Germany by land. . . . Only those who arrive by air can apply for asylum, but they would need visas to get here, and as a rule German embassies do not issue visas to people seeking political asylum. Is the only remaining possibility a flight by private plane and then a parachute jump?" (Kamm 1993: 2).

[5] Note that this strategy is similar to current U.S. policy toward asylum seekers from Haiti. By intercepting them on the high seas before they are formally in U.S. territory, the government circumvents international obligations regarding a fair hearing when the applicant arrives "in the country."

immigration and/or would extend the legal rights of undocumented persons or asylum seekers. The Belgian minister of home affairs has the power to "regularize" (legalize) undocumented persons but typically does so only on an ad hoc basis. Cases regularized by the minister tend to be extraordinary; individual amnesties are typically granted only for humanitarian reasons. An undocumented person wishing to be legalized has to apply to the minister for regularization. This requirement puts the applicant in a difficult position: undocumented migrants who do not gain "regularization" are exposed to expulsion. Potential applicants know that if they apply for "regularization" to the Ministry, the odds are against them, so most do not see this route as a practical solution to their legal problem. Others feel there is nothing to lose and use the application as a last chance or as a lottery; they are prepared to go back home.

In Belgium, unlike other EC countries such as Italy (see Calavita on Italy, this volume), there have been no attempts to grant general amnesties. It appears that many Belgians see such attempts as failures: precedent-setting blanket policies, some argue, promote further illegal immigration (Johan Leman, personal communication). For example, researchers in Leuven related the recent limited amnesty in Holland as a case in point. Undocumented workers who survived in a building damaged by the crash of an El Al airplane in December 1992 were "rewarded" with regularization by the Dutch authorities. Hundreds showed up to apply for the amnesty, many more than could have possibly been in the building at the time of the accident. It was reported that undocumented workers (mostly Tamils from Sri Lanka) even moved from Germany to apply for the limited Dutch amnesty (personal communication).

Other researchers in Brussels reported that from the Belgian point of view the recent amnesties in Italy have been a failure: relatively few undocumented workers took advantage of the law. It was also noted that the Italian amnesties probably attracted additional undocumented workers from other parts of Europe and elsewhere.

Employer Sanctions

In Belgium it is illegal to hide, help, or hire "clandestine" or undocumented migrants. Violators may be fined and even imprisoned. Researchers in Leuven and Brussels report that these laws are almost never enforced (author interviews). When they are, the sanctions appear to be symbolic. The case of a family recently charged with hiring an undocumented housekeeper illustrates this point. The family was fined a token BF 5,000 (about U.S.$161). A researcher in the field of law estimates that fewer than 0.1 percent of those employing undocumented workers are charged or fined. The authorities argue that they do not have the manpower to control the problem. Others note that there is an unwillingness to apply the laws. Failure to apply existing laws is another aspect of "non-policy" policy. On the one hand, the laws appease the right-wing political parties and the general population anxious about the "immigrant problem." On the other hand, the lack of systematic enforcement of the laws creates a space in which employers can continue to rely on more flexible undocumented workers with minimal risk.

There appears to be more public tolerance (hence less police control) of undocumented workers in certain areas of the labor market. Housekeepers are relatively invisible and in high demand, and they are in little direct competition with Belgian workers. Construction workers, on the other hand, are more visible (they typically work in public or open spaces), and they are in direct competition with Belgian workers (A.M. Van Broeck, personal communication).

Some legal scholars fear that if the police take a more active role in sanctioning, there may be clashes with issues of privacy and other basic democratic rights. Tensions have already surfaced between enforcement considerations and basic democratic principles and between local administrations and the central government when it comes to issues relating to undocumented workers. A recent case over professional "privileged information" illustrates many of these new problems.

In Belgium there is a form of aid (the Public Assistance Law of 1967) that provides "minimal security" and "dignity" to indigent people (a basic food and lodging allowance of BF 11,000 a month [$355], which undocumented immigrants may also receive). The program is handled by local centers. In the late 1980s, there was a discussion between the minister of justice and the minister for public assistance concerning the question of whether these local centers could be asked to give information to the national authorities about the people they help. A significant percentage of those receiving indigent aid are thought to be undocumented migrants. If the centers turned over the information, it would mean giving out information on the "illegals" as well. The position of the minister of justice was to press for all the information. The minister responsible for public assistance argued that the local centers should refuse, invoking the professional rule ("privileged information") that prohibits them from acting against the interests of their clients (Marie-Claire Foblets, personal communication).

On the other hand, the general public clearly opposes undocumented immigrants receiving indigent aid. These are the topics that fan the debate. Belgium's public assistance program, many fear, will be overwhelmed by demand from people who should not be in Belgium in the first place. Controls and sanctions in a liberal democracy are certain to create further tensions in the future.

Nativistic Responses

Many reject as impossible the idea that Europe will become a multi-cultural society where European and non-European traditions coexist in a benevolent and mutually beneficial order.[6] The revival of ethnocentrism and the rise of xenophobia feed the anti-immigrant sentiment (Fassmann and Münz 1992; Denton 1993; Kamm 1993). In Belgium, the anti-immigrant right-wing party Vlaams Blok, "heavy with Nazi coloration, stunned Belgium's political leadership in the most recent elections in 1991 by capturing 25% of the vote in Antwerp" (Havemann 1993: 1). The Vlaams Blok continues to gain power throughout Flanders (C. Timmerman, personal communication). The party, with its historic ties with Nazism, is one of the most articulate architects of the right-wing extremism revisiting Europe.

The significance of the Vlaams Blok is its resemblance to other European movements such as Jean-Marie Le Pen's Front National in France (see Hollifield, this volume). To an outside observer, its political agenda appears to be monomaniacally fixated on a single issue: the "immigrant problem." According to the Vlaams Blok, Belgium's problems (unemployment, crime, the budget crisis) will go away only when the immigrants go away. Eugeen Roosens, Chair of the Center for Social and Cultural Anthropology at the Catholic University of Leuven and an authority in the field of migration and ethnicity in Belgium, writes:

> By obtaining 24 percent of the vote, the Vlaams Blok became the largest political party in Antwerp. As voting is mandatory in Belgium, this means that roughly one adult out of four of the residents of that city voted for a party which propounds extreme right-wing nationalism.
>
> The most visible and basic theme that was used in the election was "the issue of the migrants." Though there are more than 300,000 French people residing in Belgium and more than 240,000 people of Italian origin, "the migrants" primarily means the Moroccans and the Turks.
>
> The program of the Vlaams Blok is very clear and widely publicized:

---

[6] A modest plan for "multiculturalism" proposed by Belgian authorities included the following points: (1) Everyone is equal before the law. Everyone has the same rights and obligations. (2) Freedom of religion. (3) All people living in Belgium must respect and live up to the Belgian principles of democracy and equality among men and women. (4) Everyone is free in all other domains.

(1) Send home immediately all migrants and their children or "the second generation" (meaning by this "the
Moroccans" and "the Turks") who are in prison. Send
home every adult migrant who is unemployed and who
receives unemployment benefits.

(2) Group the children of the migrants in special
schools, teach them their own language and culture in
order to prepare them to go home, even if they were
born in Belgium.

(3) All employers must give priority to the autochthon-
ous, so that as many Belgians as possible get jobs and a
maximum of immigrants can be sent home.

(4) The mosques of the Muslims must be concentrated
somewhere in the outskirts of the cities, where they are
less visible and would make less noise that would
disturb the other citizens.

(5) A special, unattractive regime of social security
must be established for the immigrants; they now enjoy
very generous benefits, like the Belgian citizens, which
is one of the major reasons why they stay.

(6) The Vlaams Blok, according to its leaders, does not
want to be anti-humanitarian: they propose that part of
the foreign-aid money now spent on other Third World
countries be channeled to Morocco and Turkey, and
more specifically to the regions of origin of the migrants, so that the aliens can go home and find jobs in
their own towns and villages, where they really belong
(Roosens 1993: 9).

The Vlaams Blok employs an extreme version of the doctrine of
cultural relativism: proponents argue that each culture is unique and in
some respects incommensurable with other cultures. Peoples, they note,
have a fundamental right to their own language and culture. Hence the
Vlaams Blok supported, in theory, the right of young Moroccan girls to
wear veils in school (Marie-Claire Foblets, personal communication). For
them it is a human rights issue; each group can be fulfilled only in its
own land, in its own culture. Just as the Flemish can be happy and
fulfilled only in Flanders, so the Moroccans and Turks can be happy only
in their own countries. Vlaams Blok member Steven Bosselaers said,
"We respect other people's identity. . . . We don't say one people is better
than another. We say that the only way to preserve people's identity is to

keep them apart" (Havemann 1993: 1). Hence they advocate that all migrants must eventually return home.[7]

Although many Belgians abhor the Vlaams Blok's more extreme views, surveys show that an alarming majority shares some watered-down version of their anti-immigrant agenda. A recent survey suggests that up to 70 percent of the Flemish population would like to see foreigners go home but not by any forced means (Billiet, Carton, and Huys 1990). Older people appear to be more "anti-immigrant" than younger people. Catholics appear to be more anti-immigrant than non-Catholics. However, the memories of trains full of Jews are too fresh in the minds of many Europeans for them to consider nondemocratic deportations as an acceptable option.

This anti-immigrant sentiment is at the intersection of a number of vectors. There is a general public anxiety about the budget crisis, unemployment,[8] and continued waves of undocumented immigrants and asylum seekers. There are also anxieties about the future of national cultures as boundaries collapse and the EC gains increasing relevance in the economic (and cultural) affairs of all of Europe. Another very important set of concerns relates to the problems in adaptation among previous waves of legal immigrants and their children. The high unemployment rates among non-EC migrants, about twice the rate for natives in Belgium (see table 7.3), and their reliance on the generous Belgian social security system concern many Belgians. Perhaps even more alarming is what is happening to the children of non-EC immigrants in Belgium. The high failure rates in schools and high delinquency rates among Moroccan and Turkish youths convince many that non-European immigrants will not easily adapt to European norms.

In Belgium these general anxieties find an outlet in the ideas and programs of the Vlaams Blok. The party's leadership is composed of a group of radical but charismatic personalities whose discourse constructs a simpler world divided between "us" and "them" (purity versus pollution, light versus dark, Flemish versus immigrant) (Johan Leman, personal communication). Like other xenophobic and hate movements, the Vlaams Blok seems to succeed by uniting a group that feels threatened. The threatened group develops a construct that attributes all

---

[7]Gunter Cauwenberghs, a Vlaams Blok supporter, put it succinctly: "We are in favor of letting people have their own culture in their own country. . . . We treat people [immigrants] with hospitality. They can come and they can go" (Havemann 1993: 1). Some Vlaams Blok members, whose parents or relatives were allied with the Nazis during World War II, pressure former collaborators or their relatives to take a public anti-immigrant stance (Eugeen Roosens, personal communication). The current generation of Vlaams Blok leadership sees the collapse of Communism as a vindication of the struggles of their forefathers who were disgraced after the Nazi defeat. The new generation's rage toward the immigrants is, in part, surely the result of the injuries their parents suffered for their political sins.

[8]There are some 438,000 unemployed workers in Belgium today (about 199,600 of them Flemish, 188,3400 Walloon, and the rest from other groups, including immigrants).

TABLE 7.3
UNEMPLOYMENT RATES IN BELGIUM, BY NATIONALITY
(PERCENTS)

	1987	1989	1990	1991
Nationals	10.2	7.2	6.3	6.1
EC nationals	21.7	17.4	15.8	15.0
Non EC nationals	32.7	31.4	26.3	25.1

Source: The Labour Force Survey.

unacceptable traits to an "other," which must be depreciated and disparaged. Thus, in Vlaams Blok discourse, non-EC immigrants appear as a growing force of crime-prone parasites feeding off European wealth and threatening to pollute language and culture.[9]

In a country such as Belgium, where a national identity is not relevant, concerns with ethnicity, culture, and language seem to be increasingly important. Immigrants are seen as potentially disruptive of precious cultural traditions (including language, dress, code of conduct, and the like). The display of Islamic traditional clothes, particularly by women of Moroccan origin, is often perceived as an affront to European progress and basic beliefs. The concentration of immigrants in certain areas conveys the message: we are here, we are different, we are not going to change, we will remain outsiders.

Even those who do not share the extreme views of the Vlaams Blok believe that the immigrants must adapt to the cultural norms of the dominant majority. Some argue that in the best case scenario, non-EC immigrants will culturally "disappear" in the mainstream, learning the language, adopting the clothing and mores of the dominant culture. But the process of immigrant "melting" will take a couple of generations. Belgians hope that the third generation will "look" more European in language, dress, and conduct and thus will ease the anxieties brought about by the immigrant population as a whole.[10]

As Marie-Claire Foblets, a law researcher in Leuven, put it,

---

[9]There is a mimetic quality to the majority-disparaged minority dyad. Hence non-EC immigrants in Belgium, such as the Moroccans and the Turks, do have higher unemployment rates, higher school dropout rates, and higher delinquency rates than the majority population. As in all stereotypes, kernels of truth are elaborated and magnified. Whereas the old European racism that produced, among other things, the Holocaust in Germany, was based on fears of pollution by allegedly biologically inferior groups, the new racism seems less concerned with so-called biological pollution. The fear of contamination remains but is expressed in a new idiom: now it is culture (language, manners, clothing, etc.) that must be prevented from polluting groups. Additionally, "culture" could be considered a code word for "race." Racism is illegal, but the race issue is often mentioned in informal or anonymous communication (Eugeen Roosens, personal communication).

[10]If the U.S. experience is relevant, the notion that all immigrants and minority groups will eventually disappear into a "melting pot" is questionable.

The population is in general anti-immigrant. The right-wing parties do not want to see immigrants sustained by public funding. The public prefers not to have them dependent on public funding. Illegals also have rights to some minimal social security. This is now being furiously debated. There is a movement to cut all aid to the illegals. The problem here is one of "privileged information." The agencies handling basic aid refuse to become policing institutions controlling the illegals. They do not wish to collaborate. This is one of the basic reasons why Belgium is still considered by the illegals to be paradise on earth. People from Africa can live well (comparatively speaking). They say "let us be as poor as we can be here." So that remains a basic problem (Foblets 1988).

Right-wing groups vocally advocate stopping indigent aid to undocumented migrants. It is very likely that the minister of justice will propose a law to prevent undocumented migrants from receiving indigent aid. According to some observers, the minister knows that public sentiment is against government support for undocumented immigrants; if he does not pass the law, he will be driving even more voters into the hands of the extreme right.

Others, including some left-wing parties, proclaim that immigrants have been a plus to the Belgian economy. Some observers have noted that earlier waves of immigrants contributed substantially to the European economic boom of the postwar era (Fassmann and Münz 1992). And because the undocumented immigrants have benefited Belgian society, some groups advocate that they should be "regularized."

Still others contend that there have not been any systematic studies exploring the impact of undocumented immigrants on the economy. Some studies conducted in Belgium in the 1980s suggest that legal migrants tend to produce more than they consume, and therefore regulations regarding family unification should be liberalized. As for the undocumented immigrants, there are no data on their impact in the economy. Nevertheless, as one researcher noted, "Everyone knows that the illegals are productive in the sense that for some employers they are key. Most restaurants in Brussels would just go bankrupt without the illegals" (author interview).

Yet because public opinion is generally against undocumented immigrants, many Belgians feel it would be better for the country to train and hire the unemployed Moroccan and Turkish immigrants already legally present in Belgium than to regularize or hire undocumented workers. Given the generous Belgian social security system (an unemployed legal immigrant may receive up to 80 percent of his full salary for up to a year), many think it is simply not possible to continue to support large numbers of unemployed legal immigrants.

Children of Immigrants in and out of Schools

Schools are a good starting place to approach the problems facing ethnic and immigrant minorities, because that is where many of these problems seem to begin. Researchers in Belgium (Roosens 1989a: 127–48, 1989b, 1993, n.d.; Leman 1991) and elsewhere[11] are systematically exploring the special problems of immigrant youths in schools. Many are also turning to research findings from the United States to explore what theoretical models and applied programs the U.S. record might offer (see Suárez-Orozco 1991; Roosens 1989b; Eldering 1989).

Some of the new reports on minority education and economic attainment on the continent and in Great Britain recall the early heated debates in American anthropology. Ideas and programs that flourished and then wilted in the United States in the 1960s and 1970s seem to be appearing in another cycle in European investigations. Notions that "different races have different intellectual capacities still persist in Britain, and some teachers still believe that black children have a natural lower ability" (Tomlinson 1989: 25).

The idea that some groups are "unassimilable," found in the United States at the turn of this century, is reappearing in Belgium. Islamic culture is perceived as not quite "compatible" with European culture (hence the essential educational unassimilability of young Turks and Moroccans). Some simplistic arguments over the relative influence of a so-called culture of poverty on schooling have their European counterparts. Explaining the British situation, Tomlinson writes,

> The importance of home and family background for success in education is well documented and a number of research studies in the 1960s and 1970s attributed poor ethnic minority school performance to family structures and cultural differences. This led to unhelpful stereotyping of many families. For example, single-parent Afro-Caribbean families were presented as disorganized and disadvantaging to their children, and Asian cultural segregation and language differences were presented as problems in the education of the children (Tomlinson 1989: 25).

---

[11]Including Germany (Alamdar-Niemann, Bergs-Winkels, and Merkens 1991; Boos-Nünning and Hohmann 1989), France (Vásquez 1992; Costa-Lascoux 1989, 1992; Payet 1992), Great Britain (Tomlinson 1989, 1991), the Netherlands (Eldering 1989; Pieke 1991), Scandinavia (Stromqvist 1989).

More recently, a theoretical model with U.S. counterparts explains the problems of ethnic minorities as a function of various linguistic and cognitive "cultural discontinuities" between minority and majority groups. This model, which this author and others have criticized elsewhere (see Ogbu 1982: 290; Suárez-Orozco 1989: 31–35), seems to be dominant among the competing explanatory paradigms in some European countries. The problem is no longer to be constructed along the alleged "deficiency" models of biology or cultural inferiority; rather, the problem is that the schools are failing to teach the children in a culturally appropriate idiom.

> In the 1980's, researchers in Britain are stressing factors relating to the structure and process of schooling, appropriate curriculum materials, and teacher attitudes, expectations and behaviour as important factors affecting the educational success of ethnic minority children (Tomlinson 1989: 26).

The social problems of the new immigrant minorities in Europe resemble those of ethnic minorities in the United States in important ways: discrimination (Hermans 1993; Kinzer 1993), lack of equal opportunity which results in higher unemployment and underemployment rates particularly among youths (Eldering and Kloprogge 1989), domestic poverty, generational conflict, the emergence of deviant peer reference groups fostering a countercultural identity pattern among youths, high minority dropout rates from school, and higher delinquency rates.

Scholars in Belgium and elsewhere are asking: Are the non-EC Muslim immigrants becoming more and more like America's "castelike" or "involuntary" minorities (such as African Americans)? And are the adaptations of EC immigrants from within European Christendom (Italians, Spaniards, and so on) more similar to the variations in typical immigrant experience observed in U.S. ethnic history? Another way to ask that question is: Is Europe to emerge as a segregated, castelike society, with Islam as the barrier between Islamic (non-EC) and non-Islamic (EC) minorities?

In Northern Europe, the problems of EC immigrants such as Spaniards (Morin 1984) and southern Italians (Roosens 1993; Leman 1987, 1991; Aubert 1985) are quite distinct from those of non-EC Muslim immigrants such as Moroccans and Turks (Roosens 1989a, 1989b, 1993, n.d.; Cammaert 1986a, 1986b). Non-EC Muslim immigrants develop more chronic school problems, unemployment, and delinquency (Roosens 1989b). Boys tend to develop more chronic problems than girls: whereas boys can and do turn to the streets, Muslim girls do not have that option; their lives are divided between home and school (C. Timmerman, personal communication).

Alarmingly high rates of delinquency are now appearing among some minority groups in Belgium. Drug-related activities are also emerging (Eugeen Roosens, personal communication). School dropout patterns, peer group dynamics, and the emergence of youth countercultural forms are all related to actual and perceived discriminatory practices. In addition, the current revival of Islam in Europe (Dassetto and Bastenier 1988) must be seen not only as a pan-Islamic development but also specifically as a countercultural discourse, particularly popular among the children of unwanted non-EC immigrants (see Kinzer 1993). Indeed, powerless young Muslims in Europe take up Islam as a proud banner that identifies them as belonging to an ancient and righteous tradition, and they oppose this tradition to the "decadent" postmodern malaise afflicting Europe (Roosens 1989a: 127–48).

Some Muslim youths with few possibilities for success in Belgium may turn to Islam as a "status shelter" that protects them from feelings of inferiority rooted in school failure and joblessness. Just as discriminated youths find themselves psychologically "protected" by the status system they choose to inhabit, religious fundamentalism offers them the rationale to reject the (secular) society that rejected them.

In addition to occupational and social discrimination, these youths must also contend with generationally continuous patterns of expressive exploitation or disparagement. The idea of expressive exploitation expands on the Marxist notion of "instrumental" class exploitation to include the psychological aspects of depreciation in situations of rigid class, caste, ethnic, and gender stratification (De Vos and Suárez-Orozco 1990; Suárez-Orozco and Suárez-Orozco 1993). According to this model, expressive exploitation is integral to all systems of severe inequality, be they based on class, caste, gender, or ethnic distinctions.

Stereotyping, debasement, and the projection of unspeakable traits and practices onto disparaged minorities are among the most commonly found forms of expressive exploitation. Often armed with pseudoscientific claims of biological or cultural superiority, expressive exploitation serves both to legitimate inequalities and to ventilate the status anxieties attendant on all exploitative relations. In the United States, derogatory attitudes have been more severe toward African Americans than toward immigrants from Europe and Asia. In Europe, virulent racist attitudes are now most often directed toward Moroccans (and less so Turks) and rarely toward EC migrants (Hermans 1993).

A critical issue in the study of immigrant adaptation is the experiential discontinuity separating the foreign-born from their children. In general, the first (foreign-born) generation sets for itself a clear and well-defined but arduous task: to make a decent living, secretly nurturing the dream of one day returning home. Immigrants know full well they are different, and the majority often wish to maintain some of their differences from the majority culture (Suárez-Orozco and Suárez-Orozco 1993).

In Europe, second- and third-generation (European-born) Moroccans and Turks are sometimes called "involuntary migrants," since it was their parents, not they, who chose to migrate. Children inhabit a vastly distinct psychosocial and economic atmosphere when compared with their immigrant parents (Suárez-Orozco and Suárez-Orozco 1993). They often have only fragmentary knowledge of their ancestral language and codes for behavior. Lacking their parents' cross-cultural perspectives and constant comparisons between "here" (the host country) and "there" (the home country), the second generation tend not to see their ongoing experiences and frustrations within an immigrant "dual frame of reference" (see Suárez-Orozco 1989: 88–102). The parents' country is often seen as a vaguely mythical place of origin rather than as somewhere to return to.

Second- and third-generation non-EC immigrants in Europe soon discover that they are unlike their parents, yet they are also unlike their nonimmigrant peers. They speak the language of the host country (in Belgium, the lingua franca among second-generation immigrants tends to be French, and less so Flemish, more often than Berber, Arabic, or Turkish). But these second- and third-generation Moroccans and Turks often find that they are not particularly wanted in their "new home" (Kinzer 1993). Unlike their parents, who were once courted as valuable workers to fill local demand, the new generations often do not find employment.

In Belgium, the school adaptation of non-EC minorities is typically poor. In Belgium's Limburg province 40 percent of non-EC immigrant children repeat at least one grade. With high secondary school dropout patterns, idle young Moroccans and Turks often get into trouble on the streets. Drug use is becoming a problem. Some reports suggest that close to 75 percent of all delinquency acts in the city of Brussels are committed by non-EC immigrant youths (Marie-Claire Foblets, personal communication).

Immigrant children who are in Belgium legally generally attend schools where they are instructed in Dutch or French, not the home language. However, in Limburg province, a traditional immigrant destination, there have been some pilot programs teaching in the home language for four or five hours per week. Such pilot programs have run into a major staffing hurdle: few teachers who are competent in home languages such as Arabic, Berber, or Turkish meet the teaching standards of the traditional Belgian educational system. Some experimental projects have brought in native teachers from the home countries, but the results so far are equivocal (Roosens 1989a: 142–46).

In considering the special problems of the children of undocumented immigrants in schools, we must take into account the added stresses of being in a country illegally. Under the current system, children of undocumented immigrants are not allowed to enroll in schools. Schools receive an allowance per pupil but not for the children of undocumented immigrants. Hence the parents must first convince a school principal to let their children enroll and then must pay the equivalent of the state allowance. In some cases parents are asked to pay in excess of $1,000 per year. It becomes increasingly difficult to maintain the children as they move into high school.

Many undocumented immigrant parents report that they want their children to receive an education but they do not have the funds to pay for it. On the other hand, the authorities fear that if there is a general policy allowing the children of undocumented migrants to enroll in schools, a new wave of undocumented immigrants will arrive to get a free education for their children.

Future Directions: Policy, Non-Policy, and Non-Policy as Policy

According to some Belgian observers, mainstream political parties have little to gain by tackling the "immigrant problem." Undocumented immigrants have negligible rights and power, and there is widespread anti-immigrant feeling in the population. Ministers, such as the Belgian minister of justice, have resisted addressing the problem because there is little to be gained in such volatile issues. As a researcher in Leuven expressed it,

> [The Belgian minister of justice] does not know what to do with the problem. Once you systematically address the problem, then you have to start talking about amnesties; illegals all of a sudden have individual faces. Then you have to deal with the political problem of the right wing, and the minister knows that he cannot win (author interview).

Temporary programs (similar to the immigrant worker programs that were halted in 1974) may again be needed for demographic and economic reasons. However, some Belgians fear that such programs will create a new set of problems; temporary workers will simply overstay, introducing a new wave of "illegals."

Before new temporary workers are brought in, others argue, the current population of undocumented workers must be regularized. Yet there is also some resistance to general amnesties: if undocumented workers are regularized they will command higher salaries, creating a new demand cycle for "black workers" in dangerous and undesirable jobs. The newly regularized workers would also presumably compete with Belgian workers in more desirable sectors of the job market.

Some Belgian observers argue that the problem of undocumented workers and asylum seekers will not be remedied by policing and administrative changes but rather by changing the North/South (and West/East) factors that seem to promote migration. They advocate economic aid to the "source" countries of the immigrants: primarily Morocco, India, Pakistan, and Poland. However, this kind of aid may simply shift the source of migration to other parts of the world.

Another important aspect of immigration policy has to do with bilateral relations between Belgium and the various home countries of the undocumented migrants. International issues relating to economic considerations (including oil and foreign assistance) and security considerations (including drug trafficking) affect immigration policy making. For example, certain countries (such as Morocco) were more willing to collaborate with Belgian authorities in repatriating undocumented workers when repatriation was framed in the context of a package that included development aid (personal communication).

The possible future need for a new wave of foreign workers is now, in the words of a Belgian researcher, a taboo topic. She explained,

> The problem always goes back to economics and to our economic necessity, which we can't officially recognize, to have cheap labor, cheap workers. Because of our very strict social laws, it is possible to have cheap labor only by turning to so-called black workers. If all the undocumented workers are regularized, they will no longer be cheap workers but very expensive, thus creating a new demand for cheap labor. There will then be a new reason for influx which is encouraged by some employers. They prefer to run the risk of having to pay from time to time a ticket back home for their illegal workers and pay some fines rather than having to pay the heavy social security taxes for legal workers. The control systems are not efficient, or they don't want to make them efficient, which makes the risk for them [the employers] minimal. They pay an illegal less than half what they would have to pay a Belgian worker! Why? Because the heavy costs for the employer are the so-called social costs: insurance, social security, retirement, and so on. Now unions are more concerned with these problems. For a long time unions were not concerned with the issue of migrants; now they are very concerned. Unions take on employers who rely on "black workers." At the same time some argue that you

must be realistic: the costs of legal workers are too high! There are reasons why there are so many bankruptcies! They are overwhelming our economy; the costs of legal workers are simply too high. It is inevitable that there will continue to be a search for not *regularizable* black market workers (author interview).

The future of policy in this controversial area is likely to continue to be cautious "non-policy." The contradiction between the need for a more elastic workforce and the pressures on the state to exercise its duty of controlling immigration has created a space in which paradoxes continue to unfold. As long as there are strong market pressures to rely on more flexible (and vulnerable) kinds of workers willing to migrate (Commission of the European Communities 1992), and as long as the pressures of nativistic groups can be contained, it is likely that future policy will continue to be loud official repudiation of undocumented workers coupled with symbolic—and equivocal—enforcement of controls.

References

Alaluf, Matéo. 1982. *The Education and Cultural Development of Migrants: Migrant Culture and Culture of Origin*. Strasbourg: Council for Cultural Cooperation, Council of Europe/Conseil de L'Europe.

Alamdar-Niemann, M., D. Bergs-Winkels, and H. Merkens. 1991. "Educational Conditions of Turkish Migrant Children in German Schools." In "Migration, Minority Status and Education: European Dilemmas and Responses in the 1990s," theme issue edited by Marcelo M. Suárez-Orozco. *Anthropology and Education Quarterly* 22:2:154–61.

Aubert, Roger, ed. 1985. *L'immigration Italienne en Belgique: Histoire, Langues, Identité*. Brussels: Instituto Italiano di Cultura, Université Catholique de Louvain, Louvain-La-Neuve.

Billiet, Jaak, Ann Carton, and Rik Huys. 1990. *Onbekend of onbemind? een sociologisch onderzoek naar de houding van de Belgen tegenover migranten*. Leuven: Sociologisch Onderzoekinstituut, K.U. Leuven.

Boos-Nünning, Ursula, and Manfred Hohmann. 1989. "The Educational Situation of Migrant Workers' Children in the Federal Republic of Germany." In *Different Cultures, Same School: Ethnic Minority Children in Europe*, edited by Lotty Eldering and Jo Kloprogge. Amsterdam: Swets and Zeitlinger.

Cahiers Marxistes. 1988. "Les Jeunes: Issus de L'immigration," vol. 164 (December).

Cammaert, Marie-France. 1986a. "The Long Road from Nador to Brussels," *International Migration* 24:3:635–50.

———. 1986b. "Cultural and Shifting Identity: Berber Immigrants from Nador (N. E. Morocco) in Brussels," *Journal of the Anthropological Society of Oxford* 27:1:27–45.

Cohen, Roger. 1993. "Price of European Unity is Reckoned in Lost Jobs," *New York Times*, January 10.

Commission of the European Communities. 1992. *Immigration Policies in the Member States: Between the Need for Control and the Desire for Integration*. Brussels: Directorate General, Employment, Industrial Relations, and Social Affairs.

Costa-Lascoux, Jacqueline. 1989. "Immigrant Children in French Schools: Equality or Discrimination." In *Different Cultures, Same School: Ethnic Minority Children in Europe*, edited by Lotty Eldering and Jo Kloprogge. Amsterdam: Swets and Zeitlinger.

———. 1992. "L'énfant, citoyen à l'école," *Revue Francaise de Pédagogie*, pp. 71–78.

Dassetto, Felice, and Albert Bastenier. 1988. *Europa: Nuova Frontiera dell'Islam*. Rome: Edizioni Lavoro.

Denton, Nicholas. 1993. "Illegal Immigrants Crackdown Agreed," *New York Times*, February 17.

De Vos, George A., and Marcelo Suárez-Orozco. 1990. *Status Inequality: The Self in Culture*. Newbury Park, Calif.: Sage.

Eldering, Lotty. 1989. "Ethnic Minority Children in Dutch Schools: Underachievement and Its Explanations." In *Different Cultures, Same School: Ethnic Minority Children in Europe*, edited by L. Eldering and Jo Kloprogge. Amsterdam: Swets and Zeitlinger.

Eldering, Lotty, and Jo Kloprogge, eds. 1989. *Different Cultures, Same School: Ethnic Minority Children in Europe*. Amsterdam: Swets and Zeitlinger.

Extra, Guus, and Ton Vallen. 1989. "Second Language Acquisition in Elementary School: A Crossnational Perspective on the Netherlands, Flanders and the Federal Republic of Germany." In *Different Cultures, Same School: Ethnic Minority Children in Europe*, edited by Lotty Eldering and Jo Kloprogge. Amsterdam: Swets and Zeitlinger.

Fassmann, Heinz, and Rainer Münz. 1992. "Patterns and Trends of International Migration in Western Europe," *Population and Development Review* 18:3:457–80.

Foblets, Marie-Claire. 1988. "Migration to Europe Today: International Private Law and the New Challenge of Legal Pluralism." Paper presented at the Symposium on Legal Pluralism in Industrial Societies, Zagreb, Yugoslavia, July 26.

Havemann, Joel. 1993. "A Dark Side of Europe's Cultural Hub," *Los Angeles Times*, April 9.

Hermans, Philip. 1993. "The Experience of Racism by Moroccan Adolescents in Brussels." In "The Insertion of Allochthonous Youngsters in Belgian Society," special book issue edited by E. Roosens. *Migration* 15:51–76.

Kamm, Henry. 1993. "'People Smugglers' Send New Tide of Refugees Onto Nordic Shores," *New York Times*, February 15.

Kilborn, Peter. 1993. "New Jobs Lack the Old Security in Time of 'Disposable Workers,'" *New York Times*, March 15.

Kinzer, Stephen. 1993. "Germany's Young Turks Say 'Enough' to the Bias," *New York Times*, June 6.

Leman, Johan. 1987. *From Challenging Culture to Challenged Culture: The Sicilian Cultural Code and the Socio-Cultural Praxis of Sicilian Immigrants in Belgium*. Leuven: Leuven University Press.

———. 1991. "The Education of Immigrant Children in Belgium." In "Migration, Minority Status and Education: European Dilemmas and Responses in the 1990s," theme issue edited by Marcelo M. Suárez-Orozco. *Anthropology and Education Quarterly* 22:2:140–54.

Morin, Maria Elena. 1984. "Impact of Family Life and Cultural Identity on Educational Integration. A Study of Second Generation Spanish Immigrants." Ph.D. dissertation, Catholic University of Leuven.

Nayer, André, and M. Nys. 1992. *Les migrations vers l'Europe occidentale: Politique migratoire et Politique d'intégration de la Belgique.* Brussels: Fondation Roi Baudouin.

Ogbu, John U. 1982. "Anthropology and Education." In *International Encyclopedia of Education: Research and Studies.* Oxford: Oxford University Press.

Payet, Jean-Paul. 1992. "Civilités et ethnicité dans les collèges de banlieu: enjeux, résistances et dérives d'une action scolaire territorialisée," *Revue Francaise de Pédagogie* 101:59–69.

Pieke, Frank. 1991. "Educational Achievement and 'Folk Theories of Success.'" In "Migration, Minority Status and Education: European Dilemmas and Responses in the 1990s." Theme issue, *Anthropology and Education Quarterly* 22:2:162–80.

Roosens, Eugeen. 1988. "Migration and Caste Formation in Europe: The Belgian Case," *Ethnic and Racial Studies* 11:2:207–17.

———. 1989a. *Creating Ethnicity: The Process of Ethnogenesis.* Beverly Hills, Calif.: Sage.

———. 1989b. "Cultural Ecology and Achievement Motivation: Ethnic Minority Youngsters in the Belgian System." In *Different Cultures, Same School: Ethnic Minority Children in Europe,* edited by Lotty Eldering and Jo Kloprogge. Amsterdam: Swets and Zeitlinger.

———. n.d. "The Multicultural Nature of Belgian Society Today." Manuscript.

Roosens, Eugeen, ed. 1993. "The Insertion of Allochthonous Youngsters in Belgian Society." Special book issue, *Migration* 15:5–117.

Stromqvist, Sven. 1989. "Perspectives on Second Language Acquisition in Scandinavia." In *Different Cultures, Same School: Ethnic Minority Children in Europe,* edited by Lotty Eldering and Jo Kloprogge. Amsterdam: Swets and Zeitlinger.

Suárez-Orozco, Marcelo M. 1989. *Central American Refugees and U.S. High Schools: A Psychosocial Study of Motivation and Achievement.* Stanford, Calif.: Stanford University Press.

Suárez-Orozco, Marcelo M., ed. 1991. "Migration Minority Status and Education: European Dilemmas and Responses in the 1990s." Theme issue, *Anthropology and Education Quarterly* 22:2:99–199.

Suárez-Orozco, Marcelo M., and Carola E. Suárez-Orozco. 1993. "La Psychologie culturelle des immigrants hispaniques aux États-Unis: Implications pour la recherche en Éducation," *Revue Francaise de Pédagogie* 101:27–44.

Tomlinson, Sally. 1989. "Ethnicity and Educational Achievement in Britain." In *Different Cultures, Same School: Ethnic Minority Children in Europe,* edited by Lotty Eldering and Jo Kloprogge. Amsterdam: Swets and Zeitlinger.

———. 1991. "Ethnicity and Educational Attainment in England—An Overview." In "Migration, Minority Status and Education: European Dilemmas and Responses in the 1990s." Theme issue, *Anthropology and Education Quarterly* 22:2:121–39.

Vásquez, Ana. 1992. "Études ethnographiques des enfants d'étranger à l'école francaise," *Revue Francaise de Pédagogie* 101:45–48.

Wander, Hilde. 1990. "Federal Republic of Germany." In *Handbook on International Migration*, edited by William J. Serow et al. New York: Greenwood Press.

Commentary

A Native Belgian's View of Immigration

Eugeen E. Roosens

International migrants to Belgium enter a society with a long and complex history of social and inter-ethnic oppositions. We can distinguish at least five bases for inclusion and exclusion in Belgium today: Flemish-speaking Belgians versus French-speaking Belgians (Walloons); Belgians versus natives of other European countries; Europeans (including those from other EC countries) versus non-EC immigrants, generally people of Turkish and Moroccan origin; Belgians, EC immigrants, and legal non-EC immigrants as a group versus illegal immigrants; and foreigners of high socioeconomic status (such as EC bureaucrats and managers of international firms) versus Belgian society in general.

Each of these oppositions has its own history. The oldest is the distinction between the Flemings and the Walloons, which dates back to shortly after Belgium's founding in 1830. From the beginning, Flemish leaders opposed the French speakers' domination of Belgian politics, schools, the army, and business. The Flemings eventually won this political battle, but these early tensions go a long way toward explaining Belgium's current views on immigration. Natives, who closely associate language, territory, and culture, view it as somewhat ironic that after winning their long battle against the Walloons, they are now in danger of forfeiting their cultural rights to foreigners on their own soil.

There were few problems with the early waves of immigrants to Belgium—first Italians, later Spaniards—who were actively recruited as immigrant workers after World War II. However, by 1974, when Belgium had no further need for guestworkers, there was a hardening of opinion against immigrants, including legal immigrants from EC countries; all immigrants were perceived as outsiders and were expected to return home.

Perceptions toward immigrants are undergoing another modification today, as Europe moves toward unification. As Belgians digest the message that European unity is crucial for keeping the continent competitive with Japan and the United States in the global marketplace, most of Belgian society, even the far-right Vlaams Blok, has come to accept the presence of Spanish, Italian, Greek, Dutch, and French immigrants. European leaders have been able to promote European cultural plurality in Belgium and to defend and celebrate unification with some success because European plurality could also be equated with a plurality of territories—a diversity of populations, each living on its own soil. What migration does occur within Europe is deemed to be of benefit to Belgium since it generally involves persons with high-level technical and professional skills.

This is not to say that ethnic-political movements, such as the Vlaamse Volksbeweging, have disappeared from the scene. They retain strength for two reasons. First, as the children and grandchildren of past EC-migrants to Belgium try to shed the label of immigrants, they also defend their right to retain their own ethnic, national, and cultural identities, keeping the spotlight focused on the differences between themselves and the native Belgian population. Second, ethnic-political movements continue to militate against the move to make Brussels an international capital within Europe. The movements' leaderships assert that Flemish culture will disappear, replaced in all areas of public life by a featureless "international" amalgam. They also protest the heavy concentration of foreigners in Brussels, where immigrants already account for more than 50 percent of the population.

Regarding the foreign financial and business community residing in Brussels, Flemings fear that this wealthy and influential group will eventually impose English as Belgium's lingua franca. To defuse this particular anti-immigrant current, a minister in Brussels recently released research findings that demonstrated the vital role that the wealthy foreign population plays in the Brussels economy, generating billions of Belgian francs a year.

But it is the non-EC immigrants, at the bottom of Belgium's socioeconomic structure, who are the primary targets of anti-immigrant sentiments. Many EC immigrants in Belgium view non-EC immigrants as a liability in Belgian society. Some even support the extreme-right Vlaams Blok's proposal to return Muslims to their home countries. Many of these poor immigrants have colonial ties to France and speak French, not Flemish, further exacerbating fears that Flemish culture and the Flemish language are under siege. The non-EC immigrants also have a higher fertility rate than the Flemish population, so their population share will continue to rise in the future.

The Flemings in Brussels feel squeezed on one side by rich expatriates (Eurocrats and international business executives) and on the other by non-EC, working-class migrants. The wealthy expatriates push up housing prices in the better neighborhoods, to the point that middle-class natives can no longer afford them. At the same time, more moderately priced areas are filling up with upwardly mobile working-class migrants and their families who have managed to escape the city's very poor "migrant" neighborhoods. The Flemings also feel they may lose control in another area if foreign residents are given voting rights; Flemings fear that the immigrants will vote overwhelmingly with Belgium's French-speaking population.

Exacerbating tensions further, there is a new wave of immigrants flooding into Brussels, made up of undocumented migrants, asylum seekers, and refugees from Poland, Romania, Ghana, the Philippines, and South America. Aside from the Africans, most can blend in with the majority population, but the public, fed by media accounts, remains fearful of their presence. Conditions in Belgium are still not conducive to the population adopting a view of a multi-ethnic or multicultural society as something positive or enriching. Although Belgians are increasingly tolerant of immigrants who came in response to government and business recruitment efforts and who have contributed to the country's general well-being, they are clearly not accepting of the new waves of illegal immigrants coming from a new set of sending countries. Native Belgians, EC immigrants, and legal non-EC immigrants all view this most recent wave of immigrants as a threat to their jobs and to the social order more generally. Illegal immigrants are also viewed as perpetrators of crime, and there are no organized groups in Belgian society willing to defend them. Policy makers, the police, immigrants from EC countries, and labor unions are all arrayed against them—as are legal residents from non-EC countries, who resent the negative attention that these latest newcomers bring to all foreigners in Belgium, whether documented or not.

If Belgium wants to protect its relative wealth (as it seems determined to do), the government may well be forced to legislate tight restrictions on illegal immigration and the employment of illegal immigrants. However, enforcing such measures could further degrade the position of the entire immigrant population, especially those in the lower socioeconomic strata of Belgian society, legal immigrants included. Such measures would, in effect, raise one more barrier to the realization in Belgium of a multi-ethnic and multicultural society.

8

Britain: The Would-be
Zero-Immigration Country

Zig Layton-Henry

— *"If when considering the desirability or otherwise of an alien's presence in the UK doubt arises, benefit should be given to the country not the alien."*[1]

Immigration policy in Britain, especially under recent Conservative administrations, has been based on a series of assumptions, some of which are more grounded in reality than others. The first assumption is that sovereign states have an absolute right to determine which noncitizens should be allowed to enter and remain within the territory of the state. Immigration control is thus natural and sensible, and every state has the right to refuse entry to "unwanted guests" such as criminals, spies, destitutes, the medically unfit, and others who are defined as undesirable.

A second assumption is that Britain is a small, overcrowded island that is relatively prosperous in world terms, so it is attractive to immigrants. Controls are thus necessary to prevent a tidal wave of Third World migrants invading the country, swamping its culture and traditions, and undermining its hard-won, fragile prosperity. This is a surprising assumption, since emigration from Britain has historically been higher than immigration and since the British have had a great deal of confidence in their ability to assimilate immigrants at home and maintain their culture among their citizens settled abroad (Paul 1992).

A third assumption (rarely admitted) is that while some immigrants are seen as unwelcome outsiders—competitors for jobs, housing, and welfare benefits—others are viewed as insiders or as welcome outsiders,

---

[1]Home Secretary, addressing immigration staff at Dover and Folkestone, 1924, cited in Roche 1969.

either because they are kith and kin or because they are viewed as more assimilable or as bringing essential capital investment and managerial skills. Welcome outsiders, for example, would include Japanese and American executives, while welcome insiders would include people of British descent and the Irish, who are usually regarded as insiders despite the troubles in Ulster and the often strained relations between the governments in London and Dublin.

Britain has historically relied on Ireland as her major source of unskilled migrant workers. In the early 1950s immigration from Ireland was around 60,000 a year, much higher than immigration from the New Commonwealth. During the discussions to control New Commonwealth immigration, every effort was made to ensure that immigration from Ireland should be allowed to continue, owing to its contribution to offsetting the labor shortage at that time, and also because the Irish were seen as being easily assimilable into the British population. In 1955, for example, the Committee on Social and Economic Problems arising from the growing influx into the United Kingdom of colored Commonwealth workers concluded:

> When all this has been said, however, it cannot be held that the same difficulties arise in the case of the Irish as in the case of non-white people. For instance, the Irishman looking for lodgings is generally speaking not likely to have any more difficulty than an Englishman, whereas the coloured man is often turned away. In fact, the outstanding difference is that the Irish are not— whether they like it or not—a different race from the ordinary inhabitants of Great Britain (!) [sic] and indeed one of the difficulties in any attempt to estimate the economic and social consequences of the influx from the Republic would be to define who are the Irish (Committee on Social and Economic Problems 1955: appendix 2).

The previous paragraph makes plain that the unwelcome outsiders were black immigrants from the Commonwealth, even though these were British subjects from the West Indies and the Indian subcontinent, many of whom had served Britain during the war (see table 8.1). Considerable efforts were made by postwar governments to reduce the numbers of these immigrants, and when informal means—such as persuading the Indian government to withhold passports of intending migrants—were unsuccessful, legislation was introduced.

Postwar immigration legislation was specifically aimed at controlling nonwhite immigration from the New Commonwealth. British policy makers were concerned that black immigrants would not be welcomed

TABLE 8.1
ESTIMATED NET IMMIGRATION FROM THE NEW COMMONWEALTH,
1953–1962

	West Indies	India	Pakistan	Others	Total
1953	2,000				2,000
1954	11,000				11,000
1955	27,500	5,800	1,850	7,500	42,650
1956	29,800	5,600	2,050	9,350	46,800
1957	23,000	6,600	5,200	7,600	42,400
1958	15,000	6,200	4,700	3,950	29,850
1959	16,400	2,950	850	1,400	21,600
1960	49,650	5,900	2,500	-350	57,700
1961	66,300	23,750	25,100	21,250	136,400
1962[1]	31,800	19,050	25,080	18,970	94,900

[1]First six months up to introduction of first controls
Source: House of Commons Library, 1976.

by the general public, and they did not believe that they would be easily assimilated into the British population. They feared that West Indian and Asian settlers would be met with racism and discrimination, which would result in social conflict, the creation of ghettos, and problems of law and order (Committee on Social and Economic Problems 1955: appendix 2). An additional factor underlying these concerns was the undoubted racial prejudice that existed among members of the elite. Three centuries of imperial superiority and authority over African, Asian, and Caribbean colonies had imbued not only the British public but especially the elite with feelings of European superiority and nonwhite inferiority. Black immigrants were not wanted; when they came, every effort was made to keep their numbers as low as possible. It was constantly argued that the smaller the black minority, the better this would be for race relations. Thus immigration control was assumed to be good for race relations and racial harmony. This is an assumption widely asserted by British politicians, especially those on the Conservative side.

There are a number of difficulties with the assertion that immigration control is good for race relations. First, controls may be seen to be ineffective, as not all forms of immigration can be controlled, partly because of international obligations and rights to family reunification. The public and the media may not distinguish between different types of immigration, such as, for example, migrant workers, dependants, and political refugees. Second, targeting specific groups as unwelcome at the borders hardly encourages people to be friendly to members of such groups within the borders. As Bernard Levin has argued, "You cannot by promising to remove the cause of fear and resentment fail to increase both. If you talk and behave as though black men were some kind of virus that must be kept out of the body politic, then it is the shabbiest hypocrisy to preach racial harmony at the same time" (*Times* [London], February 14, 1978).

A further assumption made by British policy makers is that immigration control is popular with the media and the electorate. Immigration and related issues have been heavily politicized in the postwar period, to such an extent that this is now a powerful constraint on policy makers. The campaigns for immigration control by Cyril Osborne and Enoch Powell in the 1950s and 1960s and the significant amount of support for the National Front in the 1970s defined the political ground on the issue. Prime Minister Margaret Thatcher happily reinforced the restrictionist position in the 1980s. The case in favor of immigration in terms of economic advantage, capital investment, expanding the labor force, international contacts and trade, and the acquiring of enterprise and entrepreneurial skills has little salience in public debates. The weight of public and media opinion tends to focus on the disadvantages of immigration and the need for tough immigration controls.

A major tacit assumption that underlies immigration policy is that control is possible. In the British case this is more realistic than is the case in most countries. The British tradition of control has always been of tight controls at the borders and relatively relaxed internal controls. The island situation of Britain has made this policy fairly effective but not, of course, completely. All states have considerable difficulty controlling movements across their frontiers and this is true for Britain. However, illegal immigration to Britain is probably relatively small, and most people in breach of immigration laws are assumed to be people who have broken their conditions of entry by overstaying or engaging in illegal work. There is also some current concern about the trade in marriages of convenience as a method of obtaining permanent residence in the United Kingdom. However, the main reasons why complete control over Third World immigration is impossible are, first, the right to family reunification which allows dependants to immigrate and, second, the right to political asylum. In spite of efforts by the Thatcher administration to restrict these rights, New Commonwealth immigration remained relatively stable during the 1980s (see table 8.2).

Current Immigration Issues

The current immigration issues in Britain concern asylum applications and the development of common European Community policies on immigration and asylum. A further issue could reemerge as 1997 draws closer—the issue of immigration from Hong Kong.

TABLE TABLE
ACCEPTANCES FOR SETTLEMENT IN THE UK, 1979–1991 ('000s)

	1979	1980	1981	1982	1983	1984	1985
New Commonwealth and Pakistan	37.2	33.7	31.4	30.4	27.5	24.8	27.1
Total	70.7	69.7	58.1	53.8	53.5	51.0	55.4

	1986	1987	1988	1989	1990	1991	
New Commonwealth and Pakistan	22.5	20.9	22.8	22.9	25.7	28.0	
Total	46.8	46.0	49.3	49.0	52.4	54.0	

Source: Home Office, Control of Immigration Statistics, UK, HMSO 1979–91.

Concern has been growing in many Western European countries over the rising numbers of asylum applications, even though only a small proportion of the world's refugee population is resident in Europe. Refugee numbers have increased substantially in the 1990s, largely due to the wars in Bosnia and Croatia, but the perception that the media and government politicians convey is not one of large numbers of European refugees from the former Yugoslavia or other parts of Eastern Europe, but rather of rising numbers of Third World people trying to circumvent the immigration laws and come to Britain. The deep recession and rising unemployment make immigrants less welcome, and rarely do governments, the public, or the media distinguish between migrant workers and people fleeing persecution and torture. All are regarded as potential competitors for jobs, housing, and welfare benefits. Governments routinely regard their asylum and refugee policy as part of their general immigration policy.

In Britain the discouraging attitude of the government toward asylum seekers has tended to keep applications low. In 1979, the number of people applying for asylum was only 1,563, and in 1988 it was still only a modest 5,700 (see table 8.3). These were very low numbers for a country the size of Britain. Nevertheless, the government reacted quickly in 1985 when there was an upsurge in applications from young male Tamils. The government, arguing that they were really economic migrants trying to bypass immigration controls, imposed a visa requirement on travelers from Sri Lanka. In 1986, visa requirements were imposed on travelers from India, Pakistan, Bangladesh, Nigeria, and Ghana, partly to discourage asylum applications. The use of visas has gradually been extended to other countries from which refugees were fleeing, such as Turkey and Haiti in 1989 and Uganda in 1991. In 1987 the government passed the Immigration (Carrier's Liability) Act to penalize

TABLE 8.3
ASYLUM APPLICATIONS, 1979–1992 ('000s)

1979	1980	1981	1982	1983	1984	1985
1.6	9.9	2.9	4.2	4.3	3.9	5.4
1986	1987	1988	1989	1990	1991	1992
4.8	5.2	5.7	16.5	30.0	44.8	24.6

Sources: 1979–90—Trends in International Migration (SOPEMI), OECD, Paris,
            1992.
         1991–92—Home Office, London 1993.

airlines and shipping companies that brought passengers to Britain
without the correct documents. Despite these measures making it more
difficult for people to come to the United Kingdom and claim asylum,
the numbers applying for asylum in the 1990s are likely to continue at a
much higher level than the low figures of the 1980s. There was, however,
a very substantial fall in applications in 1992 compared with 1991.

The significant rise in applications in 1990 and 1991 caused the
British government to introduce a series of measures to manage the
situation. First, the number of staff in the asylum determination division
at Croydon was increased. Second, document experts were sent to
airports around the world to train airport and immigration staff to try to
ensure that people without proper documents were prevented from
getting on planes. Third, the number of detention places at Heathrow,
Gatwick, and Stanstead airports was to be increased. Fourth, the
number of immigration staff who dealt with deportations was increased
(Hansard 1992a: col. 24). The final weapon in the government's armory
was the Asylum Bill, which aimed to streamline the handling of
applications and reduce the period of determination from two or three
years to twelve weeks, remove the right of appeal in certain cases, and
introduce the power to fingerprint asylum applicants to prevent multiple
applications for asylum and social security (Hansard 1992a: col. 24).

The original Asylum Bill was lost because of the calling of the
general election in April 1992. However, it was reintroduced as the
Asylum and Immigration Appeals Bill in the autumn. The bill reaffirmed the right to political asylum by incorporating into legislation the
1951 United Nations Convention on the Status of Refugees and the 1967
United Nations Protocol to the Convention. However, the objectives of
the bill were the same as those of its predecessor; namely, to speed up
the procedures for assessing applications, to remove certain rights of
appeal such as those of visitors and short-term and prospective students, to reduce fraudulent multiple applications by introducing compulsory fingerprinting, and to make it more difficult for asylum seekers

to arrive in the United Kingdom by extending the provisions of the Immigration (Carrier's Liability) Act of 1987 to passengers in transit through Britain at the discretion of the home secretary. The bill did provide for a right of appeal where a claim for asylum was refused. It also ended the obligation on local authorities to house asylum seekers irrespective of whether their existing accommodation, however temporary, was reasonable (United Kingdom, House of Commons 1992).

The home secretary confirmed, in introducing the debate on the second reading of the bill, that the government felt that good race relations were dependent on strict immigration controls and that the host population needed to be reassured that the influx from overseas was restricted to manageable numbers. If Britain was successfully to maintain its ability to receive everyone genuinely entitled to enter, it must strengthen its system for controlling entry and excluding people not entitled to enter. Asylum applications had become a means for evading immigration controls, and the bill was aimed at reducing this abuse. The bill would reduce delays and deal with bogus applicants more effectively (Hansard 1992b: col. 21).

Opposition spokesman Tony Blair argued that the new proposals were too harsh and that the priority given to weeding out false claims might well prejudice genuine claims. The time limits imposed in the appeals procedure were too tight and, as many visitors' appeals were successful, it was unjust to abolish the right, especially as refused visitors would have no redress against the refusal being entered in their passport, which might then jeopardize future applications (Hansard 1992b: col. 21).

The debate was dominated by opposition members of Parliament representing constituencies with ethnic minority electorates. All were strongly opposed to the bill. On the Conservative side, there was concern over the clause ending refused visitors the right of appeal, but otherwise the Conservative backbenchers supported the government. The opposition stressed its concern over the fact that the government, which had no money to build houses and was not prepared to release the receipts from the sale of council houses, was prepared to invest in new detention places for asylum seekers (Hansard 1992b: col. 104). The government rejected the criticism of the bill, which was given a second reading by 321 votes to 276, a comfortable majority of 45.

On the surface, Britain is out of step with her continental European partners on immigration policy, as on so many other issues. Britain has not signed the Schengen Agreement, nor does she wish to allow free movement across her borders for non-nationals, particularly non-EC citizens. She wishes to maintain her tight immigration controls. However, Britain has been strongly in favor of cooperation on immigration and security issues, initiating, for example, the establishment of the TREVI Group and the Ad Hoc Group on Immigration. The problem concerning the British government in this area is probably not so much agreeing on common policies as it is the suspicion that the policies may not be effectively implemented. The British government believes that it has the political will and the ability to control immigration to Britain but doubts whether its EC partners have either. It also feels that immigration is too important an area of national sovereignty to be delegated to a supranational body such as the EC. However, in spite of the fact that the EC has not yet agreed on common immigration and asylum policies, the pressures to develop a coherent and consistent European Community-wide policy are very strong. It is impossible to have an integrated labor market for the European Community if twelve different immigration regimes are in operation in the member states. This has already been recognized by the countries comprising the Schengen Group, whose agreement is likely to provide the blueprint for the rest of the EC.

The Schengen Agreement to abolish internal border controls and institute common policies on visas, asylum applications, control of third country nationals, the exchange of information on so-called undesirables (criminals, terrorists, illegal immigrants, rejected asylum applicants), and the imposition of Carrier's Liability would be a major step toward freedom of movement with the European Community and toward a Fortress Europe. In principle there are three British areas of concern, although many of the policies move European countries nearer to the tough British position on controls. First, a common immigration regime would involve a major loss of sovereignty—an erosion of the ability to control who has the right to enter the territory of the state. (The fact that Britain has already pooled this sovereignty with Ireland is usually overlooked.) Second, the British government might rightly feel that most other European states would not be willing or able to enforce even Schengen-type arrangements due to economic and political factors. Third, the loss of effective border controls might have two negative consequences: (1) the need for greater internal controls such as identity cards, and (2) the risk that anti-immigrant groups would be encouraged to try to mobilize support. The growing level of racist violence in many European countries against Third World immigrants and asylum seekers, and the rise in electoral support for racist parties, are matters of growing concern.

The issue of immigration from Hong Kong has slipped off the political agenda since the government passed the British Nationality (Hong Kong) Act in 1991. This gave some 50,000 persons selected on the basis of their position and skills the right to migrate to and settle in Britain with their families. The justification was to reduce the emigration of key personnel from Hong Kong and increase stability in the colony. Most people in Hong Kong with British passports are citizens of the British Dependent Territories under the British Nationality Act (1981) and do not have the right to enter and settle in Britain. As 1997 approaches, when the territories are to be handed back to China, there will exist the possibility of an upsurge of insecurity and even greater pressure to emigrate. The position of the Indian community in Hong Kong may be of particular concern. Its members will not be recognized as Chinese citizens, so Britain may have to assume responsibility for them in any event.

Historical Background

Britain has traditionally been one of the great emigration countries of the world. Its seafaring tradition, accumulation of overseas territories, and early agricultural revolution combined to promote sustained emigration which still continues though not on the same scale as in earlier times. In the last 300 years, millions of Britons have emigrated all over the world, especially to the United States, Canada, Australasia, and South Africa. Even as late as 1871–1930 there was a net outflow of some 3.4 million people from the United Kingdom. In the 1930s the balance of migration was reversed as earlier emigrants returned after failing to establish themselves overseas during the Great Depression. Between 1931 and 1940 there was a net inflow of 650,000 people. In recent years, continental Europe has become a major destination for Britain's professional workers and retired people.

Immigration to Britain has generally been on a smaller scale and was often sponsored by medieval monarchs such as the Flemings who settled in South Wales in the twelfth century. Large inflows were rare, the most notable being the 80,000 Huguenots who fled to England after the Revocation of the Edict of Nantes in 1685. More important, especially in the nineteenth century, was internal migration to England from other parts of the British Isles, especially Ireland. The 1861 census recorded 601,634 Irish-born residents in England (3 percent of the English population) and a further 204,083 resident in Scotland (6.7 percent of the Scottish population).

However, the contemporary history of British immigration policy begins with the immigration of Jewish refugees from the Russian Empire and Romania in the 1870s. Many of these refugees settled in the East End of London, where local Conservative politicians fanned anti-Jewish sentiments by into anti-immigrant agitation. The numbers involved were modest. The Royal Commission on Alien Immigration reported that the number of aliens in the United Kingdom was 135,640 in 1881; 219,523 in 1891; and 280,925 in 1901. Nevertheless, the insecurity and frustration caused by poverty, unemployment, casual work, overcrowding, and crime were projected onto the Jewish immigrants by East Enders who blamed them for social problems that had existed in profusion in the East End of London before the migration. A Select

Committee in 1889 and the Royal Commission in 1902 both came to similar conclusions: that the numbers of immigrants were small, that the immigrants were clean and healthy, that there were few criminals among them, and that their children adapted well to English schools once language problems were overcome. Despite these positive findings, the Royal Commission did recommend that certain categories of "undesirable alien" should be refused entry (Gainer 1972). The same evidence can lead to startlingly different conclusions. An immigration officer, writing in the 1960s, commenting on the Royal Commission's findings, wrote that "of the alien population of London, 2.4% were paupers; and crimes of violence committed by aliens had doubled from 28 in 1892 to 58 in 1902. It was not a pretty picture." He therefore strongly supported the recommendations to control entry (Roche 1969). The Royal Commission's positive assessment seems much more appropriate.

However, the agitation against aliens was successful, and the Aliens Act was passed in 1905. It gave the home secretary powers to refuse entry to prostitutes, pimps, people convicted of serious (extraditable) crimes, people without the means to support themselves, and people of bad character. The act applied to steerage passengers only on large ships, and immigrants had the right of appeal to an Immigration Appeals Board. Aliens had to land at a named immigration port, and transmigrants were exempt from the provisions of the act. Many immigrants were thus not covered by the legislation, and many who were covered appealed against the decision to refuse them entry. Between 1906 and 1910 some 2,731 appealed, and of these 36 percent (980) were successful.

Immigration controls over aliens were strengthened by the Aliens Restriction Act of 1914. Every person entering the country now had to produce a passport or identity document and undergo the scrutiny of an immigration officer. Aliens officers had the power to detain and examine all persons and to refuse leave to land to enemy aliens unless in possession of a permit issued by the secretary of state. An aliens officer might give leave to land to "alien friends" arriving at an approved port and attach conditions to this leave. Immigration officers could arrest without warrant any person breaking the order, including shipmasters. A host of orders were made during World War I giving the home secretary greater powers over aliens. In February 1916, for example, there was an Order in Council requiring all aliens to register with the police. Records also began to be kept of the movement of aliens to and from continental Europe. After the war the Aliens Restriction (Amendment) Act of 1919 was passed. This repealed the 1905 Aliens Act and extended the 1914 legislation for a further year.

In the following year, control of aliens was consolidated in the Aliens Order of 1920. This stated that no alien might land without the leave of an immigration officer, nor elsewhere than at an approved port; the immigration officer might refuse leave to land to any alien or might attach such conditions as he saw fit to the grant of leave to land. He was to deny leave to land to five types of aliens: those who could not support themselves, those who could not support their dependants, those seeking unauthorized employment, those who were mentally unfit, and those who had been convicted of a serious crime abroad. The immigration officer might enter or board any ship and require the production of any documents by any alien seeking to land; and every person over sixteen years of age had to produce a passport of other document satisfactorily establishing his or her national status or identity. This "temporary" legislation was renewed every year by the Expiring Laws Continuance Act until 1971, when it was superseded by the Immigration Act. It was the Aliens Order of 1920 that gave the home secretary the extraordinarily arbitrary power of being able to deport an alien if he decreed his or her presence in Britain to be "not conducive to the public good."

The only other significant development before World War II was the Coloured Seaman's Order of April 1925. This was an attempt to stop desertions by colored merchant seamen and their settlement in British ports. The order provided for the registration of colored seamen immediately upon arrival at British ports if they were unable to produce evidence that they were British subjects. A certificate was issued to them, and the immigration officer then informed the registration officer of the district to which the seaman was traveling. Chinese seamen were exempt from the order. Roche (1969: 107–08) claims that this proved to be a very efficient method of control and substantially reduced the problem of desertions.

Thus by World War II, the British Home Office had complete powers to control alien immigration. These powers were initiated in 1905 as a result of the anti-aliens agitation and were consolidated during the xenophobia inspired by World War I. The government had little power, however, to control the immigration of British subjects, and these included not only British citizens but citizens of the colonies and of independent Commonwealth countries then known as Dominions.

The history of postwar immigration to Britain has been extremely well documented (Foot 1965; Holmes 1988; Layton-Henry 1992). This author has argued that it was World War II that provided both the stimulus and the necessary conditions for postwar migration from the New Commonwealth (Layton-Henry 1992). There is considerable debate as to whether the racist response to this migration was stimulated by the political elite or was merely an elite response to grassroots racism (Studlar 1980; Foot 1965). However, the major sequences and junctures are well known.

In the early postwar period, when the labor shortage was already acute and politicians and demographers were concerned about the resumption of emigration to Australia, the United States, Canada, and parts of Africa, there were a number of sources of immigrants. First, Irish immigration was substantial and unrestricted. Second, the government was involved in a number of schemes to recruit European "volunteer workers," particularly from the displaced persons camps in Germany. These aliens, mainly Poles, Ukrainians, and Latvians, were allocated to vacancies in undermanned industries. German ex-prisoners of war were encouraged to stay, and the Polish forces that served under British command during the war were allowed to settle in Britain. There was also some immigration from Italy.

The recruitment of European labor was partly preferred because the European volunteer workers were recruited under strict conditions and could be prosecuted and deported if they broke their conditions of recruitment. But it was also assumed that European workers could easily be integrated into the workforce and assimilated into the population. There was considerable prejudice against the recruitment of black colonial workers. It was always assumed that the "absorption of large numbers of non-white immigrants would be very difficult" (Political and Economic Planning 1948; Royal Commission 1949).

The control of New Commonwealth immigration was discussed at cabinet level as early as 1950, long before substantial settlement had taken place. A draft bill was prepared in 1954 but then dropped. The first control legislation was the Commonwealth Immigrants Bill of 1962, which made Commonwealth immigrants subject to an entry voucher scheme unless they were born in the United Kingdom or held a passport issued by the British government or were included on such a passport. Other Commonwealth citizens wishing to immigrate had to have a Ministry of Labour voucher before they could enter Britain. These vouchers were to be issued under three categories: Category A for those migrants with a specific job to go to; Category B for those with special skills in short supply; and Category C for all other intending migrants who would be dealt with in order of application, with priority to those with war service. In August 1965 the new Labour government tightened the controls, imposing a quota of 8,500 a year on the recruitment of New Commonwealth immigrant workers and reserving 1,000 of these for Maltese. They also abolished Category C. In February 1968 a new bill, the Commonwealth Immigrants Act, controlled the entry of those British passport holders without a close connection with the United Kingdom. This was to facilitate a quota system imposed on British Asian migration from East Africa.

In 1971 a Conservative government introduced a comprehensive immigration bill giving the government complete control over all immigration except for "patrials," that is, people with close connections with the United Kingdom through birth or descent, who would remain free from all controls. The main provisions were that employment vouchers would be replaced by work permits, which would not carry the right of permanent residence or the right of entry for dependants. Henceforward citizens of independent Commonwealth countries and British subjects without a close connection with Britain would be treated on the same basis as aliens for the purposes of immigration control. Diagrammatically, the situation on January 1, 1973, when the Immigration Act of 1971 came into force, was as presented in table 8.4.

The Immigration Act of 1971 gave the home secretary the power to make immigration rules that guide the practice of the Immigration Service. On January 1, 1973, Britain's entry into the European Community gave new rights to enter and work to EC nationals. There was, however, little public or media interest in these provisions. European immigration was, after all, unlikely, and in any case was not a political issue.

But the potency of immigration as a political issue did not diminish with the passage of the Immigration Act of 1971. Pressure to control nonwhite immigration intensified in 1972 due to President Idi Amin's expulsion of Asians from Uganda. The acceptance of most of the Asians by the Conservative government led by Edward Heath was considered an act of betrayal by Enoch Powell and his supporters, and also by the extreme right party, the National Front. Immigration continued to be a salient issue throughout the 1970s, with the National Front exploiting a media panic over an inflow of Asians from Malawi in 1976. Although the National Front was unable to win any local government or parliamentary seats in the 1970s, its provocative marches in areas of black settlement and the modest degree of electoral support it achieved alarmed the other parties. The Conservatives in particular were pressured into adopting the most stringent policies on immigration control.

By the end of the 1970s both major parties were committed to a new Nationality Act. The Labour Party considered that a logical and nonracial immigration policy had to be based on a rational concept of British citizenship. They had produced proposals for reform as early as 1972 (Labour Party 1972). Leading Conservatives, including Powell, who was probably the first to urge this reform, were also convinced that the long-standing concept of "British subject" was anachronistic and had to be reformed. Its content had been eroded by immigration control legislation, the abandonment of Britain's imperial pretensions, and the independence of almost all of her former colonies. Britain's entry into the European Community on January 1, 1973, was viewed by many Commonwealth countries as the final act undermining the unity of the Commonwealth and ending the myth of common interest and allegiances between Britain and her former colonies. New citizenship legislation defining British nationality more narrowly to those with close links to the United Kingdom by birth, settlement, or descent from a citizen would provide a more rational and less overtly racist basis for

TABLE 8.4
BRITISH IMMIGRATION CONTROL, 1973

Not Subject to Control	Subject to Limited Control	Subject to Full Control
• British citizens (patrials)	• British Asians (from East Africa)	• Aliens
• Irish citizens	• Other EC nationals	• Other Commonwealth citizens
• Commonwealth citizens (patrials)		
• EC nationals seeking work, and their dependants		

defining who had the right of access to and abode in the territory of the United Kingdom.

The election of Mrs. Thatcher as leader of the Conservative Party in 1975 marked the beginning of the present strongly restrictionist period in Conservative immigration policy. Mrs. Thatcher was sympathetic to Powell's views. She believed that the Labour government of 1974–1979 had allowed too much New Commonwealth immigration, that popular anxieties about it were justified, and that the Conservative Party should bring it to an end. She also felt that this would be electorally popular and would undermine the basis of support for the National Front.

The Conservative Party election manifesto was vague in every policy area in 1979 except for immigration and nationality. Here a list of eight specific commitments were made that clearly had Mrs. Thatcher's wholehearted support. These commitments were:

1. We shall introduce a new British Nationality Act to define entitlement to British citizenship and the right of abode in this country. It will not adversely affect the right of anyone now permanently settled here.

2. We shall end the practice of allowing permanent settlement for those who came here for a temporary stay.

3. We shall limit the entry of parents, grandparents and children over 18 to a small number of urgent compassionate cases.

4. We shall end the concession introduced by the Labour government in 1974 to husbands and male fiancés.

5. We shall severely restrict the issue of work permits.

6. We shall introduce a register of those Commonwealth wives and children entitled to entry for settlement under the 1971 Immigration Act.

7. We shall then introduce a quota system, covering everyone outside the European Community, to control entry for settlement.

8. We shall take firm action against illegal immigrants and overstayers and help those immigrants who genuinely wish to leave this country—but there can be no question of compulsory repatriation (Conservative Party 1979).

These election commitments turned out to be too specific and led to a clash between the populist authoritarian promises of the new government and civil service pragmatism. In particular, the Conservatives were forced to drop the register of dependants and the non-EC world quota for settlement. However, they immediately set about tightening the immigration rules, in particular to deny entry to husbands and fiancés marrying or intending to marry British citizens through arranged marriages. In 1974 the Labour government had granted such persons the automatic right to enter for settlement, a right that had been limited by a previous Labour government in 1969. In November 1979 a White Paper was laid before Parliament proposing that husbands of women settled in Britain would need an entry certificate to be admitted to the United Kingdom and that this would be refused if the entry clearance officer had reason to believe, first, that the marriage was arranged solely to gain admission to Britain; second, that the husband and wife did not intend living together; or third, that the couple had not met. An entry certificate could be issued if the wife had been born in the United Kingdom. Similar conditions would apply to applications from fiancés. Elderly dependants would only be admitted if wholly or mainly dependant on sons and daughters in Britain (that is, receiving money from them), and they must also be without relatives in their own country and have a standard of living substantially below that of their own country. These conditions were clearly designed to disqualify elderly dependants from Third World countries since remittances from their children in Britain would be likely to raise their standard of living at home by a significant amount. The regulations governing change of category for people entering Great Britain as visitors or students were tightened in order to prevent such a change resulting in a right to settlement, and their right to seek employment was restricted. The new provisions relating to au pair girls were restricted to those from Western European countries.

The rules were criticized from an unexpected source. British wives living abroad (in Egypt or the United States, for example) who might wish to return to the United Kingdom to settle with their husbands lobbied Conservative backbenchers who, in turn, put pressure on the government. The government amended the rules so that the right of entry was extended to husbands and fiancés whose wives or fiancées had been born or had one parent born in the United Kingdom, providing the primary purpose of the marriage was not settlement. Also, elderly dependants would be allowed to enter Britain providing they were wholly maintained by their children or grandchildren. These new immigration rules were approved on March 10, 1980.

The new rule allowing entry to husbands and fiancés, provided the primary purpose of the marriage was not settlement in Britain, is the basis of the refusal of entry to many Asian couples, mainly from the Indian subcontinent. At present some 69 percent of applications from the Indian subcontinent are refused under the primary purpose rule.

The major political commitment that the Thatcher government of 1979–1983 did fulfill was the legislation on British nationality. The feudal and imperial concept of "British subject" had already been undermined; postwar immigration legislation meant that most British subjects no longer had the right to immigrate to the United Kingdom—though if resident in Britain, they could vote, work in the public service, and serve in the armed forces. It was felt that the way to resolve these contradictions was to create a new, narrower, and more realistic British citizenship for those with close ties to Britain, which would include the right of free entry and permanent abode. Also, since discrimination by sovereign states in favor of their own citizens was acceptable in international law, it would enable the government to cut many of its imperial obligations and at the same time make it more difficult for critics to accuse it of operating racist immigration laws. A Conservative Party policy document published in March 1980 stated: "Future immigration policies, if they are to be sensible, realistic and fair, must be founded on a separate citizenship of the UK and it is therefore essential that a reformed law of nationality should for the first time make it clear who are the citizens of the UK" (Conservative Political Centre 1980). In the longer term, the government was also concerned about the prospect of increasing pressure to immigrate coming from Hong Kong, given that the British lease on most of the territory was due to run out in 1997.

The British Nationality Act (1981) was a major milestone and a critical break with Britain's imperial past. The three messy categories of citizenship that emerged—namely, British citizenship, citizenship of the dependant territories, and British overseas citizenship—show how difficult the unscrambling was, though a neater solution could easily have been achieved. But it was a landmark, moving British nationality legislation closer to that of her neighbors and confirming her intention to divest herself of her imperial legacy and obligations. It was a change forced by postwar immigration. Its consequence was a stampede for registration and naturalization by immigrants settled in Britain. Applications for naturalization and registration rose from 38,000 in 1978 to 96,000 in 1982 despite a huge rise in fees. Naturalization fees rose from £90 in 1979 to £200 in April 1982, and those for registration from £37.50

to £70. One result of the British Nationality Act was that male and female citizens were to be treated equally under the immigration rules.

The first Thatcher government did manage to reduce immigration through its legislative and administrative actions, but only marginally. The government nevertheless claimed that it had an effective policy compared with its Labour predecessor, that it had reduced immigration, and that it had actively pursued illegal immigrants and overstayers. The Conservative justification was that good community relations depended on effective immigration controls. Its policies, it claimed, were "firm but fair." They were certainly firm on immigration controls but fair only to those who opposed New Commonwealth immigration. They were unfair to dependants, spouses, and refugees legally entitled to enter Britain but who were refused admission or kept waiting for years so that the government could claim political credit for reducing the immigration statistics.

After 1983 the focus of immigration policy switched to refugees with the Tamil crisis in May 1985 and the immediate imposition of a visa regime that was extended under pressure from immigration officers in 1986 to India, Pakistan, Nigeria, Ghana, and Bangladesh. In 1987 the Immigration (Carrier's Liability) Act made it an offense for airlines or shipping companies to bring people to the United Kingdom without proper documents and requiring these companies to enforce immigration laws and visa regulations or face a fine of £1,000 per passenger. This was to prove an increasingly intolerable burden on airlines, some of whose passengers used sophisticated forgeries or destroyed their documents during their flight.

In 1988 a new immigration bill was passed to keep control "in good repair." The absolute right of men who had settled in Britain before 1973 to bring their families was repealed. The European Court of Human Rights had ruled that this right discriminated against women; so by abolishing the right for men, both sexes were treated equally (badly). The right now became contingent on showing that dependants would receive adequate accommodation and financial support. Certain rights of appeal against refusal of entry and against deportation were restricted. Overstaying was made a continuing criminal offense, and the entry of second or subsequent wives in a polygamous marriage was banned. This last provision seemed to accord well with Mrs. Thatcher's known views. She had stated in January 1979 that "people are rather afraid that this country night be rather swamped by people of a different culture" (Thatcher 1978). Mr. Hurd, the home secretary, confirmed this view in the debate when he said, "Polygamy is not an acceptable social custom in this country" (Hansard 1987: col. 785).

The Salman Rushdie Affair

Toward the end of 1988 British Muslims became actively involved in a campaign to ban *The Satanic Verses*, written by Salman Rushdie, which they regarded as an offensive and blasphemous attack on the Islamic faith. The book was published in September and quickly brought protests from Muslin groups. On December 2 they turned to direct action: 7,000 people staged a demonstration in Bolton and burned a copy of the book to gain publicity, with little success. On January 14, 1989, a protest meeting was held outside Bradford Town Hall, and once again a copy of the book was symbolically burned. This time the protest was widely reported and condemned.

A month later, on February 14, the campaign against *The Satanic Verses* took a dramatic turn when the Ayatollah Khomeini urged Muslims throughout the world to execute Rushdie: "I inform the proud Muslim people of the world that the author of *The Satanic Verses* book, which is against Islam, the Prophet and the Koran, and all those involved in its publication who were aware of its content, are sentenced to death" (*London Evening Standard*, February 14, 1989).

There was widespread shock that a head of state could urge the death of a famous writer who was the citizen of another state. The Ayatollah's famous *fatwa* was immediately condemned in Western countries as Salman Rushdie went into hiding. Some Muslim leaders in Bradford, for example, supported the death sentence, but the Council of Mosques in Britain condemned the violence and urged Muslims to obey the law. On February 18 Rushdie apologized for the distress he had caused to Muslims, but the Ayatollah Khomeini did not accept this apology. On February 21 the British government withdrew its diplomats from Tehran and sent Iran's representative home. This action was supported by the European Community. Many writers took the lead in supporting Rushdie and defending his right to publish.

On February 24 Home Secretary Douglas Hurd addressed Muslims in the Central Mosque in Birmingham. He accepted that Muslims had been deeply hurt by the book but warned that violence or the threat of violence was wholly unacceptable and that nothing would do more damage to racial harmony than the idea that British Muslims were indifferent to the rule of law in Britain. Respect for the rule of law was a fundamental principle for which Britain stood, as were freedom of speech and tolerance of different opinions (*Independent*, February 25, 1989).

The campaign against *The Satanic Verses* raised concern about the influence of Islamic fundamentalism in Britain and efforts by Muslim groups to set up their own educational institutions, especially single-sex schools for girls. In July, John Patten, minister of state at the Home Office Responsible for Race Relations, spoke of the need for the Muslim community to integrate into British society. In a letter to the Advisory Council on Race Relations he wrote, "One cannot be British on one's own exclusive terms or on a selective basis" (*Independent*, July 20, 1989).

Those sympathetic to the Muslim campaign—who included some members of Parliament with Muslim electors—deplored the fact that the blasphemy laws applied only to Christianity and condemned the unwillingness of many liberals to understand the intensity of the offense to practicing Muslims. Some argued that British Muslims felt their values were being eroded in a hostile society, that only extreme actions enabled them to gain the attention of the media and politicians, and generally that their customs were not respected in British society. The action of the government in banning polygamous wives could be cited as an example of this view.

The Rushdie affair has brought the peaceful, hardworking Muslim community into considerable political prominence. Issues of concern to Muslims such as education, problems of adjusting to British society, and the role of the Islamic faith in a liberal secular country are receiving greater attention. The campaign divided those on the left, some of whom felt it was vital to preserve freedom of speech and publication, while others felt the campaign had unleashed considerable racist and anti-Muslim feelings that were legitimized by the actions of the Ayatollah and some protesters' threats against the publishers and bookshops. Roy Hattersley argued forcefully that the proposition that Muslims are welcome in Britain if, and only if, they stop behaving like Muslims is incompatible with the principles of a free society, but in a free society the Muslim community can be allowed to do whatever it likes only as long as the choice it makes is not damaging to society as a whole (*Independent*, July 21, 1989). The campaign against *The Satanic Verses* was unsuccessful in achieving any concessions to Muslim demands.

The General Election of 1992

In contrast to the Rushdie affair, which showed the powerlessness of British Muslims, the general election of 1992 illustrated the increasing participation and prominence of black people in mainstream politics. It also confirmed the continuing salience of immigration as a political issue. The three major parties selected nineteen African-Caribbean and Asian candidates, of whom nine were Labour, seven Conservative, and three Liberal Democrat. For the first time, the Conservatives selected ethnic minority candidates in winnable seats: Nirj Deva in Brentford and Isleworth, and John Taylor in Cheltenham. There was considerable controversy over Taylor's selection, but he was strongly supported by the party leadership.

On the Labour side, there were four African-Caribbean or Asian candidates defending parliamentary seats they had won in 1987; namely, Diane Abbott (Hackney North and Stoke Newington), Paul Boateng (Brent South), Bernie Grant (Tottenham), and Keith Vaz (Leicester East). To these must be added Ashok Kumar (Lanbaurgh) who was elected at a by-election held on November 7, 1991. Another Asian candidate, Piara Khabra, was standing in Ealing Southall, which was a safe Labour seat in West London with a large Asian electorate. None of the three ethnic minority Liberal Democrat candidates was selected for a winnable seat.

The results of the 1992 election showed that black candidates were more widely accepted by the electorate than ever before. The Labour members of Parliament, Keith Vaz and Bernie Grant, achieved large swings and greatly increased their majorities. Diane Abbott and Paul Boateng also achieved good swings, and Piara Khabra easily held Ealing Southall for the Labour Party. Ashok Kumar, however, was one of many by-election victors who failed to hold their by-election gains. Nirj Deva, elected in Brentford and Isleworth, became the first Conservative Asian member of Parliament since Sir Mancherjee Bhownagree was elected in 1895. John Taylor failed to hold Cheltenham for the Conservatives and thus failed to become, at this election, their first African-Caribbean member of Parliament. The election results suggested that parliamentary politics were slowly becoming multiracial and that prejudiced voting was very much less significant than it had been in the 1960s and 1970s.

Immigration played only a small part in the election campaign. The Conservatives promised to reintroduce the Asylum Bill (lost because of the election), which was aimed at restraining the rise in asylum applications. Labour and Liberal Democrats promised to strengthen legislation against racial discrimination, to reform the citizenship laws, and to guarantee sanctuary for genuine refugees. During the campaign the media publicized an incident in which illegal immigrants were caught being smuggled into Britain by truck (*Times*, March 24, 1992). Late in the campaign, Nicholas Fairbairn, a former Scottish solicitor general, tried to resurrect the "swamping" issue by stating the under a Labour government the country would be swamped by immigrants of every color and race (*Observer*, April 5, 1992). He was condemned by Conservative party leaders. However, this showed that some prominent Conservatives were willing to exploit racial prejudice among the electorate when they feared a Labour victory.

The persistence of prejudice against black immigration among members of the British elite could also be seen at the end of May 1993, when Winston Churchill, a member of Parliament and grandson of Sir Winston Churchill, called for a halt to the relentless flow of immigrants that was threatening to change forever Britain's way of life. He incorrectly stated that some northern English cities had populations that were over half immigrants and that in the future a typical English scene would involve muezzin calling Allah's faithful to the High Street mosque for Friday's prayers (*Times*, May 31, 1993). Churchill's remarks were widely condemned as racist and damaging to race relations, but they show that there is continuing pressure on the government from the Conservative right to maintain tough immigration controls even though immigration is only a marginal factor contributing to the growing numbers of Britain's ethnic minorities.

Conclusion

British immigration policy this century has been determined by a mixture of economic and political imperatives. The political dimension has generally been the more overt due to the mobilization of anti-alien and anti-immigrant feelings by politicians and the popular press at the turn of the century, during World War I, and in the 1960s and 1970s. The power of economic factors can be seen in the special arrangements for Ireland and the lack of public concern about free movement of EC labor or multinational company arrangements. In the postwar period it is black immigration and black refugees that have been stereotyped and against whom Conservative governments have used every conceivable administrative and legislative device to control and bar them entry to the United Kingdom. This is justified as being good for race relations within Britain, but it is in fact good electoral politics in an electorate that has on numerous occasions in the postwar period been mobilized on anti-immigration themes.

Despite draconian measures and the violation of human rights, successive governments, whether Conservative or Labour, have been unable to bring "immigration as we have known it in the post-war years to an end" (Whitelaw 1976). Acceptances for settlement continue at a stable level of 50,000–60,000 a year, half of which are from the New Commonwealth. These are now overwhelmingly dependants and are entitled to enter Britain to join close relatives. Immigration controls are horrendously tight, but as an issue immigration still seems capable of inflaming public opinion when whipped up by politicians or the tabloid press.

There are a number of unknowns when we contemplate future British immigration policies. The first is the gradual process of European harmonization and the creation of an EC immigration and refugee regime. Can Fortress Britain hold out much longer, and will Southern Europe become a gateway into Britain for Asians and Africans? Second, how will the transition to Chinese rule go in Hong Kong, and will the relatively sympathetic attitude in British public opinion toward the people of Hong Kong be maintained if an immigration panic should develop? Third, what effect would a change of government have on British immigration and nationality policy? If the Labour Party were to be returned to office, there would undoubtedly be some changes. But, given Labour's tough position on immigration from Hong Kong and their cautious proposals for reforming the immigration and nationality laws, the changes would not be significant. Conservatives have recently cited the rise of anti-immigrant parties and violence in France and Germany as justification for the "firm but fair" policy. It is unlikely that the Labour Party would risk alienating white voters by adopting more liberal immigration policies. They would emphasize integrative themes such as tougher antidiscrimination legislation to maintain their support among the black electorate while reassuring white voters that immigration control was safe in their hands. In a period of relatively high unemployment there would be no incentive to modify the restrictionist immigration regime that successive British governments have established.

References

Committee on Social and Economic Problems. 1955. *Report of the Committee on Social and Economic Problems Arising from the Growing Influx into the UK of Coloured Workers from Other Commonwealth Countries.* CAB129/77, 3, August.

Conservative Party. 1979. *The Conservative Party Manifesto.* London: Conservative Central Office.

Conservative Political Centre. 1980. *Who Do We Think We Are?* London: Conservative Central Office, March.

Foot, Paul. 1965. *Immigration and Race in British Politics.* Baltimore, Md.: Penguin.

Gainer, Bernard. 1972. *The Alien Invasion: The Origins of the Aliens Act of 1905.* London: Heinemann.

Hansard Parliamentary Debates, Commons. 1987. November 16.

———. 1992a. Vol. 205, March 2.

———. 1992b. Vol. 213, November 2.

Holmes, Colin. 1988. *John Bull's Island: Immigration and British Society, 1871–1971.* Basingstoke: MacMillan.

Labour Party. 1972. *Citizenship, Immigration and Integration: A Policy for the 1970s.* London: Labour Party.

Layton-Henry, Zig. 1992. *The Politics of Immigration: Immigration, 'Race' and 'Race' Relations in Post-War Britain.* Oxford: Blackwell.

Paul, K. 1992. "The Politics of Citizenship in Post-War Britain," *Contemporary Record* 6:3.

Political and Economic Planning. 1948. *Population Policy in Great Britain; A Report.* London.

Roche, T.W.E. 1969. *The Key in the Lock: A History of Immigration Control in England from 1066 to the Present Day.* London: John Murray.

Royal Commission on Population. 1949. "Report of the Royal Commission on Population." CMND 7695, HMSO.

Studlar, D.T. 1980. "Elite Responsiveness or Elite Autonomy: British Immigration Policy Reconsidered," *Ethnic and Racial Studies* 3:2.

Thatcher, Margaret. 1978. Verbatim report of an interview with Gordon Burns, given by Mrs. Thatcher on Monday, January 30, *World in Action*, Granada Television.

United Kingdom. House of Commons. 1992. Asylum and Immigration Appeals Bill. Session 1992/3, HMSO, October 22.

Whitelaw, W. 1976. Speech by the Rt. Hon. William Whitelaw, Conservative spokesman on Home Affairs, Conservative Party Conference, Brighton, October 5.

Commentary

Britain, the Deviant Case

Gary P. Freeman

Great Britain is in many respects a deviant case among the Western democracies considered in this volume. The British experience demonstrates that it is possible to limit unwanted migration, contrary to the implications that might be drawn from the study of other countries. Those who claim that liberal democracies are helpless to deal with contemporary immigration pressures must take account of the British anomaly.

On the other hand, Britain may well illustrate the limits on the ability of democracies to control immigration. British governments responded earlier and more vigorously to non-European immigration than other states, and Great Britain enjoyed unusual advantages such as being an island. But even the Thatcher governments were able to reduce inflows from the New Commonwealth by only a few thousand a year. The right of family reunion and the failure of voluntary repatriation saw to that. Furthermore, the fertility rates of the immigrant population and its descendants are making Britain more and more obviously multiracial, which was the outcome that policy sought to prevent.

Britain is the most interesting case of postcolonial immigration because it possessed the largest empire and had made the most expansive concessions on citizenship and immigration rights to its subjects of any colonial power. In the effort to make amends for what were clearly seen as mistakes, Britain has arguably become the only state to insert significant elements of a color bar into its immigration and citizenship laws. The distinction between British policy and that of the other European democracies that shut off new immigration for work after 1973 should not be overdrawn, of course. The policies of these states were also intended to reduce non-European migration. Britain is different because it enshrines ethnic exclusion in statutory law through the concept of patriality.

Britain is a deviant case, too, in that governments have steadfastly ignored the economic consequences of immigration, even when (as if often the case) these would almost certainly be positive. The immigration debate focuses obsessively on controlling numbers and dealing with racial tensions. The reaction of officials to the possibility of a major influx from Hong Kong is simply the latest episode confirming the primacy of politics over economics.

Britain stands apart as well with respect to its activities in the arena of intergroup relations and discrimination. The race relations law and community relations institutions have been harshly criticized as ineffectual, but a fair assessment would have to conclude that British governments have been more active and diligent with respect to these matters than the majority of European states.

Zig Layton-Henry has done a thorough job describing the evolution of British policy. But how can we explain its peculiarity? What accounts for the early, sharp, and consistent response of the government to nonwhite immigration? Why has Britain led other states in the promptness and rigor of its reaction to the asylum crisis since 1989? What contributes to the remarkable salience of immigration and race in Britain? There are at least three plausible hypotheses.

• *The racist political elite.* This hypothesis is based on the notion that the British political class, especially as it is organized in the Tory Party, is deeply racist as a result, paradoxically, of both its insularity (the Little England syndrome) and its experiences with colonialism. Elites did not need to be convinced that New Commonwealth immigration was a bad idea. In responding strongly to early entries, politicians failed in their responsibilities, contributed to grassroots reaction and violence, and blamed their own prejudiced policies on ordinary Britons. Proponents of this hypothesis usually assume that forceful leadership from the politicians would have deterred a nativist reaction by the public.

• *Populist politics.* This hypothesis emphasizes not so much the reflexive racism of the British political elite as its cynical willingness to exploit immigration and race for partisan purposes. The Conservatives in the early 1960s and Labour between 1964 and 1968 could be seen to be playing politics with the issue. The principal exhibit, however, consists of the Conservative governments after 1979 and, particularly, Prime Minister Thatcher's comments in the run-up to the 1979 general election.

• *The responsible political elite.* This hypothesis, rarely advanced, holds that the British political class, both Tory and Labour, understood that the public was little inclined to tolerate significant numbers of nonwhite immigrants. (Conversations with constituents and the outbreak of violence in the 1950s would have sufficed to indicate this.) They moved, therefore, to limit immigration in its earliest days and to reassure the public that its concerns were understood. This interpretation would take the oft-repeated argument that good race relations depended on a firm demonstration of control over numbers, not as insincere rhetoric, but as the actual logic driving policy. Elite behavior was, in this view, constrained by mass concern over nonwhite immigration and by the willingness of maverick politicians like Enoch Powell to exploit it. The behavior of the Conservative Party is consistent with its long-standing capacity to adapt to changing circumstances in order to remain electorally viable. One might even see the immigration saga in terms similar to the Disraelian social reforms of the nineteenth century. In this case, the loss of empire meant that old commitments to colonial subjects had to be jettisoned, just as traditional resistance to social reform had been set aside earlier. The virtual elimination of the anti-immigrant extreme right as a political force and the extensive effort to foster harmonious race relations also fit this interpretation.

One way of sorting out these conflicting hypotheses is to examine the institutional context within which immigration policy is made, especially institutional linkages between masses and elites. The Westminster system of responsible party government, founded on parliamentary sovereignty, is remarkably responsive to mass opinion and to constituency pressure. Mass political parties with active constituency associations are able to press claims at annual party conferences and to participate in the selection of parliamentary candidates. The Labour Party is closely tied to a trade union movement concerned about the employment effects of immigration, whose leaders are also disturbed by their limited capacity to defuse racist sentiments among the rank and file. In the Conservative constituency associations, on the other hand, one can find many members exhibiting old colonial mentalities and able to apply pressure on backbench members of Parliament. The role of a vigorous tabloid press expressing the views of the "man on the Clapham omnibus" should not be overlooked either.

The most important aspects of the British immigration policy-making process are that it is Parliament-centered and highly public. Neither a strong bureaucracy nor interventionist courts have deflected attention from the House of Commons. Debates are widely covered and have been broadcast live in recent years. They take place in a period of declining party cohesion, which is increasingly expressed in backbench criticism of governments from within their own party. The House of Lords, not being electorally accountable, has been more liberal than the Commons on immigration matters. The absence of a tradition of biparti-

sanship in Britain makes it difficult for the two major parties to depoliti-
cize immigration and race, as much as they have tried. The logic of the
Westminster system undermines such a strategy. It is not feasible to
displace immigration decision making to the bureaucracy, where it
would be out of public view. Administrative discretion is low, with
regulations implementing legislation subject to furious debate in Parliament.

In sum, British politicians are not as insulated from their constituents as their counterparts in countries like Canada, France, or Germany.
The general public, moreover, has shown itself exceedingly sensitive to
non-European immigration. All of this leads me to conclude that the
racist political elite hypothesis cannot be sustained. Rather, British
immigration policy seems to be the work of a responsible political elite
that veers from time to time toward populist manipulation of racial
issues. It is a thin line between responding to a fearful public and
exploiting their anxieties.

PART IV

Latecomers to Immigration: Italy, Spain, and Japan

9

Italy and the New Immigration

Kitty Calavita

Introduction

Italy was shaped by emigration. Since the late 1800s, millions have emigrated from Italy to settle in virtually every corner of the globe, seeking the economic opportunities abroad that eluded them at home. Emigration continued after World War II: over 7 million people left Italy between 1946 and 1975 (see table 9.1).[1] While most countries of Western Europe were recruiting guestworkers to fuel the postindustrial booms, Italy was a provider of many of the guestworkers upon whom this industrial renaissance depended.

In the late 1970s Italy suddenly became an immigrant-*receiving* country (Venturini 1991). The 1981 census showed a net increase in population that was due to return migration and new immigration (Macioti and Pugliese 1991: 6). The census also indicated that, for the first time, the number of people "present" in Italy exceeded the number of "residents," suggesting an influx of unauthorized immigrants.[2]

This chapter examines the new immigration to Italy and the responses to it on the part of both the government and various sectors of Italian society. A premise of this analysis is that this immigration is labor migration. Most of the immigrants come from Africa, Asia, and other developing countries, primarily for economic reasons. Therefore, this chapter focuses on the economic factors that made such workers needed in the Italian economy. In addition, it examines the ideological, cultural,

---

[1] Four million of these returned to Italy at least temporarily as they shuttled back and forth from jobs in Northern Europe and elsewhere to their family homes, usually in southern Italy.

[2] In every previous census the number of registered residents exceeded the number actually present, since many had left Italy to find employment abroad (Macioti and Pugliese 1991: 6).

TABLE 9.1
EMIGRATION FROM ITALY, 1876–1985
(THOUSANDS OF PERSONS)

1876–1885	1,315
1886–1895	2,391
1896–1905	4,322
1906–1914	5,854
1876–1914	13,882
1915–1918	363
1919–1928	3,007
1929–1940	1,114
1941–1945	17
1946–1955	2,471
1956–1965	3,166
1966–1975	1,714
1946–1975	7,351
1976–1985	861
Total	26,595

Source: ISTAT, cited in Antonio Goloni and Anna Maria Berindelli, "Italy." In
Handbook on International Migration, ed. W. J. Serow et al. (New York: Greenwood, 1990).

and political context in an effort to shed light on the distinctive nature of
Italy's response to the new immigration.

The first part of the chapter discusses the size of the immigrant
population, their national origins, and their regional distribution in
Italy. The second section focuses on the role of these non-EC foreigners
in the economy, providing an overview of the geographical and structural dualities crosscutting the Italian economy and of the roles of
unions and state regulations in structuring employment relationships.
The third section describes the policy response to immigration, devoting
particular attention to the laws of 1986 and 1990, which simultaneously
attempted to control illegal immigration and "regularized" those already present. The fourth section reviews studies of Italian public
opinion, emphasizing the gaps between public opinion on the immigration issue and government action. The chapter concludes with an
assessment of the ways in which the Italian experience with immigration
is similar to and differs from that of other immigrant-receiving countries.

Numbers

Two distinct developments contributed to Italy's transformation from an
emigration to an immigration country: economic growth at home and

the diversion of immigrants from Northern to Southern Europe. The economic gap between Italy and Northern Europe had narrowed by the mid-1970s, with per capita income and gross domestic product in Italy approaching that of Northern European labor recruiters (Venturini 1991: 93–94). The increased employment opportunities and higher wage levels presented by the Italian "economic miracle" attracted immigrants, much as ten years earlier Italians had been pulled north to industrial jobs in France, Germany, and Switzerland.

Italy began receiving immigrants at precisely the moment—in the mid-1970s—when Northern European receiving countries began closing their doors. To some extent, Italy became a "backdoor" to the rest of Europe or an alternative to northern destinations (Macioti and Pugliese 1991: 12). In a recent study of 1,525 legal and illegal immigrants in Italy, 40.3 percent stated that one reason they chose Italy was the relative ease of entrance; an equal number mentioned job opportunities (CNEL 1991: 43).

It is difficult to get precise counts of legal and undocumented immigrants in Italy. Official figures on the size of the legally resident population vary according to the government agency producing the data, their sources, and the specific administrative purposes of their data collection. The most reliable statistics on the number of foreigners legally resident in Italy come from the Ministry of the Interior, whose data are based on the number of residence permits extended (see Natale 1990 for a discussion of other sources). According to these data, there were approximately 850,000 foreigners residing legally in Italy in 1991, including 707,000 from outside the European Community (see table 9.2). Most (80 percent) resided in the industrial north and center of the country.

The size and distribution of the irregular or undocumented immigrant population is far more difficult to estimate (see table 9.3). In Italy there is no government entity whose primary function is the apprehension of illegal aliens, so apprehension figures are virtually useless. Instead, estimates are based on data from many sources, including Ministry of Labor surveys and applications for legalization.

Natale (1990) presents a variety of official and scholarly estimates of the total (legal and illegal) non-EC foreign population in Italy, with his own proposal putting the figure at approximately 857,000 in the early 1990s (see table 9.4). This estimate seems somewhat low in light of the 707,000 *legally* resident non-EC foreigners counted by the Ministry of the Interior. Most government officials and academics put the range at 850,000 to 1.1 million, although one research group puts the figure as high as 1.5 million.

While both men and women are represented in the total immigrant flow, a distinct gender pattern has developed. Most notably, immigrants from North Africa and the Middle East are disproportionately male,

TABLE 9.2
FOREIGNERS PRESENT IN ITALY, 1991

Number in Italy
European Community citizens   143,485
Non-European Community citizens   706,738

TOTAL   850,223

Located in:
Northern Italy   359,560
Central Italy   323,222
Southern Italy   167,456

Nationality

Nationality			
Morocco	88,103	Iran	13,214
United States	59,610	Ghana	12,632
Tunisia	46,575	India	12,103
Philippines	40,292	Romania	11,832
Germany	34,152	Somalia	11,599
Yugoslavia	31,485	USSR	8,513
Great Britain	27,392	Austria	8,206
Senegal	27,392	Pakistan	7,260
France	24,915	Holland	6,913
Albania	22,616	Nigeria	6,558
Egypt	22,520	Colombia	6,186
China	20,662	Peru	6,096
Poland	18,488	Mauritius Islands	5,884
Switzerland	18,443	Japan	5,828
Greece	16,747	Libya	5,731
Brazil	16,230	Venezuela	5,413
Argentina	14,506	Cape Verde	5,409
Spain	14,458	Bangladesh	5,309
Sri Lanka	13,485	Dominican Republic	5,237
Ethiopia	13,358		

Source: Patronata INCA CGIL, "Immigrazione a Cinque Anni dalla Prima Legge" (Rome: CSR, 1991): 5–6.

while those from the African islands and the Philippines are primarily female. The latter usually find employment as domestic servants. Furthermore, there is some indication that irregular immigrant status is more common among men (Natale 1990: 18).[3] It is unclear exactly why this is the case, but it may be that the employers of female domestic servants are more likely to sponsor, encourage, or otherwise facilitate the regularization process for their employees. In contrast, a significant minority of male immigrants are self-employed street vendors living a

[3]In one survey 61.2 percent of the women answered that they were employed "in a legal manner" (with the majority being domestics), while only 48.5 percent of the men reported that they were legally employed. Of the 51.5 percent of men admitting to illegal employment, the majority were street vendors (CNEL 1991: 68–69).

TABLE 9.3

FOREIGN POPULATION IN ITALY IN 1981–89,
ACCORDING TO THREE DIFFERENT SOURCES

	1981	1984	1987	1988	1989
1. Census	270,917				
2. Ministry of the Interior, Residence permits issued					
Total	331,665	403,923	572,103	645,423	490,388
For work	103,947	115,708	160,323	181,980	136,193
For study	75,207	95,277	107,262	113,331	67,428
For family reunification	63,084	74,295	100,979	110,856	84,669
For tourism	18,394	34,274	55,299	64,620	55,680
3. ISTAT, Standard Labor Units					
Regular foreign workers	270,917	301,569	417,847	474,291	421,942
Irregular foreign workers	321,100	464,900	548,660	554,600	572,800

Source: Alessandra Venturini, "Italy in the Context of European Migration," *Regional Development Dialogue* 12:3 (Autumn).

TABLE 9.4

ESTIMATES OF NUMBER OF FOREIGNERS IN ITALY BY GEOGRAPHIC AREA
(IN THOUSANDS)

Area	A	B	C	D	E
Northwest	144–185	119–191	213	166–249	197
Northeast	79–114	98–131	129	92–126	105
Center	170–304	180–302	329	305–390	336
South	69–102	50–54	89	105–179	133
Islands	33–47	33–36	64	68–116	86
Total	495–752	480–714	824	736–1,060	857

A Estimate of M. Natale al 1984.
B Estimate of O. Casacchia al 1984.
C Estimate of A.M. Birindelli al 1988.
D Estimate of M. Natale al 1988.
E Estimate proposed by Natale, 1990.

Source: Marcello Natale, "L'immigrazione Straniera in Italia," *Polis* 4:1 (April): 16.

marginal existence hawking their wares and frightened of the visibility that application to a legalization program would entail.[4]

One final demographic characteristic of the immigrant population is worth noting. Although most non-EC immigrants in Italy work as unskilled or semiskilled labor (to be discussed below), nonetheless as a group they are a relatively highly educated population. According to the

[4]Only a small fraction of such street vendors applied for regularization (Onorato 1989: 308).

CNEL survey (1991: 37), 33.5 percent had a high school diploma and another 13.4 percent were college graduates. Among domestic servants, particularly women from the African islands and the Philippines, the percentage of high school and college graduates is reported to be considerably higher.

The Role of Immigrants in the Italian Economy

Immigrants in Italy are concentrated in low-wage, low-prestige sectors of the economy. Macioti and Pugliese (1991: 85) underscore this status gap and the concomitant resource drain: "An investment is made in a youth in Egypt or Senegal or the Philippines for that youth to become an agricultural engineer, an economist, or a teacher, and he or she ends up in Italy as a waiter, a street vendor, or a domestic." The immigrant's place in the Italian economy is due to the economy's dualistic nature and to the extensive government and union regulation of the formal economy.

Since unification, Italy has been divided economically into a thriving industrial north and a quasifeudal, agrarian south. Although the Italian government sponsored emergency measures in the 1960s and 1970s to reverse the effects of decades of underdevelopment in the south, the results were limited to the transfer of a few large factories, many of which have subsequently relocated or closed down. This uneven development supplied northern industry with an almost limitless supply of cheap labor from the south. Italy's economic growth rate approached 6 percent annually from 1951 to 1971 and the gross national product more than doubled. Approximately 6 million people left the south from 1950 to 1975, some crossing the border to Northern Europe but many others migrating to the booming northern Italian factories.

In addition to this geographic split, a pronounced structural division crosscuts the Italian economy. Italy's economy is dualistic: it includes a few large companies like Fiat and Olivetti that have achieved international prominence, and a larger secondary and underground sector comprising small, often family-run, businesses. Estimates of the proportion of Italian economic activity that is located in the underground economy range from 14 percent to 30 percent (Venturini 1991: 106), with most estimates clustering at the high end. It is widely agreed that this duality and the prevalence of low-cost, small enterprises—a large number of which are located underground—contributed to Italy's rapid economic growth after World War II (Allum 1973; Grisoni and Portelli 1977; Venturini 1991).

Beyond these economic and regional divisions, it is important to consider the role of state regulation in the Italian economy, which is itself at least in part a product of the political strength of Italian unions. The origins of Italian union strength can be found in the recession of 1964–1965, following a decade of unprecedented economic growth. As the economy slowed and Italy's economic boom showed signs of waning, worker layoffs were commonplace.[5] In response to the crisis, the three major Italian unions—the Communist-affiliated General Italian Confederation of Workers (CGIL), the Christian Democrat Italian Labor Confederation (CISL), and the Socialist Italian Labor Union (UIL)—pledged to follow a course of solidarity. By 1966, with the major unions brought together by what they perceived to be a common enemy, a new era in labor relations began; the number of strikes doubled even as management pursued a strategy of laying off strikers. Each year strikes increased in number and intensity, and by the "hot autumn" of 1969 Fiat, Pirelli, and most other companies witnessed almost daily confrontations. Over 300 million work hours were lost in close to 4,000 major strikes that year (Grisoni and Portelli 1977; ISTAT 1970: 322).

Union contracts negotiated after the strike activity of fall 1969 gave workers substantial salary and benefit increases. Many worker demands were institutionalized in the Workers' Rights Law passed in 1970. While most of the nine political parties represented in the Italian Parliament supported some variety of workers' rights legislation, it was the Italian Communist Party—then the largest and most powerful Communist party in the West—that was most insistent that the law go beyond symbolism to guarantee to Italian workers meaningful advances in job security, occupational safety and health, salary scales, and so on.

Two items are of particular importance. First, union-negotiated national work contracts set wages and benefits for any given type of work. These salary scales and benefit packages apply to every sector of the formal economy (they exclude very small employers). Even for workers in areas of the economy that are not unionized, the courts have determined that national contracts are generally applicable, since judges have interpreted the constitutional guarantee of "reasonable compensation" to mean that which is stipulated by national work contracts. In this context, minimum wage laws are supplanted by far more advantageous union contracts.

Second, the hiring system itself is highly regulated. Except in the case of very small enterprises, employers generally must hire from government-supervised "hiring lists," with unemployed workers being hired on a first-come, first-served basis. Something akin to a union hiring hall system, these lists at least theoretically preclude the employer from shopping for worker qualities that have been called "a positive work ethic" or, alternatively, "a propensity for self-exploitation" (Venturini 1991: 107).

Taken together, these components of the Italian economy render it relatively inflexible from the employer's point of view, bringing us back to the issue of the duality of the Italian economy. The highly regulated formal

---

[5]During this two-year recession, 600,000 metalworkers were either laid off or put on part time, 150,000 construction workers lost their jobs, and 60,000 jobs in the textile industry disappeared.

economy enhances the appeal of the informal or underground sector. As early as the late 1960s, Italian employers had used the underground economy as a way to circumvent the demands of unions and to increase flexibility. Traditionally the informal economy had been made up of small firms specializing in artisanal manufacturing, as well as a variety of family-run services. However, during the labor unrest of the 1960s and 1970s, even large employers like Fiat began decentralizing and parceling out work to the underground economy (Guidi, Bronzino, and Germanetto 1974; Milanaccio and Ricolfi 1976).

Immigrants are disproportionately employed in this large underground sector as "black labor." Because of the high degree of regulation of the Italian economy, *illegal* immigrants are by definition part of the underground economy, for it is impossible to employ them without violating a wide variety of government regulations regarding the hiring process, social security contributions (which amount to approximately 40–45 percent of gross pay), and so on. While it is difficult to be precise about the size of this clandestine workforce, it was estimated in 1989 that a majority of immigrant workers were "irregular" and thus part of the underground economy (see table 9.3). The 1990 CENSIS study (CNEL 1991: 62), which followed the 1990 legalization program, reported that almost half of the legal and illegal immigrant respondents admitted to working "irregularly" in the underground economy.

Furthermore, these immigrants are generally concentrated in the service sector. According to the OECD's Continuous Reporting System of Migration (SOPEMI) (cited in Barsotti and Lecchini 1988: 423), in 1982 only 15 percent of (legal) immigrants in Italy worked in industry, while 60 percent worked in services or trade. The 1990 CENSIS survey found that 48.8 percent worked in the service sector, with another 15.9 percent making a living as street vendors. A Confindustria study (1990) based on figures from Italy's Central Statistics Institute (ISTAT) reports that among illegal immigrants, only 9.9 percent work in construction or industry, while 78.8 percent work in the service sector, broadly defined (see table 9.5).

Variations in the employment of immigrants reflect the regionality of the Italian economy. In some regions of Italy's industrial north and center—most notably Emilia Romagna—immigrants fill gaps in the industrial labor market, taking the most hazardous and/or physically demanding jobs in construction, metalwork, and foundries. One study, for example, found that in Emilia Romagna 70 percent of immigrants work in industry, 20 percent in services (primarily domestic service), and 10 percent in agriculture (Capecchi 1992: 8). In contrast, in the southern regions, particularly in rural Campania, immigrants are far more likely to be found in seasonal agricultural jobs and not infrequently competing with the local agrarian workforce (De Filippo and Morlicchio 1992).

Regional variations also exist in the proportion of the immigrant population that is irregular and working in the underground economy. As

TABLE 9.5
ILLEGAL FOREIGNERS IN THE ITALIAN WORKFORCE

	% of Illegal Foreigners Working in Sector	Illegal Foreigners as % of Workforce in Sector
Agriculture	11.2	8.6
Industry	2.2	0.3
Construction	7.7	4.0
Services	42.4	4.6
Commerce	18.4	7.9
Hotels	15.6	17.3
Transport	6.1	46.5
Domestic Services	36.4	34.6
Total	100.0	4.7

Source: Confindustria, "L'immigrazione extra-comunitaria e il Mercato del Lavoro Italiano" (mimeograph).

De Filippo and Morlicchio point out, in Campania an immigrant's "irregularity and social marginality . . . are an indispensable condition for finding employment" (1992: 45). Attempting to explain the paradoxical presence of high unemployment rates in this southern region together with a significant level of immigration and immigrant employment, De Filippo and Morlicchio argue that immigrants find work only to the extent that they are willing to work for less than local workers in illegal employment relationships. Thus immigrants do seasonal harvesting for the equivalent of approximately U.S.$20 for a ten- to twelve-hour day, while the local wage is generally more (although still substandard) (De Filippo and Morlicchio 1992).

There are other indications that such "black labor" is more prevalent among immigrants in the south, just as the underground economy is more pervasive there. For example, applications for legalization come disproportionately from the north and central regions. Legalization requires that one's employment relationship be legalized (unless the applicant is unemployed), so that an application for legalization implies a willingness on the part of worker and/or employer to "regularize" the job as well as the worker (Natale 1990: 20).[6] Fausto Bertinotti (1989: 24), secretary of the largest Italian union (CGIL), argues that immigrants play different economic roles in the north and the south. In the north they are usually "complementary" to the local workforce, taking jobs shunned by Italians; in the south they are more likely to be used

---

[6] Among legalization applicants from southern regions between 1987 and 1989, over 70 percent listed themselves as unemployed, versus 50 percent of applicants from the north and center of Italy who were similarly unwilling to list employment. The legalization law of 1986 did not allow self-employed street vendors to legalize. Therefore, street vendors who decided to apply for legalization often declared themselves "unemployed." In other cases, however, the self-categorization as "unemployed" reflected an unwillingness to expose employers in the underground economy. As Natale points out, these "two forms of legalization [as an employed worker, or as unemployed] . . . correspond to the [country's] regional economic dualism. The economic significance of these data lies . . . in the greater propensity on the part of the southern system of production . . . to employ and maintain the foreign labor force in a condition of 'immersion,' and therefore illegality" (1990: 21).

for competitive purposes, providing a reserve surplus and fueling precarious and unprotected working conditions. Bertinotti concludes, referring to Italy's regional duality and the different economic function of immigrants in the north and south, "Italy . . . includes two labor market regimes."

Some scholars have argued that the presence of a low-wage immigrant workforce has attracted capital away from the formal economy to employ immigrants clandestinely, thereby expanding the size of the informal economy and displacing Italian workers (Dell'Aringa and Neri 1987). Macioti and Pugliese (1991: 81–85), however, note that it would be an oversimplification to conclude that immigration has been the primary force behind the expansion of the underground economy. Instead, they suggest that the roots of this expansion go far deeper than the relatively recent arrival of immigrants. They argue that the postindustrial Italian economy has experienced "a crisis of the Fordist-Taylorist model," as have the economies of all developed capitalist countries (1991: 76). The result is a new organization of production characterized by decentralization and an emphasis on flexibility.

There is a strong compatibility between this new model of production and immigration from the Third World. As Macioti and Pugliese put it, "'Black labor' seems to have been the prevalent condition for immigrants, and the forced clandestineness which until now they have been constrained by has consolidated this new model [of production]" (1991: 81). Bertinotti (1989: 23) has similarly argued that the advanced capitalist societies have undergone "a third industrial revolution," characterized by high unemployment and a reorganization of production. Within this context, Third World immigration offers Italian employers an opportunity to adapt to this new economic model, with its emphasis on flexibility and the circumvention of union demands.

Available data suggest that immigration to Italy—and perhaps to other advanced capitalist societies in the 1980s and 1990s—is quite different from that of earlier generations. Immigration to the United States in the late nineteenth and early twentieth centuries, and guestworkers in West Germany, France, and Switzerland as late as the 1970s, provided those countries with a workforce with which to fuel expanding industrial production and offset labor shortages. In contrast, immigration to Italy is occurring at a time of relatively high unemployment and stagnating industrial production. Official unemployment in Italy stands at 12.4 percent, with 21.6 percent unemployed in the southern regions (U.S. Department of Labor 1989; *XXI Secolo* 1992).[7] Furthermore, the number of young people in the

---

[7]Unemployment rates are calculated differently in Italy than in the United States. A report by the U.S. Department of Labor, Bureau of International Labor Affairs, points out that in Italy part-timers who report wanting a full-time job, as well as those who have not actively sought work in the month prior to the labor survey, are listed as unemployed, thereby inflating the unemployment rate relative to that of the United States (U.S. Department of Labor 1989: 11–12).

southern regions who are in search of first jobs rose by close to 70 percent between 1984 and 1989, suggesting a "blockage at the entrance of the labor market" (*XXI Secolo* 1992: 13).

The role these immigrants play in the economy is thus structurally very different from that of the previous era in Northern Europe. Not only are they concentrated in the service sector and the informal economy rather than in heavy manufacturing, but their desirability is less related to the fact that they expand the supply of labor at a moment of absolute labor need than it is to their "irregularity" and the flexibility this provides employers in the new postindustrial economy. In contrast to the experiences of upward mobility of second-generation immigrants documented by Piore (1979) and others, these immigrants and their descendants are likely to be confined indefinitely to the margins of the Italian economy. At a time of rising unemployment and economic contraction, these immigrants serve a specific function in the labor market, offering employers a Third World source of labor with which to carry out widespread economic restructuring.

Although this immigration is distinct in important ways from the vast industrial immigrations of previous decades, it shares a number of commonalities. Most important, just as low-wage labor from southern Italy was a key factor in northern Italy's economic growth in the postwar period, so access to Third World labor from Africa and Asia may be instrumental in keeping Italy competitive in the new world economy. At a time when the increasingly global economy and the removal of trade barriers in the European Common Market intensifies economic competition, Italy's inefficient infrastructure, highly regulated economy, and relatively high salaries and good benefits (won by workers after decades of labor struggle) set it at a comparative disadvantage. Within this context, Third World immigration and the continued expansion of the informal economy may play a central role in offsetting Italy's competitive disadvantages.

Administrative and Legislative Responses

Prior to the 1980s, only two Italian laws addressed the issue of immigration. The first, passed in 1931 (Law 773) as part of a larger bill relating to public safety, laid out procedures for foreigners to apply for residence permits. The second (Law 125, passed on June 1, 1949) clarified how foreigners were to obtain permits, after having first received a residence permit, "for the purpose of work" (Adinolfi 1987). What little immigration there was prior to the 1980s was regulated primarily by administrative decrees from various government ministries.[8] Together these de-

---

[8]This practice is not uncommon in Italy, where some observers have cynically called the system "government by memo."

crees established a system of legal immigration that was driven by the needs of individual employers. The process was initiated by an employer request for a certain number of foreign workers. The Ministry of Labor issued an authorization to import these workers only after the employer had advertised unsuccessfully for thirty days for Italian workers. The process concluded with the foreign workers being issued visas "for the purpose of work"; upon entrance, these immigrants then applied to the Italian police for residence permits "for the purpose of work" and to the Ministry of Labor for work permits. No annual ceilings or quotas were set, nor did they seem necessary given the small number of immigrants involved.

The first indication that things had changed came in 1982, when a Ministry of Labor circular called a halt to all authorizations for foreign workers from outside the European Community. Also included in this circular was the first attempt at legalizing those already present in Italy and illegally employed. This first legalization program stipulated that all employers must "regularize" their illegal immigrant workers. The amnesty process required not only that employers pay all back taxes and contributions to social security, but that they post a bond equal to the cost of the return ticket for the foreign workers whom they were sponsoring for legalization.

Not surprisingly, the legalization provision was a failure, with fewer than 16 thousand immigrants being "regularized." In fact, the consequence of this law was to increase dramatically the number of irregular foreign workers in Italy. As Bonini observed, as a result in part of prohibiting any further legal immigration, "the condition of irregularity became a *modus vivendi*" (1991: 90). La Terza concurs, pointing out that the closing down of the legal immigration channel and the constraints of the legalization program vastly increased the ranks of irregular immigrants. The irony, she says, was that "the preoccupation that immigrants [brought in through legal channels] should not be allowed to compete with Italian workers has resulted in the worst kind of competition: The number of illegal immigrants has increased, meaning cheaper costs in terms of social security payments, lower wages, more flexibility, etc. Competition was enormously enhanced precisely by the fact of encouraging illegality" (La Terza 1987: 35).

On December 30, 1986, Italy passed its first comprehensive immigration law. This law, entitled Foreign Workers and the Control of Illegal Immigration (Law 943), was in large measure the product of pressure from unions and the left opposition parties who contested what they saw as the abuse of the rapidly rising number of illegal immigrants following the decree of 1982. The law consisted of three primary components: foreign workers' rights, rules on the employment of foreigners, and a regularization program.

Article 1 guaranteed that all foreign workers legally resident in Italy would receive equal treatment and full equality with Italian workers. It included a guarantee of family unification, access to housing, and nondiscrimination in services and municipal facilities like health care. The implementation of this article was left to the local regions, which in general have been slow to respond (some notable exceptions are the affluent, traditionally Communist regions of northern and central Italy). Speaking to the pronounced gap between the extensive guarantees of Article 1 and its conspicuous lack of implementation, one legal scholar complained, "The chronic vice of Italian politics is an excess of legislation and a deficit of implementation" (Onorato 1989: 307).

Article 5 of the foreign workers law removed the moratorium on importing foreign workers announced by the 1982 decree, specifying that foreign workers could be imported after the Ministry of Labor certified that Italian workers were not available (very few categories of workers have been so certified). More importantly, residence permits were separated from employment status, so that losing one's job does not mean losing residence or work permits. Article 5 further stipulated that when foreign workers lost their jobs, they were to be put on a separate hiring list specific for non-EC immigrant workers. After two years of work in Italy, foreign workers were eligible to be placed on the regular Italian hiring lists. These special lists seemed to contradict the spirit of Article 1 specifying full equality of treatment, since immigrant workers on special employment lists could only be hired if no Italian workers from the regular lists were available.

Article 12, which constitutes Italy's first employer sanctions law, consists of two parts. The first section applies to those who smuggle immigrants or hire illegal immigrants "for the purpose of exploitation," activities that can elicit a fine of Lit 2–10 million (approximately U.S.$1500–7500) per immigrant and one to five years in prison.[9]

A number of worker categories were excluded from all of these provisions, including artists, maritime workers, and others for whom there may be "more favorable rules or international agreements" (Article 14). One legal scholar argues, "This component of the law is to be criticized for its vagueness: it seems in fact to legitimate the possibility of subsequent deviations from the law through 'sub-legislative' processes. . . . It could open the way for a return to government 'by memo'" (Adinolfi 1987: 78–79).

Although the bulk of the law addressed these details of foreign worker employment, its undisputed centerpiece was an expansive regularization program. Article 16 required that all foreign workers and

---

[9]In the original House version, the proposed penalty included the fine *and* prison for each immigrant employed and for each trimester of employment. This more severe penalty was subsequently modified and liberalized in the final version (D'Harmant Francois 1988: 69).

their employers regularize their status within three months of the law's taking effect on January 27, 1987. (This deadline was subsequently extended four times through 1989.) Unlike the legalization decree of 1982, this regularization process could be initiated by either the employer or the individual immigrant. If the immigrant was employed, no retroactive fines for violation of labor laws were to be applied against his or her employer; however, the employer would be held responsible for back social security and other required employer "contributions."

If regularization was initiated by the immigrant worker rather than the employer and if the immigrant worked in the underground economy, the worker was required to denounce his or her employer. If unemployed, the immigrant would be placed on a special hiring list. Not surprisingly, it is estimated that many applicants working in the underground economy declared themselves unemployed in order to avoid denouncing their employers and risk losing their jobs. Immigrants who were regularized in this way were required to renew their status after two years, and every four years after that. Those who did not apply for regularization were subject to administrative fines and repatriation, penalties that remain largely unenforced and, some would say, unenforceable.

The thrust of this law (and of its successor, discussed below) is to control the number of immigrants who enter Italy legally or illegally, while at the same time regularizing those already present and extending them full rights. Venturini has pointed out that the 1986 law provides "the utmost protection and guarantees to the legally employed immigrant side by side with the total lack of guarantees for the clandestine immigrant worker, given the paltry employer fines and few controls over underground employment" (1989: 367).

The law was rife with "uncertainty" and "bureaucratism" (Minister of Labor Formica, quoted in Sestini 1989: 331). There is considerable confusion, for example, over how the employer sanctions provision is to be enforced. Despite the provision for possible prison terms, one Ministry of Labor official insisted that employer sanctions were entirely a civil matter (author interview). Furthermore, labor inspectors recount diverse scenarios regarding who is responsible for enforcement and how enforcement takes place. One inspector, for example, explained that the Ministry of Labor is entirely responsible and has wide discretion regarding the imposition of fines; another explained with equal certainty that upon finding employers in violation, labor inspectors are to notify the police (author interviews, July 1992). While there is some evidence that this latter interpretation is accurate, those responsible for immigration matters at the central police agency in Rome seem to be far less interested in enforcing employer sanctions than in arresting and repatriating immigrant felons (author interview, July 1992).

So obscure is the employer sanctions law that some labor inspectors had to be shown the section of the law before it was clear to them what was being referred to. It soon became apparent that Ministry of Labor officials had difficulty talking about employer sanctions as a measure distinct from other labor laws.

When an employer hires a worker in the formal economy, the government is integrally involved through the mechanism of hiring lists, or at least through a series of notification procedures. Thus, when an unauthorized immigrant is hired, there is by definition a violation not just of employer sanctions but of a wide range of other labor laws, laws that have been on the books for decades and are considered far more fundamental than this relatively obscure section of the immigration law. Indicative of this lack of attention accorded employer sanctions as a discrete measure, the Ministry of Labor does not keep a separate record of employer sanctions violations or fines. This probably reflects both the fact that they are not considered separable from other labor violations as well as the reality that there are very few such fines. When asked how many fines had been levied for employer sanctions, a senior official from the Ministry of Labor smiled and said, "What shall I say?" (author interview, July 1992).

The legalization program, while far more widely publicized than employer sanctions, was not much more successful. When the law was passed, it was estimated that there were between 600,000 and 1.2 million undocumented immigrants in Italy. Yet only about 107,000 applied for regularization under the 1986 law (Onorato 1989: 307). According to Onorato, the most important reason for the failure of this regularization program was "the bosses' interest in not regularizing black labor . . . in order to save on health and social security contributions and the minimum wage, and . . . the general vulnerability of immigrants to their employers that led them not to seek regularization for fear of losing their jobs."

As soon as the deadline for legalization passed, a new government decree was promulgated and then converted into law on February 28, 1990. The new law, the Urgent Provisions Regarding the Political Asylum, Entry, and Residence of Non-EC Foreigners and the Regularization of Non-EC Nationals and Stateless Persons Already Present in Italian Territory, is known simply as the Martelli law, after its primary author and sponsor, Deputy Prime Minister Claudio Martelli.[10] As Martelli describes it, this law consists of three main parts: "strict rules to reduce the number of illegal immigrants already here and to discourage and impede the arrival of new illegal immigrants; second, definitive rules to plan, to the best of our ability, the legal entry of other foreigners; third, to

---

[10]Martelli has since been placed under investigation for his alleged role in the widespread corruption scandals at the upper levels of Italian government and industry and has resigned his government post.

facilitate the integration of non-EC foreigners already present and regularized" (1991: 123–24).

Article 1 eliminates the geographical limits that had previously restricted applicants for asylum in Italy to European nationals. The Italian Constitution provides, "Any foreigner who in his own country is denied democratic rights guaranteed by the Italian Constitution has the right of asylum in Italy." Furthermore, Italy had ratified the Geneva Convention in 1954. Nonetheless, an Italian government decree had restricted access to the asylum process to European nationals, thereby violating both its own Constitution and the Geneva Convention. In this first piece of Italian legislation to address the refugee issue, the Martelli law eliminated this restriction and brought Italy into conformity with the European Community.

Article 2 stipulates a process through which the government will determine annually the categories of foreign workers to be admitted and the procedures to be followed; Article 3 provides that the minister of foreign affairs will issue annual decrees regarding which countries' citizens will need visas.

Despite Deputy Prime Minister Martelli's pronouncement that this law was a wide-ranging control measure, the Martelli law—like its predecessor—is above all a regularization program. Article 9 required those who were present in illegal status on December 31, 1989, to regularize within six months. Immigrants were to apply with the Italian police by presenting a valid passport and two witnesses testifying to their identity. After obtaining residence permits from the police, these newly legalized immigrants were then to apply to the Ministry of Labor for work permits. The unemployed were to register with the government hiring service, where they were placed on the same hiring lists as Italian citizens.[11]

In contrast to previous regularization programs, under the Martelli law this process was generally initiated by the immigrants themselves, rather than their employers. Furthermore, this legislation attempted to mitigate employer resistance. Not only did it stipulate that employers of illegal workers would not be fined retroactively for violating the employer sanctions law of 1986 or other labor standards, it also relieved employers from having to pay back contributions or social security taxes for regularized workers.

Residence permits under the Martelli regularization plan were valid for two years, to be renewed for four years if the immigrant could demonstrate that he or she had a monthly income for the preceding year equal to the amount of the Italian retirement pension and that this income was not earned through underground work. For those working

---

[11] A government circular [#37/89] of May 3, 1989, had already abolished the special hiring lists for foreign workers.

in the underground economy, it was possible to make an "auto-certification" of income earned, which included divulging the name of one's employer. In this latter case, renewals were to be good for two years.

Over 234,000 immigrants applied for regularization under the Martelli law. Of these, approximately 171,000 had applied for renewals by the June 30, 1992, deadline (as happened with the 1986 regularization plan, that deadline was subsequently extended). As of the June deadline, over 105,000 had been accepted for renewal, fewer than 600 had been rejected, and tens of thousands of applications were still pending (*Migration News Sheet*, July and August 1992). Only about 15,000 of those who had been processed for renewal were based on "auto-certifications" of income, probably indicating both that those working in the underground economy were underrepresented in the first phase of the regularization program and that underground workers are still reluctant to risk their jobs by denouncing their employers.

Italy's experience with the 1986 and 1990 laws points to a marked gap between the law "on the books" and the law "in action." If, as the evidence suggests, Third World immigrants are concentrated in low-wage service sectors in the underground economy, it may be precisely this function that restricts their regulation. In other words, those characteristics that make Third World immigrants attractive—their invisibility, marginality, and vulnerability—are the same qualities that make it difficult to control them (through employer sanctions) or legalize them (through regularization programs). In other words, legalization as a strategy of coping with undocumented immigration may be destined to fail in a context where immigrants' employment is partly contingent on their marginality.

Recent legislative proposals have more or less explicitly recognized the immigrants' function as a source of marginal labor. A bill proposed in November 1992 in response to pressure from city governments would initiate a temporary worker program whereby immigrants in such seasonal industries as tourism and agriculture could enter Italy legally on temporary work contracts for specified periods of time. Former minister of immigration Boniver stated that this is the most realistic response to the immigration problem (*La Stampa*, November 12, 1992).[12] In contrast to this approach but still indicative of the marginal nature of immigrant employment, then justice minister Claudio Martelli proposed a two-tiered wage system in which immigrants in some sectors— such as domestic service, hotels and restaurants, metalwork—would receive wages and benefits inferior to those in the primary sector. Martelli's proposal was designed to bring out of the shadows and institutionalize conditions in the underground economy, thereby mak-

---

[12]The Ministry of Immigration was established in the spring of 1991 to deal with the Albanian refugee crisis, and it was dissolved four months later.

ing it possible for irregular immigrants to legalize. Not surprisingly, unions condemned the "differentiated salaries" proposal, as did Boniver, who argued that a two-tiered wage system would be unconstitutional (*La Stampa*, November 12, 1992).

Despite the limited success of Italy's previous legalization programs, a third regularization process may be on the horizon. In late April 1993, a parliamentary committee overwhelmingly approved an employment bill that included a new legalization plan. The bill did not receive approval from the full Senate, in part due to extensive criticism in the Italian media and the observation that such a program would contradict commitments made by Italy under the Schengen Agreement of 1990. Nonetheless, the issue is far from dead, as Italian policy makers attempt to piece together a plan that will satisfy both their European partners who fear that Italy may become a gateway to the rest of Europe, and immigrant advocates who demand that undocumented immigrants be brought out of the shadows.

The Politics of Immigration Reform

Despite the similar economic roles that immigrants play in Italy and other developed countries, the politics of immigration in Italy is distinctive. This section traces Italian public opinion about immigration, as well as the stance of unions and their advocates in Parliament, and suggests an explanation for the relative absence of public debate on this issue.

Public opinion on immigration in Italy is increasingly restrictive, as it is in most advanced western democracies. In 1991 the independent survey firm DOXA conducted a national public opinion survey among 2,000 randomly selected Italians to determine their views on immigration and what they thought should be done to deal with it (DOXA 1991).[13] Asked whether immigration carried advantages, disadvantages, or both, 2 percent replied that there were only advantages, 24 percent saw both advantages and disadvantages, and 38 percent said immigration brought only disadvantages (see table 9.6). For those who saw at least some advantages, 32.6 percent said immigrants do work no one else wants to do. The disadvantages that respondents mentioned were that immigrants cause unemployment (41 percent), immigrants commit crimes (19.5 percent), and immigrants are a "social problem" (16.8 percent). Finally, when asked whether immigration should be encouraged or discouraged, 13 percent responded that it should be encouraged, 75 percent that it should be discouraged, and 10.9 percent that it should be prohibited altogether.

---

[13]Similar surveys had been conducted by DOXA in 1987 and 1989, providing points of comparison with which to explore trends or shifts in public opinion (see table 9.6).

TABLE 9.6
DOXA STUDY OF PUBLIC OPINIONS ON IMMIGRATION

Out of 100 Persons Who Have Noticed Immigrants in Their Area

	1991 (%)	1989 (%)	1987 (%)
Immigrants provide:			
Only advantages	2.1	5.5	6.7
More advantages than disadvantages	3.0	7.6	6.6
Advantages and disadvantages	23.9	29.0	24.1
More disadvantages than advantages	23.0	19.8	21.3
Only disadvantages	38.0	23.3	28.0
Don't know	10.0	14.8	13.3
	100.0	100.0	100.0

Source: DOXA, "Gli Stranieri in Italia," *Bollettino della Doxa* 45:9–11:113.

A smaller study by Ires Toscana (1992) focused on eighty firms in and around Florence that had hired non-EC immigrants. Ires Toscana found that while 17.7 percent of these employers thought immigration should be stopped, another 7.6 percent responded that there should be open borders. Asked why they had hired immigrants, 25 percent responded that immigrants tolerated working conditions shunned by Italians, and another 58 percent cited lack of available Italian workers. In comparing immigrant and Italian workers in general, the employers responded that immigrants were more willing to work overtime (54 percent), willing to do work refused by others (53 percent), less interested in unions (52 percent), and willing to work in illegal conditions of employment (56 percent).

Unlike most unions in the United States, Italian unions do not take a restrictionist stance on immigration. Instead they are more likely to express solidarity with Third World immigrants. Next to religious organizations, unions are the primary immigrant support group. In most major Italian cities, union caucuses and advocacy groups welcome immigrants and help them gain access to health care, housing, and other facilities. Unions have also spearheaded efforts to ensure the broad implementation of provisions of the 1986 law to help integrate immigrants and their families into Italian society.

Certain traits of Italian unions and their economic context help account for this supportive posture. First, because the formal economy is so highly regulated by national work contracts and government restrictions, immigrant workers are not perceived as a direct threat to jobs or to workers' bargaining power. The president of a major union's division of immigrant affairs noted, "The law of supply and demand in the labor market only works in an open market. . . . Here salaries go up and down not according to the availability of labor but according to how the Italian economy is doing" (author interview, July 1992). Moreover, relatively few immigrants work in the formal economy, where they would potentially compete with union workers. Protected from an open labor market by national contracts and government regulations, and insulated from competition with immigrant workers by a dual economic structure, Italian workers feel less threatened by an influx of immigrants than do their U.S. counterparts.

In addition to this economic explanation there is an ideological and political one. Italian unions have historically been influenced by progressive politics. Less narrowly focused on workplace issues than most American unions, Italian unions have traditionally maintained solidarity with oppressed people in the Third World as an important ingredient of union politics. Immigrant advocacy work is in some ways the domestic counterpart of this commitment.

The Italian unions' stance may also be the product of practical and strategic concerns. Acknowledging that immigration flows are difficult to control, and hence unlikely to disappear, Italian unions have opted to welcome the new workers. If unions can help immigrants find employment, housing, and health care, then immigrants will see the unions as allies. At a time when unions are losing ground in all advanced capitalist societies, Italian unions see in these immigrants a vital source of their future strength (author interview with a coordinator for the CGIL Office of Immigrant Affairs).

Giorgio La Malfa, former head of the small right-of-center Republican Party, noted that Italian public opinion is far more restrictionist than are most of the established political parties or the immigration policies they formulate (quoted in Bonerandi 1991: 16). There are several explanations for this discrepancy and the general failure of Italian politicians to exploit public sentiment on the immigration issue. First, leftist opposition parties and the unions with whom they are allied have historically wielded considerable power in the legislative arena and may have been responsible for blocking the more draconian control measures. They were clearly important in placing regularization at the center of the 1986 and 1990 reforms and insisting on equal treatment—including access to housing and so on—for immigrant workers and their families.

Second, union opposition to strict control measures probably reflects the role immigrants play in the economy. Despite the public perception that immigrants are a cause of unemployment, there is substantial evidence that immigrants are concentrated in sectors and jobs shunned by Italians, at least in the northern and central regions. With employers benefiting from the immigrant workforce, unions lobbying in support of immigrants, and the Italian workforce contracting, it may not be surprising that Italian politicians in general eschew restrictionism.

Last and perhaps most important, the established political parties may be protecting themselves against a wave of restrictionist sentiment that could only benefit the new conservative populism represented by independent parties like the Northern League (La Lega Nord). These independent parties' anti-south and anti-immigration rhetoric and calls for a cleanup of government corruption are attracting growing constituencies in northern Italy.[14] As Graziano Tassello, director of the Center for Immigration Studies in Rome, explained, "The established parties would rather let the immigration issue die down. It is not considered politically advantageous. The established parties are afraid of a public backlash if the can of worms is opened up, and it would be a backlash that is advantageous to La Lega" (author interview). In other words, policy makers may choose the path of least public visibility on this issue, unwilling even to launch serious debate over restrictionist measures for fear of fueling the spreading populist movement.

Discussion

The Italian experience with immigration differs from that of most other advanced democracies. First, Italy has mostly been an emigration country; only recently has it begun to receive large numbers of immigrants. Its first experience with immigration from the Third World thus comes during the current "third industrial revolution" of contraction and reorganization. Second, Italian unions are not restrictionist. Instead they have been central advocates of immigrants in the policy-making process and have provided an important support group and resource for immigrants upon their arrival in Italy. Third, Italian immigration policy has focused on bringing immigrants out of the shadows through a series of regularization programs ongoing since 1987.

There are also significant areas of convergence between the Italian experience and that of most other advanced democracies that receive immigration. First, the economic role of immigrants is comparable to the other Western European countries: immigrants take the least desirable jobs, and they provide a marginal and flexible source of labor to fill gaps in the labor market.

---

[14]With the economy deteriorating and with increasing numbers of the leaders of mainstream political parties being indicted on major corruption charges, these independent parties tap deep-seated fears and hostilities and pose a significant threat to politics as usual. In June's mayoral elections across Italy, the biggest winner was the Northern League. In Milan, Turin, and other major cities and smaller towns, the new populist party won control of city hall in resounding victories (Montalbano 1993a, 1993b; Stobart 1993).

Second, if policy makers are unable or unwilling to recognize these labor market gaps, the immigrant labor supply is likely to remain largely unauthorized. For example, although the Italian underground economy now generates between 25 and 30 percent of economic activity, most Italian policy makers are unwilling to officially endorse or legitimate conditions of employment there by proposing a guestworker program that would provide a legal supply of workers. Instead policy makers turn a blind eye to this unseemly side of the economy and limit themselves to largely unsuccessful legalization programs. Whatever the merits of former justice minister Martelli's "differentiated salaries" proposal, Italy was unwilling to officially endorse substandard working conditions for guestworkers.

Finally, even if there were a consensus over the need to control immigration—and the political will to do so—there are difficulties associated with regulating immigration. It may be virtually impossible to control an influx of Third World immigrants without resorting to police state tactics at odds with the democratic tenets upon which these societies are grounded. This dilemma is illustrated by the difficulties that Italian authorities have repatriating those apprehended in illegal status. While approximately 11,600 undocumented immigrants were apprehended in Italy and instructed to depart in the first six months of 1991, fewer than 3,000 were actually repatriated (Bonerandi 1991: 16). Given the intricacies and time-consuming nature of deportation hearings, and the reluctance of the Italian authorities to forcibly detain those it intends to repatriate, the majority fall through the cracks.[15]

A comparable dilemma exists in the realm of refugee policy, where there is a tension between the commitment to human rights and the political and practical limits of the receiving society. As Onorato points out, "Political realism may increasingly endanger the right of asylum as certain states do not want to hear of complete or universal human rights if this puts limits on their own sovereignty" (1989: 314). As its asylum requests escalate, Italy joins the rest of the European Community in confronting this dilemma.

The most striking similarity between Italy and other Western European countries is the gap between the stated aims of policy makers and the outcome of their policies. It has been argued here that this failure to enact and implement effective immigration controls is largely the result of the economic function of immigrants and the political limitations under which these liberal democratic societies operate. It is indicative of the power of such deep structural factors that countries with a variety of

---

[15]The difficulties of repatriating immigrants charged with crimes is further indicative of this dilemma. An Italian decree of April 13, 1993, provided for the expulsion before trial of any foreigner charged with a criminal offense. After approval by the Council of Ministers, the plan was rejected by the Parliamentary Committee on Legal Affairs as unconstitutional (*Migration News Sheet*, May and June 1993).

historical experiences with immigration now find themselves facing roughly the same dilemmas and using roughly the same instruments to resolve them.

References

Adinolfi, Adelina. 1987. "La Nuova Normativa Sul Collocamento dei Lavoratori Stranieri," *Rivista di Diritto Internazionale* 70:73–109.

———. 1992. *I Lavoratori Extracomunitari: Norme Interne e Internazionali*. Bologna: Il Mulino.

Allum, P.A. 1973. *Italy—Republic without Government?* New York: W.W. Norton.

Barsotti, Odo, and Laura Lecchini. 1988. "Changes in Europe's International Migrant Flows," *Journal of Regional Policy* 8:3 (July/September): 399–424.

Bertinotti, Fausto. 1989. "Cinque Domande sull'immigrazione Extracomunitaria in Italia," edited by Gianfranco Pasquino, *Problemi del Socialismo* 1 (January–April).

Bonerandi, Enrico. 1991. "Se L'immigrato Sbaglia, Espulsione Immediata," *La Repubblica*, July 13.

Bonini, Damiano. 1991. "L'immigrato e i suoi Diritti," *Perspettive Sindacali* 79/80:83–94.

Capecchi, Vittorio. 1992. "Lavoro e Formazione Professionale per Immigrate e Immigrati in Emilia Romagna," *Inchiesta* 22–95 (January–March): 1–12.

CNEL (Consiglio Nazionale dell'economia e del Lavoro). CENSIS. 1991. *Immigrati e Societa Italiana. Conferenza Nazionale dell' immigrazione*. Rome: Editalia.

Confindustria. 1990. "L'immigrazione extra-comunitaria e il Mercato del Lavoro Italiano." Mimeographed.

D'Ambrosio, Fausto. 1991. "Cittadini Extracomunitari: Regolarizzazione a Sanatoria Tutela degli Interessi e Nuovi Problemi," *Codex Convegno di Studio: Applicazione della Legge Martelli* (Florence), June 22: 35–41.

De Filippo, Elena, and Enrica Morlicchio. 1992. "L'immigrazione Straniera in Campania," *Inchiesta* 22:95 (January–March): 40–49.

Dell'Aringa, Carlo, and F. Neri. 1987. "Illegal Immigrants and the Informal Economy in Italy," *Labour* 2.

D'Harmant Francois, Antonio. 1988. "La Disciplina Legislativa del Rapporto di Lavoro dei Cittadini Extra-Comunitari," *Rivista Italiana di Diritto del Lavoro* 7:1:44–76.

DOXA. 1991. "Gli Stranieri in Italia," *Bollettino della Doxa* 45:9–11 (July 25).

Grisoni, Dominique, and Hughes Portelli. 1977. *Le Lotte Operaie in Italia dal 1960 al 1976*. Milano: Rizzoli.

Guidi, Gianfranco, Alberto Bronzino, and Luigi Germanetto. 1974. *FIAT: Struttura Aziendale ed Organizzazione dello Sfruttamento*. Milano: Mazzotta.

Ires Toscana. 1992. "Imprenditori e Lavoratori Immigrati nell'industria Fiorentina," *Quaderni di Analisi e Programmazione dello Sviluppo Regionale e Locale* 6 (March–April).

ISTAT (Istituto Centrale di Statistica). 1970. *Annuario Statistico Italiano, 1970*. Rome: Istituto Poligrafico dello Stato.

La Terza, Maura. 1987. "Innovazioni Legislative sul Lavoro degli Stranieri Extracomunitari in Italia," *Questione Giustizia* 1:29–43.

Macioti, Maria Immacolata, and Enrico Pugliese. 1991. *Gli Immigrati in Italia*. Bari: Editori Laterza.

Martelli, Claudio. 1991. "Politica d'immigrazione, una Legislazione in Via di Sviluppo," *Rassegna Informativa sulle Iniziative Relative ai Problemi dei Lavoratori Extracomunitari e delle loro Famiglie*. Ministero del Lavoro e della Previdenza Sociale 2:2 (February): 121–34.

Milanaccio, Alfredo, and Luca Ricolfi. 1976. *Lotte Operaie e Ambiente di Lavoro: Mirafiori, 1968–1974*. Turin: Giulio Einaudi Editore.

Montalbano, William D. 1993a. "Italians Say 'Basta' and Vote to Throw the Rascals Out," *Los Angeles Times*, April 20.

———. 1993b. "Depth of Voter Protest Leaves Italians at a Loss for Words," *Los Angeles Times*, June 9.

Natale, Marcello. 1990. "L'immigrazione Straniera in Italia: Consistenza, Caratteristiche, Prospettive," *Polis* 4:1 (April): 5–40.

Onorato, Pierluigi. 1989. "Per Uno Statuto dello Straniero," *Democrazia e Diritto* 6 (November–December): 303–28.

Piore, Michael. 1979. *Birds of Passage*. London: Cambridge University Press.

XXI Secolo. 1992. "Un'Italia, Due Mercati del Lavoro," vol. 4:1 (May).

Sestini, Raffaello. 1989. "La Disciplina degli Stranieri in Europa," *Democrazia e Diritto* 6 (November–December): 329–50.

Stobart, Janet. 1993. "Angry Italian Voters Stick to Their Guns," *Los Angeles Times*, June 22.

U.S. Department of Labor. Bureau of International Labor Affairs. 1989. *Foreign Labor Trends Report*. FLT 89-73. Washington, D.C.: U.S. Government Printing Office.

Venturini, Alessandra. 1989. "Il Mercato del Lavoro e i Lavoratori Extraeuropei: Una Lettura Economica," *Economia e Diritto* 6:359–71.

———. 1991. "Italy in the Context of European Migration," *Regional Development Dialogue* 12:3 (Autumn): 93–112.

Commentary

The Dualism of Italian Immigration

Alessandra Venturini

The economic structure of a destination country shapes both the type of employment available to migrants and the prospects for their social integration. This is the case in Italy, where the dual economies—the northern and the southern—diverged in the 1980s, with the north becoming more integrated with the European economic system and the south becoming more marginal.

This north-south division finds a parallel in Italy's two migration patterns: the northern one, with mainly steady and formal employment of migrants in industry and the service sector; and the southern one, with migrants filling mainly irregular jobs in agriculture and services. This dichotomy is softening somewhat today as the two migrant streams begin to converge. Migrants may find their first jobs in marginal or informal sectors, but they later seek out more structured and permanent jobs in other areas, a transition encouraged by legislation and by growing intolerance of illegal migrants.

The unskilled migrants present in Italy reinforce the country's informal sector and provide flexibility to the national economy. Most of these migrants entered Italy during the second half of the 1980s, when they served as a buffer, taking the unskilled jobs that Italian workers did not want. Today, with Italy in recession, the jobs available for migrants are increasingly marginalized, and public sentiment is turning against these workers. Although many of them would like to legalize their status and integrate into Italian society, there is little likelihood that Italy will enact a new legalization program for fear that it would only attract another wave of illegal immigrants.

While public sentiment and the right-wing LEGA party strongly oppose the migrant presence, there are no groups allied in defense of immigrants. Even employers who continue to prefer immigrant workers downplay their hiring practices in the current context of generalized economic contraction. At the policy level, the trend has shifted from tolerance of migrants toward rigid control efforts. However, the fact that there is implicit tolerance of Italy's vast underground economy reduces the authorities' effectiveness in detecting illegal migrant workers, and legal protections can hamper efforts to repatriate those who are apprehended.

In light of the economic crisis, Italy's appeal as a destination country could be expected to decline, and this has happened to a certain extent. Fewer jobs are available, and the rate of wage and income gains has slowed. Even so, these changes have produced only a slight-to-moderate reduction in migratory pressures, for at least two reasons. First, the recession is global; thus in relative terms, Italy has not become less attractive as a destination vis-à-vis most other European countries. Second, the job expectations of the Italian workforce have not diminished, and many less desirable jobs still go unfilled by native workers.

In this economic context of high unemployment combined with vacancies in low-paid, less desirable jobs, the obvious solution would be to restructure these jobs to make them attractive to nationals. However, the presence of a large pool of available foreign migrant workers discourages such restructuring. Most businesses seem to lack the will to carry out a thorough-going reorganization of production, which, together with the continuing need to fill the marginal jobs scorned by Italian citizens, suggests that the country's policy will continue to be one of keeping the backdoor partly open to immigration. Supporters of the status quo stress that Italy's falling population growth rate may require opening the front door to larger numbers of foreign workers (Italy's workforce will shrink by 2.2 million workers between 1990 and 2020). However, this projection does not take account of variations in the labor participation rate, nor a probable drop in labor demand due to technological advances.

Italy could tailor the immigrant population it accepts in the future by implementing a policy favoring foreign workers from Eastern Europe, thereby hoping to reduce migration flows from the south. Such a policy would have economic justifications (East European workers are more skilled and hence more productive) as well as political attractions (East European workers are more easily integrated). At present, East Europeans represent only 6 percent of the migrant population entering Italy (they represent an even lower percentage of migrant flows to other Southern European countries), but their numbers could be increased through international political agreements and employer preference for better qualified workers.

Although Italy can take steps as a receiving country to reduce the factors that attract international migrants, it has no control over the factors that encourage emigration from sending countries. And these push factors are intensifying. The global recession is reducing foreign investment in labor-exporting countries, inhibiting their efforts to provide jobs for their growing labor forces (Tunisia's workforce, for example, will increase by 2.3 million between 1990 and 2020; the comparable figure for Morocco during this period is 7.7 million). Increased emigration pressures in major sending countries are likely to provoke restrictive measures in Italy, including tighter control of national borders and efforts to repatriate illegal migrants to their home countries in order to maintain social peace. But Italy continues to send conflicting signals to the labor-exporting countries. While politicians may voice their determination to control migration, employers raise migrants' expectations, thereby encouraging continued migration flows.

10

Spain: The Uneasy Transition from Labor Exporter to Labor Importer

Wayne A. Cornelius

The Spanish Immigration Dilemma

During the 1980s Spain experienced a very rapid transition from labor-exporting to labor-importing country. Between 1973 and 1980 most of the more than 1 million Spanish "guestworkers" who emigrated to Northern Europe (primarily France, Germany, Switzerland, and the United Kingdom) in the 1960s and early 1970s repatriated themselves.[1] By 1985–1986 Spain was experiencing substantial immigration, attracted by the beginnings of the economic boom that coincided with Spain's entry into the European Community. The number of foreigners residing legally in Spain rose from 241,971 in 1985 to 398,148 in 1989—a 65 percent increase (Colectivo Ioé 1993: table 6.1, p. 166). By 1992, estimates of the total number of immigrants, including legal residents as well as *irregulares*,

The assistance of Cynthia R. Hibbs in the research for this paper and in translation of documents from the Catalán was essential to the completion of this chapter. I am also very grateful to Professor Juan Díez Nicolás (Universidad Complutense de Madrid and Centro de Investigaciones sobre la Realidad Social, Madrid) for his help in obtaining sample survey data and arranging interviews with key informants. Carlos Giménez Romero (Universidad Autónoma de Madrid) generously provided access to the results of numerous field studies of immigrant communities in Madrid being conducted under his supervision. This chapter is based largely on information gathered through unstructured interviews by the author with sixty-five scholars, public officials, journalists, businessmen, labor leaders, and representatives of human rights and social service organizations, interviewed in Madrid and Barcelona in 1992. Supplemental field research support from the Center for Iberian and Latin American Studies (University of California, San Diego) and the Center for German and European Studies (University of California, Berkeley) is gratefully acknowledged.

[1]A total of 466,394 returning migrants officially registered themselves in Spanish consulates between 1975 and 1988 (cited in Colectivo Ioé 1991a).

ranged from 570,000 to 835,000 (Colectivo Ioé 1991a, 1993: 149; Izquierdo Escribano 1992: 98).

Furthermore, a significant qualitative change had occurred in the foreign presence in Spain. Before the mid-1980s, foreigners were mostly relatively affluent tourists and retirees from the United Kingdom, Germany, and the Scandinavian countries who sought a warmer climate and lower living costs. Since 1985 Spain has been receiving mostly *worker* immigrants from North Africa (especially Morocco), Latin America, and Asia (mostly from the Philippines). The new immigrant flow contains many more young people, persons from lower-class backgrounds, and people whose racial, religious, and other cultural attributes clearly differentiate them from the host population.

Finally, Spain in the 1980s became a country of *destination* for many economic migrants from the Third World and Eastern Europe, supplementing its earlier function as a conduit for migrants heading for jobs in other European Community countries (especially France). Some officials estimate that more than half of those who have entered Spain illegally in recent years want to stay there; they are not in transit to any other country.[2] This change in south-north and east-west migration patterns has raised the possibility that Spain will be hosting a large, stable, and socially integrated foreign-born workforce—a prospect both unexpected and unsettling to most Spaniards.

Yet Spain, like other industrialized countries today, faces a trade-off between the sociocultural costs of admitting more foreigners, at least some of whom will settle permanently, and the economic costs of *not* importing them. Government, business, and most members of the general public want access to cheap, flexible, disposable labor for certain sectors of the economy, such as agriculture, construction, and domestic service. It is also widely recognized that the vitality of the country's very large and diversified underground economy, which supplies and otherwise supports many firms in the mainstream economy, depends on continued access to immigrant labor. Finally, the Spanish welfare state provides generous benefits (mainly unemployment compensation and other transfer payments) that reward native-born Spaniards for *not* working, at least in the formal economy. Whenever the government seeks to curtail these benefits, partly to force native-born workers back into immigrant-dominated labor markets, it meets stiff resistance.

---

[2]Interview with Celsa Pico Lorenzo, Magistrado Tribunal, Tribunal Superior de Justicia de Catalunya, May 1992. The choice of Spain as a country of destination was made more frequently by migrants seeking short-term agricultural employment than by other segments of the immigration flow. For example, temporary agricultural jobs are plentiful in southern coastal zones like Almería; North African migrants do not need to travel further north to gain employment. Nevertheless, as immigrant kinship networks become established in both rural and urban areas of Spain, it will become increasingly attractive as a country of destination for all types of migrants.

The "immigration problem" in Spain currently is defined by government officials as a delicate balancing act. They feel that they must maintain enough control over illegal flows to prevent the numbers of foreigners (especially from Third World countries) from growing too rapidly and provoking a xenophobic public backlash, while simultaneously supplying a low-cost labor force that is adequate to keep the economy growing and attracting foreign investment.

Even in the most heavily impacted cities, Barcelona and Madrid, authorities contend that the numbers of recently arrived and still arriving immigrants are "manageable." The newcomers have not overwhelmed social services, nor have they increased unemployment appreciably by competing against native-born Spaniards for desirable, formal-sector jobs. The new immigration has been highly "channelized" into certain subsectors of the economy. Nevertheless, there is a broad consensus on the need for more effective immigration control measures, and for a control system that is driven by Spain's specific labor market requirements, rather than political, cultural, or diplomatic considerations (especially pressures or mandates from the other European Community countries). The top-ranking Interior Ministry official responsible for immigration policy summarized his government's stance as follows:

> We must have a very firm, even-handed policy, giving employers the labor they need but not fanning public hostility. The policy should be, "Let all those come whom we can integrate, and for which we have an economic need." We need a positive, active immigration policy. Socialist parties of other European countries have committed serious errors in their handling of this issue. In France, they have allowed the right to seize the initiative; Le Pen has been the only winner. . . . A strict immigration control policy is the most socially progressive policy, as well as the most politically prudent (author interview with Fernando Puig de la Bellacasa, May 1992).

The number of immigrants in Spain is still small by the standards of most European countries today, representing perhaps 1.5 percent of the total population of 40 million (as compared with the European Community average of about 4 percent). But many Spaniards are aware of, and disturbed by, the potential for massive, uncontrolled immigration fueled by huge demographic and economic imbalances between Spain and its impoverished North African neighbors, just twenty kilometers away, across the Strait of Gibraltar.

While it is politically correct in Spain to criticize as extremist the views of other Europeans who warn darkly of the continent's impending

"Islamization" or "Africanization,"[3] there is growing concern, and skepticism, about Spain's capacity to absorb large numbers of Arab and African immigrants. In contrast to citizens of other industrialized countries today, Spaniards discount the notion that their country's national identity is threatened by immigration.[4] However, a multiracial, multicultural society is not seen as a desirable goal, and any immigration policy that would move Spain more quickly in this direction is to be avoided. As in France and other West European countries, many Spaniards are now questioning whether it is possible to have a "secular," nonextremist Islamic presence in their society.

Spain's preferred strategy is to avoid being cast in the role of "policeman of Southern Europe," keeping the Third World hordes at bay while persuading its fellow European Community members to step up development assistance to the labor-exporting countries of North Africa. Prime Minister Felipe González reportedly plans to give each of his EC colleagues a copy of a large photograph of Morocco taken from Spain's southern coast. "This is our Rio Grande," he seeks to remind them, pointing to the Strait of Gibraltar. "It's not far. And living standards are four, five, ten times lower on the other side" (quoted in Riding 1992).

Domestically, the goal of the Spanish government, and of all major political parties, is to have a low-profile immigration policy—one that avoids arousing public passions and inflated expectations. The political class defends immigrants and criticizes highly publicized incidents of racism and hate crimes, when they absolutely must; but a sustained educational campaign to combat anti-immigrant hostility is not likely to be undertaken.

Conveniently overlooking the similar case of Italy, Spanish leaders point with pride to their country as Europe's principal deviant case in terms of public and government tolerance for immigration. Partly, this condition is attributable to the relatively low salience of the immigration issue among the Spanish public, except in the largest metropolitan areas. It is true that Spain has largely managed to avoid the overt social tensions, recurrent violence, right-wing extremist parties, and increasingly repressive government control measures that have been provoked elsewhere by recent south-north and east-west migrations. However, violent attacks on foreigners have become more frequent, and the brutal murder of a female Dominican immigrant by a "skinhead" in November

---

[3]French demographer Jean-Claude Chesnais is frequently singled out by Spaniards as an influential proponent of this "extremist" position. See, for example, Chesnais 1990.

[4]In a recent national public opinion survey, more than two-thirds of the respondents rejected the idea that Spain's national identity could eventually be lost through large-scale immigration. See CIRES 1994. The random, stratified sample consisted of 1,200 persons at least eighteen years of age, living throughout Spain, interviewed between March 7–12, 1994, in their homes. Hereafter this study will be referred to as the CIRES survey of 1994.

1992 sparked widespread concern about the growth of xenophobic tendencies in Spain (Durán 1992).

Critics of the politicians' low-profile stance on immigration complain that it simply masks the *absence* of a real national immigration policy, as well as the lack of an administrative infrastructure and capacity that would be needed to implement an "active" immigration policy. To some observers, the reticence of the political class reflects the country's ambivalent attitudes toward the "new" immigration: many Spaniards still do not know what kind of immigration policy they really want.

With rare exceptions, the policy-making vacuum at the national level has not been filled by officials acting at lower levels. In Madrid, home to the nation's second-largest concentration of immigrants, local authorities have declined to formulate specific policies and programs to deal with foreign workers (Giménez Romero 1993a: 105). Even the powerfully entrenched ruling party in the Catalonian region wishes to avoid having the immigration issue debated in the local legislature. "It's just too complicated," observed one social scientist at the University of Barcelona (author interview with Frederic Javaloy i Mazón, May 1992).

Spain's Illegal Immigrants

By 1993, estimates of the size of Spain's illegal immigrant population by the most knowledgeable analysts ranged from 200,000 to 300,000—this after the 1991 regularization program, which legalized (at least initially) some 110,000 foreign workers. Sample surveys of Moroccan immigrants as well as data on participants in the 1991 legalization program suggest that most of the illegals are relatively recent arrivals, i.e., since 1988 (see, for example, López García 1992: 54). The immigration surge of the late 1980s is clearly related to Spain's economic boom during this period. There is widespread belief that the stock of illegal foreign workers continues to grow, albeit more slowly. The reduced growth rate can be attributed mainly to the drastic contraction in economic activity in Spain since 1992 and, according to some reports, to an increase in the numbers of native-born Spaniards who are now willing to work even in sectors of the economy characterized by the highest degree of "labor flexibility," like construction (Izquierdo Escribano 1993: 11).

Nearly half of Spain's current stock of illegal immigrants originated in Africa. Especially numerous are the Moroccans (who constituted more than 40 percent of those who regularized their status under the 1991 program), Algerians, Gambians, and Senegalese. Black Africans (Gambians, Senegalese, and Equatorial Guineans) were underrepresented in the legalization program, partly because many of them had great difficulty obtaining necessary documents from their home countries. Latin Americans comprise about one-quarter of the stock of *irregulares* (Argentina, Peru, the Dominican Republic, and Colombia are the key source countries in that region). The remainder come mainly from Asia (China, the Philippines), and Eastern Europe (Poland, Romania, the former Czechoslovakia) (Ministerio del Interior 1992: table 5).

There are striking social, economic, and demographic differences among these immigrant communities (*colectivos*, as they are known in Spain).[5] Skill and social class differences are most notable between the North Africans (who are overwhelmingly unskilled workers upon arrival in Spain) and East Europeans (skilled workers and professionals). Dominican, Filipino, and Cape Verdean immigrants are overwhelmingly female (either single women or married women who leave their spouses and children in the home country), although there is a relatively high (and rising) proportion of females in all of the immigrant *colectivos*.[6] Thirty-two percent of the *irregulares* legalized in the 1991 program were women. The substantial representation of women in Spain's immigrant stock reflects more than family reunification immigration, although this type of migration is certainly occurring and will, no doubt, be accelerated by the 1991 legalization program and more recent government actions.[7] Among the Moroccan immigrant community, for example, the rising proportion of females results from a new migration of single women, originating in large cities, who seek work in domestic service and other parts of the service sector (López García 1992: 58). The Moroccan fraction remains male-dominated, however, owing to the large numbers of Moroccan "lone males" (about half of the total) who are employed as temporary agricultural and construction workers (Izquierdo Escribano 1993: 13).

Illegal immigrants enter Spain in a variety of ways. For Latin Americans, the most common mode is entry by posing as a tourist, entering through an airport or overland by bus. While Peruvians and Dominicans are now required to have entry visas, "tourists" from other Latin American nations can enter without visas.[8] Those who enter on valid tourist or student visas can easily overstay them and seek employ-

---

[5]For a collection of highly detailed ethnographic profiles of the principal immigrant communities in Madrid, see Giménez Romero 1993b.

[6]See Giménez Romero 1992: 82–83. Among all legally resident foreigners in Spain in 1990, the proportion of women slightly exceeded that of men.

[7]In November 1993, the Interior Ministry promulgated regulations for the reunification of families headed by settled immigrants from non-European Community countries. The key requirements are that the family head must hold a job that pays enough to support him and his dependents, and he must have access to housing that meets minimum standards of habitability.

[8]Not even the imposition of visa requirements has deterred some would-be illegal entrants from the affected countries. For example, in late 1993 Spanish authorities broke up a smuggling ring that had been importing Peruvians (at U.S.$3,000 per head), using false documents and moving them by plane from Lima to Vienna, by train to Frankfurt, and finally by bus to Madrid (Ahrens 1993).

ment. With 50 million people claiming to be tourists entering Spain each year, control is difficult.

Seeking political asylum is the second most frequently used mode of entry for those who ultimately become illegal immigrants in Spain. Despite an extremely high turn-down rate, a reduction of economic assistance for asylum seekers, and a shortening of the adjudication period (see the following section on refugee policy), the asylum mechanism continues to be an attractive mode of entry for nationals of many countries.

Spain's land borders, especially the one with Portugal, are highly porous, and numerous illegal immigrants enter this way. There are virtually no control points on the Spanish-Portuguese border. Some Algerians also enter by crossing the northern border from France. Seaports represent another weak point, and stowing away on ships bound for Spain has become the newest mode of illegal entry for North Africans.

The most highly publicized mode of illegal entry, but the least significant in numerical terms, has been in small boats (*pateras*) crossing the Strait of Gibraltar. These rickety fishing boats are often dangerously overloaded and capsize in the rough waters of the Strait, drowning many of their passengers. This perilous route has been used mainly by Moroccans and black Africans. Only 1,717 would-be illegal entrants were apprehended coming ashore in *pateras* during 1991, and 1,908 during the first nine months of 1992; but unknown numbers perished at sea, and others are believed to have escaped detection, passing through Andalucia province on their way to jobs in Barcelona and Madrid. Most of this clandestine entry activity has been highly organized by people-smuggling rings based in Morocco that charge Ptas 70,000–100,000 (about U.S.$700–1,000) per head. A 1993 crackdown on these smuggling operations by Moroccan authorities, under pressure from the Spanish government, reportedly has drastically reduced the flow of illegal immigrants across the Strait of Gibraltar.[9]

Most illegal immigrants head immediately to Madrid or Barcelona because of their abundance of employment opportunities as well as kinship networks that have been established in these cities. The region of Catalonia, of which Barcelona is the capital, is also an attractive destination because of the availability of agricultural employment in the province's coastal areas. Madrid and Catalonia provinces together accounted for 63 percent of all those who legalized their status under the 1991 program.

---

[9]Goverment security forces apprehended 1,290 illegal immigrants during 1993 in the province of Cádiz, of whom only 164 had entered by crossing the Strait of Gibraltar (*El País* [Madrid], January 4, 1994). The Moroccan government may have had an economic incentive to cooperate in this crackdown on illegal immigration via the Strait: the "carrot" of an expanded fishing rights agreement with Spain.

Spain's illegal immigrants are employed predominantly (and increasingly) in the service sector, especially domestic service, gardening, hotel and building maintenance, and loading and unloading of freight. The distribution of butane gas tanks to private residences is another service niche dominated by immigrants (Pakistanis in Barcelona, Poles in Madrid).[10] Fifty-nine percent of the illegal immigrants regularized throughout Spain in 1991 were employed in services. Agriculture accounted for the second-largest group (18 percent), followed by construction (15 percent). Ironically, public works construction is a major source of employment for foreign workers in Spain. For example, many thousands of them were hired by subcontractors to build facilities for the 1992 Olympic Games, Expo '92, and the new Barcelona airport. Mining and small to medium-sized manufacturing enterprises (concentrated mainly in the Barcelona metropolitan area) offer additional employment opportunities. Finally, growing numbers of immigrants—legal as well as illegal—are self-employed, not only as street vendors but as proprietors of their own small businesses, and provide employment opportunities to other members of their *colectivo*. Immigrant-owned businesses are particularly common in sectors like apparel and shoes.

Except for the domestic service sector, there is no organized recruitment of foreign workers by employers. Upon arrival in Spain, most illegals get work quickly through social networks in the various immigrant *colectivos*. Well-organized enterprises do operate in Madrid and Barcelona to place illegal female immigrants (especially Filipinas, Dominicanas, and Peruanas) in domestic service jobs. Some of the most successful of these rings have been organized by immigrant women themselves.

Most employers do not screen job applicants for immigration status, i.e., they do not require applicants to present government-issued work permits in order to be hired. Firms that utilize foreign workers typically have mixed workforces, including both foreigners and native-born Spaniards. Frequently the natives include both legally registered employees and persons who are employed "off-the-books."

As in all countries represented in this volume, the Spanish labor markets in which immigrants participate tend to be highly segmented. In the construction sector, for example, foreigners occupy the most physically demanding, most temporary, and least skilled jobs, even though many of the African immigrants employed in such jobs are reasonably well-educated and skilled workers. In some sectors, employers seeking to hire foreigners for unskilled jobs have a preference hierarchy in hiring. In agriculture, for example, black African immigrants are the most attractive to employers, because of their image as

---

[10]Immigration experts have estimated that in Madrid over 80 percent of all foreign workers were employed in the service sector in 1990. See Colectivo Ioé 1993: table 6.15, p. 193.

very hardworking, docile, and trustworthy. Magrebíes (immigrants from Morocco, Algeria, and Tunisia) are perceived as less desirable, partly due to historically grounded prejudices against *"los moros,"* and because they are seen as "smart operators," untrustworthy, and potentially more contentious than black central Africans.

Because of labor market segmentation, instances of overt job competition between natives and foreigners have been relatively rare in Spain. The only documented cases of such competition have been in the agricultural sector. In the late 1980s, native-born citrus pickers in Valencia went on strike, and growers replaced them with Moroccan immigrants. In another region, conflicts over fruit harvesting work erupted between black Africans and poor Spaniards in 1991.

For an illegal immigrant in Spain, changing jobs is often more difficult than getting an initial toehold in the labor market. Under the 1985 immigration law (*"ley de extranjería"*), each time a foreign worker changes employers he must obtain a new work permit from the government. Even legal immigrants who lose their jobs and are unable to acquire new work permits are required to leave the country. Local branches of the national Ministry of Labor determine whether a work permit will be granted. The total number of work permits granted to foreigners has remained stable or even declined in most years since 1978, while the foreign-born population with legal *residence* permits has risen sharply (see figures 10.1 and 10.2). This imbalance has been a great boon to employers; it has helped to institutionalize a system of short-term hiring that gives them maximum flexibility to shed labor when it is not needed.

The bureaucratic obstacles to obtaining or renewing work permits in Spain are formidable. Foreigners seeking to renew their work permits must present their social security cards, but only a minority of immigrants working in certain sectors (e.g., domestic service) are able to obtain work contracts that include social security payments by the employer. Since Spanish immigration law links work permits to residence permits, most illegal immigrants are unable to obtain legal work contracts. This "Catch-22" system does not exclude them from the labor market, but it limits their options to the underground economy or to formal-sector firms that employ them off-the-books, thereby avoiding costly payments for social security and other employee benefits.

Foreign workers are typically paid less than natives if there are native-born workers employed in similar jobs in the same industries. Wage discrimination is most likely to be carried out by small subcontractors, whose wage and employment practices are rarely scrutinized by the government. Some African immigrants employed in agriculture recently were found to be receiving as little as Ptas 50 (about 50 cents) per hour, although most growers do pay the legal minimum. In some urban sectors (e.g., construction, domestic service) the chronic shortage of native-born labor puts a floor under wages paid to foreigners.

Figure 10.1

Foreigners with Legal Residence Permits in Spain, 1955-1990

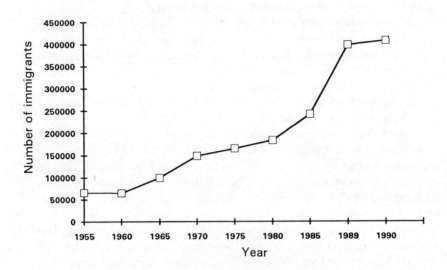

Source: Colectivo IOE, ``Rasgos generales y perfil sociodemográfico de los principales colectivos,'' in *Inmigrantes extranjeros en Madrid*, Vol. 1 (Madrid: Consejería de Integración Social, Comunidad de Madrid, 1993): table 6.1, p. 166.

Sources of Spain's Demand for Immigrant Labor

With Europe's highest official unemployment rate, ranging between 15 and 23 percent in the 1992–1994 period,[11] it would seem implausible that Spain has difficulty meeting its labor requirements without substantial foreign immigration. However, it is widely conceded that official unemployment statistics are unreliable and to some extent meaningless, given the widespread practice of collecting unemployment compensation while working in the underground economy (see below). Moreover, most social scientists agree that Spain's current shortages of labor in certain sectors of the economy are relative rather than absolute. While demographic trends clearly point toward an absolute labor deficit in the foreseeable future, labor force participation rates among women, youths, and older males are still low by comparison with other industrialized countries. Moreover, in parts of Spain where immigrants are now a fixture of the regional economy (e.g.,

---

[11]The government has estimated that 3.5 million Spaniards would be "unemployed" by the end of 1994.

Figure 10.2

Work Permits Granted to Foreigners in Spain, 1978-1991

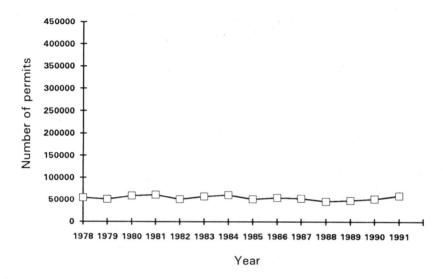

Sources: Colectivo IOE, ``Foreign Women in Domestic Service in Madrid, Spain'' (Geneva: World Employment Programme, International Labour Organisation, 1991): 3; Antonio Izquierdo Escribano, ``Los trabajadores extranjeros en Madrid: un flujo complementario que se consolida,'' *Política y Sociedad* 12 (1993): table 1, p. 23.

Andalucia, one of the country's poorest provinces), there are large pools of native-born labor theoretically available to fill the jobs now held by foreigners.

How, then, can we explain the strong demand for foreign-born labor? As noted above, the Spanish labor market is highly segmented, and there are strong disincentives for taking jobs in some sectors, causing a relative shortage of labor. Agriculture and domestic service are the two clearest examples of sectors in which native-born workers do not make themselves available in sufficient quantity.

In the case of agriculture, the temporariness of the jobs, low (but not illegal) wages, the remoteness of the work sites, and uncomfortable working conditions (working in high heat, under sheets of plastic) make it extremely difficult for employers to find and retain native workers for harvesting strawberries and other fruits. The economic boom of the late 1970s and early 1980s enabled small and medium-sized growers to invest in greenhouses, thereby creating a new demand for hand labor.[12] At the same time, many native-born former farmworkers no longer wanted to work in agriculture. This was especially true of returned Spanish emigrants, many of whom had toiled at precisely the same kinds of jobs now "reserved" for foreigners in Spain. Those who had held *better* jobs abroad were even less likely to take the bad jobs held by immigrants today (author interview with Angels Pascual de Sans, Universidad Autónoma de Barcelona, May 1992; see also Pascual de Sans and Cardelus 1990). In this way, Spain's recent experience as a country of emigration has contributed to the current demand for low-skilled foreign labor, not just in agriculture but in low-status service work as well.

Domestic service used to be provided by internal Spanish migrants from impoverished provinces like Andalucia. Since the early 1980s, however, young Spanish women have not been available for such work, particularly live-in employment. They could earn considerably more and enjoy better working conditions in other types of work, such as factory employment. It is the gap left by the virtual disappearance of Spanish-born, live-in domestic servants that has been filled by foreigners—Filipinas, Dominicanas, Peruvians, Portuguese, Moroccans, even Poles (see Colectivo Ioé 1989). At the same time, rising family incomes during the economic boom period greatly increased the demand for in-house domestic service, even in middle-class homes. Finally, the aging of the Spanish population has been creating a new demand for female immigrants, as care providers for the elderly. Domestic service is not attractive to Spaniards for most of the same reasons that lead them to shun agricultural labor: low (but usually not illegal) wages, temporariness, and poor working conditions. Spanish women now have better options.

Both employers and many public officials attribute much of the demand for foreign labor to rigidities in the labor market resulting both from restrictive labor and immigration laws and from sheer bureaucratic inefficiency. Such inefficiency has produced a huge backlog in applications for work permits. In May 1992, for example, magistrates in Catalonia were reviewing petitions submitted by employers in 1990. Critics of the existing work permit system charge that it has no utility for controlling or discouraging the hiring of illegal immigrants—quite the contrary.

The 1985 immigration law requires that an employer demonstrate that no native-born worker or citizen of a European Community member country is available to fill a job vacancy before a work permit can be issued to a non-EC foreigner. "The usual pattern," observed

---

[12]The zones of large-scale agriculture, in provinces like Andalucia and Sevilla, are mechanized and have much less need for harvest labor, in contrast to the small-scale, family-owned farms of regions like Meresme and Valencia, which depend heavily on foreign hand labor.

one legal expert, "is that no Spanish applicants come forward, and the employer just hires the foreigner illegally" (author interview with Lidia Santos Arnau, Universidad Autónoma de Barcelona, May 1992). For example, work permits are routinely denied to foreigners seeking domestic service work, on the grounds that high unemployment among native-born Spaniards makes foreign labor unnecessary. "But the unemployment statistics are too highly aggregated. No Spaniards are really available for this type of work, so the employer hires an illegal. There is a real labor demand in this sector that cannot be satisfied legally" (author interview with Magistrate Celsa Pico Lorenzo, Tribunal Superior de Justicia de Catalunya, May 1992). In fact, the number of work permits granted to foreigners for work in domestic service has declined in most years since 1986, while the number of immigrants working clandestinely in this sector has continued to rise (see Colectivo Ioé 1991b: 13–15).

Labor legislation in Spain is more restrictive and employer compliance is more costly than in most industrialized countries today. It is easy to hire workers (except foreigners who need work permits) but very difficult to fire them, and large indemnization payments are required when workers are laid off or dismissed. Social security and other employee benefits are quite costly by international standards. Many employers have highly seasonal or temporary labor requirements; they also need greater flexibility in hiring to adjust to cyclical fluctuations in the economy and quick changes in consumer preferences. Not surprisingly, Spanish business owners are usually reluctant to increase the number of permanent hires. The now-common practice of giving short-term contracts is the result. In recent years, 30 percent of all work contracts in Spain have been short term; the average has been six months (author interview with Joaquín Arango, Director, Centro de Investigaciones Sociológicas, Madrid, May 1992).

The rigidities in Spain's labor market, a legacy of Francoism, have helped to increase the demand for foreign labor in two key ways. First, they make immigrants who are willing to work on short contracts or with no contracts at all ("off-the-books") attractive as a labor source. Second, the short-term hiring system has reduced incentives for native-born Spaniards to work, at least in the formal sector of the economy. A large portion of the native-born Spanish workforce has taken advantage of the system by "jumping" from one short employment contract to another, interspersed with periods in which they collect unemployment compensation (*"el paro"*). Ministry of Labor officials and academic experts estimate that in some provinces 60 to 70 percent of the residents are on unemployment compensation and not looking for legal employment, even while they *are* working in unregistered jobs (interviews with Salvador Alvarez [Director Provincial de Ministerio de Trabajo y Seguridad Social de Catalunya], Joaquim

Saurina i Fiol [Departament de Traball de Catalunya], and Ana Cabré [Universitat Autònoma de Barcelona], May 1992). In the province of Andalucia, which has a special government-sponsored rural employment program, local politicians have facilitated taking advantage of the system by creating very short-term or fictitious, nonremunerated public works jobs, just to qualify their holders for unemployment compensation. A controversial administrative decree issued by the Felipe González government in 1992 was aimed at curbing such abuses. It remains to be seen, however, whether a general crackdown on the abuse of unemployment compensation by native-born workers will force many of them back into "immigrant jobs." The country's large underground economy will still offer alternatives for those who choose to remain outside the formal sector. Moreover, the rigidities in labor relations practices that encourage short-term hiring and enhance the attractiveness of the foreign-born labor force to Spanish employers will persist.

Meanwhile, Spain's demographic profile continues to change in ways that will make labor shortages more difficult to avert without substantial immigration. The country's total fertility rate has dropped to 1.36, among the three lowest in the world (Italy and Japan are the other two countries vying for this distinction). In 1974, 680,000 births were recorded in Spain; in 1990, only 375,000. The plummeting birthrate was associated with the end of the Franco regime, the economic crisis of 1975–1976, and a decline in the influence of the Catholic Church. When Spain's economy rebounded in the 1980s, low-fertility attitudes were already well established. According to the most recent census, the city of Barcelona lost population, in absolute terms, during the 1980–1991 period; without foreign immigration, the city's population loss would have been much greater. Alarmed by this trend, the nationalist government of Catalonia has actively promoted higher fertility (at least three children per family), but few couples seem to be paying heed.

The Spanish population is also aging rapidly. By the year 2000, Spain will have a higher proportion of elderly residents than either France or Germany; 20 percent of the population will be sixty-five years of age or older. Life expectancy is already longer than in the United States. And the "cushion" of young, entry-level labor built up during the high-birthrate years of the late Franco period will soon be gone. Assuming that these demographic trends are irreversible,[13] they will deepen the relative shortages of labor already evident in some sectors of the Spanish economy.

---

[13]Demographer Ana Cabré is the only prominent population expert in Spain who now predicts an upturn in the birthrate. She projects that by the year 2000, the total fertility rate in Cataluña province will be above two children per family, primarily due to delayed births among women over thirty-five years of age (see Cabré and Pujadas 1987).

The Evolution of Immigration Controls

Legislation and Border Controls

Before 1985, Spain had made no effort to enact a comprehensive immigration law. Its first attempt, the *ley de extranjería* (officially titled La Ley Orgánica sobre Derechos y Libertades de los Extranjeros), was approved by the Spanish Congress in April 1985 and implemented on July 1 of the same year. This law was almost entirely the result of external pressure associated with Spain's entry into the European Community on January 1, 1986, which required adherence to EC legislation restricting immigration from non-EC countries. Its main thrust was to increase government powers to deal with aliens already present in the country, rather than to strengthen border controls. It enabled the government to deport foreigners found to be engaged in "illicit activities," those who are in Spain without proper residence permits or legal temporary visas, those "implicated in activities contrary to the public order," and those who, "lacking legal means of earning a living, devote themselves to begging or other conduct considered socially unacceptable." Perhaps most importantly, the 1985 law restricts immigrants' access to formal-sector employment by requiring them to first obtain a work contract from an employer and then to solicit government work and residence permits separately, from two different ministries (Labor and Interior, respectively). As noted above, the law also requires foreigners to begin the dual application process from scratch when their initial work contract (usually for six months or less) expires and whenever they change jobs.

From the beginning, it was apparent that the bureaucratic infrastructure and security apparatus necessary for effective implementation of the 1985 immigration law did not exist; indeed, only fragments of such an infrastructure are in place even now. Until early 1992 the immigration office in the Ministry of Labor was anachronistically called the "Spanish Institute of *Emigration*." Only recently did the government initiate surveillance of "hot spots" for illegal immigration: southern coastal towns like Algeciras, the Madrid airport, and so forth. Interior Ministry officials concede that the Spanish navy and coast guard lack the resources to prevent illegal entry all along the southern coast, and they stress that an immigration policy that relies mainly on border controls will never be very effective.

There are no internal controls on population movements in Spain, so illegal immigrants who succeed in gaining entry can move about freely by highway and train. In the early 1990s, a legal tool popularly known as the *"ley corcuera"* (named after the minister of justice who introduced the legislation) was used selectively by police to stop suspected illegals on the street and demand documents (Moroccans and black central Afri-

cans were the most likely to be questioned).[14] However, very few of the
aliens who have been apprehended in this and other ways in the interior
of the country were actually processed for expulsion: only one out of
twelve in Catalonia, for example.[15] Except in central Madrid, the police
and Civil Guard do not make routine sweeps of urban areas to detect
and apprehend illegal immigrants, and there have been no mass
roundups and deportations. Another legacy of the authoritarian Franco
era is to make such highly visible, repressive actions intolerable to most
Spaniards. Finally, power struggles between the Ministries of Labor and
Justice, the two agencies principally responsible for immigration law
enforcement, have impeded a sustained, well-coordinated effort to
sweep up and expel illegal immigrants already in the country.

Employer Sanctions

Penalties against employers who knowingly hire illegal immigrants
are included in the 1985 immigration law and were implemented
beginning in 1988, but these sanctions have had no discernible
deterrent effect on either employers or illegal foreign workers. The
existing legislation prescribes administrative penalties and fines of
Ptas 500,000 (about U.S.$5,000) per alien, but no criminal penalties.
Enforcement is through comprehensive workplace inspections by the
Ministry of Labor that are *not* limited to, or even focused upon,
immigration law enforcement; inspectors look for all sorts of violations, including nonpayment of legal minimum wages, avoidance of
social security payments, health and safety violations, nonadherence
to contractual agreements on working hours, vacations, and so forth.
For example, in Catalonia (including the city of Barcelona), immigration law infractions constituted only 2.7 percent of the violations
resulting in fines that were detected through workplace inspections
during 1991. Far more important were nonpayment of social security
(48 percent of all violations) and violations of health and safety

---

[14]The "*ley corcuera*" ostensibly was aimed at drug dealers and terrorists rather than
illegal foreign workers. It gave police the right to conduct warrant-less searches of
private residences (a provision that was declared unconstitutional in December 1993)
and required all residents to carry some form of personal identification. Those who
cannot produce proof of legal residence upon demand can be detained by police for up
to six hours, then turned over to immigration authorities for deportation.

[15]Representatives of the National Police in Barcelona claim that 12,000–12,500 "apprehensions" of illegal immigrants have been made each year, on average, in Catalonia
since the 1985 immigration law was implemented. However, according to statistics
provided by Fernando Cardenal, Gobernador Civil de Catalunya, the number of aliens
actually deported from Catalonia averaged only 1,030 per year between 1988 and 1991.
The large discrepancy is attributable to the "flexibility" that local authorities reportedly
exercise in cases of "minor" infractions of the 1985 immigration law. Usually, if
foreigners have not been accused of committing crimes (other than illegal entry into
Spain) they are not detained (interview with Francisco Javier Pereira Estévez, Policía
Nacional de España, May 1992).

standards (21 percent of the total).[16] In practice, the employers who are penalized for violating the immigration law typically are those who commit the most extreme abuses of *other* labor standards; they are not prosecuted simply for employing illegal immigrants (author interview with Joaquín Arango, May 1992).

The total fines imposed on the 285 Catalonian employers accused of violating immigration laws in 1991 amounted to about U.S.$1.7 million: an average of Ptas 739,456 (U.S.$7,395) per firm. A total of just 23 illegal immigrant workers were expelled as a result of the workplace inspections that generated these fines. The Ministry of Labor in Madrid reports that 10,381 workplace inspections were conducted nationwide during 1991, resulting in 1,986 cases in which employers were fined for immigration law violations. The total fines levied in 1991 were about U.S.$14 million; the average fine, per employer, was about U.S.$7,049.[17] Catalonian officials claim that 20–30 percent of all firms in the province are inspected each year (author interview with Salvador Alvarez, May 1992), but individual businessmen say they have experienced far fewer inspections than this effort would indicate. For example, a medium-sized employer in the Barcelona apparel industry recalled having had only three or four inspections by Ministry of Labor representatives during the past twenty-six years.

Officials at all levels acknowledge that there is still no targeting strategy for the enforcement of employer sanctions by economic sector, type of firm, or other criteria. In regions most heavily impacted by illegal immigration, like Catalonia, a backlog of uninvestigated complaints (made by individual workers, labor unions, neighbors, and so on) concerning the presence of illegal immigrants has accumulated.

The Interior Ministry sometimes accuses the Ministry of Labor of being too lax in enforcement of employer sanctions, but Ministry of Labor and provincial government officials cite a host of obstacles to effective enforcement. There are special enforcement problems in agriculture, fishing, transportation, and construction. These are all sectors where the workforce is less stable, where there are open-air work sites, where it is easier to conceal illegal immigrants, and so forth.

The huge underground economy—including domestic service, street vending, and small, unregistered firms of all sorts—presents an

---

[16]Data supplied by the Ministerio de Trabajo y Seguridad Social de Cataluyna, May 1992.

[17]Data provided by the Dirección General de Migraciones, Ministerio de Trabajo y Seguridad Social, Madrid, October 14, 1992. Statistics on employer sanctions enforcement for 1991, the most recent year for which complete data are available, may be atypically low because prosecutions for this offense reportedly were suspended during the immigrant legalization program carried out during six months of that year. Even if the figures reported for 1991 were doubled, however, they would constitute little more than a symbolic enforcement effort.

even more formidable challenge to immigration control via employer sanctions. As explained by one Spanish scholar:

> The basic problem is that there is a high level of toler-
> ance for the underground economy. Rapid economic
> growth in the 1980s did not create enough permanent,
> formal-sector jobs. Therefore, a large proportion of
> illegal immigrants as well as native-born workers are
> employed in the underground economy. If it were seri-
> ously disrupted, half of the total population could be
> left without work (author interview with Lidia Santos
> de Arnau, May 1992).

Less than aggressive enforcement of such laws can also be expected because of Spain's well-entrenched *cultura del empresario* ("culture of the businessman"). Businessmen are very influential in the unconventional Socialist government of Felipe González, and numerous observers believe that the closeness of government-business ties severely limits the enforcement of employer penalties for hiring illegal immigrants, as well as sexual discrimination statutes and sanctions against "*el delito social*" — e.g., failure by employers to pay social security and other legally mandated employee benefits. Prosecutions under the "social crime" law, which has been on the books for many years, are extremely rare.

The slowness and inefficiency of the Spanish administrative-judicial system in general pose additional obstacles to fair and effective employer sanctions enforcement. It is described by one magistrate as "an incredibly inefficient, time-consuming, counterproductive system, from the standpoint of immigration control" (author interview with Celsa Pico Lorenzo, May 1992). One indicator of the problem is the fact that, ironically, many enforcement actions arise from employer requests for government approval of work permits for foreign-born employees. Eventually inspectors are sent to check whether the applicant is actually working at a given firm. The employer, who has kept the foreign worker on the payroll during the lengthy adjudication period, is fined because the applicant has not yet received his legal work permit! Some employers, faced with interminable bureaucratic delays in hiring foreign workers *por la vía legal*, prefer to pay a fine rather than sacrifice a large order and lose market share within their industry.

Employers who find it difficult to recruit a legally resident workforce also have the option of "going offshore." This was the outcome of the most widely publicized case of employer sanctions enforcement in Spain to date. In June 1990 a large textile factory in the small Catalonian city of Vic was raided, and 76 of its employees—mostly illegal immigrants from Mo-rocco—were apprehended. The employer paid a heavy fine and imme-diately recruited native-born replacement workers from Andalucia, which has the highest regional unemployment rate in Spain. Even though the firm was paying at or above the legal minimum wage, it failed to retain the Andalusian workers, most of whom left after three weeks on the job, complaining that the work was not to their liking, that the city of Vic was "boring," and that they were too far from their families and hometowns. Eventually the employer gave up and moved his factory to Morocco.[18]

The same route—moving labor-intensive manufacturing operations to Third World countries having cheap, abundant labor supplies—is being chosen by increasing numbers of Spanish firms of all sizes. The owner of a leather products company in Barcelona summed up his options as follows: "[Because of labor market rigidities], the only way to survive is to turn Spain-based firms into commercializing and design operations, and do the manufacturing elsewhere" (author interview, May 1992). This businessman has already moved most of his manufacturing operations to Pakistan and India, reducing the workforce in his Barcelona plant from 135 in 1975 to 32 by mid-1992.

Various proposals have been made in recent years to strengthen the penalties for employers who hire illegal foreign workers. Under one proposed amendment to the penal code, such employers would be subject to fines of up to Ptas 15 million per worker (vs. the current fine of Ptas 500,000), as well as criminal penalties (jail terms of three months to six years). However, there is widespread skepticism, even among senior government officials, that such draconian penalties would ever be applied if approved by the Congress.[19] Moreover, a fine of about U.S.$150,000 per worker could easily put many small employers—the most likely offenders—out of business. Legal experts predict that much stiffer employer sanctions, if enacted, will actually *reduce* application of the law. Judges will consider the penalty disproportionate to the crime, and acquittals will be even more common than they already are (author interview with Lidia Santos Arnau and Blanca Vila Costa, Universidad Autónoma de Barcelona, May 1992).

Rather than vigorously pursue employers of illegal immigrants, the government's current preference is to focus enforcement efforts on the well-organized smuggling rings that introduce illegals into the workforce.[20] In 1994, for example, a selective crackdown was ordered on "*las mafias chinas*"

---

[18]This case illustrates an additional factor that tends to reduce the effective supply of native-born labor in Spain: the limited spatial mobility of much of the potential workforce. Spaniards traditionally have had stronger cultural and emotional ties to their local community and region than to the nation-state (see Pérez-Díaz 1993: 194–235). Despite significant internal migration from southern to northern Spain in the 1960s and 1970s, most workers remain resistant to uprooting themselves and their families from their native region.

[19]The Interior Ministry's top official for immigration policy, Fernando Puig de la Bellacasa, frankly conceded that "judges will be reluctant to apply such harsh penalties to businessmen" (author interview, May 1992).

[20]Statements by Fernando Puig de la Bellacasa, Undersecretary of the Interior (in *El País* 1994).

that supply illegal workers, mostly to Chinese-owned restaurants and garment factories, by having them pose as bona fide applicants for political asylum. The number of asylum applicants from China had risen suspiciously from just 26 in 1992 to 701 in 1993.

Visa Policy

Spain's second most important immigration policy concession to the other members of the European Community, after the 1985 immigration law, has been a tightening of visa control. Before 1991, entry visas were not required for citizens of the Magreb countries, and more than a half-million of them came to Spain, ostensibly as tourists, mostly by plane. In 1990 alone, more than 70,000 would-be illegal immigrants from the Magreb countries were "rejected" by Spanish authorities at coastal ports of entry, mostly in Algeciras, where ferries from Morocco land. Since the imposition of a visa requirement in 1991, fewer than 120,000 Magrebíes have entered Spain on visas issued in their home countries. The 1991 change in visa policy clearly has made entry into Spain from the Magreb countries more difficult, but there is no evidence that the clandestine flow of Magreb immigrants lacking visas has ended.

Spain's next concession to the European Community was to impose visa requirements on nationals of certain Latin American countries. This was a much more politically and diplomatically sensitive step than restricting entries from the Magreb countries. For several decades, many Latin American countries have had dual-nationality agreements with Spain, and Latin Americans are hardly perceived by Spaniards as "foreigners," given their shared linguistic and cultural attributes. "Requiring visas for Latin Americans posed great problems for the Spanish government. . . . It ran contrary to the policy followed by every Spanish government from Franco to the present Socialist government," which has played a leading diplomatic role in trying to forge an Iberoamerican community of nations (Díez Nicolás 1992).

The Latin American nations selected thus far for special visa treatment are Peru and the Dominican Republic, both countries that have been important sources of illegal immigration to Spain since the mid-1980s (especially women seeking domestic service jobs). To justify the selectivity of the visa policy shift, government officials cited advertisements promoting emigration to Spain that were placed in the newspapers of Lima, Peru, by people-smuggling rings which were transporting would-be illegal immigrants by air from Lima to Madrid via Paris (author interview with Fernando Puig de la Bellacasa, May 1992). The issuance of visas to citizens of Peru and the Dominican Republic is now highly restricted; among other requisites, evidence of substantial home-country financial assets and round-trip plane tickets must be presented. The burden of control has now been passed to the international airlines, which must repatriate at their own expense any Peruvians and Dominicans lacking proper entry visas upon arrival at Spanish airports.

Spanish officials see visa restriction as potentially a more effective instrument of immigration control than either border controls or employer sanctions. Nevertheless, there are clear economic limits to this approach for a country as dependent on tourism income as Spain. Spain ranks third in the world (after the United States and France) in the number of tourists it receives—more than 50 million per year. Tourism constitutes such an important sector of the Spanish economy that authorities cannot impose draconian visa restrictions on citizens of many labor-exporting countries without risking major economic damage.

Refugee Policy

In yet another effort to achieve harmonization with EC immigration policies, Spain in recent years has also tightened its refugee admissions policy. The task of adjusting its refugee policy posed greater legal difficulties for Spain than passing a general immigration law (the 1985 *ley de extranjería*). This is because Title One, Article Thirteen of the liberal, democratic constitution adopted by Spain after the demise of the Franco regime in 1978 includes the right to asylum as a fundamental, constitutionally protected human right, and states that "for humanitarian reasons," asylum petitioners "have the right to housing, public education, and social assistance" (Rives López 1989: 26).

Spanish officials explain that when the otherwise harsh 1985 immigration law was passed, it did not include restrictive provisions on refugee admissions because "we didn't anticipate the massive abuse of this mechanism that has occurred since then" (author interview with Fernando Puig de la Bellacasa, May 1992). The 1985 law even prescribes that persons whose applications for refugee status have been *denied* will have an additional three-month period in which they can apply for work and residence permits "through the normal procedure," i.e., as *economic migrants*, without risk of deportation.

The number of asylum applicants grew rapidly during the second half of the 1980s. New applications averaged about 11,600 per year during the 1990–1993 period. As the number of unfounded claims for refugee status mounted, the government raised the denial rate. By 1990, 93 percent of asylum applications were being rejected; in 1991 the rejection rate was nearly 96 percent, which was maintained through 1993.

Refugee advocates dispute the officially reported incidence of fraud in asylum claims. One of the largest refugee counseling groups estimates that if administrative deficiencies in the agencies responsible for processing refugee applications were eliminated, the valid rejection rate would be 70–75 percent rather than the present 96 percent. The alleged deficiencies include a virtual absence of serious investigation of individual cases on their merits; instead, determinations are made on the basis of "totally inadequate" reports filed by Spanish embassies on generalized political persecution conditions in the asylum seekers' countries of origin (CEAR 1991: 7).

Legitimate asylum applicants end up being "sacrificed" through this procedure, according to refugee advocates (author interview with María de Jesús Arsuaga, Director, Comisión Española de Ayuda al Refugiado, May 1992). They charge that Spanish officials now operate with a list of sending countries that dictates which refugee applications shall be rejected a priori—i.e., on the basis of country of origin alone. These countries are mainly African. Even the most minimal appearances of "democracy" (e.g., the holding of elections in authoritarian systems like that of Zaire) are considered sufficient for these countries to be declared free of political persecution. Under current policy, persons from former Soviet bloc countries in Eastern Europe can still apply for asylum, but economic assistance is denied to applicants from these countries because the government assumes that they are actually *economic* migrants whose petitions for refugee status will ultimately be denied. As noted above, asylum applications from Chinese nationals are now automatically assumed to be bogus because of the frequent use of the asylum mechanism by professional Chinese "people smugglers." Most immigrants from Morocco—who constitute the largest single contingent of illegal immigrants—do not even attempt to apply for refugee status.

It is obvious that significant—but hardly massive—numbers of purely economic migrants to Spain *have* tried to take advantage of the refugee mechanism. In response, the government shortened the adjudication process from one to two years before 1991 to a claimed average of about three months (author interview with Fernando Puig de la Bellacasa, May 1992). However, several specific immigrant *colectivos* (Peruvians, Angolans, Zairians) have reported that the adjudication period for their members still averages two to three years.

As a further disincentive to would-be asylum seekers, the government has also reduced the period of assured financial support for applicants. Economic assistance, provided by the government through the Red Cross and other nongovernmental organizations, is now limited to six months in most cases. The aid is also being dispensed more selectively, with asylum applicants from certain African, Latin American, and East European countries receiving nothing. Poles, for example, do not receive such assistance because they originate in a country now defined by the government as "democratic"; nevertheless, they constituted 29 percent of the applicants for refugee status during the 1990–1992 period.

Direct support payments to asylum applicants in 1992 were about U.S.$340 per month for an individual and U.S.$510 for a married couple, plus U.S.$50 per dependent child. The nongovernmental organizations that dispense this financial assistance point out that it is not sufficient for asylum seekers (especially family units) to support themselves in cities like Barcelona and Madrid, which have extremely high living costs. Therefore, virtually all refugee applicants work clandestinely to supplement their incomes (asylum applicants are *not* eligible to receive legal work permits).

The government claims, and refugee advocates agree, that the shortening of the refugee adjudication process (in most but clearly not all cases) and the new limits on economic support have discouraged illegal entry by this means. However, the flow of would-be refugees continues, albeit at a much diminished pace, and refugee advocates suggest that the only way to further diminish it would be to shorten the adjudication period even more drastically.

What happens to asylum seekers whose claims are denied? As noted above, they are legally entitled to an additional three-month period during which they may attempt to regularize their situation by obtaining work and residence permits. However, the vast majority of rejected refugee applicants fail even to attempt this last-ditch legalization maneuver; they simply disappear into the underground economy, and most are neither harassed nor expelled from the country. Like most industrialized countries today, Spain has no police or administrative apparatus capable of tracking rejected refugee applicants (or other foreigners whose visa status is temporary) and expelling them. Spain's de facto policy of denying virtually all asylum claims but allowing the applicants to remain in the workforce is criticized even by some officials as a thinly veiled, economically driven, backdoor immigration policy. "It is a policy that simply disguises what is really going on" (author interview with Celsa Pico Lorenzo, May 1992).

Legalization Programs

Spain has had three different legalization ("regularization") programs since 1985, the largest and most successful of which was conducted during the period of June 10–December 10, 1991. The earliest program— attempted in 1985–1986, at a time of great fear and confusion within the immigrant population caused by the recent enactment of the *ley de extranjería*—was poorly planned and publicized. It had little credibility in the eyes of distrustful illegal immigrants, and only 40,000 applications were received, of which 23,000 were approved (Colectivo Ioé 1992).

The government's next attempt was a special legalization program for Moroccans, conducted in the first quarter of 1991, ostensibly to rectify "administrative errors" in the previous, 1985–1986 legalization program. The "rectification" program succeeded in legalizing fewer than 3,000 Moroccans, again because of credibility and information dissemination problems. The legalization program begun in June 1991 was preceded by a government survey which found that the vast majority of illegal immigrants already residing in Spain intended to stay and eventually bring their families. These results are believed to have contributed to the government's decision to undertake a more extensive regularization program (author interview with Celsa Pico Lorenzo, May 1992).

The 1991 program was also a product of domestic politics. Major newspapers had published inflated estimates of the numbers of illegal immigrants, alarming public opinion; labor unions and immigrants rights and church groups were pressing for a broad amnesty. The government presented the 1991 legalization to the Spanish public as the "lid" to unwanted immigration—a program that would help those illegals already settled in the country while limiting access to Spain for potential newcomers (Hibbs 1994: 63). The program was implemented despite objections from other European Community nations, which opposed any sort of regularization program in Spain on the grounds that it would only encourage more illegal immigration from non-EC countries.

The main legalization program of 1991 was much more successful than its predecessors in getting people to apply.[21] To increase the credibility of the program, information and application materials were widely disseminated through NGOs, labor unions, and immigrant associations. Enforcement of employer sanctions through workplace inspections was temporarily suspended. Applicants were required to demonstrate that they had been living in Spain prior to May 15, 1991; that they had work contracts from employers; and that they had *arraigo* ("roots") in their local community, which could be demonstrated with children's school enrollment records, long-term housing rental contracts, membership in voluntary associations, and other means. A total of 110,067 illegal immigrants were regularized under this program and a much less successful follow-up effort to legalize family members of the primary applicants. Only about 6,500 dependents applied, reportedly because of distrust generated by long delays in delivery of legalization papers to the primary applicants.

Moroccans were the principal beneficiaries of the 1991 legalization program, accounting for more than 40 percent of the 128,127 applicants. According to immigrant service organizations, most of the 18,060 illegals whose applications for regularization were denied (in most cases because of missing or fraudulent documents) probably stayed in Spain;

---

[21]The best description of the program's structure and procedures can be found in Sagarra Trias et al. 1991.

theoretically, all of them are locatable and at risk of deportation. But, as in the case of foreigners who enter Spain on tourist or student visas and overstay them, there is no real tracking system; nor do the police have the manpower to round up and deport them.

The government estimates that as many as 200,000 illegal immigrants did not apply for regularization in 1991. Nevertheless, top immigration officials are adamant that the legalization program will not be repeated, despite considerable public support for further regularization efforts (see the penultimate section of this chapter). They contend that most of the new illegal immigration experienced by Spain since 1991 was encouraged by the regularization program. According to these officials, some of the post-1991 arrivals were deceived by people smugglers into thinking that they could still benefit from the 1991 amnesty; others simply hoped that they could participate in some future regularization program (author interviews with Fernando Puig de la Bellacasa and Raimundo Aragón Bombín, Director General de Migraciones, Ministerio de Trabajo, Madrid, 1992).

There is fragmentary evidence that the regularization program has encouraged some additional family reunification immigration. For example, newly regularized Moroccans are now bringing their spouses and children from the home country or intend to do so eventually, whatever the legal obstacles (Pumares 1993: 160–61). In any event, the government firmly believes that any debate over the need for another legalization program would only stimulate further illegal flows. Independent analysts dismiss as unrealistic the notion that 1991 will be Spain's last regularization.

Finally, there is growing concern about the fate of the newly legalized immigrants once their initial work contracts expire. Those regularized under the 1991 program were given only a one-year work permit, which limited them to a specific employer in a specific region. The employment instability inherent in Spain's now routinized short-term hiring practices, coupled with the legal requirement that regularized immigrants must renew their work permits annually for five years, may cause a large portion of them to drop into *la clandestinidad* again if their work contracts are not extended by employers.[22] Government statistics indicate that this is, in fact, occurring. By 1993, more than 25 percent of those who regularized themselves under the 1991 program had either been denied renewal of their initial work permits or did not seek renewal (Izquierdo Escribano 1993: 14–15). At this rate,

---

[22]The Ministry of Labor issues three types of work permits to foreigners. "A"-type work permits are for strictly temporary (under one year) employment in Spain; "B" permits are for one year but can be renewed annually for five years, after which the holder is eligible to apply for a "C" permit. The "C" permit is a long-term work permit for permanent legal immigrants; it is granted initially to only a minority of immigrants, mainly Latin American nationals. Illegal immigrants regularized through the 1991 program received "B" permits.

much of the beneficial effect of the legalization program will soon be undone.

The Social Integration of Immigrants

As yet, Spain has no comprehensive, well-defined policy to promote the social integration of foreign workers and their dependents. However, the government has not attempted to limit access to public schools or health care facilities for immigrants and their children, regardless of legal status. All immigrant children are encouraged to enroll in schools, and most are attending. The National Health Service offers free care and covers 100 percent of the population, including immigrants. There has been no attempt to limit emergency room and in-patient care for foreigners; a residence permit is, however, required to receive out-patient care (author interview with Jesús de Miguel, Universidad Central de Barcelona, May 1992). The Red Cross, Caritas, S.O.S. Racismo, and other nongovernmental agencies provide a variety of social services to immigrants, irrespective of legal status. These services, often dispensed through *centros de acogida* (social service centers) operated by the NGOs, are funded primarily by the government and the Catholic Church. They include child care for working mothers, Spanish language instruction, and legal aid. Illegal immigrants cannot collect unemployment compensation since they lack the work and residence permits necessary to qualify them for such assistance.

There is no evidence thus far that social service utilization by immigrants is excessive or fiscally burdensome to governments at any level. During 1992, for example, the Red Cross in Barcelona, one of the country's principal service providers for immigrants, handled an average of thirty-two new cases per month. Public officials who fund the services provided through NGOs do not complain of the costs, and social service utilization by foreigners has not yet become a public issue. However, most provincial and municipal governments have not established social service programs designed especially for immigrants, perhaps in hopes of avoiding complaints from native-born residents.

Spain's treatment of the "second generation"—the children born in Spain to illegal-immigrant parents—is much more problematic. These offspring have practically no legal rights or assured access to basic human services. For example, the 1985 immigration law guarantees public education only to the children of *legal* immigrants. While the public schools usually do not discriminate against the children of illegals in terms of enrollment, such children are not eligible for scholarships for post-elementary study; nor do they have access to vocational training at public institutions. Because of their irregular status, children of illegal immigrants finishing elementary school do not receive a *certificado de escolaridad* (diploma), and they are not eligible for work permits when they enter the labor force. Therefore it is exceptional for the native-born child of an illegal immigrant to gain legal entry into the labor market; most are limited to employment in the underground economy. "The practical consequence is that the immense majority of these children stay 'irregular' throughout their lives" (author interview with Lidia Santos Arnau and Blanca Vila Costa, May 1992).

In Spain, the nationality of children is determined by their parents' nationality (*jus sanguinis*), regardless of their place of birth. Foreigners can acquire Spanish citizenship through residence in the country, but it must be legal and continuous residence. Naturalizations are few (averaging 8,000–9,000 in recent years), with Moroccans, many of them residents of Spain since the early 1970s, accounting for more than a third of recent naturalizations.[23]

Access to housing is often more limited for immigrants, irrespective of legal status, than access to employment or social services. A great deal of antiforeigner discrimination is practiced by landlords, who claim to be concerned about potential drug traffic and other crime problems. As a result, severe overcrowding problems have developed in immigrant communities, with twenty persons (four to ten families) sometimes occupying a single apartment, and forty to fifty people living in a single garage (author interview with Isidoro Barba, S.O.S. Racismo, May 1992). In Madrid, Third World-style squatter settlements populated entirely by foreign workers and their families are proliferating, often occupying undeveloped plots of land sandwiched between middle- and upper-class residential areas. The city council of Madrid has recognized the existence of several of these settlements, affixing numbered metal plaques to each *chabola* (shack), which is typically constructed of discarded construction materials and sheets of plastic. Most of these irregular settlements do not have urban services except for electricity, which is "borrowed" from lines in adjacent neighborhoods. One of Madrid's most consolidated squatter settlements, begun five years ago, now has between 400–500 residents, virtually all of them Moroccans (Pumares n.d.). There are no known squatter settlements in Barcelona, where newly arriving immigrants have occupied low-rent apartments abandoned by earlier waves of internal migrants to Catalonia.

Overcoming housing discrimination and residential segregation is often cited as the acid test of the Spanish government's effort to promote immigrant assimilation (author interview with Raimundo Aragón Bombín, May 1992). Unfortunately, little progress can be identified in this area. More generally, officials as well as nongovernmental observers concede that not much social integration has occurred thus far among first-generation immigrants, especially those from Third World coun-

---

[23]Data from the Interior Ministry, Madrid.

tries. The principal exceptions are Latin American nationals, who are considered easy to assimilate because of their shared language and cultural traits. The sociocultural integration of other immigrant groups has been highly uneven. For example, Senegalese and other black Africans who arrive relatively well educated are incorporated readily into the economy and suffer from less historically grounded prejudice than immigrants from the Magreb countries. The Spain-born children of immigrants, regardless of nationality, seem to be integrating well, at least linguistically, through the public school system; the vast majority of such children are bilingual. However, if their parents are illegal immigrants, they face the formidable post-school barriers to economic mobility described above.

Public Opinion and the Politics of Immigration

On the surface Spaniards are remarkably tolerant of the influx of "new immigrants" that has occurred since the mid-1980s, especially by comparison with their counterparts elsewhere in Western Europe and the United States. Sample surveys reveal that their general attitudes toward immigrants are benign and even, in some respects, sympathetic. Most Spaniards accept the need for controls on immigration from less developed countries (majorities of 59 percent and 61 percent in two recent national opinion surveys),[24] but only a third or less believe that there are too many foreigners living in Spain (33 percent in the CIS survey of 1991; 28 percent in the CIRES survey of 1994).[25]

This high level of acceptance is all the more remarkable given the fact that Spaniards are willing to blame foreigners for exacerbating a variety of social and economic problems in their country. In one survey, 59 percent agreed that immigrants from less developed countries have caused more unemployment among Spaniards; 42 percent believed that they depressed wages for native-born workers; and 56 percent blamed immigration for an increase in crime (CIRES 1994). In this and earlier opinion surveys, hostility toward foreigners was found to be greater among lower-class Spaniards (presumably because they are more likely to view immigrants as potential competitors for jobs) and among residents of the largest metropolitan areas (where crime, overcrowding, and other "big city" problems are more likely to be blamed on immigrants).

---

[24]Respectively: CIRES 1994; CIS 1992. The CIS survey involved a nationwide probability sample of 17,800 persons interviewed in April and May 1991.

[25]CIRES 1994; CIS 1992. A 1991 national survey of Spanish public opinion toward immigration, also conducted by CIRES, found only 12 percent expressing the view that too many foreigners were living in the country—evidence that anti-immigrant sentiment has risen significantly during the 1990s.

At the same time, Spaniards in general claim to be highly supportive of the rights of the foreigners already working in their country. Eighty percent believe that illegal immigrants should be given a chance to regularize their status, at least if they have regular employment; only 20 percent feel that they should be forced to return to their country of origin. Two out of three Spaniards believe that the government should guarantee immigrants' access to housing; more than 80 percent believe that it should also guarantee access to public health care. Two-thirds believe that foreigners working legally in Spain should be able to vote in all elections. However, Spaniards are evenly divided on the issue of whether permanent settlement of immigrants (with their dependents) should be encouraged or whether the foreigners should remain temporary workers, sans family members (CIRES 1994; CIS 1992).

Disaggregated analyses of public opinion data reveal some important variations in tolerance, depending mainly on country of origin. The results of several national and regional survey studies show a clear hierarchy of acceptance or preference regarding the integration of various nationalities into Spanish society, with Latin Americans at the top, followed by East Europeans, black central Africans (Senegalese, Gambians, etc.), and North African Arabs (Moroccans, Algerians, Tunisians) at the bottom. For example, 58 percent consider the social integration of North African Arabs to be problematic or very problematic, while only 30 percent see Latin American and East European immigrants as difficult to assimilate.[26]

Much of the Spaniards' hostility toward North Africans is rooted in centuries-old fear of *"los moros,"* who are today associated with Islamic fundamentalism as well as a high propensity to commit crimes. Anti-Moroccan attitudes also reflect the strong bias of many Spaniards against anyone of lower social-class background. Even some public officials candidly admit that the countries of origin for much of Spain's new immigration constitute a "problem," and they express a longing for "better quality, more skilled labor. . . . We want more Poles and other East Europeans, and fewer Africans" (author interview with a senior official in Barcelona, May 1992).

Setting aside these variations in tolerance for different nationalities, how can we explain the generally positive view of immigrants that is revealed in surveys of Spanish public opinion? One factor is the widespread belief that parts of Spain's economy could not function without foreign workers. "What the public accepts without complaint is having cheap labor" to perform tasks shunned by the average Spaniard (author interview with Carlota Solé, Universidad Autónoma de Barcelona, May 1992). Interestingly, survey data also show that while a majority (54

---

[26]CIRES 1994. These results are mirrored by those of the CIS national survey of 1991, and a 1991 survey of 1,600 Barcelona residents directed by Carlota Solé (unpublished data, Depto. de Sociología, Universidad Autónoma de Barcelona).

percent) of Spaniards believe that foreign workers are performing the jobs that Spaniards don't wish to do, only a small minority believe that foreign labor is absolutely necessary to supplement domestic labor supplies. For example, 62 percent agree that foreign workers occupy jobs that *could* be filled by Spaniards, particularly young people (CIS 1992).

Pro-immigrant attitudes on human and political rights issues may be another element of the Franco legacy. Since the democratization movement that began in 1976, Spain has been seized by the goal of becoming a "modern, European democracy": liberal, tolerant, with sensitivity for social justice, defense of the weak, and so forth. Racist, xenophobic attitudes would be incompatible with these ideals. The same explanation is frequently given for the absence in Spain of any overtly anti-immigrant movement or political party, which distinguishes Spain from all other West European countries today. The conventional wisdom among political professionals and social scientists is that most Spaniards would label anyone espousing explicitly nativist views as a right-wing extremist—a throwback to the discredited Fascist past. Since the only votes for nativist policies are on the far right, no Spanish political party, they argue, would dare to latch onto the immigration issue.

Moreover, Spain's principal business and labor organizations are either indifferent or openly pro-immigrant. While not taking an explicit, public position on immigration policy, the Confederación Española de Organizaciones Empresariales (CEOE), the nation's largest employers association, expresses concern about the deepening labor shortage in some sectors of the economy and sees importation of foreign labor as a necessity to deal with it (author interview with the director, Depto. de Asuntos Laborales, CEOE, May 1992). The two principal labor union confederations, the Comisiones Obreras (CCOO) and the Unión General de Trabajadores (UGT), welcome immigrants, legal or illegal, as members. They provide some direct support services to immigrants and press the government to do more to provide them with decent housing, education, and social services in order to accelerate their social and economic integration (interview with Immaculada Simón and Inés Ayala, UGT, May 1992; UGT/CCOO 1991). In sum, "nowhere on the political spectrum do you find a significant group capable or willing to try to whip up nativist sentiment" (author interview with Jesús de Miguel, May 1992).

While most observers accept this as an accurate characterization of the politics of immigration in Spain at present, some warn that high levels of tolerance for immigration, particularly from the Third World, may be only a temporary phenomenon in Spain. They point out that, in regions like Catalonia, most residents have little consciousness of the fact that the new foreign immigrants are different from earlier waves of internal migrants who were successfully assimilated into the local culture; that Spaniards in general have had very little personal interaction with the foreigners in their country;[27] that they get most of their information about immigrants from the mass media, which convey an unremittingly negative image of foreigners as sources of various societal problems; and that many interviewees in public opinion surveys may be giving "politically correct" or "socially desirable" answers that are not indicative of their true feelings.[28] Still others point to the long tradition of racism directed at one of Spain's domestic minority groups, the Gypsies (*gitanos*), who are almost universally identified in the public mind with crime. Because a significant minority of immigrants are also involved in petty crime, it is argued that anti-*gitano* hostility could easily be transferred to foreigners (interview with Tomás Calvo Buezas, Universidad Complutense de Madrid, May 1992; see also Calvo Buezas 1990).

The working hypothesis among some Spanish social scientists and public officials concerned about the evolution of public attitudes toward immigration is that intolerance will prove to be a threshold phenomenon: its emergence is simply a question of time and numbers. Eventually the growth of the foreign worker population, especially the permanent settler component, will be sufficient to provoke a public backlash. This outcome could easily be accelerated by prolonged economic recession or by any attempt by immigrants to assert their cultural differences, "like the Arab girls in France who insist on attending school with veils."[29] Already, according to a content analysis of newspaper coverage, the incidence of hate crimes and threats against immigrants in Catalonia has risen sharply, and "skinhead" attacks on black African and Dominican immigrants have occurred recently in both Madrid and Barcelona.[30]

Other knowledgeable observers insist that an anti-immigrant backlash in Spain is not inevitable, especially if strong labor market segmentation persists. As long as foreigners do not compete for the kinds of jobs held by native Spaniards, the economic benefits of their presence will

[27]In a national sample of Spaniards interviewed in September 1990, 82 percent of the respondents rated themselves as "poorly informed" or "not informed at all" about the issue of immigrants in Spain (CIS 1991). In the CIRES survey of 1994, only 10 percent of the respondents reported having immigrants from less developed countries as co-workers, and only 11 percent lived in a neighborhood with an appreciable Third World immigrant presence.

[28]Many respondents in these surveys portray *themselves* as highly accepting of immigrants, but they attribute lower tolerance for foreigners to their "*relatives and friends*" and to the Spanish population as a whole. To one analyst of these results, they suggest that "respondents give the answers that they consider more socially acceptable, and project onto others their own true attitudes" (Díez Nicolás 1992: 22).

[29]Interview with Joaquim Saurina i Fiol, May 1992. Fernando Cardenal, civil governor of Catalonia, expressed similar concerns: "There is a lot of paternalism and sentimentality about immigrants in Spain—an explosive combination. Most Spaniards reject the notion that they are racists, but when they have a personal experience of some sort, this 'tolerance' is put to the test. It's still a big deal if your daughter marries someone from the next village!" (author interview, May 1992).

[30]Unpublished data provided by Federic Javaloy i Mazón, Departament de Psicología Social, Universidad de Barcelona.

override cultural-racial objections and ambivalent attitudes toward immigration will continue. After all, they point out, Spain until relatively recently was a country of emigration, and the many thousands of Spaniards who themselves were international migrants have a sense of solidarity with the foreigners in their midst.[31]

Spain's Alternative Immigration Futures

Tightening Immigration Restrictions under EC Pressure

In 1985, Spain responded to its European neighbors worried about the laxity of Spanish immigration controls by passing the *ley de extranjería*. The initiation of a visa requirement for the Magreb countries in 1991, and for selected Latin American countries in 1992, was another response to pressure from the European Community. With anti-immigrant sentiment on the rise throughout Europe, reinforced by persistent economic stagnation or slow growth, Spanish officials anticipate continuing pressure from other members of the European Community as well as the Schengen Group (to which Spain belongs) to tighten Spain's immigration controls. Under these conditions, how much latitude will Spain have to fashion its own policy in this area?

It is generally conceded that Spain must take its share of responsibility for securing the European Community's external borders. At least half of the general public appears to support adherence to EC-mandated restrictions on immigration.[32] The Felipe González government insists that Spain must be one of the six or seven key players in achieving the goals of the Maastricht Treaty on European union, and it has invested considerable political capital in convincing the Spanish public that achieving "convergence" with the rest of the EC is the best route to higher economic growth and living standards in Spain. Thus Spain cannot afford to sully its image in Europe by appearing to ignore immigration pressures.

All this leads some critical observers to predict that Spain will be increasingly, perhaps excessively, responsive to external pressures for immigration restriction in the remainder of the 1990s. Government spokesmen insist that they will fight to have a "realistic" immigration

---

[31] Other scholars and public officials are not so sanguine about the potential moderating effect of Spain's emigration experience of the 1960s and early 1970s on contemporary public attitudes toward foreign immigration. Even former migrants, they point out, can be strongly prejudiced, especially toward immigrants (e.g., Moroccans, black Africans) who are culturally and racially very different from the host population.

[32] In the 1991 CIS national survey of public opinion on immigration (CIS 1992), 50 percent expressed the view that the Spanish government should abide totally or partially by the restrictive measures imposed by the EC; 22 percent felt that the Spanish government should reject such measures and do whatever it considers best for the country; and 28 percent had no opinion.

policy. As stated by one of the top two immigration policy makers in the González government:

> Other EC members talk about the need for a "zero-immigration" policy, but this is completely unrealistic for Spain, and even for countries like France, Germany, and Italy, which continue to have a need for large numbers of foreigners in some sectors of their economies. Other countries are being blind and hypocritical. . . . We want them to recognize Spain's objective need for foreign labor. Spaniards won't do certain kinds of jobs, and we need to channel foreign labor to meet these needs.[33]

This argument is echoed by many Spanish intellectuals, who are scathingly critical of what they regard as the "bad faith" shown by EC countries that criticize Spain for being the backdoor for unauthorized immigration to Europe:

> All the other EC countries have their labor supply assured, but we're told not to import any foreign workers. In an era of stiff international competition, it would be irrational for Spain to accept this. If certain sectors of the economy don't have an adequate labor supply, this could be detrimental to Spain's overall economic performance (author interview with Ana Cabré, May 1992).

Spain is likely to pursue a three-pronged strategy in its effort to address both EC pressures and domestic needs in this policy area. First, it will accept without complaint the Schengen Group's insistence on police-type control measures, which will not shut off the flow of foreign labor but will provide a convenient rationalization for making some policy changes that the Spanish government wants to make anyway. These "concessions" to the other European countries carry a low domestic political cost, and they can be exchanged for EC concessions in other areas of greater importance to the Spanish government (such as the amount of deficit reduction, inflation control, and other macroeconomic policy changes needed to achieve "convergence" with other EC countries).

Second, Spain will continue its recently adopted policy of "differentiation" in visa requirements for Latin Americans. Having abandoned its

---

[33] Author interview with Fernando Puig de la Bellacasa, May 1992. These comments were echoed in a more recent interview (see *El País* 1994).

traditional policy of allowing entry by all Latin Americans without visas, Spain will now require them of citizens of a growing list of Latin American countries that pose special problems (actual or potential) for EC countries: drug traffic, terrorism, or illegal immigration (author interview with Guadalupe Ruiz-Giménez, Spanish member of the European Parliament, May 1992).

Third, Spain will try to convince its EC partners to invest more heavily in the economic development of the Magreb countries. Spanish officials complain that the other EC countries worry too much about east-west migration (a temporary phenomenon that will stabilize within a few years) and too little about south-north migration (a long-term, structural problem). Spain will argue that substantial development assistance targeted to key labor-exporting countries must be part of the European immigration control effort (author interviews with Fernando Puig de la Bellacasa and Ricardo Aragón Bombín).

Such a package, if accepted by Spain's EC partners, does offer a certain margin of flexibility for Spanish immigration policy. Already Spain seems to be moving to take advantage of the latitude it expects to have in this area, which may be even greater if plans for more complete European union continue to disintegrate.

Gradually Expanding Immigration through a Quota System

By 1992 a consensus had formed in Spanish officialdom around the need to design a system that would legally admit the number of foreign workers that Spain needs economically and is capable of integrating socioculturally. Despite the deepening recession, such a quota system (*política de cupos*) was implemented in 1993, with the first-year ceiling set at 20,600.[34] The basic idea of the "*cupos*" policy is that the government will work with employers to ensure that their labor requirements are met, while conveying to the general public the sense that the policy makers are "in control" and "doing something" about unwanted immigration.

Immigration quotas already existed in some subsectors of the Spanish economy (e.g., in the tourist sector, for tour guides; in the education sector, for English language instructors; in the agricultural sector, for grape pickers in Catalonia). The new system sets labor quotas for broad sectors of the economy (domestic service, construction, agriculture, etc.) and for each region of the country. It is ostensibly modeled on the U.S. immigration quota system but in fact is much more labor market- and employer-driven than the U.S. system. "The basic principle will be that our economy can absorb x number of workers in a given

---

[34]This quota is drastically scaled down from the 100,000 figure widely discussed among officials during most of 1992. Clearly it was feared that the larger quota would be too politically sensitive at a time when Spain's economic recession was deepening.

sector, in a given region" (author interview with Joaquim Saurina i Fiol, May 1992). Quotas proposed by the Ministry of Labor will be negotiated with employers and labor unions in various sectors of the economy on an annual basis. Two types of work permits are offered under the new quota system: long-term (permanent) and temporary (duration unspecified).

The government claims to have the administrative capacity to implement a labor market-driven quota system, using information supplied by the National Unemployment Survey (conducted monthly using government employment offices), the National Institute of Employers, various professional organizations (*colegios, gremios*), and the country's two principal labor confederations. Nevertheless, questions abound: Which economic sectors and job categories will be included each year, and according to what criteria? How will the appropriate mix of temporary and permanent workers be determined? What mechanism will be created to ensure the repatriation of workers with temporary permits? (The government promises to conclude agreements with key sending countries, especially Morocco, "to guarantee return once the worker's contract has expired" [*El País* 1992].) The government acknowledges the complexity of working out such a system but considers full implementation feasible within a few years, and expects it to have broad public support.[35]

The government also hopes that channeling foreign workers to the most labor-short sectors of the economy through a quota system will retard the flight of Spanish manufacturing enterprises to Morocco and other Third World, cheap-labor countries and provide incentives for new foreign investment in Spain. "Spain still promotes itself to foreign investors as having a cheap labor supply," observed one official, "but it can no longer *deliver* that labor supply without foreign immigration" (author interview with Joaquim Saurina i Fiol, May 1992). In fact, Spain is in some danger of pricing itself out of the foreign investment market. In recent years, wage increases have been some three points above the rate of inflation, and while labor is still considerably cheaper in Spain than in Germany, industrial wages are nearly equivalent to those in Britain (see *Economist* 1992: 18).

A temporary worker program limited to Moroccans was considered by the government during 1992, but the newly established quota system subsumes this idea by creating a small, de facto guestworker program

---

[35]The 1992 CIRES survey found that 47 percent of the public would support a quota system that included limits on the occupations that could be filled by foreigners, their nationality, the length of time they would spend in Spain, or other types of restrictions. The 1994 CIRES survey found that 34 percent of the public would support a quota system with such restrictions. However, an additional 11 percent indicated that they would support an *unrestricted* quota system, and only 29 percent of the total sample felt that a quota of 20,000 immigrants per year was excessive. ("Don't know" and missing responses are excluded from these tabulations.)

not limited by nationality. Clearly, foreigners with temporary work permits will fit the needs of some sectors with highly variable labor demand (e.g., hotels, agriculture, construction) better than other sectors requiring stable, year-round labor (domestic service, most kinds of manufacturing). But, based on much European and U.S. experience, "leakage" of some holders of temporary work permits into permanent jobs in the mainstream economy will be impossible to prevent. If such leakage is viewed as excessive, it could be politically costly to the government. Many Spaniards have a preference for *temporary* migrants who arrive without dependents, and they want to avoid family reunification immigration. A national survey conducted in 1992 found that Spaniards preferred unaccompanied, temporary workers over permanent immigrants with dependents by a 46 to 36 percent margin; a comparable 1994 survey found public opinion evenly divided on this question.[36]

The performance of the quota system implemented in 1993 remains in doubt. By October 1993, only 3,600 workers had been admitted under this system. Interior Ministry officials blamed the economic recession, which sharply reduced job offers, for the failure to fill the first-year quota of 20,600. However, it is equally plausible that many employers who use foreign labor are comfortable with well-established, informal recruitment mechanisms and simply wish to avoid further entanglement in government bureaucracy. A true test of the system, and of the breadth of public support for it, must await Spain's recovery from the 1990s recession.

A Severely Restrictive Immigration Policy Driven by Nativist Backlash

To most Spanish officials and academics, this is the "worst case" scenario. Its underlying assumption is that Spain harbors a latent current of racist, xenophobic sentiment that could eventually be mobilized by an extremist, "Le Pen"-style party or movement.[37] In a deep, prolonged economic recession, public tolerance for immigration could diminish rapidly.

Some members of the government favor pursuing a more restrictive immigration policy now, to prevent a generalized anti-immigrant backlash in the future. Others hope to avert such a reaction primarily by cracking down on "alien crime," which they consider to be the greatest potential source of xenophobia (see, for example, *El País* 1994). Indeed, surveys show that the average Spaniard perceives a strong relationship

---

[36]CIRES surveys of 1992 and 1994. "Don't know" and missing responses are excluded from the tabulations.

[37]There is no Spanish "Le Pen" on the scene, as yet. The mayor of the small city of Marbella in Andalucia province is the only overtly racist, anti-immigrant politician in the country who has received any media attention, and his following is highly localized.

between immigration and crime, especially street crime and drug traffic.[38] Graffiti expressing this association is omnipresent in Madrid and Barcelona.

Statistically, foreigners do not commit a disproportionate share of crime in Spain. Of the 128,000 illegal immigrants who applied for regularization in 1991, fewer than 3,000 were found to have any criminal record (author interview with Fernando Puig de la Bellacasa, May 1992). Even in Barcelona, which has the country's highest per capita concentration of foreign-born people, only 15 percent of all crimes in 1991 were committed by aliens.[39] Moreover, a high percentage of the crimes committed by foreigners in Spain are petty thefts and other "economic survival" crimes. Nevertheless, officials report an upward trend in alien crime, due primarily to the growing involvement of foreigners in drug trafficking as well as more frequent recourse to crime in order to get by during the 1990s recession (author interviews with Francisco Javier Pereira Estévez, Jefe de la Sección Operativa de Extranjeros, Policía Nacional de España, and Fernando Cardenal, Gobernador Civil de Catalonia, May 1992). Politicians who are increasingly fearful of a nativist backlash favor changes in the existing legal system, which makes it very difficult to deport aliens accused of crime in a timely manner.

Of course, the three "alternative futures" of Spanish immigration policy sketched above are not mutually exclusive. Indeed, some combination of the first two scenarios, in which economic considerations rather than political-cultural variables drive the policy, seems most plausible. The "worst case" scenario of draconian restrictions enacted under intense public pressure is one that probably can be avoided through a combination of moderate immigration control measures like those now being implemented.

If the currently unfolding experiment with a quota system for immigration proves unsuccessful, Spain's long-term strategy may be to export as many as possible of its labor-intensive activities to Third World countries with cheap, abundant labor supplies. However, in the view of most experts on the Spanish economy, the costs of such an approach would outweigh the conceivable benefits, while leaving intact all the rigidities and inefficiencies of the Spanish labor market and bureaucratic structure that helped to create the present illegal immigration problem. These analysts would concur with the assessment of the Ministry of

---

[38]For example, the CIS survey of 1991 (CIS 1992) found that 52 percent of a national sample saw a strong or very strong relationship between the presence of immigrants in Spain and drug trafficking; 44 percent perceived such a relationship with crime in general (*"la inseguridad ciudadana"*). In the 1994 CIRES survey, drug trafficking was mentioned by more respondents (35 percent) than any other problem that they saw being caused by immigrants.

[39]Data provided by Fernando Cardenal, May 1992.

Labor's senior immigration policy maker Raimundo Aragón Bombín:
"For Spain, there is simply no alternative to immigration" (author
interview, May 1992).

References

Ahrens, J.M. 1993. "Desmantelada una red que introdujo ilegalmente a per-
uanos en España," *El País* [Madrid], November 5.

Cabré, Ana, and Isabel Pujadas. 1987. "La fecundidad en Cataluña desde 1922:
análisis y perspectivas." Papers de Demografía 20. Barcelona: Centre d'Es-
tudis Demogràfics, Universitat Autònoma de Barcelona.

Calvo Buezas, Tomás. 1990. *¿España racista? — Voces payas sobre los gitanos*. Barcelona: Anthropos.

CEAR (Comisión Española de Ayuda al Refugiado). 1991. "Puntos de vista de
CEAR sobre la comunicación del Gobierno al Congreso de los Diputados
sobre '*La situación de los extranjeros en España: líneas básicas de la política española
de extranjería*'." Madrid: CEAR. Unpublished.

Chesnais, Jean-Claude. 1990. "The Africanization of Europe?" *American Enterprise*, May–June.

CIRES (Centro de Investigaciones sobre la Realidad Social). 1994. "Survey on
Attitudes toward Immigrants." Madrid: CIRES. Unpublished report.

CIS (Centro de Investigaciones Sociales). 1991. "Estudio C.I.S. NÁ 1882: Inmigración y racismo." Madrid: CIS.

———. 1992. "Estudios C.I.S. NÁ 1964: Inmigración." Madrid: CIS. Unpublished.

Colectivo Ioé. 1989. *El servicio doméstico en España: entre el trabajo invisible y la
economía sumergida*. Madrid: Juventud Obrera Cristiana de España.

———. 1991a. "Inmigrantes indocumentados en España," *L'Evenement Européenne* (Paris) 11: 135–54.

———. 1991b "Foreign Women in Domestic Service in Madrid, Spain." Working
Paper MIG WP.51.E. Geneva: World Employment Programme, International
Labour Organisation.

———. 1992. "Los trabajadores extranjeros en España: informe para el Instituto
Sindical de Estudios." Madrid: Colectivo Ioé. Unpublished.

———. 1993. "Rasgos generales y perfil sociodemográfico de las principales
colonias." In *Inmigrantes extranjeros en Madrid, Tomo I*, edited by Carlos
Giménez Romero. Madrid: Consejería de Integración Social, Comunidad de
Madrid.

Díez Nicolás, Juan. 1992. "Cultural and Economic Factors That Shape Spanish
Attitudes toward Immigrants." Paper presented at the Center for U.S.-Mexican
Studies, University of California, San Diego, November.

Durán, Luis Fernando. 1992. "Un inmigrante dominicano, brutalmente agredido
en Madrid," *El País*, December 30.

Economist, The. 1992. "A Survey of Spain," April 25–May 1.

El País [Madrid]. 1992. "[Ministerio del] Interior fijará un cupo anual de inmigrantes a partir de 1992," September 26.

———. 1994. "Fernando Puig de la Bellacasa: 'Seremos inflexibles con la delin-
cuencia extranjera,'" January 10.

Giménez Romero, Carlos. 1992. "Madrid y la cuestión inmigrante," *Alfoz* (Madrid) 91–92.

———. 1993a. "Madrid y el desafío de la inmigración." In *Inmigrantes extranjeros en Madrid, Tomo I: Panorama general y perfil sociodemográfico*, edited by C. Giménez Romero. Madrid: Consejería de la Integración Social, Comunidad de Madrid.

Giménez Romero, Carlos, ed. 1993b. *Inmigrantes extranjeros en Madrid, Tomo II: Estudios monográficos de colectivos inmigrantes*. Madrid: Consejería de Integración Social, Comunidad de Madrid.

Hibbs, Cynthia R. 1994. "Immigration Policy and the Quotidian Hassles of Being: Foreign Workers in Madrid and San Diego." M.A. thesis, University of California, San Diego.

Izquierdo Escribano, Antonio. 1992. "España: la inmigración inesperada," *Mientras Tanto* (Fundación Giulia Adinolfi) 49 (March–April).

———. 1993. "Semejanzas y diferencias en el perfil demográfico y laboral de los marroquíes que solicitaron la regularización en 1985 y en 1991." Madrid: Universidad Complutense de Madrid. Unpublished.

López García, Bernabé. 1992. "Las migraciones magrebíes y España," *Alfoz* 91–92.

Ministerio del Interior. 1992. "Regularización de inmigrantes 1991." Madrid, March 10.

Pascual de Sans, Angels, and Jordi Cardelus. 1990. *Migració i historia personal: investigació sobre la mobilitat des de la perspectiva del retorn*. Barcelona: Bellaterra.

Pérez-Díaz, Víctor M. 1993. *The Return of Civil Society: The Emergence of Democratic Spain*. Cambridge, Mass.: Harvard University Press.

Pumares, Pablo. 1993. "La inmigración marroquí." In *Inmigrantes extranjeros en Madrid, Tomo II*, edited by Carlos Giménez Romero. Madrid: Consejería de Integración Social, Comunidad de Madrid.

———. n.d. Ph.D. dissertation in progress, Consejo Superior de Investigación Científica, Madrid.

Riding, Alan. 1992. "For González, 10 Years in Power, One More Race," *New York Times*, October 26.

Rives López, Isabel. 1989. *La Ley de Extranjería*. Madrid: Decálogo.

Sagarra Trias, Eduard, et al. 1991. *El trabajador extranjero y la regularización de 1991*. ITINERA Cuadernos, No. 1. Barcelona: Fundación Paulino Torras Domènech.

UGT/CCOO. 1991. "Proceso de regulación de trabajadores extranjeros: resolución adoptada por UGT y CCOO." Madrid: UGT/CCOO, December 10.

Commentary

Bringing International Political Economy into the Immigration Picture

Colectivo Ioé
(Carlos Pereda, Miguel A. de Prada, and Walter Actis)

The subjects of immigration policy can only be understood from an international perspective. Although immigrants are employed in industrialized countries, we must necessarily refer to their countries of origin as a point of reference. In the case of undocumented immigrants, this is generally the countries of the Third World. Because immigrants are part of this larger picture, it is not sufficient to consider only the economic, legislative, and administrative features of industrialized countries. We must also examine the conditions in labor-exporting countries and, especially, the relationship that exists between them and the labor importers.

According to classical political economy, this relationship is a three-sided process of exchange: of capital, commodities, and labor. Since 1982 the balance of capital flows between North and South has favored the North; in the second half of the 1980s the net transfer of capital generated in the South and absorbed by the North was equivalent to four Marshall Plans (or U.S.$300 billion). Regarding the exchange of commodities, the North (including Europe, Japan, and the United States) has raised tariff and nontariff barriers against the more competitive products of the countries of the South. Labor flows move relatively freely in a north-south direction, following investment capital and export commodities, but they are strictly controlled when the flow goes from south to north (with the exception of highly skilled workers, who are privileged under certain policies, such as in the U.S. quota system).

Translated by Aníbal Yáñez.

Wayne Cornelius accurately defines Spain's position within the international community. After the Franco era ended, Spain joined the OECD, NATO, and the European Community, and it is currently a candidate for membership in an expanded Group of Seven. Thus, despite Spain's intermediate level of development, it is clearly positioned economically, politically, and militarily alongside the most industrialized Western countries. In the area of immigration, this translates into ever tighter restrictions on the entry of immigrants from the Third World (through visa requirements for Filipinos, North Africans, and Latin Americans, stricter entry requirements for political refugees, and so on) at the same time that Spain opens her borders to the wealthy nations—the EC member countries and the United States.

Most immigration to Spain comes from Morocco (there were approximately 64,000 Moroccans residing legally in Spain in 1992). Morocco has, since 1983, been following an economic adjustment program dictated by the World Bank and the International Monetary Fund (with the backing of the developed countries). This economic program has required sharp cutbacks in social spending and in the level of support for export agriculture, with dramatic social consequences: a crisis of the traditional peasantry, internal migration to and overcrowding in urban areas, and a generally deteriorating standard of living. A portion of Morocco's displaced populations is forced to emigrate, often to Spain as illegal workers. Although the wealthy nations support the adjustment strategy that the World Bank and the IMF imposed on Morocco as necessary to correct that country's severe economic imbalances, these same nations accept no responsibility for the social consequences of adjustment, including emigration.

Within European capitalism we are witnessing an important evolution from the Keynesian or Fordist model toward a neoliberal model. Examining this shift and its social effects may help clarify how new immigrants are admitted to and channeled within the labor markets of receiving countries. Factors to consider include increased labor market segmentation, the proliferation of temporary jobs, the crisis of the welfare state, and the new roles assigned to labor unions.

The evolution of Spain's economy after World War II followed the course of Europe as a whole, but with some lags and peculiarities. Cornelius describes the process in terms of a shift from the "rigidities" of Francoism to the "flexibility" of liberal democracy. However, this characterization may overemphasize the juridical and political aspects of the process while slighting its economic and social dimensions, which have as much or more explanatory weight as the former. If we examine the economic and social aspects, we find that in the 1965–1970 period the foundations were laid for an urban, industrial society with the expansion of the middle class and the emergence of an incipient welfare state. Full employment was possible in this period thanks to the emigration to

Central Europe of more than 1 million Spaniards displaced by agricultural modernization. Their remittances contributed significantly to the financing of Spain's development (representing nearly 3 percent of GDP and 15 percent of gross capital formation in the early 1970s).

When postwar Europe's model of capitalist development entered into crisis in the early 1970s, the impacts in Spain coincided with the beginning of that country's democratic process. In the 1980s, the Socialist Party government based its economic strategy on opening to the international economy (including membership in the European Community) and supporting major domestic and foreign capital. Social concertation agreements between the government and unions reduced workers' purchasing power for several years. By the time the economy recovered, between 1986 and 1991, the features of the labor market differed significantly from what they had been under the protectionist state of the late 1960s and early 1970s. By the last half of the 1980s the salient features of Spain's labor market were: (1) the spread of temporary employment to one-third of the workforce; (2) the increased importance of the informal economy; and (3) structural unemployment (over 15 percent of the economically active population were unemployed during the 1980s). These features explain what followed when recession reappeared in 1991: temporary employment quickly became unemployment when a half-million jobs disappeared within a six-month period, and the unemployment rate rose to 21 percent of the economically active population by March 1993.

A contributing factor was the spread in the international economy of new technologies in the areas of information and robotics, with very important impacts in terms of the location of production, the type of labor that was required, and so on. New technologies mobilize and fragment labor markets, reinforcing labor market segmentation. All this helps to explain why, with unemployment hovering above 20 percent in the mid-1990s, Spain still has a high demand for unskilled foreign immigrants, mostly as domestics, agricultural day laborers, and unskilled workers in construction, mining, commerce, and the hotel industry.

11

Japan: The Illusion of Immigration Control

Wayne A. Cornelius

Immigration and the Changing Japanese Labor Market

Japan represents perhaps the most intriguing and important laboratory in the world today for studying the interplay among private market forces, cultural tolerance for immigration, and government attempts to regulate it. Until recently Japan has not had to deal with appreciable numbers of culturally and ethnically distinct people in its society. Since overrunning (but not completely exterminating) the indigenous Ainu and Okinawan cultures on the islands occupied by Japan, the Japanese have enjoyed centuries of ethnic and cultural stability. Table 11.1 presents a breakdown of the legally registered foreign population, by nationality, from 1920 to 1991. Between 1950 and 1988 the percentage of foreigners in the total population of Japan was consistently about 0.6 percent.

Indeed, supposedly "immigrant-free" Japan has often been offered by U.S. social scientists as definitive proof that an advanced industrial society has no need of foreign labor, especially unskilled foreign labor, to

The research and translation assistance of Takeyuki Tsuda, Akiko Harada, and Emiko Kiyochi is gratefully acknowledged. Keiichi Tsunekawa, Director of the Center for Latin American Studies, University of Tokyo-Komaba, and Tatsuya Tanami, Program Director of International House of Japan, provided invaluable help in identifying potential information sources and arranging interviews. This chapter draws heavily upon interviews with fifty-seven government officials, diplomats, academic researchers, journalists, business and labor leaders, and representatives of nongovernmental social service organizations, con-ducted by the author in July and November 1992 in the cities of Tokyo, Yokohama, Fujisawa, and Oizumi. This fieldwork was supported, in part, by an Abe Fellowship awarded by the Japan Foundation Center for Global Partnership, through the Social Science Research Council. The comments of John C. Campbell, Dept. of Political Science, University of Michigan, and Takeyuki Tsuda, Dept. of Anthropology, University of California, Berkeley, on an earlier draft were extremely helpful.

TABLE 11.1
LEGAL REGISTERED ALIENS IN JAPAN, BY NATIONALITY, 1920–1991[1]

Year	TOTAL	Korean	Chinese	Other Asian	Brazilian	Other Latin American	U.S.A.	Other
1920	78,061	40,755 (52.2)	24,130 (30.9)	na	na	na	3,966 (5.1)	9,210 (11.8)
1930	477,980	419,009 (87.7)	44,051 (9.2)	na	na	na	3,640 (0.8)	11,280 (2.4)
1940	1,304,286	1,241,315 (95.2)	45,825 (3.5)	na	na	na	4,755 (0.4)	12,391 (1.0)
1947	639,638	598,507 (93.6)	32,889 (5.1)	na	83 (0.0)	na	2,249 (0.4)	5,640 (0.9)
1950	598,696	544,903 (91.0)	40,481 (6.8)	na	169 (0.0)	na	4,962 (0.8)	8,181 (1.4)
1955	641,482	577,682 (90.1)	43,865 (6.8)	na	361 (0.1)	na	8,566 (1.3)	11,008 (1.7)
1960	650,566	581,257 (89.4)	45,535 (7.0)	2,618 (0.4)	240 (0.0)	207 (0.0)	11,594 (1.8)	9,115 (1.4)
1965	665,989	583,537 (87.6)	49,418 (7.4)	4,617 (0.7)	366 (0.1)	373 (0.1)	15,915 (2.4)	11,763 (1.8)
1970	708,548	614,202 (86.7)	51,481 (7.3)	6,597 (0.9)	891 (0.1)	597 (0.1)	19,045 (2.7)	15,645 (2.2)
1975	751,842	647,156 (86.1)	48,728 (6.5)	10,900 (1.5)	1,418 (0.2)	1,362 (0.2)	21,976 (2.9)	20,302 (2.7)
1980	782,910	664,536 (84.9)	52,896 (6.8)	17,044 (2.2)	1,492 (0.2)	1,871 (0.2)	22,401 (2.9)	22,670 (2.9)
1985	850,612	683,313 (80.3)	72,924 (8.6)	31,492 (3.7)	1,955 (0.2)	2,447 (0.3)	29,044 (3.4)	26,328 (3.1)
1989	984,455	681,838 (69.3)	137,499 (14.0)	32,011 (3.3)	14,528 (1.5)	na	34,900 (3.6)	83,679 (8.5)
1990	1,075,317	687,940 (64.0)	150,339 (14.0)	86,281 (8.0)	56,429 (5.2)	16,436 (1.5)	38,364 (3.6)	39,528 (3.7)
1991	1,218,891	693,050 (56.9)	171,071 (14.0)	110,430 (9.1)	119,333 (9.8)	35,465 (2.9)	42,498 (3.5)	47,044 (3.9)

[1]Figures in parentheses are percentages of the annual total of registered aliens. Rows may not sum to 100.0% due to rounding.

Sources: (For 1920–1985 and 1990:) Susumu Watanabe, "The Lewisian Turning Point and International Migration: The Case of Japan," *Asian and Pacific Migration Journal* 3:1 (1994): table 6, p. 136. (For 1989:) Shigemi Kono, "International Migration in Japan: A Demographic Sketch," in Wilbert Gooneratne, Philip L. Martin, and Hidehiko Sazanami, eds., *Regional Development Impacts of Labour Migration in Asia* (Nagoya, Japan: United Nations Centre for Regional Development, Research Report Series, No. 2, 1994), table 8.1, p. 143.

Notes: "Chinese" includes Taiwan; "Korean" includes both North and South Korea.

ensure a prosperous, growing economy.[1] Japan was the only major industrialized country that, since the 1950s, had managed to avoid reliance on foreign-born workers to fill significant numbers of low-level jobs. This was interpreted, erroneously, by some West European and U.S. analysts as the result of a deliberate societal and/or governmental choice not to introduce foreign labor, in anticipation of future technological innovations and rationalization of the native-born workforce that would keep labor supplies adequate. However, as one Japanese immigration specialist has pointed out, most Japanese in the 1960s and 1970s "never considered employing foreign workers to make up for the labor shortage" (Kajita 1994: 7). Thus the myth of "Japanese exceptionalism" has been extended to the area of immigration policy.

During the 1980s, however, Japan clearly lost its exceptional-case status, due to a combination of factors summarized in the following section. Actually, for Japan the demographic tipping point between country-of-emigration and country-of-immigration seems to have occurred in the mid-1960s, at the end of a fifteen-year period of unprecedented economic growth (Watanabe 1994; Abella 1994: 5). However, the shift was not noticeable prior to the influx of foreign workers who arrived to meet labor shortages that became acute in the second half of the 1980s.[2]

By the year 2000, according to government projections, the foreign-born population in Japan could be between 1.3 and 1.8 million, excluding those resident Koreans who have not yet been naturalized (perhaps an additional 300,000 people). A plausible, mid-range projection of the foreign-born population for the year 2015 is 3.2 million, or about 2.6 percent of the total population (Kono 1994: table 8.2, p. 148).

A Rapidly Deepening Labor Shortage

The labor shortage that developed in the second half of the 1980s reflected the combined effects of several key factors:

---

[1] The following is an example of this line of thought: "Japan is the prime example of a technologically advanced nation that depends on its own population for nearly all of its workers. . . . Japan's ability to maintain a high living standard with virtually no dependence on immigrant labor reflects some distinctive aspects of Japanese culture, religious philosophy, and nationalism" (Muller 1993: 287–88). The author goes on to explain that the Japanese have avoided importation of foreign labor by paying high wages for even low-skill, manual jobs, attaching high societal value to menial work, and developing an educational system that produces "disciplined" workers for all skill levels and abilities. One of the few analyses of contemporary Japan by a U.S. scholar to note the significant and growing presence of foreign labor can be found in Sassen 1991, especially pp. 307–15.

[2] One Japanese labor economist has argued persuasively that Japan might have needed a substantial foreign-born workforce much earlier (e.g., in the mid-1970s) if the Middle Eastern oil crisis had not occurred. That crisis accelerated the introduction of labor-saving technologies in Japanese industries and postponed any serious discussion of foreign labor importation until well into the 1980s. See Iyotani 1992.

- *The country's extremely low fertility rate*, which has declined by 27 percent since 1965 to 1.53 children per family—the world's lowest total fertility rate (and it continues to go down). Another key factor is the rapid aging of Japan's population, which is growing old more rapidly than that of any other industrial nation. Recent estimates show Japan becoming the first country in the world with one-fifth of its population above age sixty-five. At present, 10 percent of the Japanese population are age sixty-five or older. By the year 2000, Japanese in this age cohort will constitute 17 percent of the total population; by the year 2007, their proportion will have risen to 20 percent; and by the year 2025, 27.3 percent of the population—33.2 million people—will be sixty-five years or older. The "dependency ratio" will shift accordingly. In 1990, one elderly retiree was supported by 5.5 members of the economically active population; projections show that by the year 2020 he or she will be supported by only 2.3 workers.[3]

- *The depletion of Japan's formerly large labor reserve in rural areas*, which was drawn upon heavily during the post-World War II era of reconstruction and rapid reindustrialization.[4] Having supplied about 10 million workers (equal to the total number of jobs added to Japan's industrial sector during this period), this rural labor reservoir was virtually exhausted by the second half of the 1960s (see Iyotani 1991: table 1). Even the flow of seasonal migrant workers from northern parts of Japan used mostly by the construction and automotive industries has decreased continuously.

- *The government's new policy of strongly encouraging firms and workers to reduce working hours*. In 1990, the number of hours worked by the average Japanese was 10 percent higher than in the United States and the United Kingdom, and 25 percent higher than in Germany and France (*International Economic Insights* 1992: 14). The rationale for reducing working hours (in particular, by taking two days off per week) is to increase domestic consumption and ease trade frictions with the United States. Reducing working hours is also supposed to increase Japanese workers' level of job satisfaction and cement their loyalty to the firm—something that is advantageous to employers in a tight labor market (Jameson 1992). The traditional Japanese practice of working long hours and putting in lots of overtime served to delay the entry of foreign workers into some firms and job categories. Now employers

---

[3]Projections by the Population Research Institute, Nihon University, Japan, based on 1990 census data. By contrast, the United States will require thirty-two years for one-fifth of its population to reach sixty-five and older, Switzerland will take fifty-four years, Germany will take sixty-two years, and Sweden sixty-six years. For comprehensive discussions of how rapid population aging will reflect various aspects of Japanese society and public policy, see Martin 1989; Campbell 1992.

[4]For a description of Japan's pre-World War II urbanization process, see Nakamura 1993.

who are successful in getting their regular employees to go home must seek substitute labor.

Pre-recession estimates of Japan's aggregate labor shortage by the year 2000 ranged from a low of 500,000 workers (the estimate of one Ministry of Labor official) to a high of 5 million, which was the estimate of Keidanren, Japan's most powerful business organization.[5] Academic experts have estimated a shortfall of 1–2 million workers by the end of the 1990s.

A survey of 266 small and medium-sized firms in the Tokyo metropolitan area conducted at the end of 1988 found that about 60 percent suffered from a "very serious" shortage of labor, especially of young male workers. Fifty-seven percent of these employers believed that, given the labor shortage, the use of foreign workers was unavoidable and that the government should allow it as a matter of survival of small-scale companies. One-quarter of the firms surveyed were either employing or had previously hired foreign workers.[6]

While the labor shortage has been felt most acutely in small and medium-sized manufacturing firms, many Japanese economists and social scientists see the greatest potential for future labor shortages in the service sector. They expect a robust growth of demand for unskilled workers in hotels, restaurants, convalescent homes, janitorial services, and many other services provided outside the home. A significant increase in the employment of foreigners in this sector is anticipated once the current generation of native-born workers employed in low-skill, low-wage service occupations retires (Morita and Sassen 1994: 157–58). There is little interest in these kinds of jobs among young, well-educated Japanese.

The Rapid Growth of the Japanese Economy

The economic boom experienced by Japan during the period from 1986 to 1991 increased total employment by some 4.4 million workers (or 1.8 percent) and produced an influx of low-skilled, mostly illegal immigrant workers into the construction industry and into small and medium-scale industrial enterprises. One key indicator of the rapid buildup in the immigrant stock is the estimated number of visa overstayers, which more than doubled in the fifteen-month period from July 1990 to November 1991. The "bubble economy" of the 1980s, based largely on real estate and financial speculation, has now burst, and Japan is

---

[5]See Keidanren 1992. The organization's estimate is based on an average GNP growth rate (real terms) of 3.5 percent per annum and an average productivity increase of 3.5 percent in the period to the year 2000. "Based on these macroeconomic assumptions, our estimate is that the labor force in 2000 will fall about 5 million short of demand" (p. 8).

[6]Findings of the Joint Research Group on "The Internationalization of the Japanese Economy and Regional Restructuring," as reported in Morita and Iyotani 1994: 195.

recovering slowly from what it regards as a severe recession. During this three-year economic slowdown, Japan's unemployment rate edged up by only a few tenths of a point, to about 2.2 percent,[7] and the labor market in most sectors of the economy remained tight.

The Appreciation of the Japanese Yen

Shortly after the Plaza Agreement of September 1985, the yen began a steep climb against other currencies. This sudden change in the exchange rate combined with strong population pressures and low living standards in developing countries to make Japan a much more attractive destination for economic migrants from throughout the Pacific Basin. Even before the yen's revaluation, disparities in the average wage and in per capita income between Japan and its neighbors in the Asia-Pacific region had become very large. In 1986, for example, Japan's per capita income was eighty times higher than that of Bangladesh.[8] Such gaps widened rapidly in the remainder of the decade, creating an overwhelming economic "pull" factor for would-be migrants to Japan.

Basic Societal Changes within Japan

For all practical purposes, Japan-born workers, especially the youngest generation, are no longer willing to take so-called "3K" jobs—the Japanese acronym for jobs that are dirty (*kitanai*), dangerous (*kiken*), and physically arduous (*kitsui*). Young Japanese are increasingly well educated: 95 percent of them enter high school, and almost all graduate; a large proportion go on to universities. Thus educated, and having been raised in an affluent society that until recently offered seemingly limitless, highly paid employment opportunities, young working-age Japanese now seek upper-level service jobs. The youngest generation has moved particularly away from skilled, blue-collar work in construction and manufacturing, even as the number of such job openings has increased sharply since 1988 (Japan Institute of Labor 1992: 50).

Moreover, Japanese parents strongly discourage their children from taking manual-labor jobs. The labor shortage itself enables and *encourages* Japanese youth to shun such jobs. Given the tightness in the labor market, with so many higher-status job openings available, Japanese young people no longer need to settle for low-status, unskilled, or even skilled manual jobs. Thus the reluctance of the newest generation of Japanese workers to take "3K" jobs is both a cause and a result of the labor shortage.

[7]Japan excludes from its unemployment statistics anyone employed for more than one hour during the last week of the month. The unemployment rate would be somewhat higher if calculated by U.S. or European methods, but still far below the levels of other industrialized countries during the current recession.

[8]Kono 1994: 146. Today, average wages in Japan are thirty to forty times higher than in most of the labor-exporting Asian countries.

Taking all of these factors into account, most academic experts on the Japanese labor market believe that (1) it is impossible to eliminate "3K" jobs from those sectors of the economy where they presently exist in large numbers; and (2) it is equally impossible to change the attitudes of Japanese youths toward these jobs, especially those located in small and medium-sized firms that cannot afford to offer substantial nonwage incentives (shortened working hours, more holidays, annual bonuses, health insurance, pension plans, a more attractive work environment, and so forth).

Specifying Japan's Immigration Problem

By the beginning of the 1990s, for the first time in its history Japan had a large, *voluntary* foreign labor force.[9] While a plurality of today's foreign workers are clustered in the Tokyo-Yokohama, Osaka, and Nagoya metropolitan areas, smaller concentrations can be found in many parts of Japan, as far north as Hokkaido island, and the general trend is toward greater geographic dispersion. Small industrial towns like Ohta, Oizumi, Tatebayashi, and Isesaki in the eastern region of Gunma Prefecture and the Hamamatsu area of Shizuoka Prefecture are known to have far more foreign workers per capita than Japan's largest cities, attracted there by the jobs available in the small components-producing factories that surround the huge manufacturing plants owned by industrial giants like Sanyo, Toyota, and Mitsubishi.

The forced immigration and labor of some 400,000 Koreans in Japan during World War II represents a special case but one that enters into contemporary debates over Japanese immigration policy. Currently there are about 600,000 Koreans residing permanently in Japan; most of them are second and third generation, born in Japan. They are slowly being naturalized—given Japanese citizenship—if they have a Japanese mother or father. Some Koreans continue to migrate, illegally, to Japan, because the wage differential in construction and other sectors is still large enough to be attractive, especially after the rapid appreciation of the Japanese yen in the latter half of the 1980s (Chung 1992: 1). Even though most members of the settled Korean minority are culturally assimilated (they speak and behave completely as Japanese and try to hide their ethnicity), they still are not *accepted* and continue to be severely discriminated against, both socially and economically. This treatment derives from a highly derogatory, deeply ingrained Japanese perception of Koreans as innately inferior.

Some Japanese officials argue that, after more than fifty years, the Korean assimilation problem has not yet been "solved," and until it *has*

---

[9]The World War II era, in which huge numbers of migrant workers were involuntarily imported from Korea and other countries occupied by Japan, is discussed below.

been "solved" it is pointless to consider importing large numbers of foreigners of other nationalities, at least as permanent resident aliens. Given the deep cultural and historical roots of the "Korean problem" and the extremely low probability that it will be "solved" in the foreseeable future, Japanese who make this point may simply be using it to disguise their fundamental opposition to accepting foreign workers—regardless of nationality—on a permanent basis.

The Japanese government defines its current immigration problem primarily in terms of the number of visa overstayers—foreigners who were legally admitted to Japan on short-term visas as tourists, students, or "entertainers,"[10] but who never went home. By comparing legal entry and exit records, the Immigration Bureau estimates that the number of visa overstayers present as of November 1, 1993, was 296,751 (see table 11.2). Government officials assume that over 90 percent of these overstayers are in the workforce.

These numbers are still quite small compared with the United States and most other industrialized countries today. Foreign workers—including both legals and illegals—constitute only 1 percent or less of the Japanese labor force: perhaps 500,000–700,000 out of a total workforce of 65 million.[11] (These figures do not include the Korean legal permanent residents, who number about 600,000.) Nevertheless, the trend since the late 1980s has been sharply upward. As shown in table 11.2, the estimated number of visa overstayers nearly tripled between 1990 and 1993.

Significantly, this large increase in the stock of illegally resident foreigners *followed* the implementation in 1990 of a more restrictive immigration law, including stiff sanctions against employers of illegal foreign workers and the tightening of visa requirements for nationals of key sending countries (see below). Moreover, the government has reported that the "brokering" of jobs for illegal foreign workers is becoming increasingly organized and sophisticated, with growing involvement of crime syndicates based in Hong Kong, Taiwan, Thailand, and the Philippines, as well as the Japanese *yakuza* (Mafia-like families) (*Mainichi Daily News* 1994a; United Press International 1994).

---

[10]This type of temporary visa has been used most often by women originating in the Philippines, Thailand, and South Korea. The vast majority of those who have entered Japan with an "entertainment" visa work in small-scale service, food, and bar businesses. Among Japan's illegal worker population, these *Japayuki-san* are the most likely to have their basic human and labor rights violated, by both employers and gangster-like labor brokers. The most extensive field research on this subject has been done by David Groth, Dept. of Political Science, University of Hawaii at Hilo. See also Fukushima 1991.

[11]The estimate of 500,000 foreign workers, ca. 1991, has been used by officials of the Ministry of Labor (Iguchi 1992: 3). Economist Junichi Goto has estimated that about 700,000 foreign migrant workers were in Japan's workforce in 1991, of whom 266,369 were legally employed (Goto 1993).

In recent years the principal source countries for visa overstayers have been Thailand, the Philippines, Malaysia, South Korea, mainland China, Iran, and Bangladesh (see table 11.2). The construction industry has been by far the most important employer of male illegal foreign workers (accounting for nearly half of those detected by the government in 1991), followed by manufacturing (especially small and medium-sized firms that operate as subcontractors to large corporations). According to one analysis of official statistics, these two sectors—construction and manufacturing—together employed more than 80 percent of illegal foreign male workers apprehended from 1987 to 1990.[12] Within the manufacturing sector, illegal immigrants are especially likely to be employed in "dirty" industries like metal and plastic processing, plating, materials coating, and printing and binding, and with small subcontractors who make electrical machinery. In third place is the retail sector, including restaurants, where illegals are employed as dishwashers and other kitchen helpers. Among women, nearly half of those apprehended in 1991 were employed as "bar hostesses" or "entertainers"; about 14 percent worked in manufacturing industries; 8 percent as prostitutes; and 8 percent as dishwashers in restaurants.[13]

Interestingly, only 3.5 percent of the female illegal foreign workers detected by the government in 1991 were working as housecleaners. That is a major difference from the United States and most of the West European countries, where domestic service is one of the most common occupations for female immigrants, especially illegals. In Japan the labor market for maids, in-home providers of child care, and housekeepers is limited mainly to foreign professionals and diplomats who are temporarily posted there. This is a major reason why so many female immigrants from Asian countries have been forced into Japan's "entertainment" sector; in other countries many of them would be working as live-in maids.

More generally, foreign workers in Japan are significantly underrepresented in the service sector (except the so-called entertainment industry) by comparison with all other industrialized countries. In Japan, jobs like housecleaning, street sweeping, and garbage collecting—which in other industrialized, labor-importing countries are now heavily immigrant-dominated occupations—are still performed mainly by Japanese. The Japanese anomaly is explained partly by the fact that some low-social-status service jobs actually pay quite well (garbage

---

[12]Morita and Sassen 1994: 157. A 1992 survey of 8,410 firms in Kanagawa Prefecture that employ foreigners, conducted by the local government, found a similarly high proportion of foreign workers employed in these two sectors: 63.8 percent in manufacturing and 22.1 percent in construction.

[13]Unpublished data provided by the Immigration Office, Ministry of Justice, Tokyo, November 1992. This distribution of occupations is roughly consistent with the findings of numerous independently conducted sample surveys of immigrants in various Japanese cities and prefectures.

TABLE 11.2

ESTIMATES OF UNAUTHORIZED VISA OVERSTAYERS,
BY NATIONALITY, 1990–1993[1]

Nationality	July 1, 1990	May 1, 1991	Nov. 1, 1991	May 1, 1992	Nov. 1, 1992	May 1, 1993	Nov. 1, 1993
TOTAL	106,497	159,828	216,399	278,892	292,791	298,646	296,751
Thailand	11,523 (10.8)	19,093 (12.0)	32,751 (15.1)	44,354 (15.9)	53,219 (18.2)	55,383 (18.6)	53,845 (18.2)
South Korea	13,876 (13.0)	25,848 (16.2)	30,976 (14.3)	35,687 (12.8)	37,491 (12.8)	39,455 (13.2)	41,024 (13.8)
China	10,039 (9.4)	17,535 (11.0)	21,649 (10.0)	25,737 (9.2)	29,091 (9.9)	33,312 (11.2)	36,297 (12.2)
Philippines	23,805 (22.4)	27,228 (17.0)	29,620 (13.7)	31,974 (11.5)	34,296 (11.7)	35,392 (11.9)	36,089 (12.2)
Malaysia	7,550 (7.1)	14,413 (9.0)	25,379 (11.7)	38,529 (13.8)	34,529 (11.8)	30,840 (10.3)	25,653 (8.7)
Iran	764 (0.7)	10,915 (6.8)	21,719 (10.0)	40,001 (14.3)	32,994 (11.3)	28,437 (9.5)	23,867 (8.0)
Peru	242 (0.2)	487 (0.3)	1,017 (0.5)	2,783 (1.0)	6,241 (2.1)	9,038 (3.0)	11,659 (3.9)
Bangladesh	7,195 (6.8)	7,498 (4.7)	7,807 (3.6)	8,103 (2.9)	8,161 (2.8)	8,069 (2.7)	7,931 (2.7)
Taiwan	4,775 (4.5)	5,241 (3.3)	5,897 (2.7)	6,729 (2.4)	7,283 (2.5)	7,457 (2.5)	7,677 (2.6)
Pakistan	7,989 (7.5)	7,864 (4.9)	7,923 (3.7)	8,001 (2.9)	8,056 (2.8)	7,733 (2.6)	7,414 (2.5)
Myanmar	1,041 (1.0)	1,676 (1.1)	2,712 (1.3)	3,661 (1.3)	4,149 (1.4)	4,511 (1.5)	4,686 (1.6)
Others	17,305 (16.2)	21,645 (13.5)	28,236 (13.1)	32,290 (11.6)	36,005 (12.3)	37,511 (12.6)	38,954 (13.1)

[1]Figures in parentheses are percentages of the estimated total of visa overstayers. Columns may not sum to 100.0% due to rounding.

Source: Immigration Bureau, Ministry of Justice, Japan. Statistics are derived from computerized cross-checking of individual entry and exit records. Because of several potential sources of error in this methodology, the figures should be regarded as best estimates rather than precise statistics. The figures do not refer to unauthorized immigrants who have been apprehended by the immigration authorities, but only to those whose presence in Japan has been detected by the government through the cross-checking of records. The assistance of Kiriro Morita (University of Tokyo) and Katsuhiko Fujimori (Fuji Research Institute, Tokyo) in obtaining the latest data from 1993 is gratefully acknowledged.

collectors, for example). Another reason is that many employers in the retail and service sectors do not want to use foreigners in highly visible jobs where they might offend their Japanese customers. They prefer, instead, to use them in invisible, "back-of-the-house" jobs.[14]

The exclusion of foreigners from domestic service jobs can be attributed partly to persistent male chauvinism (even working wives are expected to do all the household chores themselves[15]), as well as to traditional female gender expectations. The Japanese woman is socialized to regard care of the family and the home as her main purpose in life, and delegating this expected social role to a foreign household servant would invite social ostracism as well as intense personal guilt feelings (see Gelb and Palley 1994). The centuries-old concept of "purity/impurity" that is embedded in Japanese culture may also explain some of the hesitancy to accept foreign workers in the home. According to this cultural construct, everything external to the home is considered to be "impure," as symbolized by the practice of removing one's shoes and leaving them in the *genkan*—a small, square space at the entrance of a Japanese home or apartment. Everything outside the home is regarded as dirty; "outside" is where cultural and biological germs (especially "people dirt") are located (see Ohnuki-Tierney 1984: 21–31). Having a foreigner working in the home could be regarded as a particularly egregious form of impurity.[16] In addition to these cultural factors, there are some very practical reasons why some Japanese families may choose not to hire domestic workers, such as the lack of space in the typical Japanese house and the cost of outside labor. Whatever the explanation, the phenomenon does have significant labor supply implications. If Japanese families were not reluctant to hire domestic help, this would enable more women to work outside the home for longer periods and for more years of their lives.

Current Government Policy and Policy Making on Foreign Workers

As in the other two industrialized nations represented in this book that only recently became labor importers (Spain and Italy), Japanese immigration policy is inchoate, with little consensus evident within the government on the basic directions of the policy. The policy-making

---

[14]This employer preference is by no means limited to Japan; the restaurant industry in the United States provides abundant examples of the same phenomenon. See Morales 1985.

[15]A government survey found that a Japanese husband whose wife was in the labor force spent an average of only six minutes per day doing household work (Prime Minister's Office 1980).

[16]Latin American immigrants of Japanese ancestry (the *Nikkeijin*) may escape this stigma. For example, some Brazilian-Japanese women have been employed in Tokyo as live-in care providers for the elderly.

process in this area most often resembles a tug-of-war involving competitive segments of the bureaucracy having different interests and constituencies, with the Prime Minister's Office exerting little or no leadership.

To define its general stance on the immigration issue and generate specific policy recommendations, each of the ministries most concerned with immigration has appointed at least one "study group" chaired by a prominent "outside" academic with close ties to the bureaucracy. After an appropriately long review period, the study group's findings are issued as the official (or unofficial) opinion of the ministry that appointed it.[17] The political parties—including the long-ruling Liberal Democratic Party, prior to its defeat in the 1993 elections—have played only marginal roles in this process of policy formulation, even though they, too, have established "study groups" or ad hoc committees focusing on immigration policy.

Among the key players, the Ministry of Justice has taken the hardest line, insisting on sanctions against employers who hire illegal foreign workers and resisting expansionary policies that might damage the interests of Japanese workers. Its preferences are reflected in the 1990 amendments to Japan's immigration law. The Ministry of Labor has been more concerned with facilitating employer access to legal foreign labor and providing support services to the growing foreign-born workforce. On the expansionary end of the policy spectrum can be found the ministries most deeply involved in Japan's "internationalization" (Foreign Relations, International Trade and Industry) and those representing the interests of labor-short sectors of the economy (e.g., Fisheries, Transportation).[18]

Despite these differing emphases and concerns within the government bureaucracy, three fundamental tenets can be identified as the basis for Japan's current immigration policy:

- *Admitting foreign workers, on whatever basis, should be a last resort*—something that is done only after all alternatives for solving the labor shortage are exhausted. The alternatives most frequently cited are making greater use of female and elderly workers, and inducing more small and medium-sized manufacturing firms to "go offshore" for their unskilled labor—i.e., to move their labor-intensive production to Third World countries. Small and medium employers can also be urged or financially incentivized by the government to introduce more labor-saving technologies, on the assumption that these firms are not already on a "mechanization plateau."

---

[17]In the Japanese system, this indirect, informal approach to policy making is by no means confined to the immigration arena. See, for example, Zhao 1993: 12, 71–76.

[18]For a more detailed description of the immigration policy positions taken by these and other government ministries in the period preceding the 1990s recession, see Sassen 1991: 312–14.

- *No unskilled workers (what the Japanese call "simple labor") should be admitted*—only highly skilled workers and professionals, or workers who may enter unskilled but who will become skilled during a relatively brief training program in Japan and then return to their home countries.

- *All foreigners should be admitted on a temporary basis only.* An insistence on temporariness will prevent the social conflicts that permanent settlers could generate among the Japanese public, and it also relieves governments at all levels of the burden of providing expensive social services to a settled population that includes women and children, not just unaccompanied males. Moreover, by adhering to a strict-rotation system of foreign labor importation, Japan can minimize the kinds of sociocultural assimilation problems with which the United States and the West European countries are now struggling, and the notion of Japan's ethnic and racial homogeneity can be preserved.

In the remainder of this section, I will explain how all three of these supposedly inviolable principles of Japanese immigration policy are, in fact, being disregarded or seriously undermined, both by Japanese companies and by the government itself.

Government documents and public statements overflow with rhetoric about the need to pursue all other alternatives before sanctioning the importation of foreign labor.[19] Nevertheless, one gets the clear sense that these admonitions are half-hearted, and that no one really believes they will do enough to solve the country's labor shortage in the long run.

Take, for example, the option of making greater and more effective use of female labor. While Japan has one of the highest rates of female labor force participation in the industrialized world, exceeding 50 percent in recent years, many Japanese women with college-level educations still leave the labor force in mid-career, following childbirth, and do not return, at least until the children have been raised. Several studies have found that, among Japanese women, educational level is negatively or insignificantly related to the probability of being employed outside the home. For women, "education is a resource for the marriage market-. . . for being a good wife and wise mother . . . but not for the labor market" (Tanaka 1986).

There are numerous sociocultural barriers to the full, lifetime participation of women in the Japanese workforce. Most importantly, Japanese males still expect their children to be cared for at home by their natural mothers, even though public day care is better and more readily available in Japan than in many other countries. Moreover, the financial incentives for

---

[19] A typical compendium of such remedies is the recent book *Coping with the Age of Labor Shortage*, edited by the Placement Bureau, Ministry of Labor (Tokyo, 1991), which presents the final report of the Research Committee on the Direction of Employment Policy to Resolve the Problems Caused by the Change of Labor Supply Structure.

women to stay employed or return to their jobs are weak: in general, Japanese women earn only about one-half as much as similarly experienced men. Even when variables like age, occupation, and job seniority are taken into account, there is still a large male/female wage differential (see Saso 1990: 66–72; Osawa n.d.). There is also a very obvious "glass ceiling" problem for women employed in major companies, which prevents them from advancing to higher-paying jobs. A 1981 government survey found that 45 percent of companies offered no promotion opportunities for women at all (Prime Minister's Office 1982; see also Cook and Hayashi 1980).

Women have found that even entry-level jobs have been harder to get during the economic downturn of the 1990s. A Ministry of Labor survey of 1,000 firms completed in late 1993 found that more than half were reducing the hiring of new female employees so that they could continue hiring males in the usual numbers. The common explanation by personnel managers was that males are likely to stay with a firm far longer than women and virtually never request child-care leaves.[20] Even though Japan since 1986 has had an equal employment opportunity law that forbids such discrimination, it is widely disregarded by employers. The fault, contends the Federation of Employers Associations, lies with the women themselves, who fail to seek jobs in smaller and medium-sized companies.[21]

Therefore, to achieve any significant increase in female labor force participation—for example, among the numerous middle-aged women who are not presently employed—Japan would need to make some fundamental cultural changes, especially in gender and family roles. Moreover, the severe financial disincentives for women to work would have to be removed (see Osawa n.d.). Finally, a serious effort would have to be made to enforce laws and government regulations forbidding systematic discrimination against women in the workplace. No one expects any of this to happen very soon.[22]

The elderly present other types of challenges as a supplemental labor force. Japan has many millions of elderly, but a large proportion of them

---

[20] As reported in Sanger 1994. Yoshio Teresawa, head of Japan's Economic Planning Agency, has acknowledged that employers still treat women unfairly, in the belief that men do better work, and lamented the fact that foreign firms "are hiring away good women graduates, while Japanese firms are giving up on them" (*Wall Street Journal*, June 6, 1994).

[21] *Wall Street Journal*, June 6, 1994. In fact, government statistics show that a majority of female workers are already employed in small and medium-sized firms—a higher proportion than males.

[22] The difficulty of accomplishing such changes is suggested by the following observation: "Though Japanese women work before marriage and after raising children, they are mainly confined to lower-rank and temporary positions in a culture that assumes that women cannot and will not be as serious, dedicated, and capable on the job as men. Mostly, young women work to prepare themselves for marriage, and older women work because of economic necessity and boredom. Those who wish to break the glass ceiling and compete professionally, full-time, at the same level with men eventually encounter resistance from within both the firm and the family" (personal communication from Takeyuki Tsuda, Dept. of Anthropology, University of California, Berkeley, January 1993). For corroborating evidence, see Yashiro 1984.

are already in the labor force. Traditionally, Japanese workers retire from their so-called lifetime job with a single company at the age of fifty-five (recently this has been raised to sixty years). They then go on to a second career, working until age sixty-five or later, even if the work is much lower-paying and part-time. Older workers simply do not drop out of the Japanese labor force as often as they do in other industrialized countries, partly because of lifetime work habits (no one wants to be idle in Japan!), partly because they need the income. Pension benefits are relatively low, although they have improved considerably for more recent retirees from larger companies. Thus in 1990, 44 percent of Japanese workers aged fifty-five and over were employed—a much higher labor force participation rate for this age cohort than the OECD countries' average. And this statistic probably does not include the numerous older Japanese workers who are employed only part-time. All this means that it is very difficult to conceive the older population as an underutilized segment of the labor force, waiting to be tapped. Moreover, there are many kinds of jobs now performed by foreign workers (e.g., hard and/or dangerous manual labor in the construction industry) for which older people would not be regarded as appropriate.

The option of reducing labor requirements through robotics or some other form of technological innovation is one that already has been pursued extensively. The majority of the small and medium-sized firms that have suffered most from the labor shortage since the mid-1980s say that they cannot afford more technological improvements.[23] Others argue that they have already mechanized as much as possible, given the nature of their business. Indeed, illegal immigrants in Japan today are found working not only in "backward," declining industries but in highly mechanized, technologically advanced factories, which remain labor-short. "The labor shortage is, in fact, quite serious among those companies that are shifting to high-value-added products and are rationalizing their operations" (Morita and Iyotani 1994: 196).

Labor requirements can also be reduced by moving production abroad, although this option is not available to most small to medium-sized service businesses or firms that engage in construction activities. Following the nearly complete liberalization of capital export in the early 1970s, numerous Japanese manufacturing companies of all sizes moved production to low-cost sites all around the Pacific Rim, from China to Thailand, Malaysia, and Mexico. The number of overseas subsidiary firms established by Japanese corporations rose from 339 in 1975 to 1,307 in 1987 (Machimura 1992: table 1).

Today, with only a few exceptions, Japanese economists view this relocation of production to Third World countries as a process that is

---

[23]See the results of a national-level sample survey of small and medium-sized employers, reported in Inagami et al. 1992.

reaching its limits. They point out that large Japanese corporations need to maintain a certain number of small subcontractors within Japan to enable them to meet short production deadlines and give them a "cushion" in times of economic recession (excess labor can be shed more easily by the subcontractors than by the larger firms that they supply). Therefore, the option of continuing to move capital abroad seems unrealistic as a long-term solution to the domestic labor shortage.

What are the explicit policy instruments that Japan has used thus far to regulate immigration flows, and how have they functioned?

Visa Issuance Policy

Since 1989, the government has used visa issuance policy to shut off the flow of illegal immigrants from certain countries, beginning with Bangladesh and Pakistan. Like most of the unskilled illegal immigrants now working in Japan, Bangladeshis and Pakistanis typically had entered as tourists and then stayed to work. Since January 15, 1989, nationals of Bangladesh and Pakistan have been required to obtain entry visas, from which they had previously been exempted. To obtain even a tourist visa they must now meet stringent requirements, including having a "sponsor" in Japan, and must demonstrate substantial financial assets. This policy change has sharply reduced the flow of new immigrants from Bangladesh and Pakistan. However, most Bangladeshis and Pakistanis already working in Japan in 1989–1990 appear to have remained, as visa overstayers (see table 11.2).

Virtually as soon as Bangladesh and Pakistan lost their visa exemption, Iranian workers began to flood into Japan. Partly because of their concentration each weekend in two of Tokyo's largest public parks to socialize and engage in petty commerce, Iranians quickly became the most visible segment of Japan's illegal immigrant population. This produced a strongly negative public reaction, and the government acted within a year to impose new visa requirements on Iranians.[24] The government estimates that there are still more than 40,000 illegal Iranian immigrants in the country, employed mainly by construction firms and factories.[25] Nevertheless, the loss of Iran's visa exemption has had the short-term effect of sharply reducing the flow of new would-be immigrants from that source.

However effective it has been thus far in keeping out unskilled workers from certain sending countries, there are limits to the policy of using stiff visa requirements to deny entry to potential illegal immigrants. In 1992, for example, more than 3.8 million foreigners entered

[24]Much of Tokyo's Yoyogi Park, one of the Iranians' favorite weekend gathering places, was also closed in 1993, ostensibly for "refurbishing."

[25]Data from a survey of 143 Iranians interviewed in Ueno Park, Tokyo, in June 1992 (see Yamazaki et al. 1992). Ueno Park attracts so many Iranian migrants on a regular basis that it is popularly called "Little Teheran."

Japan for various reasons, mostly as tourists and businessmen. Two-thirds of these ostensibly short-term visitors came from other Asian countries with which Japan wants to have good diplomatic and economic relations (both trade and tourism). Government officials acknowledge that it is not in Japan's own economic interest to restrict excessively the entry of people from its Asian neighbors. Moreover, some immigration authorities express skepticism that visa controls can even be a long-term solution to the problem of clandestine immigration from the sending countries upon which they have been imposed. "The demonstration effect by returnees is strong enough to motivate others to look for [other] ways to come to Japan, and this has led to various types of illegal attempts at entry," including the use of forged passports and visas provided by labor brokers (Sasaki 1994: 161, 164).

Employer Sanctions

Illegal immigrants are supposed to be denied access to Japan's labor market by an employer sanctions law, which went into effect on June 1, 1990. It is similar in concept and construction to the employer sanctions laws enacted by the United States in 1986 and by the West European countries in the mid-1970s and early 1980s.

On paper, Japan's employer sanctions are draconian: large fines (up to 2 million yen per alien, equivalent to about U.S.$20,400 in mid-1994), and criminal penalties of up to three years in prison. These penalties are supposed to apply both to employers who knowingly hire illegal aliens and to the labor brokers or contractors who often recruit foreign workers for Japanese firms.

Enforcement is another matter. An objective assessment could only conclude that no more than a token effort is being made at present to enforce the employer sanctions provision of Japan's 1990 immigration law. The available statistics support such an assessment. Only about 350 Japanese employers per year were penalized for violations of the new immigration law in 1991 and 1992.[26] And far more illegal foreign workers appear to have returned home voluntarily, in anticipation of the implementation of employer sanctions in 1990, than have been detected and deported since then as a result of workplace inspections.[27]

This symbolic enforcement effort is explained by local-level officials as a recognition of the essential role now played by foreign workers—

---

[26]Data provided by Tadashi Nagai, Policy Development Department, Immigration Bureau, Ministry of Justice, Tokyo, July 1992.

[27]During the week preceding the effective date for employer sanctions, some 23,000 illegal migrants surrendered themselves at Immigration Bureau offices, apparently in response to an unfounded rumor swirling through Japan's immigrant communities that the new penalties would be imposed on the workers themselves rather than their employers (Sasaki 1994: 157–58).

legal and illegal—in certain sectors of the Japanese economy.[28] Another, obvious explanation is the fact that Japan has only about 1,800 immigration officers who have the legal authority to inspect for violations of the employer sanctions law, in a country with millions of private businesses. Enforcement is also hampered by the low visibility of illegals employed in small factories and retail businesses.

The rapid expansion of job brokerage networks in recent years is cited by immigration authorities as another key obstacle to enforcement. Japanese employers, like their U.S. counterparts following passage of the 1986 Immigration Reform and Control Act, have turned increasingly to subcontractors and labor brokers to insulate themselves against prosecution under the 1990 law. Large numbers of such employment brokers now operate freely in urban areas where foreigners dwell, even though they, too, are nominally subject to prosecution under Japan's employer sanctions law.[29] Finally, foreign workers can still be hired easily on a part-time basis without documents. In sum, the Japanese experience with employer sanctions seems to be paralleling that of all other industrialized countries that have tried this approach to immigration control.

Refugee Admissions Policy

There is no West European-style refugee problem in Japan because, with the exception of about 8,000 Southeast Asians admitted during the 1970s and early 1980s as political refugees from the Vietnam War, Japan simply has not accepted applications for refugee or asylum status, and there are no plans to do so.

The contemporary German "refugee horror story" is all the evidence that most Japanese need for avoiding a liberal asylum policy. To Japanese policy makers, the difficulty of distinguishing legitimate political refugees from economic migrants seems insurmountable. Public opinion polls show a majority of Japanese opposing the acceptance of economic refugees, especially from countries like China, with its 1.2 billion population. Moreover, accepting refugees as permanent residents would contravene one of the basic tenets of Japan's current immigration policy—i.e., that no foreign workers should be admitted on a permanent basis.

Immigration Control: Paths Not Taken

Several theoretically available options for immigration control exist that seem to have been ruled out by the Japanese government, at least for the

---

[28]Interviews with Shuji Shirota, Director, Fujisawa Labor Hall, Fujisawa, Japan, November 1992; and Kenji Yamanari, Counsellor, Labour Affairs Division, Kanagawa Prefectural Government, Yokohama, November 1992.

[29]Such brokerage activities have expanded throughout Japan, contributing to the trend toward dispersion of illegal foreign workers from big cities to small towns (Sasaki 1994: 161). See also Kuwahara 1992: 11.

time being. First, while the number of apprehensions rises each year,[30] there has been no large-scale, systematic roundup and deportation campaign to reduce the population of illegal foreign workers. In 1992, for example, 67,824 illegal immigrants were apprehended by the government, in one way or another.[31] Of these, only 3,992 were caught in the act of illegal entry or "illegal landing." (Most of these unlucky foreigners were "boat people" originating in China.) Over 93 percent of the illegal immigrants detected in 1992 were visa overstayers; it is unclear how many of these illegals were actually deported. The most concerted roundup and deportation effort thus far, carried out by immigration officials in several major cities during November and December 1993, netted 2,773 persons—fewer than 1 percent of the stock of approximately 300,000 foreign workers estimated to be in Japan illegally at that time.[32]

More sweeping and systematic immigration law enforcement efforts of this type would certainly be feasible. Japan's illegal immigrant population exhibits a rather high degree of residential segregation, with obvious concentrations in particular cities, neighborhoods, and apartment buildings. Local police stations in every Japanese neighborhood keep close tabs on residents within their jurisdictions. Presumably they have the knowledge and capability to round up virtually every foreigner living illegally in their neighborhood and deliver them to the immigration authorities for deportation. Instead, local police as well as Immigration Bureau agents operate almost entirely on the basis of specific complaints lodged by a neighbor or someone else against an illegal foreign resident. "They are far too busy doing other things to bother with foreign workers," one informant told me. In some cases, the authorities merely "apprehend" illegals who turn themselves in.[33]

Perhaps more importantly, there is a growing recognition that foreign workers are supporting vital sectors of the Japanese economy

---

[30] Apprehensions of illegal entrants or residents rose from 2,536 in 1982 to 67,824 in 1992, according to statistics from the Immigration Bureau, Ministry of Justice.

[31] An additional 25,762 unauthorized aliens were "denied landing" at legal ports of entry, mostly at Narita International Airport, because of fraudulent entry documents. (Statistics from the Immigration Bureau, Ministry of Justice.)

[32] Statistics from the Ministry of Justice, reported in *Mainichi Daily News* 1994b.

[33] A book written by a former illegal immigrant in Japan from the Philippines describes how he finally surrendered to the authorities, not out of fear of capture, but for personal and family reasons. He describes his interrogation by the local official to whom he turned himself in. The nonthreatening official already knows just about everything about the immigrant's life and that of many of his friends, and produces a detailed map of the neighborhood showing where all the foreigners live. The illegal immigrant leaves the Enforcement Division without being detained. He is allowed to go home and return to his job at a construction site, while bureaucrats do the paperwork needed for his deportation. Returning several days later, he receives his completed papers from an immigration officer, who informs him that he would be free to return to Japan, legally, in a year's time. (Summarized from Ventura 1992: 168–73.)

and that their removal would have adverse economic impacts on the businesses and communities in which they are working. "[Even] the sleekest and most modern car assembly plant that Toyota operates would soon run out of parts, were it not for 'just-in-time' deliveries from hundreds of parts-makers, large and small, who rely at least partially on foreign labor" (Oka 1993). Not surprisingly, local government authorities seem far more willing to accommodate immigrants than their national government counterparts, especially in "company towns" where the health of local businesses (and therefore the flow of tax revenues) is heavily dependent on the continued availability of foreign labor.[34]

Second, beyond a few small human rights and immigrants' advocacy groups, there seems to be no effective constituency for a large-scale "amnesty" or legalization program to reduce the population of illegals. The general public claims to be more accepting of this option than the government. In a nationwide poll done in 1989, for example, 45 percent of the respondents favored legalizing the foreigners already in Japan who lacked authorization to work.[35] But government officials and other key actors seem strongly convinced that a large, U.S.-style legalization program would only encourage more illegal immigration. Among organized groups, only some labor unions have urged legalization of unauthorized foreign workers.[36]

The same logic is being applied to the option of a European-style "guestworker" or temporary worker program, which had been proposed during the 1980s by the Ministry of Labor but was successfully resisted by the Ministry of Justice. Most members of the Japanese political and economic elite now seem to fear that any such program would touch off mass emigration from surrounding countries, especially China. The number of workers soliciting participation in a guestworker program would vastly exceed the number of visas available, and the overflow would try to come illegally. An even greater fear among the general public, rooted in the West European experience of the 1970s and 1980s, is that the "guests" would never go home—that rates of "leakage" out of the program, permanent settlement, and family reunification in Japan would be excessively high.

This preoccupation with maintaining the temporariness of Japan's foreign workforce, and with preventing family reunification immigration, is clearly reflected in the available data from opinion surveys. For example, in a nationwide survey conducted for the Prime Minister's Office in November–December 1990, a surprisingly high proportion of

---

[34]For a case study of Ohta, a "company town" 90 km. north of Tokyo that has experienced rapid growth of immigrant employment since 1985, see Koga 1994.

[35]Data from a poll conducted by the *Asahi Shimbun* Opinion Poll Department, provided by Makoto Ushida, analyst.

[36]See *Yomiuri Shimbun* 1992. The national-level Japanese Trade Union Confederation (Rengo) has not yet endorsed this position.

interviewees—over 70 percent—declared themselves in favor of allowing the admission of *unskilled* foreign laborers. This would be a radical departure from current government policy, which is to deny entry to all unskilled workers (a policy endorsed by only 14 percent of the poll respondents). However, the majority felt that the employment of such workers should be subject to certain conditions; most frequently mentioned (by 48 percent of the respondents) was a specific time limit on their stay in Japan.[37]

Informal Mechanisms for Importing Foreign Labor

Undoubtedly the most interesting elements of current Japanese immigration policy are its various informal, "side-door" mechanisms for importing unskilled foreign labor, in some cases on a de facto permanent basis. These measures are being implemented even while the government maintains the official stance that (1) no *unskilled* immigrants shall be admitted, and (2) no foreigners, regardless of skill level, should be admitted on a *permanent* basis.[38]

In recent years, these informal labor-importation devices have supplied about 150,000 legal, essentially unskilled foreign workers to Japan per annum. This figure falls far short of the number of workers that were actually needed to meet Japan's unskilled labor demand, especially in the pre-recession period. However, the foreigners admitted through these mechanisms were supplemented by the nearly 300,000 visa overstayers whose presence the government now acknowledges.

Importing "Japanese-Latin Americans"

Numerically the most important of Japan's side-door mechanisms for labor importation has been the policy of allowing the descendants of Japanese emigrants to Latin America (the *Nikkeijin*) to immigrate to Japan. Since 1989–1990, Latin America-based persons of Japanese ancestry, including the first (*issei*), second (*nisei*), and third (*sansei*) generations, have had essentially unrestricted access to the Japanese labor market. Under the 1990 amendments to Japan's immigration law, there are no numerical ceilings on the number of immigrants of Japanese

---

[37] Prime Minister's Office 1991. Results are based on 3,681 valid cases. A national poll taken in 1989 by Japan's largest newspaper, *Asahi Shimbun*, found that 56 percent of the Japanese public favored the admission of foreign workers—even unskilled ones—with the same kinds of conditions (e.g., their length of stay should be limited; dependents should remain in the home country).

[38] As John Creighten Campbell points out (personal communication, January 1993), this approach to immigration policy making is perfectly consistent with the traditional "Japanese tolerance, or even preference, for strict laws combined with winking at exceptions." He notes that the same kind of behavior can be observed in the health care field, in which the government maintains a strict fee schedule but allows quasi-legal "extra" charges and ignores large, under-the-table "gifts" by patients to prominent physicians.

ancestry who can enter. As a matter of de facto policy, no restrictions exist on where or how they can be employed, regardless of the generational status distinctions included in the 1990 immigration law. The initial visa issued to the *Nikkeijin* is for three years, but it can be renewed an unlimited number of times. Essentially, the *Nikkeijin* can become permanent residents if they choose to; and many do, easily finding employment in manufacturing industries (especially the auto-parts subsector) and bringing their dependents to live in small "company towns" outside of metropolitan Tokyo.[39]

The policy of highly liberal immigration opportunities for the *Nikkeijin* from Latin America is seen by Japanese officials as a politically low-cost way of helping to solve the labor shortage, since immigrants of Japanese ancestry are not supposed to upset the country's mythical ethnic homogeneity:

> Official documents dating from before the 1989–1990 reform [of Japanese immigration law] suggest that maintenance of cultural and "racial" homogeneity was a major concern of policy makers and the ruling Liberal Democratic Party. Such documents often refer to Japan's possession of "one ethnic group, one language" as a key contributing factor to its post-war economic miracle. The *Nikkeijin* were acceptable because, as relatives of Japanese, they "would be able to assimilate into Japanese society regardless of nationality" (Yamanaka 1992: 7).

That most second- and third-generation Brazilian and Peruvian *Nikkeijin* initially have little or no competence in the Japanese language, and that they behave culturally as Latin Americans rather than Japanese, are facts conveniently overlooked. Furthermore, because they typically have not maintained close contacts with their relatives in Japan, the Latin America-based *nisei* and *sansei* must rely on labor brokers rather than family ties in order to gain employment in Japan, at least during their initial sojourn (Kajita 1994: 30).

The Japanese-Latin Americans are considered highly desirable as a labor source for various reasons. To many Japanese employers, they have been a godsend, because "*Nikkeijin* workers are virtually the only *legal* [foreign] workers who can take on *unskilled* jobs" (Inagami et al. 1992: 45, emphasis added). Not only can the *Nikkeijin* be hired legally to do any type of job; they also tend to be well educated and occupationally skilled

---

[39]The largest sample survey of the Latin American *Nikkeijin* population to date is International Cooperation Enterprise Group 1992. The sample includes 1,027 respondents located in various regions of the country. The study was directed by Hisatoshi Tajima, Dept. of Humanities, Josai International University, Chiba.

by comparison with the population of origin and even by Japanese standards. Surveys show that most Latin American *Nikkeijin* are people who were white-collar office workers and professionals in their home countries, but who are willing to do manual work in Japan given the huge pay differential.

Some Japanese companies, either individually or as part of employer associations, have recruited workers directly in the five Latin American countries where the *Nikkeijin* are concentrated: Brazil, Peru, Argentina, Bolivia, and Paraguay. Many other companies have relied on professional labor contractors to deliver their *Nikkeijin* workers. Serious abuses of worker rights are committed by some of these brokers, who operate in a totally illegal fashion, through travel agencies and similar enterprises.

The government recognized the presence of approximately 150,000 *Nikkeijin* workers in June 1991, up from only 29,000 in 1989 (Iguchi 1992: 2). By 1993, according to some estimates, their numbers had reached about 200,000. Given the limited number of source countries and the small size of the Japanese-ancestry populations within them, the *Nikkeijin* alone cannot possibly supply Japan with the number of foreign workers that its economy seems to demand. For example, in 1992 more than 90 percent of the *Nikkeijin* in Japan were from Brazil. The total number of Japanese descendants in Brazil has been estimated by the Japanese government at 1,280,000, at least 131,000 of whom—more than 10 percent—are already in Japan. Some Japanese scholars believe that the number of Brazilian *Nikkeijin* working in Japan could eventually rise to nearly half a million, which would represent 39 percent of the theoretically available pool. However, that is an upper-end estimate; most others are considerably lower. In Peru, the potential recruitment pool is just 80,000, an estimated 38 percent of whom were in Japan by 1992 (Inagami et al. 1992: 45). Argentina has an estimated 30,000 Japanese émigrés and descendants; Paraguay, 7,000; and Bolivia, 6,000.

Corporate Trainee Programs

Potentially more important in the future, especially as the pools of Latin American *Nikkeijin* are exhausted, is another of Japan's currently operating backdoor immigration policies, the "company trainee" programs. In 1991, 43,649 foreigners were admitted to Japan as trainees of private companies; about the same number were admitted in 1992, mostly from mainland China, Thailand, the Philippines, Korea, Vietnam, and Indonesia.

The Japanese government officially justifies the company trainee programs as a form of development assistance to poorer countries—a vehicle for skill and technology transfer. However, independent observers consider this to be diplomatic window dressing, since most of the skills acquired by company trainees are not directly transferable to jobs in their home countries unless the Japanese firms that provide the training have established subsidiaries or joint-venture plants there. The government has been planning a major expansion of the company trainee programs, which began in 1993. In the future, once the economy has regained its pre-recession robustness, Japan may be admitting between 200,000 and 300,000 foreign trainees per year, according to government informants. More than 500 recruitment networks are being established by the Japanese government with the cooperation of main-land Chinese local government councils, and a new government-to-government agreement to stimulate emigration of aspiring company trainees has been negotiated with Indonesia.

Interestingly, the Japanese government has been moving ahead with plans to expand and liberalize the company trainee programs even in the face of Japan's most prolonged and severe recession of the post-World War II era. The most plausible explanation is that the officials responsible for these programs, like the private employers who have come to rely upon foreign workers, are taking the long view of Japan's labor supply situation. They do not see the domestically unmet demand for unskilled labor as being cyclical; rather, they consider it a structural feature of the Japanese economy in the last decade of the twentieth century and beyond. While the recent economic downturn may have taken some pressure off labor-short small and medium-sized businesses, these same firms remain deeply concerned about future supplies of young workers.

The company trainee approach to solving the country's long-term labor shortage has won strong support from Japan's business organiza-tions, several of which have developed and presented to the government their own designs for foreign-worker training programs (see, for exam-ple, Japan Foodservice Association 1990; Tokyo Chamber of Commerce 1989). The government has cooperated by liberalizing the terms of employment for foreign company trainees, to enable employers to get greater use out of their trainees as production workers. Under the so-called Practical Trainee program, initiated in April 1993, employers are permitted to retain their foreign trainees for two full years. In the first year, one-third of the trainee's time is supposed to be spent in classroom instruction in Japanese language and culture; another third is devoted to formal training in job skills; and the rest goes to "on-the-job" training (i.e., working on production lines, applying the newly acquired skills). The trainee's second year in Japan is devoted entirely to "on-the-job" training.

This modification has intensified criticism of the company trainee programs, primarily by intellectuals, on the grounds that most jobs held by foreign trainees are exactly those that Japanese citizens will not do; that many employers provide very little actual training; and that most companies are simply using the trainees as a source of cheap, unskilled labor.[40] Indeed, some firms are already lobbying the government to amend the Practical Trainee program to allow foreign workers admitted under the program to stay longer than two years in Japan (Ikezawa 1994).

Because foreign trainees during their first year in Japan are not considered regular employees under Japanese labor law, they do not receive regular wages, health insurance, workmen's compensation, or other fringe benefits. They get only a "living stipend" and housing provided by the employer. Foreign trainees are, in fact, somewhat cheaper to the firm than the average Japanese employee. Employers pay no recruitment fees and have no long-term obligations to their foreign trainees. Only if the employer opts to retain a trainee for a second year *and* the foreign trainee passes a certifying examination given by the Ministry of Labor does he become an officially recognized employee with standard benefits and protections.

Those who criticize the company trainee system as nothing more than a "side-door" foreign labor importation scheme point out a basic lack of fit between the system's stated objectives of human capital development and technology transfer and the kinds of firms that are most in need of foreign "trainees." Those are, of course, small and medium-sized businesses, which typically lack the capacity to provide an adequate training program for unskilled foreign workers (see, for example, Kajita 1994: 26–27).

Finally, there is no adequate enforcement mechanism in place to ensure that foreign workers granted entry as participants in these programs actually return to their home countries once their stipulated training and post-training employment period has ended. The government simply accepts assurances from companies with approved programs that their trainees have been repatriated. As the company trainee system currently operates, assured repatriation seems to be mainly the responsibility of sending-country governments. For example, China reportedly is selecting its very best workers to participate in Japanese company trainee programs, and the Chinese government is very strict about repatriating those that they send; other countries are less selective and vigilant.

Despite these drawbacks (some would say *because* of them), company trainee programs seem likely to serve as Japan's principal acceptable vehicle for legal foreign labor importation in the foreseeable future. The demand for places in these programs is likely to remain quite strong. Even the first-year living stipend for a company trainee averages about 80,000 yen per month, equal to two full years of wages at a Chinese factory. There will be plenty of "takers" for company trainee-

---

[40]See, for example, Komai 1992. Some companies reportedly have even used the trainee system to obtain brides for their Japan-born workers from various Asian countries (Kajita 1994: 25).

ships, even if many of the trainees have actually experienced downward mobility in occupational status by coming to Japan.

A greatly expanded company trainee system could be the functional equivalent of a quota system for immigration, but it would probably be more effective in maintaining the strict-rotation principle than a U.S., Canadian, or Spanish-style quota system.[41] The company trainee approach offers other advantages. It is attractive to employers (any Japanese company can participate if it agrees to abide by the government's rules), is more acceptable to the Japanese public than a formal quota system, and avoids the diplomatic sensitivities of allocating visas among the sending countries that are Japan's close neighbors. Some academic experts believe that the political difficulties raised by a formal quota system would paralyze the government bureaucracy. Therefore, expanding the company trainee program is both a more realistic and a preferred option.

Importing Part-time "Student" Labor

The admission of foreigners on student visas represents yet another of Japan's current "backdoor" immigration policies. Persons admitted to Japan in this way are supposed to be taking Japanese language courses or be enrolled in various kinds of vocational training programs. Foreign students are legally entitled to work four hours per day, or a total of twenty hours per week, to supplement their incomes. In fact, most students work considerably more than that; and a substantial part of the so-called foreign student population is, de facto, a part of the regular, full-time labor force, whether or not they were bona fide students attending legitimate schools at the outset of their stay in Japan.

The government has recognized the presence of more than 50,000 foreign, part-time "student" workers as of June 1991 (Iguchi 1992: 2). Clearly many of them were bogus students to begin with; and some Japanese employers are taking advantage of student-visa holders as another source of unskilled labor. In 1994, the Ministry of Justice estimated the accumulated stock of student visa overstayers at 22,000 (*Japan Times* 1994). Nevertheless, despite a recently proposed tightening

---

[41] In the view of labor economist Haruo Shimada, one of Japan's leading authorities on immigration, company trainee programs need not and *should* not be used to maintain the strict-rotation principle. Shimada has developed a highly detailed proposal for a "work-and-learn program" that would enable unskilled foreign workers to acquire job and Japanese language skills and, if they chose to settle in Japan permanently at the end of their three-to-five-year workplace-based program, would facilitate their integration into Japanese society. Precisely because of its emphasis on the inevitability of foreign labor importation and the need to deal with foreign *workers* admitted to Japan (through whatever mechanism) as potential permanent *residents*, Shimada's proposal will undoubtedly meet stiff resistance from key sectors of the government bureaucracy and may raise serious concerns in the minds of average Japanese. However, the proposal merits serious consideration. See Shimada 1994, especially pp. 83–144.

of visa issuance requirements,[42] the long-standing government policy of gradually increasing the number of legally admitted foreign students (with a ceiling of 100,000 per year) remains in effect. In 1992, some 27,000 foreigners were permitted to enter on student visas, ostensibly to study at Japanese "language academies," compared with 13,900 in 1991.

The Public Opinion Constraint: Can Japan Become a Multiethnic Society?

Most government officials, political party leaders, many business leaders, and other policy influentials in Japan see general public opinion as a very real constraint on what the government can do in the area of immigration policy. Academic opinion seems divided on whether public opinion is a real constraint, or merely a pretext for inaction or a justification for the various "backdoor" and "side-door" immigration policies that allow Japan to cope with its labor shortage while not stirring up the native-born population and requiring the government to expend any political capital.

Is the tolerance of the Japanese public for higher levels of immigration really increasing or decreasing? According to various public opinion surveys sponsored by newspapers and government agencies since 1989, public acceptance—at least of a substantial, *temporary* foreign presence in the workforce—is much greater than was suspected before scientific measurement of public attitudes toward foreign workers began in Japan. The data reveal a marked generational divide in public opinion, with young people generally more tolerant and older Japanese more hostile toward immigrants, especially unskilled workers.[43] Such findings suggest that the government does have some degrees of freedom in immigration policy making that it does not acknowledge.

Looking beneath the surface of general public opinion, however, one finds considerable ambivalence and inconsistency among the Japanese. As a general proposition, immigration is fine so long as it meets certain conditions (e.g., temporariness). The most commonly given reasons for this acceptance are that foreign workers are helping to solve the country's labor-shortage problem and that they are a

---

[42]In early 1994 an advisory council appointed by the Ministry of Justice recommended that applicants for visas to study the Japanese language should be required to meet higher standards of Japanese proficiency, to help reduce the abuse of such visas by illegal foreign workers. Under existing regulations, a visa for language study in Japan can be obtained by any high school graduate, regardless of his demonstrated Japanese language competence.

[43]See, for example, results from a large 1988 survey by the Agency of Management and Coordination, reported in Sassen 1991: note 28, p. 312. The same positive correlation between age and anti-immigrant hostility has been found in surveys done in the United States and Germany, although the evidence is somewhat mixed for Canada and the United Kingdom. See Hoskin 1991: 110–12.

source of cheap labor. As yet, there is little fear of direct job competition with foreigners; pluralities of survey respondents say it is acceptable to give jobs that Japanese people shun to foreigners if they want to do them (see, for example, Prime Minister's Office 1991: 5).

Nevertheless, when Japanese have been asked whether they would be willing to live next door to an African, Iranian, or a Chinese, or whether they would be willing to have their daughter marry a foreigner, the responses were more cautious, even though large pluralities still expressed "pro-immigrant" views. A survey conducted by the city government of Tokyo found that 64 percent of Tokyo residents disliked having foreigners in their neighborhoods; only 28 percent welcomed outsiders (*Wall Street Journal* 1994).

Japanese interviewed in various surveys have been distinctly more pessimistic about the tolerance of *others*—which is perhaps a more accurate indicator of their own attitudes. In a 1991 survey done by the polling unit of the *Asahi Shimbun* newspaper, fully one-half of the respondents agreed with the statement that "Japan is a country with strong racial discrimination."[44] The same proportion agreed that "Japan is a country that does not understand, and is closed toward, accepting political refugees from abroad." Nevertheless, the same poll found that only 20 percent of the public wants an absolutely "closed-door" immigration policy; and a large plurality (48 percent of those who have actually seen or had some other contact with foreign workers) favors legalization of visa overstayers.

The Japanese in general are highly sensitive to racial/phenotypical differences, and some social scientists are convinced that those who are not *racially* Japanese, regardless of how *culturally* Japanese they may become, will never be accepted on an equal basis in Japanese society (the "Korean problem").[45] But there are at least some indications that these differences are not the insurmountable barriers to social assimilation that they have been in the past. For example, the rate of intermarriage between Japanese and Koreans has risen sharply; about 80 percent of permanent-resident Koreans now are marrying Japanese (see Kojima 1990). Since the late 1980s, marriages between Japanese and Filipinos and between Japanese and Latin American *Nikkeijin* have also become increasingly common.[46]

---

[44] In the more recent survey of Tokyo residents, 57 percent said that the Japanese discriminate against foreigners (*Wall Street Journal* 1994).

[45] As Takeyuki Tsuda points out, if this analysis is correct, virtually the only group of foreigners that could ever be successfully assimilated into Japanese society are the Latin American *Nikkeijin*, who are at least *racially* Japanese (personal communication, January 1993).

[46] In the past five years, 19,372 marriages between Japanese and Filipinos have been recorded by the Japanese Embassy in Manila; in more than 90 percent of these cases, the husband was Japanese (*Japan Times*, January 31, 1994).

Some academics argue that those Japanese who complain about the foreigners in their midst do so not primarily on racial or cultural grounds, but because of so-called "practical" difficulties that could be remedied with education and longer residence in Japan. For example, foreigners often do not know how to sort their garbage correctly into recyclable and nonrecyclable bins, they turn up their radios too loud, and so forth. Most Japanese are monolingual except for the limited English competence that they develop through the required pre-university curriculum; therefore, the language barrier is often cited as a key source of tensions and misunderstandings between foreigners and natives. "Once the foreigners learn enough Japanese, a lot of the tensions will disappear," one sociologist predicted (author interview, July 1992). Finally, while government officials frequently justify their actions in terms of what is necessary to maintain Japan's cultural purity, only 6.7 percent of the respondents in a national survey mentioned "the threat to Japan's unique culture" as a reason for opposing the employment of unskilled foreign laborers (Prime Minister's Office 1991: 7). Far more respondents were concerned about possible crime problems,[47] rising unemployment, and conflicts in local communities.

How are we to interpret this apparent bundle of contradictions? Can Japan really make the transition to a multicultural, multiethnic society without serious social and political conflict? On this crucial issue there is little consensus among Japanese public officials, business leaders, journalists, and academics; some are sanguine, others deeply skeptical or pessimistic. Perhaps the modal view is that much will depend on how rapidly the number of foreign workers increases, and perhaps on how they are distributed geographically and sectorally.

Some thoughtful Japanese intellectuals genuinely fear a right-wing backlash, à la Germany in the early 1990s, if the numbers of immigrants rise too quickly. They note that further overcrowding, especially in major cities, could amplify hostility toward foreigners. Moreover, if Japan is to make the transition to a multiethnic society — not just an "internationalized workforce" — deeply embedded negative stereotypes and intolerant attitudes toward non-Caucasian for-

---

[47]Media reports on crime statistics often focus on the number of crimes committed by foreigners, especially South Koreans and Iranians, who are viewed by most Japanese as actual or potential delinquents. However, there is no evidence that foreign workers are, as yet, a major source of urban crime in Japan. In 1992 the number of foreigners of all nationalities arrested for committing crimes (mostly petty larceny) was 5,961; the crime rate among non-Japanese was lower than that of the population as a whole (*Mainichi Daily News* 1993). The specific crime most commonly attributed to foreign workers in Japan in the early 1990s was the buying and selling of illegally doctored telephone calling cards which can be used to make free long-distance calls from pay phones. The allegedly brisk traffic in altered phone cards in the Iranian bazaar that used to be held in Tokyo's Yoyogi Park was one of the pretexts used by authorities to close the park temporarily in 1993.

eigners as well as exclusionary concepts of "Japanese-ness" must be altered.[48]

On the other hand, there seems to be a growing recognition that Japan's labor shortage is acute enough to "bottleneck" future economic growth, at least at the rates to which Japan has been accustomed. If the alternatives to foreign worker importation prove inadequate to deal with the labor shortage (as most experts believe they will be), then, most starkly put, the issue facing Japan will be: How much future economic growth and prosperity are the Japanese willing to sacrifice in exchange for maintaining ethnic homogeneity?

One potentially critical difference between public attitudes toward immigrants in Japan and those encountered in Germany today is that the Japanese are more likely to see foreign workers as playing a positive economic role, supporting a still-viable, labor-hungry economy. This perception is reflected even in public opinion surveys conducted during the 1990s recession, in which majorities of respondents continued to express the belief that foreign workers are employed primarily in jobs shunned by native-born Japanese. Many Germans, by contrast, see the foreigners in their midst as feeding off a troubled economy; people who merely took advantage of a once overly generous political asylum system.

The Future of Japanese Immigration Policy

Haruo Shimada recently summed up Japan's current dilemma in this way:

> The Japanese people don't want to face up to the requirements of a formal national immigration policy—the need for a real social integration policy, efforts to combat exploitative labor practices and discrimination against foreigners, solutions for housing problems, education of immigrant children, and so forth. They want to avoid open confrontations and debates on basic principles, like "one nation, one people." But the Japanese are a very realistic, pragmatic people. So they support the development of employer-based networks [the company trainee programs] to accommodate foreigners as their employees. This amounts to a de facto immigration policy, but without laws, rules, principles, or public debates. Moving

[48]For example, a Japanese official has argued that his country's ability to come to grips with a larger foreign worker presence is constrained by its long history of limited contacts with the outside world. "In such a confined environment, cultural ties bound the nation more closely and to such an extent that Japanese often understand each other without the need for explicit language. . . . [This] renders many Japanese incapable of communicating effectively with people who have different customs and traditions. For Japanese who have never lived abroad, more time is needed to learn how to associate with a foreign neighbor" (Muto 1993: 350).

> toward a formal immigration policy with explicit accep-
> tance criteria and proper control mechanisms will be a
> painful process for Japan. But we must bring foreigners in
> as human beings—or we shouldn't bring them in at all![49]

A number of ongoing structural transformations in the Japanese economy and society will probably force the government to come to grips, sooner rather than later, with the policy issues posed by Shimada. These processes include: the inexorable "greying" of the population; further segmentation of the labor market; the casualization of work (as evidenced by a major increase in part-time jobs and the proliferation of businesses that provide temporary workers to other firms needing them[50]); the interna-tionalization of the economy (which will inevitably strengthen both eco-nomic and social ties between Japan and labor-exporting countries of the Asia-Pacific region); the relative decline of the manufacturing sector; and the growth of the service sector (which has caused a proliferation of "small, freestanding firms not incorporated into the large economic groupings into which much of the Japanese economy is still organized" [Sassen 1991: 315]).

These fundamental transformations, perhaps coupled with further deregulation of the economy (as advocated by the succession of "reform" governments that have held power since the fall of the Liberal Demo-cratic Party regime in 1993), can be expected to create many additional spaces in the labor market for foreign workers, especially once Japan's "normal" rate of economic growth has been restored. Many economists believe that the Japanese economy still has a long-term real growth potential of 4 percent per annum, and some have argued that growth at that rate must be maintained to satisfy the population's desire for higher living standards.[51]

---

[49]Personal interview with Haruo Shimada, Dept. of Economics, Keio University, November 1992. For a fuller exposition of Shimada's views, see Shimada 1994, especially chap. 8.

[50]According to Ministry of Labor survey data, the proportion of part-timers in Japan's workforce increased from 7 percent in 1970 to 12 percent in 1987. Among women, part-time workers nearly doubled, from 12 percent to 23 percent, during the same period (statistics cited in Sassen 1991: 242). Today, part-time workers may constitute as much as 20 percent of the total labor force. Sociologist Takamichi Kajita reports that the Japanese food service industry and supermarkets, in particular, "cannot do without" such part-time workers, whose ranks increasingly include foreign workers as well as Japanese students and housewives. He also points out that in Japan, labor unions usually are not powerful enough to prevent this kind of "casualization" if management opts for greater flexibility in its workforce (Kajita 1994: 10, 58).

[51]See, for example, Koshiro 1991: 3. According to Koshiro's simulation, without a more expansionary immigration policy, wage-push inflation will raise consumer prices by more than 6 percent by the end of the current decade, even if economic growth does not exceed 2 percent per annum. If 1 million immigrants are admitted and the labor supply is further expanded through greater utilization of female and elderly workers, the simulation shows that wage-push inflation would be effectively restrained while maintaining a 4 percent annual economic growth rate.

The effect of Japan's most recent recession on the demand for foreign labor has not yet been investigated systematically. However, preliminary indications are that the impact has been much less than might have been expected. The growth of the illegal immigrant population may have leveled off during the recession of the 1990s, and the estimated stock of visa overstayers declined from May 1 to November 1, 1993, but only by 0.6 percent (see table 11.2). Businesses seem to have avoided laying off their foreign employees if at all possible, although most of these workers had their previously generous overtime pay reduced severely or eliminated altogether. Anecdotal evidence suggests that some employers became more selective during the recession, preferring to hire only Japanese-speaking immigrants; but the employment of foreign workers, even those with little or no Japanese language competence, did not cease.[52]

There is no evidence that the 1990s recession shut off the flow of new foreign workers, nor that it induced those already employed in Japan to return home prematurely. Even though prospective immigrants perceived a contraction of job opportunities in Japan as a result of the recession (perhaps more than warranted by objective labor market conditions), such perceptions were not strong enough to deter them from emigrating to Japan.[53] Moreover, the government's persistent failure to keep illegal foreign workers under stricter control, even in the depths of recession, sends a powerful message: "[It] makes foreigners feel that Japan is relatively easy to enter and that Japan actually accepts foreign workers" regardless of skill level (Kajita 1994: 20). Further encouragement is provided by local governments that continue to provide basic social services to foreign workers, often regardless of legal status,[54] and even by local-level Immigration Bureau officials who in some areas have begun granting residence permits to illegal immigrants who have married Japanese nationals.[55]

---

[52]Tomichi Ichimura (1993) quotes one factory manager as follows: "The problem is that despite the recession, there just aren't any young Japanese who are willing to work and put in overtime at a factory like this [a small die casting factory in Isesaki that makes pots and auto components from aluminum alloy]. We're saved, thanks to the foreigners [six Pakistani workers]."

[53]Field research conducted by Takeyuki Tsuda (Dept. of Anthropology, University of California, Berkeley) among *Nikkeijin* in two Brazilian cities in 1993–1994.

[54]In the 1993 and 1994 fiscal years, prefectural governments in the Tokyo metropolitan area, Gunma, and Kanagawa all adopted policies of helping to pay the medical bills of foreign workers, on "humanitarian" grounds. The Tokyo government's plan covers up to 70 percent of such workers' medical expenses (*Mainichi Daily News* 1994c). Some towns in these prefectures having large foreign-worker populations maintain considerably more elaborate social support systems (see, for example, *Asahi Evening News* 1994).

[55]The growing number of mixed marriages and indications of a more lenient stance by the Immigration Bureau have led to a sharp increase in the number of residency applications submitted by illegal-alien spouses. To justify these applications, lawyers have been citing the International Convention on the Rights of All Migrant Workers and Members of Their Families, approved by the United Nations General Assembly in December 1990, which stipulates the right of migrant workers and their dependents to live together. See Irie 1994; Hune 1991.

The available evidence, however fragmentary, suggests that in Japan, as in other advanced industrial countries, the demand for foreign labor has become largely insensitive to cyclical fluctuations in the economy. Future demand is more likely to be affected by such factors as the country's demographics (extremely low fertility, rapid aging of the native-born population); long-term labor shortages in certain sectors (e.g., small and medium-sized manufacturing firms, subcontractors, construction) and in certain low-social-status job categories; noneconomic "pull" factors like the desire for family reunification (which may be encouraged by more protracted company trainee programs and unlimited visa renewals for Latin American *Nikkeijin*); and the institutionalization of labor brokerage networks anchored in both the sending and receiving countries. If the post-1980 experience of other industrialized nations is any guide, a strong demand for immigrant labor driven by such factors will be increasingly resistant to government interventions—if and when the Japanese government summons the political will to close the side doors and backdoors to foreign workers.

Meanwhile, the lack of consensus on immigration evident in both the bureaucracy and the general public makes it prudent for the government to pursue a policy of playing for time. As one Japanese immigration specialist has observed, "The government seems to want to keep its options open concerning foreign worker policy, while satisfying the needs of small and medium-sized companies for foreign labor. It tries to leave some room for introducing tough controls over foreign workers, to use if economic conditions warrant. Once the government has adopted a formal, front-door [immigration] policy, amendments of the policy will become difficult" (Kajita 1994: 34).

References

Abella, Manolo I. 1994. "Introduction," special issue of *Asian and Pacific Migration Journal* 3:1.

Asahi Evening News (Tokyo). 1994. "Model Town Extends Helping Hands to Foreign Residents," January 1–2.

Campbell, John Creighton. 1992. *How Policies Change: The Japanese Government and the Aging Society.* Princeton, N.J.: Princeton University Press.

Chung, Chin Sung. 1992. "Illegal Korean Workers in Japan." Paper presented at the Yokohama City University Symposium on Foreign Workers, Yokohama, Japan, November.

Cook, Alice H., and Hiroko Hayashi. 1980. *Working Women in Japan: Discrimination, Resistance, and Reform.* Ithaca, N.Y.: Cornell University Press.

Fukushima, Mizuho. 1991. "Immigrant Asian Workers and Japan: The Reality I Discovered at HELP [Women's Shelter]." Paper presented at the conference "International Manpower Flows and Foreign Investment in Asia," Tokyo, September 9–12.

Gelb, Joyce, and Marian L. Palley, eds. 1994. *Women of Japan and Korea*. Philadelphia: Temple University Press.

Goto, Junichi. 1993. *Gaikokujin rodosha to nihon keizai*. Tokyo: Yuhikaku.

Hoskin, Marilyn. 1991. *New Immigrants and Democratic Society: Minority Integration in Western Democracies*. New York: Praeger.

Hune, Shirley. 1991. "Migrant Women in the Context of the International Convention on the Protection of the Rights of All Migrant Workers and Members of Their Families," *International Migration Review* 25:4 (Winter): 800–17.

Ichimura, Tomichi. 1993. "Illegal Workers Getting a Raw Deal," *Japan Times*, November 11.

Iguchi, Yasushi. 1992. "Foreign Workers and the Labour Market in Japan." Paper presented at the International Organization for Migration Symposium on Foreign Workers, Tokyo, October.

Ikezawa, Kenichi. 1994. "Foreign Apprentices Train for Future," *Nikkei Weekly* (Tokyo), May 2.

Inagami, Takeshi, Yasuo Kuwahara, and General Research Institute of People's Financial Savings. 1992. *Small and Medium-Size Enterprises That Use Foreign Workers*. Tokyo: Small and Mid-size Enterprise Research Center.

International Cooperation Enterprise Group. 1992. "Report on the Examination of Actual Conditions of the Nikkeijin Working in Our Country." Tokyo, February. Mimeo.

International Economic Insights. 1992. "Japan's Labor Market Gets Even Tighter." Washington, D.C.: Institute for International Economics, September–October.

Irie, Gaku. 1994. "Illegal Immigrants Fight for Basic Family Rights," *Nikkei Weekly*, February 14.

Iyotani, Toshio. 1991. "Foreign Labor and the Japanese Economy." Tokyo: Tokyo University of Foreign Studies. Manuscript.

———. 1992. "The Unavoidable Challenge: Foreign Workers in Postwar Japan" ("Sakerarenai kadai: Sengo Nippon keizai ni okeru gaikokujin rodosha"). In *Theory of Foreign Workers (Gaikokujin rodosha ron)*, edited by T. Iyotani and Takamichi Kajita. Tokyo: Kobundo.

Jameson, Sam. 1992. "Japan Trying to Get Workers Out of Factories and into Stores," *Los Angeles Times*, July 21.

Japan Foodservice Association. 1990. "Proposal to Accept Foreign Workers." Tokyo: The Association, May.

Japan Institute of Labor. 1992. *White Paper on Labour 1991: Present State and Problems and Female and Young Workers*. Tokyo: Ministry of Labor.

Japan Times. 1994. "Standards Eyed for Language Visas," March 31.

Kajita, Takamichi. 1994. "Characteristics of the Foreign Worker Problem in Japan." Tokyo: Faculty of Social Sciences, Hitosubashi University. Manuscript.

Keidanren. 1992. "Toward Sustainable Growth and Adequate Labor Supply." Tokyo.

Koga, Masanori. 1994. "The Impact of Immigrant Workers on the Regional Economy: A Case Study." In *Regional Development Impacts of Labour Migration in Asia*, edited by Wilbert Gooneratne, Philip L. Martin, and Hidehiko Sazanami. Research Report Series, no. 2. Nagoya, Japan: United Nations Centre for Regional Development.

Kojima, Hiroshi. 1990. "Research Note on Intermarriage Rates," *Journal of Health and Welfare Statistics* (Health and Welfare Statistics Association, Tokyo) 12:39–45.

Komai, Hiroshi. 1992. "Are Foreign Trainees in Japan Disguised Cheap Laborers?" *Migration World* 20:13–17.

Kono, Shigemi. 1994. "International Migration in Japan: A Demographic Sketch." In *Regional Development Impacts of Labour Migration in Asia*, edited by Wilbert Gooneratne, Philip L. Martin, and Hidehiko Sazanami. Research Report Series, no. 2. Nagoya, Japan: United Nations Centre for Regional Development.

Koshiro, Kazutoshi. 1991. "Labour Shortage and Employment Policies in Japan." Paper presented at the Second Japan-ASEAN Forum on International Labour Migration in East Asia, United Nations University, Tokyo, September 26–27.

Kuwahara, Yasuo. 1992. "To Tie the Untied String: Migrant Workers and Japan's Economic Cooperation." Working Paper MIG WP.70. Geneva: World Employment Programme, International Labour Organisation, May.

Machimura, Takashi. 1992. "The Urban Restructuring Process in Tokyo in the 1980s: Transforming Tokyo into a World City," *International Journal of Urban and Regional Research* 16:1.

Mainichi Daily News (Tokyo). 1993. "Blame for Crime Rise Laid on Foreigners," November 28.

———. 1994a. "Organized Crime Muscles in on Foreign Labor Market," February 21.

———. 1994b. "2,733 Illegal Foreign Workers Nabbed," February 22.

———. 1994c. "Tokyo to Help Cover Unpaid Medical Fees of Foreigners," January 9.

Martin, Linda G. 1989. "The Graying Of Japan," *Population Bulletin* 44:2 (July).

Morales, Richard A. 1985. "Under One Roof: Mexican Immigrant and Native-Born Workers in the Non-Union Restaurant Industry of San Diego County." Ph.D. dissertation, University of California, Berkeley.

Morita, Kiriro, and Toshio Iyotani. 1994. "Japan and the Problem of Foreign Workers." In *Regional Development Impacts of Labour Migration in Asia*, edited by Wilbert Gooneratne, Philip L. Martin, and Hidehiko Sazanami. Research Report Series, no. 2. Nagoya, Japan: United Nations Centre for Regional Development.

Morita, Kiriro, and Saskia Sassen. 1994. "The New Illegal Immigration in Japan, 1980–1992," *International Migration Review* 28:1 (Spring).

Muller, Thomas. 1993. *Immigrants and the American City*. New York: New York University Press.

Muto, Masatoshi. 1993. "Japan: The Issue of Migrant Workers." In *The Politics of Migration Policies*, edited by Daniel Kubat. 2d ed. New York: Center for Migration Studies.

Nakamura, Hachiro. 1993. "Urban Growth in Prewar Japan." In *Japanese Cities in the World Economy*, edited by Kuniko Fujita and Richard C. Hill. Philadelphia: Temple University Press.

Ohnuki-Tierney, Emiko. 1984. *Illness and Culture in Contemporary Japan: An Anthropological View*. New York: Cambridge University Press.

Oka, Takashi. 1993. "Foreign Workers in Japan Alter Industries and Viewpoints," *Christian Science Monitor*, October 20.

Osawa, Machiko. n.d. *Economic Change and Women Workers (Keizai Henka to Joshi Rodo)*. Tokyo: University of Tokyo Press, forthcoming.

Prime Minister's Office. 1980. "Basic Survey of Social Life." Tokyo.

———. 1982. "Survey on the Employment Management of Female Workers." Cited in "Formal and Informal Work in Japan: A Life Cycle Analysis of Women's Employment Opportunities," by Kazuko Tanaka (Iowa City: University of Iowa, 1986), manuscript.

———. 1991. "Public Opinion Survey on Foreign Workers: Summary." Tokyo: Foreign Press Center, March.

Sanger, David E. 1994. "Job-Seeking Women in Japan See Discrimination," *New York Times*, May 27.

Sasaki, Shoko. 1994. "Clandestine Labour in Japan: Sources, Magnitude and Implications." In *Regional Development Impacts of Labour Migration in Asia*, edited by Wilbert Gooneratne, Philip L. Martin, and Hidehiko Sazanami. Research Report Series, no. 2. Nagoya, Japan: United Nations Centre for Regional Development.

Saso, Mary. 1990. *Women in the Japanese Workplace*. London: Hilary Shipman.

Sassen, Saskia. 1991. *The Global City: New York, London, Tokyo*. Princeton, N.J.: Princeton University Press.

Shimada, Haruo. 1994. *Japan's "Guest Workers": Issues and Public Policies*. Tokyo: University of Tokyo Press, distributed by Columbia University Press.

Tanaka, Kazuko. 1986. "Formal and Informal Work in Japan: A Life Cycle Analysis of Women's Employment Opportunities." Iowa City: University of Iowa. Manuscript.

Tokyo Chamber of Commerce and Industry. 1989. "Proposals on the Establishment of a Training System for Foreign Workers." Tokyo: The Chamber, December.

United Press International. 1994. "Illegal Workers on the Rise in Japan." UPI dispatch, Tokyo, May 16.

Ventura, Rey. 1992. *Underground in Japan*. London: Jonathan Cape.

Wall Street Journal. 1994. "World Wire." June 6.

Watanabe, Susumu. 1994. "The Lewisian Turning Point and International Migration: The Case of Japan," *Asian and Pacific Migration Journal* 3:1:119–47.

Yamanaka, Keiko. 1992. "Unskilled Foreign Workers and the New Immigration Policies of Japan." Revised version of a paper presented at the 44th Annual Meeting of the Association for Asian Studies, Washington, D.C., April.

Yamazaki, Yoshihiko, et al. 1992. *Iranians and the Ueno Community: Their Conflict and Coexistence*. Tokyo: Dept. of Health Sociology, University of Tokyo.

Yashiro, Atsushi. 1984. "Employment Management of Female Employees: A Case Study of a Large Department Store," *Mita Business Review* 27:5:67–84.

Yomiuri Shimbun. 1992. "Some Labor Unions Welcome Unskilled Foreign Workers," August 7.

Zhao, Quansheng. 1993. *Japanese Policy Making: The Politics Behind Politics— Informal Mechanisms and the Making of China Policy*. Westport, Conn.: Praeger.

Commentary

Theory versus Reality in Japanese Immigration Policy

Keiko Yamanaka

Contemporary Japan is no exception to the developed world's pattern of migration streams, as Cornelius's chapter convincingly demonstrates. Japan's long-closed labor market recently has proven to be porous, and, like every other advanced economy, Japan now relies increasingly on foreign labor to fill low-skill jobs. Driving the influx of foreign workers are the same factors seen elsewhere, including restructuring of the domestic and international economies, and a demographic transition to an older population. Also like its counterpart countries, Japan has had little success in controlling immigration by means such as employer sanctions and tightened visa issuance.

The cross-national comparative approach used in this book does not permit in-depth examination of the sociopolitical conditions and historical contexts informing a country's immigration policy. Yet Cornelius is good at deciphering the ambiguous, often disguised, messages in the statements and writings of Japanese policy makers, business leaders, and mainstream academics. From his analysis we can identify several key gaps between theory and reality:

- "Official" immigration policy is to admit only skilled professionals, yet several ad hoc measures have opened backdoors to unskilled foreign workers.

- The long-term solutions to labor market imbalances proposed by neoclassical macro-economic theory are countered by pragmatic market forces operating to fill an immediate labor shortage.

- Japan embraces the democratic ideals of a modern welfare state even as the nation divides along nationality, ethnicity, and gender lines.

No observer can miss the strong contradiction between the firm government rule that only skilled foreign labor is to be admitted, on the one hand, and the presence in Japan of a half-million unskilled workers from Asia and South America on the other. Ad hoc government measures since the mid-1980s have enabled Japanese-Brazilians, Japanese language students, company trainees, and tourists to enter and work in Japan under various legal constraints.

Conspicuous among these backdoor entrants are the so-called Asian female entertainers. New arrivals in this category totaled 64,100 in 1992; Filipinas were the largest group, followed by Koreans and Taiwanese. Thailand is believed to be another significant source, since numerous Thai women enter Japan as tourists but remain to work. Entertainers are admitted as professionals, yet this group is in fact a source of cheap labor for positions shunned by Japanese women: as singers, dancers, bar hostesses, and prostitutes. Despite the involvement of racketeers as employers and labor brokers, Japanese policy makers have been slow to address the situation of these exploited female immigrants, whose working conditions often approximate slavery. (Interestingly, while women formed the first wave of Japan's "guestworkers" in the late 1970s, it was only after men began to arrive in large numbers in the mid-1980s that the foreign worker problem rose to prominence). The growing incidence of AIDS in Japan has prompted new fear of and revulsion toward these Asian women, but few scholarly studies have addressed the behavior of female entertainers and their association with the disease.

Cornelius appropriately emphasizes the gap between the long-term labor policies endorsed by Japanese labor economists and adopted by the Ministry of Labor, on the one hand, and the realities of labor market forces on the other. My own research in the labor market of Hamamatsu-shi, Central Japan, revealed that small manufacturing subcontractors were simply not able to attract good workers in the late 1980s, when demand for labor shot up. Women and older workers were either not available or were not desired by local employers, who turned instead to foreign workers, especially Japanese-Brazilians. Conveniently, an amendment to Japan's Immigration Control and Refugee Recognition Act in December 1989 legalized the employment of this population. South Americans thus functioned as a safety valve for Japanese employers, who could hire them during economic expansion and let them go in periods of recession.

Underlying this employment pattern is Japan's dual industrial structure of a few large firms and numerous small subcontractors. My Hamamatsu data indicate that smaller firms had difficulty securing workers in 1989, when the economy was growing rapidly. Firms with more than 300 employees had increased their hiring of young Japanese men by 20–50 percent during the preceding year, while small firms' ability to attract young male workers fell by 8–20 percent, even though they offered competitive wages. This association between firm size and labor shortages points to the need for empirical research in two areas. The first concerns the emerging patterns of wage stratification and division of labor by industry and occupation among foreign workers according to their legal status, nationality, ethnicity, and gender. The smallest labor-short firms may have found Japanese-Brazilians hard to attract because they were legally entitled to work, and therefore commanded higher wages and better working conditions. The weakest employers must then have turned to unauthorized or disguised cheap laborers.

The second area where research is needed relates to how the hierarchical labor market for foreigners is linked to and interacts with a preexisting labor market that places certain types of Japanese workers (women, the elderly, and contract workers) at the bottom. The lifetime employment system commonly found in large Japanese organizations, including the bureaucracy, involves on-the-job skill development and extremely low turnover rates within internal labor markets. Outside those domains, there is a large labor market in which workers are hired on a temporary basis only. Since the 1980s, foreign workers have joined the pool of short-term labor. How have they been incorporated into this labor market, and what has been the impact of that process on the groups traditionally comprising it?

Yet another gap between theory and reality in Japan's immigration policy is suggested by the contradiction between the ideals of civil society and actual practice. It was generally assumed in the postwar period that economic prosperity would spawn all-encompassing social justice. The racial homogeneity myth epitomized by the slogan "one nation, one ethnicity" has played an important role in this construct: Japan's democracy is based on the idea that everyone is equal because everyone is Japanese. But the myth of homogeneity has long been belied by the presence of ethnic and national minorities, including ethnic Koreans and Chinese. (The forced assimilation of Okinawans and aboriginal Ainu is another case in point.) Ironically, the myth of racial homogeneity has denied basic human rights to the ethnic Koreans who are permanent residents in Japan, where they were born and educated.

Legal barriers based on nationality and gender began to give way in the mid-1980s as the economy internationalized. Under the nationality law in effect until 1985, Japanese nationality was handed down through paternal lineage. Thus a child of a Japanese mother and non-Japanese father was not a Japanese national. Bowing to the United Nations Convention on the Elimination of All Forms of Discrimination against Women, Japan amended the nationality law in 1985 to allow Japanese nationality to be passed through either parent. The new nationality law represented a victory for feminists as well as Koreans and Japan's other immigrant groups. The majority (80 percent) of ethnic Koreans marry Japanese nationals; their children now automatically become Japanese. It is premature to evaluate fully the amendment's impact, but it could portend wider acceptance of multiculturalism in a country that has long pretended to be monocultural. The recent emergence of the Japanese-Brazilian community will test further Japan's willingness to integrate immigrant groups, old and new.

What do these multiple gaps between theory (ideals) and reality imply for an understanding of Japan's immigration policy and its implementation? Analysis of the areas of contradiction discussed above suggests that many of the sociopolitical forces that are shaping international migration to Japan today have deep historical and cultural roots. The arrival of substantial numbers of foreign workers may catalyze challenges to the myths of social harmony and racial homogeneity that are purported to have driven Japan's postwar economic miracle and encouraged belief in a Japanese exceptionalism. As a latecomer to the world market and global community, Japan was able, until very recently, to appropriate ideas and technologies from the West for its own economic and social progress. But there are no models for Japan to follow in coping with its contemporary immigration problems. Japan must develop its own philosophy and policies in this area. It can no longer dismiss its de facto guestworker program as an "overstayer" problem. The world will be watching closely to see how this traditionally closed country will open its doors to migrants from poor and war-torn countries.

Statistical Appendix

This appendix presents basic population, workforce, and immigration data for the nine countries examined in this volume. These nine countries include the richest of the industrial democracies; although together they contain only about 13 percent of the world's population, their combined GDP, which totals over $13.3 trillion, is approximately one-half of the world's GDP. All of these countries have slow-growing populations and native-born workforces.

Comparative data on foreigners or immigrants must be interpreted with caution. Germany, for example, considers the child of Turkish parents who have been in Germany for twenty years to be a foreigner, while the United States counts as a citizen the U.S.-born child of an illegal alien who just recently slipped into the country. An international migrant to one of these countries is recorded when an individual enters that nation's territory and is classified as an immigrant by government officials. This means that official immigration statistics will underestimate the number of foreign-born persons present to the extent that individuals enter clandestinely, without undergoing a document inspection, and they will overestimate the size of the immigrant population if migrants' exits from the country are not recorded, which is frequently the case. The data in table A.11 represent the gross, or one-way, inflows of immigrants. High numbers, such as for France in 1982 and the United States in 1990–1991, reflect amnesties under which aliens who were present illegally were regularized (i.e., recognized as immigrants).

The baseline economic data must be interpreted with caution as well. Definitions of labor force, sectors, and unemployment vary among the nine countries. Thus cross-sectional comparisons should take account of local statistical methods. With few exceptions, however, the time series data within each country were gathered using the same methodology.

TABLE A.1
TOTAL POPULATION (THOUSANDS OF PERSONS)

Year	Belgium	Canada	France	Germany	Italy	Japan	Spain	UK	USA
1970	9,651	21,324	50,772	60,651	53,661	103,720	33,876	55,632	205,052
1971	9,673	21,595	51,251	61,302	54,015	104,750	34,190	55,907	207,661
1972	9,709	21,822	51,701	61,672	54,400	106,180	34,498	56,079	209,896
1973	9,739	22,072	52,118	61,976	54,779	108,660	34,810	56,210	211,909
1974	9,768	22,395	52,460	62,054	55,130	110,160	35,147	56,224	213,854
1975	9,795	22,727	52,699	61,829	55,441	111,520	35,515	56,215	215,973
1976	9,811	23,027	52,909	61,531	55,701	112,770	35,937	56,206	218,035
1977	9,822	23,295	53,145	61,400	55,730	113,880	36,367	56,179	220,239
1978	9,830	23,535	53,376	61,327	56,127	114,920	36,778	56,167	222,585
1979	9,837	23,768	53,606	61,359	56,292	115,880	37,108	56,227	225,055
1980	9,847	24,070	53,880	61,566	56,416	116,800	37,386	56,314	227,757
1981	9,853	24,366	54,182	61,682	56,503	117,650	37,751	56,379	230,138
1982	9,856	24,604	54,480	61,638	56,639	118,450	37,961	56,335	232,520
1983	9,855	24,803	54,729	61,423	56,825	119,260	38,180	56,377	234,799
1984	9,855	24,995	54,947	61,175	56,983	120,020	38,342	56,488	237,011
1985	9,858	25,181	55,170	61,024	57,128	120,750	38,505	56,618	239,279
1986	9,862	25,374	55,394	61,066	57,221	121,490	38,668	56,763	241,625
1987	9,870	25,644	55,630	61,077	57,331	122,090	38,716	56,930	243,942
1988	9,921	25,939	55,884	61,450	57,441	122,610	38,809	57,065	246,307
1989	9,938	26,254	56,160	62,063	57,525	123,120	38,888	57,236	248,762
1990	9,967	26,620	56,420	63,232	57,647	123,540	38,959	57,411	251,523

Source: Labour Force Statistics, 1970–1990 (Paris: OECD, 1992), pp. 18–19.

TABLE A.2
TOTAL CIVILIAN LABOR FORCE (THOUSANDS OF PERSONS)

Year	Belgium	Canada	France	Germany	Italy	Japan	Spain	UK	USA
1970	3,675	8,395	20,857	26,318	20,329	51,530	12,549	24,936	82,771
1971	3,699	8,639	21,024	26,457	20,285	51,860	12,721	24,861	84,382
1972	3,710	8,897	21,182	26,592	20,146	52,000	12,671	24,917	87,034
1973	3,748	9,276	21,456	26,922	20,309	53,260	12,946	25,272	89,429
1974	3,812	9,639	21,690	26,884	20,503	53,100	13,074	25,331	91,949
1975	3,837	9,974	21,764	26,660	20,717	53,230	13,023	25,557	93,775
1976	3,873	10,203	22,013	26,502	21,032	53,780	13,078	25,775	96,158
1977	3,893	10,500	22,322	26,505	21,329	54,520	13,011	25,897	99,009
1978	3,918	10,895	22,463	26,682	21,423	55,320	13,008	26,039	102,251
1979	3,964	11,231	22,666	26,996	21,743	55,960	13,030	26,314	104,962
1980	3,979	11,573	22,800	27,417	21,997	56,500	13,046	26,517	106,940
1981	4,000	11,899	22,953	27,770	22,129	57,070	13,079	26,406	108,670
1982	4,027	11,926	23,163	28,026	22,220	57,740	13,228	26,354	110,204
1983	4,047	12,110	23,142	28,067	22,490	58,890	13,398	26,288	111,550
1984	4,042	12,316	23,304	28,135	22,722	59,270	13,487	26,939	113,544
1985	4,023	12,532	23,357	28,366	22,890	59,634	13,586	27,389	115,461
1986	4,019	12,746	23,445	28,659	23,225	60,200	13,819	27,469	117,834
1987	4,024	13,011	23,555	28,854	23,415	60,840	14,333	27,660	119,865
1988	4,034	13,275	23,606	29,075	23,683	61,660	14,633	27,939	121,669
1989	4,054	13,503	23,740	29,246	23,700	62,700	14,823	28,119	123,869
1990	4,091	13,681	23,929	29,829	23,744	63,840	15,021	28,133	124,787

Source: Labour Force Statistics, 1970–1990 (Paris: OECD, 1992), pp. 30–31.

TABLE A.3

EMPLOYMENT IN INDUSTRY (THOUSANDS OF PERSONS)

Year	Belgium	Canada	France	Germany	Italy	Japan	Spain	UK	USA
1970	1,535	2,449	7,975	12,908	7,591	18,190	4,335	10,908	27,029
1971	1,534	2,470	8,031	12,710	7,617	18,450	4,373	10,534	26,092
1972	1,503	2,532	8,092	12,570	7,469	18,600	4,472	10,297	26,766
1973	1,508	2,685	8,241	12,651	7,454	19,570	4,632	10,455	28,225
1974	1,522	2,784	8,301	12,273	7,614	19,380	4,713	10,428	28,194
1975	1,453	2,720	8,056	11,606	7,636	18,730	4,772	9,987	26,288
1976	1,410	2,812	7,985	11,430	7,526	18,880	4,606	9,699	27,354
1977	1,369	2,782	7,951	11,369	7,617	18,890	4,593	9,673	28,402
1978	1,324	2,869	7,831	11,385	7,577	18,930	4,489	9,653	29,889
1979	1,298	3,002	7,725	11,534	7,583	19,140	4,351	9,707	30,918
1980	1,270	3,055	7,664	11,592	7,699	19,560	4,165	9,426	30,313
1981	1,193	3,111	7,459	11,383	7,647	19,700	3,957	8,607	30,191
1982	1,139	2,815	7,341	11,029	7,527	19,650	3,784	8,168	28,256
1983	1,100	2,726	7,150	10,689	7,352	19,930	3,699	7,787	28,253
1984	1,077	2,816	6,902	10,645	7,045	20,080	3,513	7,718	29,892
1985	1,061	2,850	6,695	10,684	6,896	20,250	3,377	7,662	30,047
1986	1,048	2,908	6,573	10,771	6,823	20,180	3,475	7,468	30,338
1987	1,027	2,989	6,470	10,774	6,716	19,970	3,681	7,468	30,475
1988	1,022	3,140	6,413	10,717	6,750	20,520	3,829	7,595	30,965
1989	1,045	3,203	6,450	10,836	6,754	20,990	4,036	7,755	31,287
1990	1,056	3,094	6,503	11,111	6,845	21,290	4,202	7,703	30,901

Source: Labour Force Statistics, 1970–1990 (Paris: OECD, 1992), pp. 38–39.

TABLE A.4

EMPLOYMENT IN INDUSTRY (AS PERCENT OF CIVILIAN LABOR FORCE)

Year	Belgium	Canada	France	Germany	Italy	Japan	Spain	UK	USA
1970	41.8	29.2	38.2	49.0	37.3	35.3	34.5	43.7	32.7
1971	41.5	28.6	38.2	48.0	37.5	35.6	34.4	42.4	30.9
1972	40.5	28.5	38.2	47.3	37.1	35.8	35.3	41.3	30.8
1973	40.2	28.9	38.4	47.0	36.7	36.7	35.8	41.4	31.6
1974	39.9	28.9	38.3	45.7	37.1	36.5	36.0	41.2	30.7
1975	37.9	27.3	37.0	43.5	36.9	35.2	36.6	39.1	28.0
1976	36.4	27.6	36.3	43.1	35.8	35.1	35.2	37.6	28.4
1977	35.2	26.5	35.6	42.9	35.7	34.6	35.3	37.4	28.7
1978	33.8	26.3	34.9	42.7	35.4	34.2	34.5	37.1	29.2
1979	32.7	26.7	34.1	42.7	34.9	34.2	33.4	36.9	29.5
1980	31.9	26.4	33.6	42.3	35.0	34.6	31.9	35.5	28.3
1981	29.8	26.1	32.5	41.0	34.6	34.5	30.3	32.6	27.8
1982	28.3	23.6	31.7	39.4	33.9	34.0	28.6	31.0	25.6
1983	27.2	22.5	30.9	38.1	32.7	33.8	27.6	29.6	25.3
1984	26.6	22.9	29.6	37.8	31.0	33.9	26.0	28.6	26.3
1985	26.4	22.7	28.7	37.7	30.1	34.0	24.9	28.0	26.0
1986	26.1	22.8	28.0	37.6	29.4	33.5	25.1	27.2	25.7
1987	25.5	23.0	27.5	37.3	28.7	32.8	25.7	27.0	25.4
1988	25.3	23.7	27.2	36.9	28.5	33.3	26.2	27.2	25.5
1989	25.8	23.7	27.2	37.1	28.5	33.5	27.2	27.6	25.3
1990	25.8	22.6	27.2	37.2	28.8	33.3	28.0	27.4	24.8

Source: Labour Force Statistics, 1970–1990 (Paris: OECD, 1992), pp. 30–31, 38–39.

TABLE A.5
EMPLOYMENT IN SERVICES (THOUSANDS OF PERSONS)

Year	Belgium	Canada	France	Germany	Italy	Japan	Spain	UK	USA
1970	1,892	4,866	9,602	10,999	7,749	23,890	4,575	12,686	48,083
1971	1,931	5,027	9,797	11,434	7,684	24,630	4,706	12,867	49,765
1972	1,965	5,237	10,010	11,741	7,792	25,110	4,680	13,107	51,787
1973	2,001	5,503	10,277	12,052	8,070	25,970	4,909	13,525	53,265
1974	2,050	5,762	10,516	12,184	8,377	26,240	5,021	13,676	54,987
1975	2,071	5,999	10,652	12,230	8,594	26,890	4,925	14,046	56,051
1976	2,100	6,103	10,949	12,395	8,858	27,400	5,113	14,125	57,944
1977	2,132	6,316	11,224	12,572	9,044	28,190	5,132	14,181	60,189
1978	2,182	6,544	11,478	12,811	9,217	28,820	5,097	14,364	62,609
1979	2,240	6,803	11,672	13,176	9,485	29,520	5,170	14,706	64,395
1980	2,271	7,070	11,816	13,534	9,715	30,030	5,157	14,924	65,461
1981	2,279	7,290	11,953	13,749	9,982	30,540	5,151	14,765	66,687
1982	2,287	7,242	12,167	13,844	10,248	31,250	5,252	14,784	67,700
1983	2,291	7,359	12,341	13,842	10,472	32,090	5,279	14,895	69,040
1984	2,310	7,528	12,452	13,986	10,947	32,460	5,247	15,576	71,644
1985	2,347	7,796	12,638	14,186	11,316	32,730	5,310	15,932	73,765
1986	2,386	8,053	12,848	14,484	11,550	33,400	5,642	16,169	75,909
1987	2,426	8,306	13,074	14,759	11,699	34,250	5,980	16,696	78,565
1988	2,486	8,549	13,358	15,041	12,012	34,850	6,256	17,423	80,677
1989	2,524	8,747	13,631	15,361	12,133	35,660	6,626	18,055	82,678
1990	2,570	8,947	13,904	15,874	12,383	36,700	6,890	18,305	83,658

Source: Labour Force Statistics, 1970–1990 (Paris: OECD, 1992), pp. 40–41.

TABLE A.6
EMPLOYMENT IN SERVICES (AS PERCENT OF CIVILIAN LABOR FORCE)

Year	Belgium	Canada	France	Germany	Italy	Japan	Spain	UK	USA
1970	51.5	58.0	46.0	41.8	38.1	46.4	36.5	50.9	58.1
1971	52.2	58.2	46.6	43.2	37.9	47.5	37.0	51.8	59.0
1972	53.0	58.9	47.3	44.2	38.7	48.3	36.9	52.6	59.5
1973	53.4	59.3	47.9	44.8	39.7	48.8	37.9	53.5	59.6
1974	53.8	59.8	48.5	45.3	40.9	49.4	38.4	54.0	59.8
1975	54.0	60.1	48.9	45.9	41.5	50.5	37.8	55.0	59.8
1976	54.2	59.8	49.7	46.8	42.1	50.9	39.1	54.8	60.3
1977	54.8	60.2	50.3	47.4	42.4	51.7	39.4	54.8	60.8
1978	55.7	60.1	51.1	48.0	43.0	52.1	39.2	55.2	61.2
1979	56.5	60.6	51.5	48.8	43.6	52.8	39.7	55.9	61.4
1980	57.1	61.1	51.8	49.4	44.2	53.2	39.5	56.3	61.2
1981	57.0	61.3	52.1	49.5	45.1	53.5	39.4	55.9	61.4
1982	56.8	60.7	52.5	49.4	46.1	54.1	39.7	56.1	61.4
1983	56.6	60.8	53.3	49.3	46.6	54.5	39.4	56.7	61.9
1984	57.1	61.1	53.4	49.7	48.2	54.8	38.9	57.8	63.1
1985	58.3	62.2	54.1	50.0	49.4	54.9	39.1	58.2	63.9
1986	59.4	63.2	54.8	50.5	49.7	55.5	40.8	58.9	64.4
1987	60.3	63.8	55.5	51.2	50.0	56.3	41.7	60.4	65.5
1988	61.6	64.4	56.6	51.7	50.7	56.5	42.8	62.4	66.3
1989	62.3	64.8	57.4	52.5	51.2	56.9	44.7	64.2	66.7
1990	62.8	65.4	58.1	53.2	52.2	57.5	45.9	65.1	67.0

Source: Labour Force Statistics, 1970–1990 (Paris: OECD, 1992), pp. 30–31, 40–41.

TABLE A.7

UNEMPLOYMENT (AS PERCENT OF LABOR FORCE)

Year	Belgium	Canada	France	Germany	Italy	Japan	Spain	UK	USA
1970	1.9	5.6	2.5	0.6	5.3	1.1	2.5	2.2	4.8
1971	1.8	6.1	2.7	0.7	5.3	1.2	3.3	2.8	5.8
1972	2.3	6.2	2.8	0.9	6.3	1.4	2.8	3.1	5.5
1973	2.4	5.5	2.7	1.0	6.2	1.3	2.5	2.2	4.8
1974	2.5	5.3	2.8	2.1	5.3	1.4	3.0	2.1	5.5
1975	4.5	6.9	4.0	4.0	5.8	1.9	4.3	3.2	8.3
1976	5.9	7.1	4.4	3.9	6.6	2.0	4.4	4.8	7.6
1977	6.7	8.0	4.9	3.8	7.0	2.0	5.1	5.2	6.9
1978	7.2	8.3	5.2	3.6	7.1	2.2	6.8	5.1	6.0
1979	7.5	7.4	5.9	3.2	7.6	2.1	8.4	4.6	5.8
1980	7.9	7.4	6.3	3.2	7.5	2.0	11.1	5.6	7.0
1981	10.2	7.5	7.4	4.5	7.8	2.2	13.8	9.0	7.5
1982	11.9	10.9	8.1	6.4	8.4	2.4	15.6	10.4	9.5
1983	13.2	11.8	8.3	7.9	9.3	2.6	17.0	11.2	9.5
1984	13.2	11.2	9.7	7.9	9.9	2.7	19.7	11.1	7.4
1985	12.3	10.4	10.2	8.0	10.1	2.6	21.1	11.5	7.1
1986	11.6	9.5	10.4	7.6	10.9	2.8	20.8	11.6	6.9
1987	11.3	8.8	10.5	7.6	11.8	2.8	20.1	10.4	6.1
1988	10.3	7.7	10.0	7.6	11.8	2.5	19.1	8.3	5.4
1989	9.3	7.5	9.4	6.8	11.8	2.3	16.9	6.1	5.2
1990	8.7	8.1	9.0	6.2	10.8	2.1	15.9	5.5	5.4

Source: Labour Force Statistics, 1970–1990 (Paris: OECD, 1992), pp. 32–33.

TABLE A.8

STOCK OF MIGRANTS (THOUSANDS OF PERSONS)

Year	Belgium	Canada	France	Germany	Italy	UK	USA
1970							9,619.3
1971							
1972							
1973							
1974							
1975							
1976							
1977							
1978							
1979							
1980			3,440.0	4,453.3	298.7		14,079.9
1981	885.7	3,848.3		4,629.8	331.7		
1982	891.2		3,714.2	4,666.9	358.9		
1983	890.9			4,534.9	381.3		
1984	897.6			4,363.7	403.9	1,601.0	
1985	846.5			4,378.9	423.0	1,731.0	
1986	853.2	3,908.0		4,512.7		1,820.0	
1987	862.5			4,630.2		1,839.0	
1988	868.8			4,489.1		1,821.0	
1989	880.8			4,845.9		1,949.0	
1990	904.5		3,607.6	5,241.8		1,875.0	

Source: SOPEMI, Trends in International Migration (Paris: OECD, 1992), pp. 131, 149, 151.

TABLE A.9
STOCK OF MIGRANTS (PERCENT OF TOTAL POPULATION)

Year	Belgium	Canada	France	Germany	Italy	UK	USA
1970							4.7
1971							
1972							
1973							
1974							
1975							
1976							
1977							
1978							
1979							
1980			6.4	7.2	0.5		6.2
1981	9.0	15.8		7.5	0.6		
1982	9.0		6.8	7.6	0.6		
1983	9.0			7.4	0.7		
1984	9.1			7.1	0.7	2.8	
1985	8.6			7.2	0.7	3.1	
1986	8.7	15.4		7.4		3.2	
1987	8.7			7.6		3.2	
1988	8.8			7.3		3.2	
1989	8.9			7.8		3.4	
1990	9.1		6.4	8.3		3.3	

Source: SOPEMI, *Trends in International Migration* (Paris: OECD, 1992), pp. 131, 149, 151.

TABLE A.10
FOREIGN LABOR STOCKS (THOUSANDS OF PERSONS)

Year	Belgium	France	Germany	UK
1980		1458.2	2115.7	
1981		1427.1	2096.3	
1982		1503.0	2029.0	
1983	190.6	1574.8	1983.5	
1984	182.5	1658.2	1854.9	744.0
1985	179.7	1649.2	1823.4	808.0
1986	179.2	1555.7	1833.7	815.0
1987	176.6	1524.9	1865.5	815.0
1988	179.3	1557.0	1910.6	871.0
1989	196.4	1593.8	1940.6	960.0
1990		1553.5	2025.1	933.0

Source: SOPEMI, *Trends in International Migration* (Paris: OECD, 1992), p. 133.

TABLE A.11
INFLOWS OF MIGRANTS (THOUSANDS OF PERSONS)

Year	Belgium	Canada[1]	France	Germany	Italy[2]	UK	USA
1970							373.3
1971							370.5
1972							384.7
1973							400.0
1974							394.9
1975							386.2
1976							398.6
1977							462.3
1978							601.4
1979							460.3
1980	46.8	143.1	59.4	523.6	298.7	69.8	530.6
1981	41.3	128.6	75.0	451.7	331.7	59.1	596.6
1982	36.2	121.1	144.4	275.5	358.9	53.9	594.1
1983	34.3	89.2	64.2	253.5	381.1	53.5	559.8
1984	37.2	88.2	51.4	295.8	403.9	51.0	543.9
1985	37.5	84.3	43.4	324.4	423.0	55.4	570.0
1986	39.3	99.2	38.3	378.6	450.2	47.8	601.7
1987	40.1	152.1	39.0	414.9	572.1	46.0	601.5
1988	38.2	161.9	44.0	545.4	645.4	49.3	643.0
1989	43.5	192.0	53.2	649.5	490.4	49.7	1090.9
1990	52.3	213.6	63.1		701.1	52.4	1536.5

[1]Inflows of permanent settlers.
[2]Residence permits granted.
Sources: SOPEMI, *Trends in International Migration* (Paris: OECD, 1992), pp. 67, 132, 150; *1990 Statistical Yearbook of the Immigration and Naturalization Service* (Washington, D.C.: U.S. Government Printing Office, 1991), p. 47.

TABLE A.12
ASYLUM SEEKERS (INFLOWS, IN THOUSANDS OF PERSONS)

Year	Belgium	Canada[1]	France	Germany	Italy	Spain	UK	USA[2]
1980	2.7	40.4	18.8	107.8			9.9	95.2
1981	2.4	15.0	19.8	49.4			2.9	178.3
1982	3.1	16.9	22.5	37.2			4.2	76.2
1983	2.9	14.0	22.3	19.7	3.1	1.4	4.3	92.5
1984	3.7	15.3	21.6	35.3	4.6	1.1	3.9	99.6
1985	5.3	16.8	28.8	73.8	5.4	2.3	5.4	80.7
1986	7.6	19.2	26.2	99.7	6.5	2.8	4.8	67.3
1987	6.0	21.6	27.6	57.4	11.0	3.7	5.2	85.8
1988	4.5	26.8	34.3	103.1	1.4	4.5	5.7	105.0
1989	8.1	37.0	61.4	121.3	2.2	4.0	16.5	190.6
1990	13.0	39.7	54.7	193.1	4.7	8.6	30.0	135.3
1991	15.2		50.0	256.1	27.0	8.0	57.7	
1992	17.7	37.7	27.5	438.2	2.5	11.7	32.0	103.5
1993	26.9	20.5	26.5	322.6	1.3	12.9	28.5	150.4

[1]Figures for Canada include both convention refugees and "designated class" (those who do not strictly meet the UN Convention).
[2]Figures for the United States are for applications for asylum filed with the INS.
Sources: SOPEMI, *Trends in International Migration* (Paris: OECD, 1992), pp. 131, 150; *1990 Statistical Yearbook of the Immigration and Naturalization Service* (Washington, D.C., U.S. Government Printing Office, 1991), p. 102.

TABLE A.13
ALIENS APPREHENDED (THOUSANDS OF PERSONS)

Year	USA
1970	345.4
1971	420.1
1972	505.9
1973	656.0
1974	788.1
1975	766.6
1976	1097.7
1977	1042.2
1978	1058.0
1979	1076.4
1980	910.4
1981	975.8
1982	970.2
1983	1251.3
1984	1247.0
1985	1348.7
1986	1767.4
1987	1190.5
1988	1008.1
1989	954.2
1990	1169.9

Source: 1990 Statistical Yearbook of the Immigration and Naturalization Service (Washington, D.C., U.S. Government Printing Office, 1991), p. 166.

TABLE A.14
NATURALIZATIONS (THOUSANDS OF PERSONS)

Year	Belgium	Canada	France	Germany	Spain	UK	USA
1970							110.4
1971							108.4
1972							116.2
1973							120.7
1974							131.7
1975							141.5
1976							190.7
1977							159.9
1978							173.5
1979							164.2
1980							157.9
1981							166.3
1982							173.7
1983							178.9
1984							197.0
1985							244.7
1986							280.6
1987							227.0
1988	1.7	58.8	46.4	46.8	8.3	64.6	242.1
1989	1.9	87.5	49.3		5.8	117.1	233.8
1990		104.3	54.4		7.0	57.3	270.1

Sources: SOPEMI, *Trends in International Migration* (Paris: OECD, 1992), p. 36; *1990 Statistical Yearbook of the Immigration and Naturalization Service* (Washington, D.C.: U.S. Government Printing Office, 1991), p. 144.

Index